1/25/99
60
ABF-4556

DATE DUE

MAY 11 2000

This is an indispensable guide to one of the most influential and important dramatists of the theatre. The volume offers a wide-ranging study of Shaw with essays by a team of leading scholars. The Companion covers all aspects of Shaw's drama, focusing both on the political and theatrical context, while the extensive illustrations showcase productions from the Shaw Festival in Canada. In addition to situating Shaw's work in its own time, the Companion demonstrates its continuing relevance, and applies some of the newest critical approaches.

Topics include Shaw and the publishing trade, Shaw and feminism, Shaw and the Empire, as well as analyses of the early plays, discussion plays and history plays.

CAMBRIDGE COMPANIONS TO LITERATURE

THE CAMBRIDGE
COMPANION TO
GEORGE BERNARD
SHAW

At the end of *The Simpleton of the Unexpected Isles*, George Bernard Shaw and his survivors look ahead to an uncertain future, in the Shaw Festival's 1996 productrion

THE CAMBRIDGE
COMPANION TO

GEORGE BERNARD SHAW

EDITED BY
CHRISTOPHER INNES
York University, Ontario

CAMBRIDGE
UNIVERSITY PRESS

PUBLISHED BY THE PRESS SYNDICATE OF THE UNIVERSITY OF CAMBRIDGE
The Pitt Building, Trumpington Street, Cambridge CB2 1RP, United Kingdom

CAMBRIDGE UNIVERSITY PRESS
The Edinburgh Building, Cambridge CB2 2RU, United Kingdom
40 West 20th Street, New York, NY 10011–4211, USA
10 Stamford Road, Oakleigh, Melbourne 3166, Australia

First published 1998

Printed in the United Kingdom at the University Press, Cambridge

Typeset in Sabon 10/13 pt. [CE]

A catalogue record for this book is available from the British Library

Library of Congress cataloging in publication data

The Cambridge companion to George Bernard Shaw / edited by Christopher Innes.
p.   cm. – (Cambridge companions to literature)
Includes bibliographical references and index.
ISBN 0 521 56237 6 (hardback). – ISBN 0 521 56633 9 (paperback)
1. Shaw, Bernard, 1856–1950 – Criticism and interpretation.
I. Innes, C. D.   II. Series.
PR5367.C27   1998
822'.912 – dc21   97-42229
CIP

ISBN 0 521 56237 6 hardback
ISBN 0 521 56633 9 paperback

CONTENTS

ILLUSTRATIONS

CONTRIBUTORS

FREDRIC BERG is Associate Professor and Director of Theatre at Georgia College and State University. His publications include various articles on theatre, including one on *The Simpleton of the Unexpected Isles* which appeared in *Modern Drama*. He is currently working on a study of Shaw's use of dramatic structure in the early plays.

CHARLES A. BERST is a Professor of English at UCLA, where he has taught modern drama and English literature for thirty years. His publications include *Bernard Shaw and the Art of Drama* (1973); an edited collection of essays, *Shaw and Religion* (1980); *Pygmalion: Shaw's Spin on Myth and Cinderella* (1995); and numerous articles on Shaw's life and plays. At UCLA he has received a Distinguished Teaching Award, a University Service Award, and served as chair of the College of Letters and Science faculty, and chair of the faculty senate.

RONALD BRYDEN is literary adviser to the Shaw Festival in Niagara-on-the-Lake, Ontario. During the 1960s, he was a theatre critic in London, writing for the *New Statesman* (1964–66) and *Observer* (1966–71). From 1971 to 1975 he was play adviser to the Royal Shakespeare Company. From 1976 to 1993 he taught drama at the University of Toronto.

TRACY C. DAVIS is Associate Professor of Theatre, English, and Performance Studies at Northwestern University. She is the author of *Actresses as Working Women: Their Social Identity in Victorian Culture* (1991), *George Bernard Shaw and the Socialist Theatre* (1994), and dozens of articles on nineteenth and twentieth-century performance and culture.

T. F. EVANS was formerly Tutor, Lecturer, and Deputy Director in the Department of Extramural Studies of the University of London. He has been Editor of *The Shavian* since 1963 and has edited *Shaw: The Critical Heritage* and *Shaw and Politics*.

ROBERT G. EVERDING is a Professor of Theatre and Dean of the College of Fine Arts and Communication at the University of Central Arkansas. He was the founder and artistic director of the Houston Shaw Festival and his articles on Shaw have appeared in *Shaw, English Language Notes*, and other journals.

DAVID J. GORDON is a Professor of English at Hunter College and the CUNY Graduate Center. Among his publications are *D. H. Lawrence as a Literary Critic* (1976), *Bernard Shaw and the Comic Sublime* (1990), and *Iris Murdoch's Fables of Unselfing* (1995).

CHRISTOPHER INNES is a Distinguished Research Professor at York University, Ontario, and a Fellow of the Royal Society of Canada. He is the General Editor of the Cambridge "Directors in Perspective" series, as well as one of the editors for *Modern Drama*, and has published widely on twentieth century theatre: his most recent books being *Modern British Drama: 1890–1990* (1992), *Avant Garde Theatre: 1892–1992* (1994), and *The Theatre of Gordon Craig* (1998).

KATHERINE E. KELLY is an Associate Professor of English at Texas A&M University. She is the general editor of *Modern Drama by Women 1880s–1930s: An International Anthology* (1996), co-editor of *British Playwrights, 1880–1956* (1996), author of *Tom Stoppard and the Craft of Comedy* (1991) and has published articles on G. B. Shaw and Woman Suffrage, Elizabeth Robins, and the Actresses' Franchise League. Her current projects include a study of the modernity of modern drama and a casebook on Tom Stoppard.

JAN McDONALD is James Arnott Professor of Drama in the Department of Theatre, Film and Television Studies at the University of Glasgow. Publications in the area of the "New Drama" include: "The Promised Land of the London Stage – Acting Style at the Court Theatre, London 1904–1907," *Proceedings of the Congress of the International Federation for Theatre Research* (1978); "New Actors for the New Drama," *Themes in Drama. Drama and the Actor* (1984); *The New Drama 1900–1914* (1986); "New Women in the New Drama," *New Theatre Quarterly* (1990); "The Origins of the Modern Stage," in *Literature and Criticism – A New Century Guide* (1990); "'The Second Act was Glorious': the Staging of the Trafalgar Square Scene in Elizabeth Robin's *Votes for Women* at the Royal Court Theatre," *Theatre History Studies* (1995).

FREDERICK J. MARKER, a Professor of English and Drama at the University of Toronto, has written extensively on many aspects of modern theatre and drama. His books include studies of Hans Christian Andersen, Kjeld Abell, Ingmar Bergman, Edward Gordon Craig, Henrik Ibsen, and others. He is also a former editor of the journal *Modern Drama*.

SALLY PETERS has published widely on modern drama, dance, and cultural studies and is the author of the biography *Bernard Shaw: The Ascent of the Superman* (1996). Vice-president of the Bernard Shaw Society and member of the editorial board of *The Annual of Shaw Studies*, she teaches literature in the Graduate Liberal Studies Program, Wesleyan University.

KERRY POWELL is Professor of English and director of graduate studies at Miami University, Oxford, Ohio. He is the author of *Oscar Wilde and the Theatre of the 1890s* (1990) and *Women and Victorian Theatre* (1997), both from Cambridge University Press. He is a contributor to *The Cambridge Companion to Oscar Wilde* (1998), as well as to a forthcoming collection of articles on the Salome legend from the University of Chicago Press. His essays on Victorian theatre and Oscar Wilde have appeared in *Philological Quarterly*, *Modern Drama*, *Nineteenth Century Theatre* and *Papers on Language & Literature*.

MATTHEW H. WIKANDER, Professor of English at the University of Toledo, is the author of *The Play of Truth and State: Historical Drama from Shakespeare to Brecht* (1996) and *Princes to Act. Royal Audience and Royal Performance, 1578–1792* (1993), and contributor of an essay to *The Cambridge Companion to Eugene O'Neill* (1998).

J. L. WISENTHAL's work on Shaw includes *Shaw's Sense of History* (1988), *Shaw and Ibsen* (1979), and *The Marriage of Contraries: Bernard Shaw's Middle Plays* (1974). He is currently writing about Victorian historical narratives, and is also engaged in an interdisciplinary project on the Madame Butterfly theme in opera, drama, film, and prose fiction. Professor Wisenthal is a member of the English Department at the University of British Columbia.

PREFACE

Bernard Shaw was possibly the most prolific of all twentieth-century authors. In addition to writing plays – accompanied by prefaces frequently longer than the dramatic scripts – Shaw was a novelist, lecturer, and journalist, who established a significant reputation as a music critic and published several volumes of dance and theatrical criticism, social commentary and political theory, as well as carrying out a voluminous correspondence through the whole of an unusually long and active lifetime. He also directed many of the first productions of his earlier plays and subsequently exercised tight control over the way his work was staged, designed costumes and settings for some of his plays, and later adapted several for film-versions. However, while recognizing other aspects of his writing, *The Cambridge Companion to George Bernard Shaw* focuses primarily on Shaw's theatre.

The volume covers his plays from the 1890s up to the decade before his death in 1950, and the wider theatrical context against which Shaw established himself, as well as contemporary stagings of his work. The chapters deal with his whole career; but since Shaw has over fifty plays to his credit, ranging from the eight-hour *Back to Methuselah* to short sketches and interludes, detailed attention can only be given to his major plays. His novels, political lectures and pamphlets, musical and theatrical reviews are referred to primarily where these contribute to the understanding of his drama. At the same time, attention is also paid to his publishing practices, since Shaw was the first modern dramatist to establish his plays as literature – indeed his aim was to persuade the public that drama (which at the end of the nineteenth century was widely despised as a genre) was no less worthy of serious attention than the novel. In that sense, as well as the specific influence of his plays on other writers, Shaw could be seen as the father of modern British drama, having created the conditions that attracted later authors to write for the theatre.

Shaw is still very much a living presence on the stage; and the illustrations have been selected to showcase the work of the Shaw Festival in Niagara-on-the-Lake. Founded in 1962, and with a professional company operating every summer, the popularity of the Shaw Festival is indicated by its expansion to a six-month season and into three different theatres: a main stage (constructed in 1973), the Court House Theatre (an intimate space inside a historic building), and the Royal George Theatre (a small restored vaudeville house). Christopher Newton, the artistic director of the Festival since 1980, has the ambition to present every one of Shaw's plays during his tenure, although Shaw's major works are frequently remounted in new productions. This is reflected in some illustrations that take examples from different productions of the same play. The mandate of the Festival is to present not only the works of Bernard Shaw, but also of his contemporaries, which provides a rich image of the wider cultural context in which Shaw was working. However, the illustrations here focus solely on the performances of Shaw's plays. In writing his plays, Shaw of course was always closely attuned to theatrical requirements, and the dialogue frequently imposes specific physical relationships among the actors. So even if some of the stage interpretations represented in these photos have been quite untraditional, there is a surprisingly close correspondence between the visual record and the points brought out in the various chapters.

There are several complete editions of Shaw's plays and their prefaces available, but the text generally accepted as standard is *The Bodley Head Bernard Shaw: Collected Plays with their Prefaces*, edited by Dan Laurence (London, 1970–74), or the American edition (*Bernard Shaw: Collected Plays with their Prefaces*, edited by Dan Laurence [New York, 1975]). Quotations from Shaw's plays in this *Companion* are generally to one of these editions. However, in some cases other editions have been used, particularly in chapters dealing with the early plays where the argument requires reference to the original texts. Wherever this occurs, full bibliographical details are given in the endnotes to the relevant chapter.

Most of the major critical studies, as well as recent biographies of Shaw, are listed in the endnotes to the various chapters. Additional information on Shaw criticism and scholarship is supplied in the lists of "further reading."

CHRISTOHER INNES
Toronto, 1998

ACKNOWLEDGMENTS

We would like to thank Christopher Newton and the staff of the Shaw Festival, particularly Denis Johnston, for their invaluable aid in making this photographic record available. We are extremely grateful to all the members of the company appearing in the various productions illustrated, who have been so generous in allowing permission to reproduce their work, and whose names are listed in the captions. In addition, we would like to thank the designers who created the visual context, and the photographers who captured the images. Specifically, listing the productions in the order they appear throughout the book, these are:

The Simpleton of the Unexpected Isles, 1996 (Frontispiece, and Nos. 1, 2, 23, 25); *Misalliance*, 1990 (No. 15); and *Pygmalion*, 1992 (No. 28); Designer: Leslie Frankish   Lighting Designer: Robert Thomson Photo: David Cooper

Shakes versus Shav, 1989 (No. 4); Designer: Ronnie Burkett   Photo: David Cooper

Mrs. Warren's Profession, 1997 (Nos. 5, 8); and *The Philanderer*, 1995 (No. 6); Designer: Leslie Frankish   Lighting Designer: Kevin Lamotte   Photo: David Cooper

Widowers' Houses, 1992 (No. 7); Set Designer: Yvonne Sauriol Costume Designer: Sean Breaugh   Lighting Designer: Graeme S. Thomson   Photo: David Cooper

Arms and the Man, 1994 (No. 9); and *Man and Superman*, 1989 (No. 12); Designer: Eduard Kochergin   Lighting Designer: Robert Thomson Photo: David Cooper

Arms and the Man, 1994 (No. 10); Designer: Michael Levine with Charlotte Dean   Lighting Designer: Jeffrey Dallas   Photo: David Cooper

Man and Superman, 1977 (No. 11); Designer: Brian H. Jackson   Lighting Designer: John Stammers   Photo: Robert C. Ragsdale

Major Barbara, 1987 (No. 13); and *Caesar and Cleopatra*, 1983 (Nos. 17, 18); Designer: Cameron Porteous   Lighting Designer: Jeffrey Dallas   Photo: David Cooper

Getting Married, 1989 (No. 14); Designer: Christina Poddubiuk   Lighting Designer: Robert Thomson   Photo: David Cooper

Heartbreak House, 1985 (No. 16); Designer: Michael Levine   Lighting Designer: Jeffrey Dallas   Photo: David Cooper

Saint Joan, 1993 (Nos. 19, 29, 30); and *The Millionairess*, 1991 (No. 24); Designer: Cameron Porteous   Lighting Designer: Robert Thomson   Photo: David Cooper

Candida, 1993 (No. 20); Set Designer: Yvonne Sauriol   Costume Designer: Cameron Porteous   Lighting Designer: Kevin Lamotte   Photo: David Cooper

Captain Brassbound's Conversion, 1979 (No. 21); Set Designer: Michael Eagan   Costume Designer: Astrid Janson   Lighting Designer: Robert Thomson   Photo: Robert C. Ragsdale

Too True To Be Good, 1994 (No. 22); Designer: Peter Hartwell   Lighting Designer: Robert Thomson   Photo: David Cooper

The Man of Destiny, 1993 (No. 26); Designer: Kenneth Shaw   Lighting Designer: Aisling Sampson   Photo: David Cooper

The Philanderer, 1971 (No. 27); Set Designer: Maurice Strike   Costume Designer: Tiina Lipp   Lighting Designer: Donald Acaster   Photo: Robert C. Ragsdale

CHRONOLOGY

For the plays, dates of composition and first professional production in Britain have been given, as well as details of copyright and amateur or foreign performances where these occured earlier.

Unfinished/unperformed playscripts are also indicated. In addition, novels and major essays, or collections of essays, have been included to show the wider dimensions of Shaw's career.

1856	(July 26) Born: Dublin
1876	First essays (as a music critic) published
1878	"Passion Play" (unfinished)
1879	*Immaturity* (first published 1930)
1882–83	*Cashel Byron's Profession* (first published 1886, revised 1899, 1901)
1886	First essays (as an art critic) published
1887	*An Unsocial Socialist* (first serialized in *Today*, 1884)
1898	"The Gadfly or The Son of the Cardinal" (adaptation of the novel by Ethel Voynich – unfinished)
1889	"Un Petit Drame" (unfinished)
1889	*Fabian Essays*
1889–90	"The Cassone" (unperformed)
1891	*The Quintessence of Ibsenism* (revised 1913)
1885–92	*Widowers' Houses* (An Original Didactic Realistic Play) First presented: December 9 and 13, 1892, Independent Theatre Society at the Royalty Theatre in London

First presented in public: October 7, 1907, by Miss
Horniman's Company at the Midland Theatre in Manchester

1893   *The Philanderer* (A Topical Comedy in Four Acts of the Early
        Eighteen-Nineties)
        Copyright performance: March 30, 1898, at the Bijou
        Theatre, Bayswater, London
        First presented: February 20, 1905, by the New Stage Club at
        the Cripplegate Institute, London
        First presented in public: February 5, 1907, by J. E. Vedrenne
        and Harley Granville Barker at the Court Theatre, London

1893–94 *Mrs. Warren's Profession* (A Play in Four Acts)
        First presented: January 5, 1902, by the Stage Society of New
        Lyric Club, London
        First presented in public: October 27, 1905, by Arnold Daly
        at the Hyperion Theatre, New Haven, CT, USA
        First publicly performed in England: July 27, 1925, by the
        Macdona Players at the Prince of Wales Theatre, Birmingham

1894   *Arms and the Man* (A Romantic Comedy in Three Acts)
        First presented: April 21, 1894, by Florence Farr at the
        Avenue Theatre, London

1894   *Candida: A Mystery*
        Copyright performance: March 30, 1895, at the Theatre
        Royal, South Shields
        First presented in public: July 30, 1897, by the Independent
        Theatre Company at Her Majesty's Theatre, Aberdeen
        First presented in London: July 1, 1990, by the Stage Society
        at the Strand Theatre
        First publicly presented in London: April 26, 1904, by
        Vedrenne and Barker at the Court Theatre

1895   *The Man of Destiny* (A Trifle/A Fictitious Paragraph of
        History)
        First presented: July 1, 1897, by Murray Carson at the Grand
        Theatre, Croydon
        First presented in London: March 29, 1901, by J. T. Grein at
        the Comedy Theatre

1895–96 *You Never Can Tell* (A Pleasant Play in Four Acts)
        Copyright performance: March 23, 1898, at the Bijou
        Theatre, Bayswater, London

First presented: November 26, 1899, by the Stage Society at the Royalty Theatre, London
First presented in public: May 2, 1900, by James Welch and Yorke Stephens at the Strand Theatre

1896–97   *The Devil's Disciple: A Melodrama*
Copyright performance: April 17, 1897, at the Bijou Theatre, Bayswater, London
First presented: October 1, 1897, by Richard Mansfield at the Hermanus Bleeker Hall, Albany, New York
First presented in public in England: September 26, 1899, by Murray Carson at the Prince of Wales Theatre, Kennington, London

1898   *The Perfect Wagnerite*

1898   *Caesar and Cleopatra: A History*
Copyright performance: March 15, 1899, by Mrs. Patrick Campbell's Company at the Theatre Royal, Newcastle upon Tyne
First presented: May 1, 2, 3, 1901, by students of the Anna Morgan Studios for Art and Expression at the Fine Arts Building, Chicago
First presented professionally in German: March 31, 1906, by Max Reinhardt at the Neues Theater, Berlin
First presented in England: September 16, 1907, by Forbes Robertson at the Grand Theatre, Leeds

1899   *Captain Brassbound's Conversion: An Adventure*
Copyright performance: October 10, 1899, at the Court Theatre, Liverpool
First presented: December 16, 1900, by the Stage Society at the Strand Theatre, London
First presented in public: May 12, 1902, by Harold V. Neilson at the Queen's Theatre, Manchester

1900   *Love Among the Artists*

1901   *The Admirable Bashville* or *Constancy Unrewarded* (Being the Novel of *Cashel Byron's Profession* Done into a Stage Play in Three Acts and in Blank Verse)
First presented: December 14, 1902, by amateurs at the Pharos Club, Covent Garden, London
First presented professionally: June 7, 8, 1903, by the Stage

Society at the Imperial Theatre, London
First presented in public: September 22, 1905, by Harold V.
Neilson at the Queen's Theatre, Manchester

1901–03 *Man and Superman: A Comedy (and a Philosophy)*
Copyright performance: June 29, 1903, at the Bijou Theatre,
Bayswater, London
First presented: May 21, 1905, by the Stage Society at the
Court Theatre, London (without Act 3)
First presented in public: May 23, 1905, by Vedrenne and
Barker at the Court Theatre, London (without Act 3)
First production of *Don Juan in Hell* (Act 3 Scene 2): June 4,
1907, presented by by Vedrenne and Barker at the Court
Theatre as a one-act play, subtitled *A Dream from "Man and
Superman"*
First presented in its entirety: June 11, 1915, by the
Travelling Repertory Company (Esme Percy and Kristeen
Graeme) at the Lyceum Theatre, Edinburgh

1904 *John Bull's Other Island*
First presented: November 1, 1904, by Vedrenne and Barker
at the Court Theatre, London

1904 *How He Lied to Her Husband*
First presented: September 26, 1904, by Arnold Daly at the
Berkeley Lyceum, New York
First presented in England: February 28, 1905, by Vedrenne
and Barker at the Court Theatre, London

1905 *The Irrational Knot*

1905 *Major Barbara* (A Discussion in Three Acts)
First presented: November 28, 1905, by Vedrenne and Barker
at the Court Theatre, London

1905 *Passion, Poison, and Petrification* or *The Fatal Gazogene* (A
Brief Tragedy for Barns and Booths)
First presented: July 14, 1905, in "The Theatre Royal" at the
Theatrical Garden Party, Regent's Park, London

1906 *Our Theatres in the Nineties* (Shaw's theatre criticism for
The Saturday Review, 1895–98)

1906 *The Doctor's Dilemma* (A Tragedy in Four Acts and an
Epilogue)

First presented: November 20, 1906, by Vedrenne and Barker at the Court Theatre, London

1906–7   *Dramatic Opinions and Essays*

1907   *The Interlude at the Playhouse / The Inauguration Speech: An Interlude*
First and only performance: January 28, 1907, at the reopening of the Playhouse Theatre, London

1908   *The Sanity of Art: An Exposure of the Current Nonsense about Artists Being Degenerate*

1908   *Getting Married: A Conversation* (A Disquisitory Play)
First presented: May 12, 1908, by Vedrenne and Barker at the Haymarket Theatre, London

1909   *The Shewing-Up of Blanco Posnet: A Sermon in Crude Melodrama*
First presented: August 25, 1909, by Lady Gregory and W. B. Yeats at the Abbey Theatre, Dublin
First presented in England: December 5, 1909, by the Abbey Theatre Company, under the auspices of the Stage Society, at the Aldwych Theatre, London
First publicly presented in London: March 14, 1921, by Norman Macdermott at the Everyman Theatre, Hampstead

1909   *The Glimpse of Reality: A Tragedietta*
First presented: October 8, 1927, by the Glasgow Clarion Players (amateur) at the Fellowship Hall, Glasgow
First presented professionally: November 20, 1927, at the Arts Theatre Club, London

1909   *Press Cuttings* (A Topical Sketch Compiled from the Editorial and Correspondence columns of the Daily Papers during the Woman's War in 1909)
First presented: July 9, 12, 1909, by the Civic and Dramatic Guild at a "Private Reception" at the Court Theatre, London
First presented: in public: September 27, 1909, by Miss Horniman's Company at the Gaiety Theatre, Manchester

1909   *The Fascinating Foundling* (A Disgrace to the Author)
First presented by amateurs: 1909, organized by Elizabeth Asquith, Princess Bibesco

First presented professionally: January 28, 1928, by the Arts
Theatre Club, London

1909–10   *Misalliance* (A Debate in One Sitting)
First presented: February 23, 1910, by Charles Frohman in
his repertory season at the Duke of York's Theatre, London

1910   *The Dark Lady of the Sonnets: An Interlude*
First presented: November 24, 25, 1910, by the Committee
of the Shakespeare Memorial National Theatre at a charity
matinée at the Haymarket Theatre, London

1911   *Fanny's First Play: An Easy Play for a Little Theatre*
First presented: April 19, 1911, by Lillah McCarthy at the
Little Theatre, London

1912   *Androcles and the Lion: A Fable Play*
First presented: September 1, 1913, by McCarthy and Barker
at the St. James's Theatre, London

1912   *Overruled: A Demonstration*
First presented: October 14, 1912, by Charles Frohman at
the Duke of York's Theatre, London

1912–13   *Pygmalion* (A Romance in Five Acts)
First presented (in German): October 16, 1913, at the
Hofburg Theater, Vienna
First presented in England: April 11, 1914, by Herbert
Beerbohm Tree at His Majesty's Theatre, London

1913   *Great Catherine (Whom Glory Still Adores)* (A Thumbnail
Sketch of Russian Court Life in the XVIII Century)
First presented: November 18, 1913, by Norman McKinnel
and Frederick Whelen at the Vaudeville Theatre, London

1913   "Beauty's Duty" (unfinished)

1913   *The Music Cure: A Piece of Utter Nonsense*
First presented: January 28, 1914, by Kenelm Foss at the
Little Theatre, London as a curtain-raiser to celebrate the
100th performance of G. K. Chesterton's *Magic*

1914   *Common Sense About the War*

1915   *O'Flaherty, VC: A Recruiting Pamphlet* (A Reminiscence of
1915)
First presented: February 17, 1917, by officers of the 40th

Squadron, RFC, on the Western Front at Treizennes, Belgium (amateur)
First presented professionally: June 21, 1920, by the Deborah Bierne Irish Players at the 39th Street Theatre, New York
First presented in England: December 19, 1920, by the Stage Society at the Lyric Theatre, Hammersmith, London

1916   *The Inca of Perusalem: An Almost Historical Comedietta* (by "A Member of the Royal Literary Society")
First presented: October 7, 1916 by Barry Jackson at the Repertory Theatre, Birmingham

1916   "Macbeth Skit" & "Glastonbury Skit" (unfinished)

1916   *Augustus Does His Bit: A True-to-Life Farce* (An Unofficial Dramatic Tract on War Saving and Cognate Topics by the Author of *The Inca of Perusalem*)
First presented: January 21, 1917, by the Stage Society at the Court Theatre, London
First presented in public: December 10, 1917, by the Drama League Players (amateur) at Polio's Theatre, Washington, DC
First public professional production: March 12, 1919, by John D. Williams at the Comedy Theatre, New York

1917   *Annajanska, The Wild Grand Duchess / Annajanska, The Bolshevik Empress: A Revolutionary Romancelet* (From the Russian of Gregory Bessinoff)
First presented: January 21, 1918, at the Coliseum, London, in a variety bill

1919   *Heartbreak House* (A Fantasia in the Russian Manner on English Themes)
First presented: November 10, 1920, by the New York Theatre Guild at the Garrick Theatre, New York
First presented in England: October 18, 1921, by J. B. Fagan at the Court Theatre, London

1918–20   *Back to Methuselah: A Metabiological Pentateuch* (A Play Cycle in Five Parts)
First presented: Parts I and II February 27, 1922, Parts III and IV March 6, 1922, Part V March 13, 1922, by the New York Theatre Guild at the Garrick Theatre, New York
First presented in England: Part I October 9, 1923, Part II October 10, 1923, Part III October 11, 1923, Part IV October

	11, 1923, Part v, October 12, 1923, by Barry Jackson at the Repertory Theatre, Birmingham
1921–22	"The War Indemnities" (unfinished)
1922	*Jitta's Atonement* (By Siegfried Trebitsch, English Version by G. Bernard Shaw) First presented: January 8, 1923, by Lee Shubert at the Shubert-Garrick Theatre, Washington First produced in England: January 26, 1925, by the Partnership Players at the Grand Theatre, Fulham, London
1923	*Saint Joan: A Chronicle Play* (A Chronicle Play in Six Scenes and an Epilogue) First presented: December 28, 1923, by the New York Theatre Guild at The Garrick Theatre, New York First presented in England: March 26, 1924, by Mary Moore and Sybil Thorndike at the New Theatre, London
1926	*Translations and Tomfooleries*
1927	"The Yahoos" (unfinished)
1928	*The Intelligent Woman's Guide to Socialism and Capitalism*
1928	*The Apple Cart: A Political Extravaganza* (A Political Extravaganza in Two Acts and an Interlude) First presented (in Polish): June 14, 1929, at the Teatr Polski (Director, Arnold Szyfman), Warsaw First presented in England: August 19, 1929, by Barry Jackson at the Festival Theatre, Malvern
1931	*Music in London 1890–94: Criticisms contributed Week by Week to The World*
1931	*Our Theatres in the Nineties: Criticisms contributed Week by Week to the Saturday Review from January 1895 to May 1898*
1931	*Immaturity*
1931	*Pen Portraits and Reviews*
1931	*Too True To Be Good: A Political Extravaganza* First presented: February 20, 1932, by the New York Theatre Guild at the National Theatre, Boston, MA First presented in England: August 6, 1932, by Barry Jackson at the Festival Theatre, Malvern

1931   *Doctors' Delusions: Crude Criminology: Sham Education*

1932   *What I Really Wrote About the War*

1932   *The Adventures of the Black Girl in her Search for God*

1933   *Village Wooing* (A Comediettina for Two Voices in Three
        Conversations)
        First presented: April 16, 1934, by the Little Theatre
        Company at the Little Theatre, Dallas, Texas, USA
        First presented in England: May 1, 1934, by the Wells
        Repertory Players at the Pump Room, Tunbridge Wells, Kent
        First presented in London: June 19, 1934, by the People's
        National Theatre at the Little Theatre

1933   *On the Rocks: A Political Comedy*
        First presented: November 25, 1933, by Charles Macdona at
        the Winter Garden Theatre, London

1934   *Short Stories, Scraps and Shavings*

1934   *Prefaces*

1934   *The Simpleton of the Unexpected Isles: A Vision of Judgment*
        (A Play in a Prologue and Two Acts)
        First performed: February 18, 1935, by the New York
        Theatre Guild at the Guild Theatre, New York
        First presented in England: July 19, 1935, by Barry Jackson
        at the Festival Theatre, Malvern

1934   *The Six of Calais* (A Mediaeval War Story in One Act by Jean
        Froissart, Auguste Rodin and Bernard Shaw)
        First presented: July 17, 1934, by Sydney Carroll and Lewis
        Schaverien at the Open Air Theatre, Regent's Park, London

1934–35 *The Millionairess* (A Jonsonian Comedy in Four Acts/
        A Comedy in Four Acts)
        First presented (in German): January 4, 1936, by the
        Burgtheater at the Akademie Theater, Vienna
        First presented in English: March 7, 1936, by the McMahon
        Players at the King's Theatre, Melbourne
        First presented in England: November 17, 1936, by the
        Matthew Forsyth Repertory Company at the De La Warre
        Pavilion, Bexhill-on-Sea, Sussex
        First presented in London: May 29, 1944, by Jack de Leon at
        the "Q" Theatre, London

1935	"The Garden of the Hesperides" (unfinished)
1935	The Girl with the Golden Voice" (unfinished)
1936	*Geneva* (A Fancied Page of History/Another Political Extravaganza) (revised 1939, 1940, 1947) First presented: August 1, 1938, by Roy Limbert at the Festival Theatre, Malvern
1936	"Arthur and the Acetone" (unfinished)
1937	*London Music in 1888–89 As Heard by Corneto di Bassetto*
1937	"Sequence for the King's People" (unfinished)
1937	*Cymbeline Refinished* (A Variation on Shakespear's Ending) First presented: November 16, 1937, by the Embassy Play Producing Society (Ronald Adam) at the Embassy Theatre, Swiss Cottage, London
1939	*"In Good King Charles's Golden Days": A True History that Never Happened* (A History Lesson in Three Scenes) First presented: August 12, 1939, by Roy Limbert at the Festival Theatre, Malvern
1944	*Everybody's Political What's What?*
1936–37 and 1945–47	*Buoyant Billions: A Comedy of No Manners* First presented (in German as *Zu Viel Geld*): October 21, 1948, at the Schauspielhaus, Zurich, Switzerland First presented in England: August 13, 1949, by Roy Limbert at the Festival Theatre, Malvern
1948–50	*Farfetched Fables* First presented: September 6, 1950, by the Shaw Society at the Watergate Theatre, London
1949	*Sixteen Self Sketches*
1949	*Shakes Versus Shav* (A Puppet Play) First performed: August 9, 1949, by the Waldo Lanchester Marionette Theatre at the Lyttleton Hall, Malvern First presented in London: June 10, 1951, at the Riverside Theatre, Festival Gardens, Battersea Park
1950	*Why She Would Not: A Little Comedy* (A Comedietta) – Only five of the six scenes finished
1950	(November 2) Dies: Ayot St. Lawrence

POSTHUMOUS PUBLICATIONS

1950 *Bernard Shaw's Rhyming Picture Guide To Ayot Saint Lawrence*

1952 *"The Voice:" An Autobiographical Exploration*

1958 *An Unfinished Novel*, ed. Stanley Weintraub (written 1887–88)

1980 *Collected Screenplays*, ed. Bernard F. Dukore

Many of Shaw's essays, speeches and reviews, covering the whole of his career from 1876–1950, have also appeared in anthologies and collections published since his death.

1958 *Shaw on Theatre*, ed. E. J. West

1961 *How To Become A Musical Critic*, ed. Dan H. Laurence and Rupert Hart-Davis

1961 *Shaw on Shakespeare: An Anthology of Bernard Shaw's Writings on the Plays and Productions of Shakespeare*, ed. Edwin Wilson

1961 *Platform and Pulpit*, ed. Dan H. Laurence

1962 *The Matter With Ireland*, ed. Dan H. Laurence and David H. Greene

1963 *The Religious Speeches of Bernard Shaw*, ed. Warren Sylvester Smith

1963 *George Bernard Shaw On Language*, ed. Abraham Tauber

1965 *Selected Non-Dramatic Writings of Bernard Shaw*, ed. Dan H. Laurence

1967 *Shaw on Religion*, ed. Warren Sylvester Smith

1971 *Bernard Shaw: The Road to Equality: Ten Unpublished Lectures*, ed. Louis Crompton

1972 *Bernard Shaw's Nondramatic Literary Criticism*, ed. Stanley Weintraub

1976 *Bernard Shaw: Practical Politics*, ed. Lloyd J. Hubenka

1981 *The Bodley Head Bernard Shaw: Shaw's Music, The Complete Musical Criticism in Three Volumes*, ed. Dan H. Laurence

1985   *Bernard Shaw. Agitations. Letters to the Press 1875–1950,* ed. Dan H. Laurence and James Rambeau

1991   *Bernard Shaw's Book Reviews* (two volumes), ed. Brian Tyson

1993   *The Drama Observed / Bernard Shaw,* ed. Bernard F. Dukore

In addition, much of Shaw's correspondence and some personal papers have appeared in print, as well as some secondary material.

1951   *Shaw's Plays in Review,* ed. Desmond MacCarthy

1952   *Bernard Shaw and Mrs. Patrick Campbell: Their Correspondence,* ed. Alan Dent

1965–88   *Bernard Shaw: Collected Letters,* (four volumes), ed. Dan H. Laurence

1982   *The Playwright and the Pirate. Bernard Shaw and Frank Harris: A Correspondence,* ed. Stanley Weintraub

1982   *Bernard Shaw and Alfred Douglas: A Correspondence,* ed. Mary Hyde

1986   *Bernard Shaw's Letters to Siegfried Trebitsch,* ed. Samuel A. Weiss

1986   *Bernard Shaw: The Diaries: 1885–1897* (two volumes), ed. Stanley Weintraub

I

THE SOCIAL AND CULTURAL CONTEXT

I

SALLY PETERS

Shaw's life: a feminist in spite of himself

By his seventieth birthday, Bernard Shaw was one of the most famous people in the world. Yet despite intense scrutiny, perhaps no other figure of his stature and visibility has been so thoroughly misunderstood. The only Nobel laureate also to win an Academy Award (for the screenplay of *Pygmalion*), he was recognized as much for his wit and his eccentric personality as for his writings. Certainly the celebrity made unfailing good copy as he voiced opinions on everything from European dictators to child-raising. But for too long he insisted on caricaturing himself as a clown and buffoon. Late in life, he lamented that he had been all too persuasive, the overexposed G. B. S. figure trivializing views of both man and artist. Then, too, there had always been an undercurrent of antagonism toward the self-proclaimed genius who insisted on the satirist's right to skewer societal foibles – that insistence marked him as guilty of a disconcerting detachment from the mass of his fellow human beings according to his detractors, a detachment noticeable in the personal sphere as well.

In addition to his own part in misleading critics and would-be biographers, Shaw managed to elude attempts to understand him simply because of the enormity of the task. Not only was he the author of some five dozen plays, his mountain of writings includes five completed novels, a number of short stories, lengthy treatises on politics and economics, four volumes of theatre criticism, three volumes of music criticism, and a volume of art criticism. Add to that total well over a hundred book reviews and an astonishing correspondence of over a quarter of a million letters and postcards.

Then there was the sheer length of the life. G. K. Chesterton's *George Bernard Shaw* preceded his subject's death by a full forty years. As Shaw steadfastly outlived his contemporaries, he noisily called attention to his façades, while quietly destroying correspondences and prevailing over biographers. Always needing to control, where his biography was concerned, Shaw was obsessive, coercing, directing, managing. Both Archibald

3

Henderson, North Carolinian mathematician and three-time authorized biographer, and Hesketh Pearson, a long-time friend, more or less willingly submitted. After the death of Frank Harris, Shaw earned the widow's gratitude by completing his own biography, admittedly "quite the oddest" task of his life (Harris, *Bernard Shaw*, p. 419). When American professor Thomas Demetrius O'Bolger proved both independent and curious, Shaw blocked publication of O'Bolger's work. Although Shaw made clear that his early life was less than idyllic, not until after his death did much darker intimations of family life appear – in the works of St. John Ervine, B. C. Rosset, and John O'Donovan.

A wealth of information about Shaw's life is now available. Dan H. Laurence has edited the massive four-volume *Collected Letters*, while individual collections abound. There are correspondences to admiring women such as Florence Farr, Ellen Terry, Mrs. Patrick Campbell, and Molly Tompkins; and to men such as Frank Harris, Lord Alfred Douglas, German translator Siegfried Trebitsch, and actor-playwright Harley Granville Barker. Currently, an ongoing ten-volume project includes the correspondences with H. G. Wells, with film producer Gabriel Pascal, and with Fabian Socialists Sidney and Beatrice Webb. Shaw's diaries, edited by Stanley Weintraub, cover the period of 1885–97, the two volumes offering a snapshot of Shaw's activities, rather than a journal of intimate thoughts and feelings.

A plethora of reminiscences and memoirs abound – everyone from Shaw's cook, secretary, and neighbors to the famous and once famous have recorded glimpses of the man. Serious biographical studies include the thoughtful analysis of critic William Irvine, now a half century old. More recently biographer Margot Peters has spotlighted the actresses in Shaw's life, weaving a richly detailed narrative. In another vein, both Daniel Dervin and Arnold Silver have invoked Freudian analysis to explain Shaw, Dervin citing unresolved Oedipal feelings and narcissism, Silver finding "homicidal tendencies." Michael Holroyd, meanwhile, has followed the interpretations of previous biographers, disappointing scholars.

Although many bright Irish Protestant boys endured difficult circumstances, it was the relatively unknown Bernard Shaw who in 1889 loudly proclaimed: "My business is to incarnate the Zeitgeist" (*Collected Letters*, vol. I, p. 222). Certainly no other playwright has exercised exactly his influence on society. How did Shaw circumvent the fate that seemed to have decreed that he live and die a clerk in Dublin?

Exploring the many contradictions Shaw presented reveals another Shaw, his real nature intimately but disjunctively connected with his art. Far more enigmatic and complex than the fabricated G.B.S. image, the real

Shaw was a man whose relation to the feminine – in himself and others – hailed from a highly extravagant inner life. As he struggled heroically against his own ambivalences, the artist emerged triumphant. Nurtured too in such rich soil was Shaw the feminist, not only by the standards of the nineteenth century but also by today's criteria as we approach the twenty-first century. What was the nature of the man that eluded detection for so long?[1]

Bernard Shaw was born in Dublin on July 26, 1856, the third child and first son of Lucinda Elizabeth Gurly Shaw (Bessie) and George Carr Shaw. As a member of the much resented Protestant ascendancy, the Shaws laid claim to a relatively high rung on the ladder of prestige. Bessie, the motherless daughter of a country gentleman, displeased both her father and her very proper aunt when she married a matrimonial adventurer nearly twice her age. George Carr Shaw, a civil clerk turned wholesale corn merchant, boasted of his kinship to a baronet. But the family had more pretensions than money. "I was a downstart and the son of a downstart," wailed Shaw (Preface to *Immaturity*, p. x).[2] Yet he held to the unverified research of Alexander Macintosh Shaw that the Shaws were descended from Macduff, slayer of Macbeth: "It was as good as being descended from Shakespear, whom I had unconsciously resolved to reincarnate from my cradle" (p. xii). Indeed Shaw spent a lifetime in rivalry with his literary "father," fashioning a dialogue with his powerful precursor that extends through the puppet play *Shakes versus Shav*, written the year before his death.

Behind the Shaw family façade of snobbery and pretense lurked the reality of daily humiliations incurred by both parents. George Carr Shaw boasted of his teetotalism but slipped away to drink in solitary and morose fashion. His embarrassing alcoholism led to the family's banishment from the home of the baronet, Sir Robert Shaw of Bushy Park. Even more portentously for the young Shaw, the drunken father tried to throw his son into a canal. The sudden terrible recognition of his father's fallibility was aggravated by Bessie Shaw's response: contempt for her husband and a refusal to comfort her young son. The man claimed to be marked for life by that disillusioning incident. Quite early the boy learned that his father's drunkenness had to be "either a family tragedy or a family joke," thereby embracing a polarized approach to life (Preface to *Immaturity*, p. xxvi).

Bessie Shaw offered her own humiliations. For she defied the Shaw family creed by singing in Roman Catholic churches and entertaining Catholic musicians in her home. Even more devastating for her son was the *ménage à trois* formed with her voice teacher, George J. Vandeleur Lee, who moved in with the family when Shaw was ten, and soon arranged for them all to share a cottage in rural Dalkey, outside Dublin. Although Shaw insisted that it was an innocent arrangement, his preoccupation with his mother's virtue suggests that he feared otherwise. Meanwhile the influence of the mesmeric Lee on Shaw proved profound and lifelong.

Late in life Shaw claimed to reveal "a secret kept for 80 years": the shame he endured in attending the Central Model Boys' School with the sons of Catholic tradesmen (*Sixteen Self Sketches*, p. 20). As a result he was ostracized by the sons of Protestant gentlemen. In recalling his shame and schoolboy difficulties, Shaw omits a crucial piece of information – that he was subjected to taunts because of a highly visible effeminacy. That effeminacy was the reason he was later chosen to play Ophelia in a production of *Hamlet* at the Dublin English Scientific and Commercial Day School.

Although there was always money for alcohol, George Carr Shaw had no money to give his son a university education and Shaw never forgave his father for sending him to work at age fifteen. Becoming an ill-paid clerk for a land agency was one of the few acceptable forms of employment for a gentleman's son; the lucrative retail trade was contemptuously dismissed. Despite himself, the adolescent Shaw proved so competent that after the cashier absconded with office funds the young stopgap landed the job. Later transferred to make room for his employer's nephew, the incensed Shaw claimed he had resigned to follow his self-perceived destiny as Shakespeare's heir; "For London as London, or England as England, I cared nothing. If my subject had been science or music I should have made for Berlin or Leipsic. If painting, I should have made for Paris ... But as the English language was my weapon, there was nothing for it but London." (*Preface to Immaturity*, p. xxxviii).

There was another incentive for Shaw to leave his native land – reunion with his mother. For three years earlier Bessie Shaw had abandoned her son and husband to follow Lee to London. She took her eldest daughter Agnes, and sent for daughter Lucinda Frances (Lucy). Shaw arrived in England just a few days after Agnes had died from consumption, moving in with his mother and sister. Bessie was teaching singing and Lucy was trying to make a career singing in *opéra bouffe*. Both women rebelled against their gender-defined roles and were crucial in Shaw's sympathy with the plight of the independent woman. But it was his mother's assertion of female power and her defiance of assigned female roles concerning sexuality, respectability, and career fulfillment that most affected Shaw. When Lee began forcing his attentions on Lucy, Bessie took the "Method," his yoga-like approach to teaching voice, and set up shop herself. It was a more radical move than that of Eliza in *Pygmalion* (another Elizabeth) who only threatened to appropriate Higgins's method of voice articulation. In *Pygmalion*, Shaw explores the intersection of male artistic creation and female self-creation.

During the next nine years, Shaw contributed virtually nothing to his own support, although he made desultory and mostly abortive attempts at finding employment. His first meager pay came from acting as ghostwriter for Lee. His brief buzzings as a weekly pseudonymous music critic for the soon defunct *Hornet* would evolve into the sparkling witticisms and musical perceptions of "Corneto di Bassetto" for *The Star* and of G.B.S. for *The World;* his music criticism would culminate with *The Perfect Wagnerite* (1898), his reading of Wagner's *Ring*. He became a book reviewer for the *Pall Mall Gazette* (1885–88) and an art critic for *The World* (1886–90). He also established himself as a theatre critic, being seemingly omnipresent in that capacity during a stint for the *Saturday Review* (1895–98).

In 1880, the budding critic had not hesitated to launch an attack on the powerful and preeminent actor-manager Henry Irving for his "mutilation" of Shakespeare (a theme Shaw would continually return to even as he denounced "Bardolatry," unconditional admiration of the Bard). His last piece of dramatic criticism would be a May 1950 defense of his own drama of ideas against an attack by playwright Terence Rattigan. The nonagenarian drove home the point: "my plays are all talk, just as Raphael's pictures are all paint, Michael Angelo's statues all marble, Beethoven's symphonies all noise" (*The Drama Observed*, vol. IV, p. 1524). Meanwhile, in the intervening seven decades, Shaw produced some fifteen hundred pages of vigorous prose, peppered with classical, literary, and biblical allusions. Not content merely to review, he campaigned for his vision of the theatre and proselytized for his theories of art; he offered practical advice on stage technique and acting, celebrated the intensity of puppets, and analyzed the relation of the cinema to the theatre. His pieces are so interlaced with provocative commentary on social, moral, and artistic issues that they offer a lens into the very fabric of his society – everything from diet to the penal code. In various guises, he ponders male/female relations in a restrictive society: "I cannot for the life of me see why it is less dishonorable for a woman to kiss and tell than a man"; and "Can any sane person deny that a contract 'for better, for worse' destroys all moral responsiblity?" Married people should be "as responsible for their good behavior to one another as business partners are" (*The Drama Observed*, vol. II, p. 629; vol. III, p. 1036). Outfitted with sound judgment, discriminating taste, and an unfailing wit, Shaw produced the finest body of dramatic criticism since William Hazlitt.

But before the mature journalist and critic emerged there was a time of apprenticeship. He spent his days at the British Museum Reading Room learning his craft. His evenings were occupied with the myriad societies he joined – debating societies, literary societies, political societies. Already he had set himself to the task that would occupy him for more than seven decades: fashioning himself into political and social activist, cultural commentator and satirist, playwright and prophet.

Shaw's development as a playwright cannot be understood apart from his socialism, a cause for which he labored for more than sixty-five years. One September evening in 1882, he heard the American orator Henry George speak on land nationalization and the importance of economics suddenly flashed on him. A few months later, after struggling with the French translation of the first volume of *Capital*, he underwent a "complete conversion" to Marx (*Sixteen Self Sketches*, p. 58). Shaw, who felt compelled to polarize life's possibilities, found Marx's dialectic of history psychologically appealing. Now with a mission in life, Shaw brought the gospel of Marx to the people, speaking in streets and parks, in halls and drawing rooms. Like his hero Sidney Trefusis in *An Unsocial Socialist* (1883), his fifth novel, written during this time, Shaw saw his calling as that of "saviour of mankind" (*Collected Works*, vol. V, p. 110).

The flirtation with Marx was brief. In May, 1884, intrigued by the pamphlet *Why are the Many Poor?* he turned up at a meeting of the newly formed Fabian Society. The name was derived from the Roman general Fabius Cunctator, for the Fabians were attracted to what was believed to be his battle strategy against invading Carthaginian general Hannibal. The Fabian credo declared: "For the right moment you must wait, as Fabius did most patiently, when warring against Hannibal, though many censured his delays, but when the time comes, you must strike hard, as Fabius did, or your waiting will be in vain, and fruitless."

As the socialist group struggled to define itself and to reconcile its visionary and practical elements, Shaw contributed *A Manifesto*, Fabian Tract no. 2, which wittily declared that "Men no longer need special political privileges to protect them against Women, and that the sexes should henceforth enjoy equal political rights." Thanks to Shaw, the equal rights of women were firmly established as a Fabian principle from the outset. Meanwhile the pamphleteer was in his glory as he turned out tract after tract on socialism.

Believing that human nature is "only the raw material which Society manufactures into the finished rascal or the finished fellowman" (*The Road to Equality*, p. 96), Shaw collaborated with staunch Fabian friends like Sidney Webb, Sydney Olivier, and Graham Wallas ("the Three Musketeers & D'Artagnan") to forge a better society (*Collected Letters*, vol. II, p. 490).

Everywhere he preached that human potential was being stymied and depraved by inequality. Challenged by hecklers or socialists of other stripes, the accomplished platform speaker demolished the opposition with his devastating wit.

Although devoted to socialism, Shaw was no Utopian, one of the four chief strains of socialist thought in the nineteeth century, along with the Fabian, Marxist, and Christian Socialist. Unlike artist-poet-socialist William Morris, Shaw feared a "catastrophic policy for simultaneously destroying existing institutions and replacing them with a ready-made Utopia" (*Road*, p. 31). He sought a revolution that would be "gradual in its operation" (*Road*, p. 35). The Fabian policy of "permeation," of infiltrating key organizations, fits perfectly with his psychological need to overturn the *status quo* covertly.

As a critic and platform speaker, Shaw was now a highly visible figure in Victorian London. Four of the five novels he had produced methodically during days spent at the British Museum Reading Room were serialized in little magazines. *Cashel Byron's Profession*, his fourth novel (1883), based on his own acquaintance with the boxing ring, was also published in book form, and to some popular acclaim. In 1901, to protect the novel from theatrical piracy, he transformed it into a play himself. Written in blank verse in one week, it emerged as *The Admirable Bashville*. However, the satiric view of Victorian morality and sentimentality that characterized the novels doomed the author to remain essentially unsuccessful as a novelist.

The novels, all autobiographically revealing, document Shaw's early feminist sympathies. In the conclusion of *Immaturity*, Harriet Russell advises Shaw's hero, the jejune Robert Smith, that marriage is "not fit for some people; and some people are not fit for it" (*Collected Works*, vol. I, p. 437). Shaw explores that view further in *The Irrational Knot*, the title a reference to the matrimonial knot. The pregnant Marian Conolly has had a romance, left her husband, and refuses to return even after he tells her she "may have ten romances every year with other men... Be anything rather than a ladylike slave and liar" (*Collected Works*, vol. II, p. 349). Similarly *Love Among the Artists* praises unconventional women who place their professional identities before domesticity. *Cashel Byron's Profession* wittily overturns cultural stereotypes on two fronts: Cashel, boxing champion supreme and Shaw's first vital genius, cheerfully gives up his career to marry Lydia Carew, who claims she wants him for eugenic purposes – *her* intellect and *his* physique. In *An Unsocial Socialist*, Shaw playfully satirizes his hero as a political firebrand who, at novel's end, has met his match in the down-to-earth woman who will marry him and tame him. Throughout the novels, Shavian barbs are aimed at Victorian hypocrisy surrounding love and marriage.

Shaw's growth as a writer during his apprenticeship period was paralleled by the crafting of the persona eventually known as G.B.S. Part of that persona involved an array of seemingly idiosyncratic personal interests and habits. Probing them uncovers a psychological minefield.

Shaw's conversion to vegetarianism in 1881 was more than a trendy cheap alternative to the badly boiled eggs he ate at home. His most famous pronouncement was to a packed meeting of the newly formed Shelley Society where he trumpeted that he was, like Shelley, "a Socialist, Atheist, and Vegetarian" (*Sixteen Self Sketches*, p. 58). It was not mere showmanship because for Shaw vegetarianism had links to the artistic, the political, and the religious. Not only did it fuel his great energy, vegetarianism was necessary in his quest for "fragility" (*Collected Letters*, vol. II, p. 27). Fighting his appetite and watching his weight scrupulously, he attacked meat-eating as a form of cannibalism; it was repugnant to his nature – the higher nature. He invested food and eating with ritualistic meaning, embracing vegetarianism the way saints embrace vigils and fasts. Avoiding alcohol, tea, and coffee, feasting on wheatmeal porridge and lentils, he became a missionary whose creed was celebrated with barley water.

He longed, like his Don Juan, to escape the tyranny of the flesh with its eternal counter-pull to the rank crawling underground world of weasels, stoats, and worms that made him shudder, the stupid "forces of Death and Degeneration" (*Collected Plays*, vol. II, p. 661). From the mire of such a dread world arose his militant antivivisectionism. Shaw explicitly equated experiments on animals with those on human beings. The butcher uses animal bodies as an end, the vivisectionist as a means, and both kill animals in the service of human desires. Shaw's seeming high-minded stand may have issued from a buried fear that the hand that smote the rabbit could well smite him. In his outrage at vivisection, Shaw never incriminated Lee or called him vivisector. Yet Lee experimented on cadavers and the heads of birds in his effort to locate the secret of bel canto. Lee's dark secrets were all too closely associated with Bessie, his star pupil.

Shaw suffered from a bout of smallpox in May 1881. He claimed to be unblemished but it left his chin and jaw pockmarked, marks concealed by the famous beard that he then nurtured for the first time. His psychological scars were deeper and not so easily concealed. He launched a lifelong campaign against doctors as well as against the vaccination that failed to give him full protection. The one-hundred-page 1911 Preface to *The Doctor's Dilemma* and the 1931 collection of articles known as *Doctors'*

Delusions are major prose examples of doctors as perpetrators. The theme of victimization appears as early as an 1887 book review attacking vivisection and as late as comments in *Everybody's Political What's What?* (1944). In his hatred of the medical profession and scientific medicine, he specifically attacked Edward Jenner, Louis Pasteur, and Joseph Lister. The three men had one thing in common: their fame rested on controlling micro-organisms.

Shaw's hatred stemmed from a peculiar sense of being assailed by an unseen world of germs, which he evidenced in a virulent hypochondria. At the same time, he scoffed at that concept of total health known as *mens sana in corpore sano*, the belief of Victorian intellectuals that training the body resulted in a vigorous mind. For Shaw, who longed for the power to will one's destiny, only the reverse would do: "it is the mind that makes the body and not the body the mind" (Preface to *Doctors' Delusions*, p. xiv and *Everybody's*, p. 247; see also "The Revolutionist's Handbook," *Collected Plays*, vol. II, p. 795).

In his drama, Shaw learned to take the materials of his life and transform the virulent into the playful. In *The Philanderer* (1893), he satirizes the vivisector in the character of Dr. Paramore, whose reputation rests on discovering a microbe in the liver that means certain death. When his discovery cannot be confirmed, he is inconsolable, even though it means perfect health for his misdiagnosed patient. Four decades later, in *Too True to be Good* (1931), Shaw satirizes the doctor who cures no disease while blaming the microbe. Comically, Shaw has the microbe appear on stage and lament that humans infect microbes, but Shaw was dead serious.

In the early 1880s Shaw immersed himself in boxing, which interested him as both a science and an art. In 1883, having acquired some reputation as a boxer, the author of *Cashel Byron's Profession* entered his name in the Queensberry Amateur Boxing Championships in both the middleweight and heavyweight ("Any Weight") divisions. Although he was not given the chance to compete, The Fighting Irishman from the British Museum carefully preserved the program. His fascination for the sport as a trial of skill never waned as he commented and analyzed in articles and letters, always disdaining the slug fest. Shaw implied that boxing was a reenactment of primitive rites, a reaching back into Greek origins with its celebration of the male body. In *Cashel Byron's Profession*, Shaw's reveals his masculine ideal – and reverses the usual voyeurism of gazing at a female – as Lydia is dazzled by the sight of Cashel's body, whose "manly strength and beauty" is compared to the Hermes of Praxiteles (*Collected Works*, vol. IV, p. 38). Meanwhile in the drama, Shaw's characters use their fists or threaten to use them in *How He Lied to Her Husband* (1904), *Major*

Barbara (1905), *The Fascinating Foundling* (1909), *Overruled* (1912), *The Millionairess* (1934), and *Shakes Versus Shav* (1949).

Shaw's most visible eccentricity was his adoption of the clothing system of German health culturist Dr. Gustav Jaeger, who touted the hygienic effects of wearing wool. In 1885, with the insurance money from his father's death, the desperately shabby Shaw ordered new clothes. Embracing Jaegerism, he decked himself out in the knitted one-piece wool suit that buttoned up to the neck and along one side, so that he looked something like a gymnast. Eventually he would give up the extreme style of the combination for more conventional tailoring, but his favorite outfit resembled a Norfolk jacket with knee breeches. It was no mere affectation. Nor was it simply part of the attack on the unhealthy and irrational in dress launched by contemporary dress reformers like Edward Carpenter and Henry S. Salt. Shaw's wool clothes were a way to fight the dirt of life. With wool the pores could breathe. Wool let out body dirt and secretions while protecting against contamination in the external world. Carrying his woolen bedsheets with him when he traveled, pulling on gloves to keep his hands clean in the streets, wearing digital socks, garbed in the yellowish red suit, the scrupulously clean Shaw was an immaculate walking mannequin, an elaborate advertisement for the hygienic way of life.

Despite his unflagging intellectual commitment to feminism, deep ambivalences colored his personal relations with women. Pursued all over London by the most advanced women – actresses, artists, and intellectuals – Shaw nevertheless kept his virginity until age twenty-nine. Then he surrendered it to Jane (Jenny) Patterson, a tempestuous Irish widow some fifteen years his senior, and his mother's close friend. A long and stormy affair followed during which Shaw treated her as a mere convenience, while the jealous Jenny stole his mail, stalked him, threw violent tantrums, or pleaded pathetically for time with her young lover.

Undeterred, Shaw flirted with abandon and charmed women all over London. He admitted to trying to impress Eleanor Marx, the youngest daughter of Karl Marx, who confided in him her most intimate feelings, including those concerning her unhappy relations with common law husband Edward Aveling. Having engaged the affections of the irrevocably married orator and social activist Annie Besant, he fled in terror after she surprised him by drawing up a pseudo-marriage contract. He contentedly listened while writer Edith Bland told tales of husband Hubert's infidelities but refused to go any further than tea and talk with his friend's wife, thereby infuriating her. He acted as confidant and advisor to Kate Salt, whose marital difficulties turned out to stem from her lesbianism. He stole actress Florence Farr from William Butler Yeats, only to avoid her once she

1 Shaw in his Jaeger suit: Al Kozlik in the Shaw Festival's 1996 production of *The Simpleton of the Unexpected Isles*

was divorced from her absent husband. He moved in with the newly married May Morris (daughter of the great William Morris), destroying her marriage to Henry Halliday Sparling; years later May scoffed as Shaw blamed the result on a violated "Mystic Betrothal" between the two of them ("Morris," p. xxvii). All along his path were strewn the broken hearts of innumerable young Fabian women. But except for Jenny Patterson, his love affairs remained platonic.

While the relationship with May Morris was Shaw's most romanticized in-the-flesh love affair, his most ethereal romance took the form of his correspondence with Ellen Terry, the famous paper courtship between the fledgling playwright and the world-renowned actress. During the years 1895–1900, Shaw wooed her entirely through the mails. In Ellen, nine years his senior, he found a woman of great sympathy and understanding, a woman to whom he could reveal many of his deepest fears and longings. He wanted her for his plays, but shied away from meeting her so that she might admire the epistolary persona he so artfully created. Although Ellen thought otherwise, as far as Shaw was concerned, the correspondence was a completely satisfactory love affair.

The Quintessence of Ibsenism (1891), Shaw's exposition of Ibsen, contains a chapter titled "The Womanly Woman." There Shaw decries the "reckless self-abandonment" that transforms woman's passionate sexual desire into the "caresses of a maniac," a description that suggests more than his revulsion toward Jenny Patterson's feverish passion (*Collected Works*, vol. XIX, p. 38). It also reveals his own deep antipathies toward sex. Intellectually, however, he harbored no qualms in asserting a strong feminism. In order to emancipate herself, Shaw thought the Womanly Woman must repudiate "her womanliness, her duty to her husband, to her children, to society, to the law, and to everyone but herself" (p. 44).

Both his tangled personal relations with women as well as his feminist sympathies are evident very early in his drama. The playwright emerged with *Widowers' Houses* (1892), originally conceived in 1884 as a collaboration with drama critic William Archer, and based on the French formula Shaw derided shortly after in the *Saturday Review* as "Sardoodledom." Shaw's bitter satire on slum-landlordism, with its resonances to his Dublin experience in the land agency, scandalized critics. They especially detested its heroine, the darkly melodramatic Blanche Sartorius, who beats her maid.

The offstage drama surrounding his first play had its own scandalous side since Shaw's heroine was based on Jenny Patterson. Moreover, Florence Farr, who played Blanche, was being squired around town by Shaw. One evening, a screaming, swearing Jenny burst in while Shaw was visiting Florence. A "shocked and upset" Shaw determined to be finished with Jenny (*Diaries*, vol. II, p. 902). That final real-life scene is dramatized as the triangular opening scene of *The Philanderer* (1893), Shaw's second play. Leonard Charteris, the philanderer, is portrayed as cool, collected, and in control, exactly what his creator was not.

Shaw's third Unpleasant Play, *Mrs. Warren's Profession* (1893), reveals his feminist stance as he portrays the successful brothel-keeper as making a practical career choice in a society that underpays and undervalues women. From Mrs Warren's perspective, marriage is prostitution: "The only way for a woman to provide for herself decently is for her to be good to some man that can afford to be good to her. If she's in his own station of life, let her make him marry her; but if she's far beneath him she cant expect it" (*Collected Plays*, vol. I, p. 314).

Shaw's dissatisfaction with the British ideal of marriage was lasting. In the 1911 Preface to *Getting Married* (1908) – the play itself offering more than a dozen views of marriage – he calls the difference between marriage and prostitution simply the "difference between Trade Unionism and unorganized casual labor" (*Collected Plays*, vol. III, p. 501). In writing the play, Shaw was influenced by the proddings of actress Janet Achurch and Fabian Beatrice Webb, as well as the less than respectable career moves of his mother and his sister.

The Lord Chamberlain denounced *Mrs. Warren's Profession* as "immoral and otherwise improper for the stage," refusing to license the play. However to those men "surprised to see ladies present" at a private performance of the play given by the Stage Society, Shaw declared in a 1902 preface to the play that it was written for women and that it had been performed and produced mainly through the determination of women (*Collected Plays*, vol. I, p. 253).

Two other Shaw plays were to be banned. *The Shewing-up of Blanco Posnet* (1909), which the playwright called "a religious tract in dramatic form," shocked the censor into declaring it blasphemous because of the way Posnet, an accused horse thief and convert to Christianity, refers to God (*Collected Plays*, vol. III, p. 674). Shortly after the banning, Shaw flagrantly flouted the censor with *Press Cuttings* (1909). He created two characters whose satirical names were instantly recognizable, thereby brazenly violating the code which forbade offensive representations of living persons on the stage. Shaw protested that his General Mitchener was not the late Lord Kitchener and that Prime Minister Balsquith (who first appears on stage cross-dressed as a suffragette) was neither Lord Alfred Balfour nor Liberal politician Herbert Henry Asquith.

Shaw's three banned plays amounted to 10 percent of the thirty plays competely banned by the censor between 1895 and 1909, out of some eight thousand plays submitted for licensing. In the one-hundred page Preface to *The Shewing-up of Blanco Posnet*, Shaw spells out the case against stage censorship, one battle in his long struggle against all forms of censorship – including the censorship of social behavior. In his view, "much current morality as to economic and sexual relations" was "disastrously wrong" (*Collected Plays*, vol. III, p. 698).

Despite his reservations about marriage, in 1898 he married Charlotte Payne-Townshend, a wealthy Irishwoman who had led a largely social life in London since her arrival twenty years earlier from County Cork. Having been thrown together with her in a country house rented one summer by the Webbs, the eligible philanderer immediately began wooing the receptive Charlotte. Characteristically, he also retreated from her for close to two years. But then his health broke down and with it, he claimed, all objection either to his own death or to his marriage. Charlotte's first important role as wife was nurse to the bridegroom, who proceeded to suffer a series of accidents that kept him on crutches or in a wheelchair into the second year of their marriage. Sex was out and Shaw confided that the marriage was never consummated. Safe from pursuing women, the married playwright became the successful playwright.

Man and Superman (completed 1902) offers glimpses of Shaw's view of his own marriage. John Tanner warns the poet Octavius that after a week of marriage he would find even the glamorous Ann Whitefield no more inspiring than a plate of muffins. Don Juan wants to flee to heaven to escape sexual demands; there the women are so dowdy they "might be men of fifty," that is, middle-aged and sexually indistinguishable, like Charlotte (*Collected Plays*, vol. II, p. 683).

Shaw, having long associated the Don Juan myth with himself, used his play as a vehicle to elevate his ambivalent feelings toward women to a cosmic plane. The pursuing woman and the retreating philsophical Don Juan are inversions that reverse the cultural stereotype of passive women and active men. Nevertheless, Shaw reinforces the conventional dichotomy of woman as body, man as mind. As the Life Force courses through the determined Ann – a vitalist genius like Cashel Byron – she becomes nothing less than Woman Incarnate relentlessly seeking her mate for the sake of the children she will bear. In so doing, Shaw integrates the Don Juan myth into Creative Evolution, his private evolutionary myth, both myths depending on the power of sex.[3]

Like Blake, Shaw created his own system so he would not be enslaved by another man's. Socialism and philosophy, biology and metaphysics, merged into the religious-philosophical theory of Creative Evolution that he was to dramatize in *Back to Methuselah* (1918–20). The term declared Shaw's affinity to Henri Bergson's identically titled book, *Creative Evolution*. But before Bergson had published his discourse on the *élan vital*, Shaw had already incorporated what he called the Life Force into *Man and Superman*, for Bergson's book did not appear until 1907.

2   Eugenic fables of female superiority: the Reverend Phosphor Hammingtap (Ben Carlson)
is borne aloft by Maya, Kanchin, and Vashti (Lisa Waines, Shaun Phillips, and Janet Lo)
in the Shaw Festival's 1996 production of *The Simpleton of the Unexpected Isles*

Celibate himself, Shaw's abiding interest in human sexuality is evidenced
in his drama, in Creative Evolution, and in his consuming interest in the
science of eugenics. His concerns, which focus on the need for the human
race to evolve, are epitomized in the figure of the superman. Like his view
of himself, Shaw saw his superman as saint, artist, and genius – the
complete outsider. Many of the supermen Shaw admired – such as
Shakespeare, Goethe, Michelangelo – were considered by certain of Shaw's
contemporaries to be examples of homosexual geniuses. Shaw was also
influenced by the view of his friend Edward Carpenter, the homosexual
poet and reformer who believed that the artist's very homosexuality was
the source of his genius.

The youth in Dalkey had dreamed of amours on the plains of heaven; the
man worshipped female beauty. Fascinated and inspired by women, the
artist created the most powerful female characters on the English stage
since Shakespeare – even while believing that "[n]o fascinating woman ever
wants to emancipate her sex: her object is to gather power into the hands
of Man, because she knows that she can govern him" (*Collected Letters*,
vol. II, p. 260). His heroines variously overturn custom, care not a whit for
propriety, or pretend to be docile and submissive while joyously insisting
on their status as fully-fledged human beings.

To Ellen Terry, Shaw billed *Candida* (1894) as "THE Mother Play" (*Collected Letters*, vol. I, p. 641). His heroine is worshipped by both her husband, the Reverend James Mavor Morell, and the effeminate poet Marchbanks. Candida encompasses three female roles raised to exaltation – domestic maid, enchantress, angel – and the play exposes patriarchal assumptions concerning love and marriage when she gives herself to "the weaker of the two," the tearful Morell (*Collected Plays*, vol. I, p. 591). Shaw later contended that it was meant as a "counterblast" to Ibsen since in the typical doll's house "it is the man who is the doll," a view representing his own experience at least (*Collected Plays*, vol. I, p. 603).

Lady Cicely Waynflete (created with Ellen Terry in mind), a woman of the managing type like Mrs. Warren, is the sole woman in *Captain Brassbound's Conversion* (1899), where she instructs a brigand and overpowers everyone she meets. With God's work still to be done, Barbara Undershaft, in *Major Barbara*, agrees to marry her "dear little Dolly boy," but ideology more than love plays Cupid (*Collected Plays*, vol. III, p. 184). Lina Szczepanowska, the valiant aviator and acrobat in *Misalliance* (1909), wears male garb and triumphantly eschews female roles – especially bourgeois marriage – affirming her independent womanhood in one of the finest bravura pieces in Shaw. Similarly Joan wears clothes that reflect her true role – leading soldiers for God – and rises to lyricism as she expresses her need for unfettered freedom, even at the cost of her earthly body (*Saint Joan*, 1923). Millionairess Epifania Ognisanti di Parerga Fitzfassenden is a judo expert who talks like a man and uses her fists on her passionless bridegroom (*The Millionairess*, 1934). Meanwhile female creations like Mrs. George in *Getting Married* (1908) and Hesione Hushaby in *Heartbreak House* (1917) are drenched in a seemingly supernatural sexuality. In Shaw's comic universe, women are more than equal to the ineffectual men around them.

Given Shaw's outspokenness on gender issues and his depiction of strong women in his artistic works, it is not surprising that women sought his political backing. In 1912 when actress Lena Ashwell, president of the female Three Arts Club, asked him to speak on equal rights for professional women, he readily agreed. But he was not always so agreeable where the Woman Suffrage Campaign was concerned. Although Shaw was in sympathy with the suffragettes' goal, he tailored the role he played to fit his own agenda. Privately to his sister, Lucy Carr Shaw, he insisted that women were better off speaking for themselves and, besides, his views on the subject were well known (*Collected Letters*, vol. II, p. 904). Publicly he exaggerated his reluctance, declaring that men at public meetings "brought forward between petticoats . . . looked so horribly ignominious and did it so much worse" than women (*Fabian Feminist*, p. 229). There were other ways to help. With his assistance, American actress and feminist Elizabeth Robins succeeded in getting her suffrage play, *Votes for Women!*, produced at the Royal Court Theatre in 1907.[4]

Shaw was often prompted by events. In addition to numerous comments on the subject, he penned half a dozen essays devoted to woman suffrage. When Sir Almroth Wright posited a specifically feminine mind as a case against woman suffrage, Shaw countered that woman's mind is "exactly like Man's mind" (*Fabian Feminist*, p. 244). In an address in March 1913, he attacked the practice of forcible feeding of suffragettes, expanding the issue of woman's rights beyond suffrage to a more inclusive "commonsense" issue. He asserted that "the denial of any fundamental rights" to a woman is really "a violation of the soul" and an attack "on that sacred part of life which is common to all of us"(*Fabian Feminist*, p. 235). In May 1913, after the government had attempted to suppress *The Suffragette*, the organ of the Woman's Social and Political Union, he protested the action. A few weeks later he wrote three newspaper pieces remonstrating against the government's barbaric treatment of suffragettes, whom he referred to as martyrs.

But Shaw also annoyed suffragettes by suggesting that what was needed was a "coupled vote," every vote cast to be for a pair consisting of a man and a woman so that there would be an equal number of men and women in the elected body. A decade after women had been enfranchised in England, he returned to the idea of the "coupled vote" in the Preface to *"In Good King Charles's Golden Days"* (1939), writing that women, as he had predicted, had used their vote "to keep women out of Parliament" (*Collected Plays*, vol. VII, p. 208).

Feminists might disagree with his assessment of the way women used the vote; nevertheless Shaw still subscribed to the belief he had uttered in 1907 during a rare appearance at a meeting of the National Union of Women's Suffrage Societies: "I deny that any social problem will ever be satisfactorily solved unless women have their due share in getting it solved. Let us get this obstacle of the political slavery of women out of the way and then we shall see all set to work on the problems – both sexes together with a will" (*Fabian Feminist*, p. 254).

Shaw, as always, preferred to lead his own movement, not to march under someone else's banner. He saw his work as that of guiding the Fabians toward a new society to benefit both women and men. And, as is suggested below, he also actively pursued his own covert agenda for gender and sexual tolerance.

Shaw's feminist comment that "a woman is really only a man in petticoats" has often been noted. The ignored second half of his aphorism is just as striking. Writing that "a man is a woman without petticoats," he makes the petticoats the essential mark of gender (*Platform and Pulpit*, p. 174). That is, he confers on woman the signifying power of gender, thereby reversing the way gender was determined in his phallocratic society. Similarly – and cryptically – in the Preface to *Saint Joan*, Shaw writes that "it is not necessary to wear trousers and smoke big cigars to live a man's life any more than it is necessary to wear petticoats to live a woman's" (*Collected Plays*, vol. VI, p. 35).

Decades earlier, during a noisy scandal in 1889 involving a male bordello, Shaw wrote a carefully worded letter to the editor of *Truth* under the banner of "moral responsibility." Well aware that "men are loth to meddle" because they might be suspected of acting in their own personal interest, he nevertheless spoke out against the "principle of the law" that inflicted "outrageous penalties" upon consenting adults (*Collected Letters*, vol. I, pp. 230–32). The letter, which showed familiarity with both current and historical views on homosexuality, was never published.

Shaw's stands on the subject remained progressive. He became an early member of the British Society for the Study of Sex Psychology, a membership he kept so quiet that it has escaped the notice of his previous biographers. Established in 1914 to educate the public on issues of sex, the Society was specifically dedicated to reforming the laws on homosexuality. Significantly, the nucleus of the Society was composed of former members of the Order of Chaeronea, a secret society formed in the 1890s by literary and professional men to work for homosexual liberation. Only a few of the Order's members have been conclusively identified.

There is a pattern of evidence in Shaw's life, including his preoccupation with questions of heredity, genius, and "inversion," that suggests that he secretly viewed himself as a "noble invert" – an ascetic artist whose gifts were linked to a homoerotic source. Of his many friendships with men, the closest was with Harley Granville Barker, twenty-one years his junior, a young genius whose gifts he extolled.

Shaw entered into a triumphant theatrical partnership with Barker and John Eugene Vedrenne at the Royal Court Theatre from 1904 to 1907. Brilliant productions from Euripides to contemporary drama, especially Shaw, were mounted. Until then, despite success overseas, Shaw had only a coterie following. Now his work accounted for 70 percent of the Royal Court performances and established him as a successful playwright, even as he cast, directed, and staged his own plays.

Shaw's association with Barker proved an extraordinarily productive one as the men wrote plays in virtual dialogue with one another, themes of one playwright resonating in the work of the other. Shaw plays written during the Court Theatre years were *John Bull's Other Island, How He Lied to Her Husband, Major Barbara, The Doctor's Dilemma.* As the friendship continued, the plays continued to flow: *Getting Married, The Shewing-Up of Blanco Posnet, Misalliance, The Dark Lady of the Sonnets, Fanny's First Play, Androcles and the Lion, Overruled,* as well as several playlets and his prose tract *Common Sense about the War.* Having written *Pygmalion,* he fell in love with his own creation one pleasant afternoon as he read it to Mrs. Patrick Campbell, for whom he had created Eliza Doolittle. As Shaw raved about Stella, London buzzed with gossip. But the resurrected Don Juan image was a sham – the much too public indiscretions only a game and so carefully revealed to Ellen Terry for *her* pleasure (*Collected Letters,* vol. III, p. 111).

Then disaster struck. Barker was swept off his feet by Helen Huntington, wife of the American millionaire, Archer M. Huntington. He divorced actress Lillah McCarthy, the two having fallen in love a decade earlier playing John Tanner and Ann Whitefield during the first production of *Man and Superman.* Jealous of Barker's relationship with Shaw, Helen Huntington forbade all contact between the two men. Losing Barker was a tragedy for Shaw. Feeling "suicidal," he began writing *Heartbreak House* (*Bernard Shaw and Mrs. Campbell,* p. 209). Captain Shotover's warning to the cultured leisure class was also a warning to Barker, whom Shaw thought seduced by luxury into a drifting existence: "Navigation. Learn it and live; or leave it and be damned" (*Collected Plays,* vol. V, p. 177). *The Secret Life,* Barker's haunting and subtle drama (published 1922), can be read as his melancholy response to Shaw's plea – sometimes only the unattainable can content one and sometimes irrevocable loss brings relief. Although Shaw futilely hoped that the two could reconcile, Barker was a lost cause and his creative life was submerged. Not even T. E. Lawrence (Lawrence of Arabia), a mutual friend whose help Shaw enlisted, could rescue Barker from what Shaw viewed as a life of damnation with Helen.

As wishfulness, longing, and didacticism merged, more and more in his drama Shaw turned to allegory, a form he perfected with *Heartbreak House.* Indeed the play may be the premier example in twentieth-century drama of didactic intention shaping art. Openly amenable to fantasy, in allegory Shaw had a flexible forum to state his beliefs unhampered by the demands of character psychology, as in plot-structured works, or the strictures of negative statement, as in satire.[5]

Shaw's longing for a bodiless ethereal realm is the most startling characteristic of *Back to Methuselah,* the huge allegory he called his "Metabiological Pentateuch." *In the Beginning* opens in the Garden of Eden with Adam, Eve, and the Serpent, the very first *ménage à trois.* It is the Serpent who reveals the guilty secret of human sexuality to a stricken Eve; his laughter makes the Fall a dirty joke. In *The Gospel of the Brothers Barnabas*, set in the first years after World War I, Creative Evolution is posited as promising the longevity needed to advance the human race. In *The Thing Happens*, two unexceptional characters from the former play are the seeming rulers of the British Islands in the year 2170 and an African woman "the real president" (*Collected Plays*, vol. V, p. 477). By 3000 AD, *The Tragedy of an Elderly Gentleman*, the seemingly emotionless, soulless longlivers outnumber the shortlivers, who are highly susceptible to discouragement. Finally, in the year 31,920 AD, *As Far as Thought Can Reach*, human beings hatch from eggs, quickly advance beyond the physical, spend hundreds and hundreds of years in contemplation, and long for life without flesh, "the vortex freed from matter . . . the whirlpool in pure intelligence" (*Collected Plays*, vol. V, p. 630).

In *Saint Joan*, Shaw's next play, he turned from imagining an elusive bodiless future to portraying a historical figure, specifically a figure who had been both elevated and denigrated in the various tellings of her story. Cutting through the carapace of legend, Shaw depicts Joan as a spiritual heroine and an "unwomanly woman." She is both practical and passionate by nature, a woman whose virginity stems from strength, not from mere Victorian purity. As she exercises her individual will and insists on her private vision, she becomes a conduit of evolutionary thought and behavior.

Joan bears striking parallels to the playwright. Like her creator, she was almost drowned by a terrible father, unflinchingly fights hypocrisy, is a vital genius, is the rare Galtonic visualizer (one whose mind's eye is like a magic lantern), and has been forced to live precariously among those who persecute the superior individual. Shaw's self-identification with his androgynous heroine – martyred for revealing her true feelings – results in a play where tragic overtones are tempered by the satiric wit and the generically comic form. The play opens as farce but steadily darkens until the epilogue of Shaw's irreverent divine comedy. Then Joan's brief return to earth signals the comic turn, as those who praise her vanish at the prospect of her resurrection. Only in some future time will saints – and geniuses – be safe on "this beautiful earth" (*Collected Plays*, vol. VI, p. 208).

Saint Joan resulted in a canonization of sorts for the playwright, who received the Nobel Prize for 1925, but, refusing the money, transferred the funds to the newly created Anglo-Swedish Literary Foundation. Meanwhile there was creative silence while Shaw labored on *The Intelligent Woman's Guide to Socialism and Capitalism*. Then Barker published *His Majesty*, his last play, and Shaw responded with *The Apple Cart*, and his own impotent king. Remarkably, Shaw's career stretched forward another two decades.

Addressing the International Congress of the World League for Sexual Reform, the ascetic speaker elicited a laugh when he presented himself as an expert on sex. He visited Russia and met Stalin, Gorki, and Stanislavsky. He met Ghandi. He wrote a prose fable, *The Adventures of the Black Girl in Her Search for God* (1932), and made his first visit to America the following year. He wrote a dramatic eugenic fable, *The Simpleton of the Unexpected Isles* (1934), too blithely satirized the European dictators in *Geneva* (1936, final revision 1947), and again wrote his own brand of history with *"In Good King Charles's Golden Days."* As late as *Farfetched Fables* (1948), he was still wedding allegory and eugenics in his drama.

The world-famous Shaw lived half his life in the tiny village of Ayot St. Lawrence. There he spent his days writing in the little hut that revolved to catch the sun. He wrote virtually to the end of his days with a mind clear and unclouded by age. To celebrate his ninety-fourth birthday, he wrote *Why She Would Not.* He was working on a rhyming picture guide to Ayot St. Lawrence at the time of his death, the result of a fall in his garden. On his death bed, he spoke of Barker whose death four years earlier had prompted a public written tribute from the ancient playwright.

He remained a vegetarian, an antivivisectionist, an antivaccinationist, a wool-wearer, a eugenicist, a Fabian, and a feminist. Whatever Shaw's personal unhappiness, the extraordinarily productive life featured an upward trajectory, as he imposed his will and exercised his fancy on seemingly intractable materials, spinning out glorious comedies and enduring parables. Always his vision of the stage was as the apex of human endeavor, a place of beauty and spirituality. Believing that the fates of artists, homosexuals, and women are intertwined, insisting that all great art is didactic, he valiantly worked for a society unblemished by the inequalities of class or gender. "This is the true joy in life, the being used for a purpose recognized by yourself as a mighty one"(*Collected Plays*, vol. II, p. 667).

NOTES

1 For a full spelling out of the ideas in this essay, see my biography, *Bernard Shaw: The Ascent of the Superman* (New Haven: Yale University Press, 1996).

2 Quotations are from the following: *Bernard Shaw: Collected Letters*, ed. Dan H. Laurence, 4 vols. (New York: Dodd, Mead, 1965, 1972, New York: Viking, 1985, 1988); *The Bodley Head Bernard Shaw: Collected Plays with Their Prefaces*, ed. Dan H. Laurence, 7 vols. (London: Max Reinhardt, The Bodley Head, 1970–74); *The Collected Works of Bernard Shaw*, Ayot St. Lawrence edition, 30 vols. (New York: William H. Wise, 1930–32); *Bernard Shaw: The Diaries, 1885–1897*, ed. Stanley Weintraub, 2 vols. (University Park: Pennsylvania State University Press, 1986); *Bernard Shaw: The Drama Observed*, ed. Bernard F. Dukore, 4 vols. (University Park: Pennsylvania State University Press,

1993); Bernard Shaw, *Everybody's Political What's What?* (New York: Dodd, Mead, 1947); *Fabian Feminist: Benard Shaw and Woman*, ed. Rodelle Weintraub (University Park: Pennsylvania State University Press, 1977); Frank Harris, *Bernard Shaw* (New York: Garden City, 1931); May Morris, "Morris As I Knew Him," in *William Morris: Artist, Writer, Socialist, Volume the Second: Morris as a Socialist*, pages ix-xl; (1936, rpt. New York: Russell and Russell, 1966. *Bernard Shaw*, Preface to *Doctors' Delusions*, in *Collected Works*, vol. XXII; *Bernard Shaw*, Preface to *Immaturity*, in *Collected Works*, vol. I; *Bernard Shaw: Platform and Pulpit*, ed. Dan H. Laurence (New York: Hill and Wang, 1961); *Bernard Shaw: The Road to Equality: Ten Unpublished Lectures and Essays, 1884–1918.* ed. Louis Crompton (Boston: Beacon Press, 1971); Bernard Shaw, *Sixteen Self Sketches* (London: Constable, 1949); *Bernard Shaw and Mrs. Patrick Campbell: Their Correspondence*, ed. Alan Dent (New York: Knopf, 1952).

3 On the role of myth in the structure of *Man and Superman*, see my essay "Ann and Superman: Type and Archetype," in *Fabian Feminist*. Reprinted in *George Bernard Shaw: Modern Critical Views* and *George Bernard Shaw's Man and Superman: Modern Critical Interpretations*, both ed. Harold Bloom (New Haven: Chelsea House, 1987).

4 On Shaw's reluctance, Margot Peters sees Shaw as feeling emasculated by the movement as well as disagreeing with both the guerilla tactics and the conservative politics of Emmeline and Christabel Pankhurst; see *Bernard Shaw and the Actresses* (Garden City, New York: Doubleday & Co., 1980), p. 314. Katherine E. Kelly traces Shaw's differences with the suffragettes and sees a fear of female power and of feminization; see "Shaw on Woman Suffrage: A Minor Player on the Petticoat Platform," in *The Annual of Bernard Shaw Studies*, 14: 1992: *Shaw and the Last Hundred Years*, ed. Bernard F. Dukore (University Park: Pennsylvania State University Press, 1994), pp. 67–81.

5 For a structural analysis of *Heartbreak House* as allegory, see my essay "*Heartbreak House*: Shaw's Ship of Fools," *Modern Drama*, 21, 3 (1978), pp. 267–86.

2

KATHERINE E. KELLY

Imprinting the stage: Shaw and the publishing trade, 1883–1903

Shaw's efforts to publish his plays for a large reading public helped define the "New" or "Modern" Drama as a reading as well as performing canon.[1] Deliberately following the example of Henrik Ibsen whose plays often circulated in printed translations before being produced, Shaw aimed to fashion his plays as "high" art by giving his published scripts the material look and poetic weight of fiction and poetry. Shaw promoted play publication not to devalue stage production but to reclaim for the playwright from the actor-manager both legal ownership and primary authorship of the written script. Determined to strengthen playwrights' economic and cultural leverage by establishing their status as authors, Shaw argued for the literary merits of drama and for the author's exclusive right to the script as a property.[2] Grounding his economic plan for selling his labour in Fabian socialist principles, Shaw anchored his aesthetic plan for publishing his plays in a modest adaptation of William Morris's revolutionary return to the arts of papermaking, printing, and bookbinding.

By all indications, Shaw's program to reform the profession of playwright was long overdue. Before 1911, the weakness of nineteenth-century copyright protection for dramatic scripts and the absence of a significant reading public for drama made it virtually impossible for most playwrights to earn a sustained income from their published works.[3] Playwrights not only failed to make money from their writing but also lacked the legal means to protect their rights as authors. As J. R. Stephens has noted, "For effective copyright protection, the drama requires a formula which covers not merely the words on the page but the representation of that text in public performance on the stage" (*The Profession of the Playwright*, p. 84). In the absence of such a formula, unethical publishers had a long established practice of printing versions of plays still in manuscript, while unscrupulous theatre managers planted groups of longhand writers in audiences to copy particular characters' parts, which, when combined, amounted to a full manuscript of a play gotten merely for the cost of the

25

copiers' labor. To the dramatist's peril, the drama posed an anomalous case for copyright legislation, which the law effectively ignored and/or failed to enforce until the Copyright Act of 1911, which improved dramatists' odds of winning damages.

By 1886, Shaw was earning the attention of literate intellectuals as an art critic, but disappointing notice as a novelist, with editors variously informing him that readers "are not much interested in socialism."[4] Undaunted, Shaw wrote to Hubert Bland in 1889, "My one line of progress is from writing stories, reviews, and articles, more and more towards writing fully and exhaustively what I like."[5] But what Shaw "liked" was as influenced by his shrewd assessment of the business of publishing as it was by his socialism. With one eye on the popularity of Ibsen among "discriminating readers," and another eye on the censor's banning of Ibsen's plays, Shaw eventually set out to write and publish plays as mid-priced works of literature – a mode of literary production that publishers and readers customarily associated with prose fiction and poetry. Correctly anticipating the dawn of a mass reading market,[6] Shaw looked for a way to create in England and the US what he believed could be a play-reading habit. Writing to publisher T. Fisher Unwin in September of 1895, Shaw hinted broadly at his interest in being published: "If I thought that people were picking up the French trick of reading dramatic works, I should be strongly tempted to publish my plays instead of bothering to get them performed" (*Collected Letters*, vol. I, p. 557).[7] The playwright who could encourage this trick might realize a decent income from publication rights and avoid the pitfalls of dramatic piracy, so entrenched in the British theatre that three attempts at legal reform (1833, 1842, and 1911) were needed to change the practices of managers, publishers, and agents accustomed to dividing among themselves the benefits owed the playwright.

Shaw improvised a strategy for writing, designing, printing, binding, and marketing his plays that would recognize the value of his labor while fashioning his authorial persona as a literary socialist with high-art appeal. Even as he planned to publish his plays, he pushed to have them produced in England and the US, hoping they would succeed in drawing large numbers of spectators, which they eventually did. But he recognized that, more often than not, the economics of play production and the power of the censor worked against the challenging dramatic author. Under the right conditions, the book-selling market would permit him greater access and control over the production of his works than the collaborative and traditionally exploitative system of play production. If he could write and publish inexpensively a "literary" drama, that is, entertaining drama that called attention to its commerce with politics, philosophy, science, and fiction, he could extricate his labor from the grip of the censor and the playwriting pirates while creating for himself a position in the canon of an emerging "modern" drama.

By 1884, when Shaw's third novel, *An Unsocial Socialist*, was being published serially in *To-Day*, the new "Monthly Magazine of Scientific Socialism," he had already decided against assigning his copyright to a publisher indefinitely. He wrote to Swan Sonnenschein & Co. in February of 1885, "I am willing that you shall have the exclusive right to publish the book for five years on the conditions named. But the copyright must remain my property, and the book come under my control again to alter, withdraw, or do what I please with" (*Collected Letters*, vol. I, p. 117). When Swan et al. responded by offering him a fifteen year lease at a 10 percent royalty, Shaw refused, demanding a higher percentage, which he justified by sketching the future of the publishing industry over the next fifteen years. Shaw correctly predicted falling printing costs, rising values of monopoly copyrights, the bankrupting of compositors, the lowering of profits for the selling and publishing of works with competitive value, and a new preference for publishing on commission. In the event of an International Copyright Treaty, Shaw also correctly predicted that authors of reputation would deal directly with publishers in the US (*Collected Letters*, vol. I, pp. 124–25). After agreeing in the main with Shaw's forecast, the firm offered a compromise of a seven years' lease at 10 percent royalty, renewable at their option at 20 percent. Shaw accepted on condition of specifying additional points and concluded by proposing a 33 percent royalty rate on foreign copyrights. When the revised contract arrived, there were more amendments, the most sensitive of them touching on the issue of copyright assignment. Shaw wrote, "I have altered 'shall be the property of' to 'is hereby assigned by the author to.' Although a copyright is personal property, I believe we have no power to declare by a deed that it is the property of anyone in particular" (*Collected Letters*, vol. I, p. 129). Shaw clearly claimed the copyright as his and his alone.

The serializing of *An Unsocial Socialist* brought Shaw no payment from the editors of *To-Day*, but it did bring him to the attention of William Morris and Annie Besant, the socialist publisher of *Our Corner*, who eventually ran two more of his novels in serial form. The novels never drew much notice beyond this circle, and Shaw eventually abandoned attempts to write long works of prose fiction, announcing five years after completing his third and last novel, "I tried novelizing again . . . but I could not stand the form: it is too clumsy and unreal. Sometimes in spare moments I write dialogues. . . . When I have a few hundred of these dialogues worked up and interlocked, then a drama will be the result" (*Collected Letters*, vol. I, pp. 221–22). Shaw the failed novelist had no desire to court further rejection, while Shaw the Fabian socialist suspected that sermonizing in dialogue repudiated "individualism" more readily than sermonizing in long narrative blocks. In the 1887 appendix to *An Unsocial Socialist*, Shaw expressed what Michael Holroyd has called his puritan preference for romantic fiction over social fact (*Bernard Shaw*, p. 121). But the uneasiness also could be read as Shaw's suspicion of a single-voiced narrative that crowds out social facts.[8] In the "hundred of these dialogues worked up and interlocked," Shaw may have anticipated a social reality emerging from the interplay of voices in conflict. In any case, looking back fifty years later, Shaw claimed "I really hated those five novels . . . I wrote novels because everybody did so then; and the theatre, my rightful kingdom, was outside literature." (*Collected Letters*, vol. IV, p. 675) During the 1890s, Shaw would work to bring Modern Drama within the realm of literature by securing the publication of his plays in carefully prepared editions aimed at the growing market of literate readers.

While struggling to write novels he would later claim to hate, the Shaw of the 1880s was formulating a political identity that would have implications for his dealings with the publishing trade. Shaw's reading of the first volume of Karl Marx's *Das Capital* (in French translation) is widely described as occurring against the backdrop of his prior reverence for Henry George's land nationalism and single tax doctrine, his flirtation with H. M. Hyndman's Social Democratic Federation (SDF), and his early involvement with Secularism, Iconoclasm, and other varieties of free-thinking.[9] Joining the Fabian Society on May 16, 1884, and its executive committee in January of 1885, marked Shaw's shift from anarchism and the Marxism of the SDF toward the middle-class evolutionary socialism of the Fabians. By 1886, the Fabians had broken with the revolutionary SDF and with the anti-constitutional anarchists and the Socialist League. The Fabian Manifesto of 1887 declared their "permeation" strategy by which they would influence national policy by becoming politically active at all levels, especially the local, or municipal level. From such local activism, a national socialist movement would grow.[10]

Like most English readers of Marx throughout the 1880s, Shaw sub-scribed to three essential political principles: a belief in "a labour theory of value, an iron law of wages, and the idea that monopolies underlie exploitation" (Bevir, "The Marxism of George Bernard Shaw," p. 303). Beyond these commonly held principles, Shaw had unique beliefs with regard to human nature and economic competition, several of which he illustrated in his early novels.[11] The practice of economics, believed Shaw, grew from the essentially self-interested nature of each human being.

Competition between capitalists would favor the economy of larger firms, thus creating a tendency toward monopolies and trusts. Breaking up and preventing monopolies and trusts would "naturally" lead to a free-trade utopia (Bevir, "The Marxism of George Bernard Shaw," pp. 305–06).

Shaw encouraged capitalist publishers to compete for his work as a means of safeguarding his authorial interest and securing favorable royalties and other terms. His efforts in this regard could only be described as prodigious, as witnessed by his exchange of letters with publishers and editors. In March of 1885, *Time* published Shaw's short story of sixteen pages, "The Miraculous Revenge," together with his book review of Michael Davitt's "Leaves from a Prison Diary," a review Shaw undertook at the request of *Time* publisher Miss Abdy-Williams, who requested the review at a meeting of the Fabian Society. When sent a check from *Time* publishers Swan Sonnenschein & Co. for £3 3s 0d, Shaw returned it with the request that he be paid the full amount owing him, £9 9s 0d. Soon thereafter he wrote Miss Abdy-Williams for clarification, explaining, "[I]t is quite impossible for me to express to you how emphatically I would have refused to review Michael Davitt for a capitalist magazine for nothing ... We said nothing at all about payment: I concluding that there would be no question about the usual terms" (*Collected Letters*, vol. I, p. 122). Shaw defined for Swan et al. the "usual terms" to be $\frac{1}{2}$ guinea per page, "the usual rate of payment for a shilling magazine," adding acidly, "and the rate paid to the contributors to Time when it was $\frac{1}{2}$ its present price" (*Collected Letters*, vol. I, p. 123).

Shaw delivered to the same publisher in October of 1885 a brief lesson on the role of the free market in setting his value as a writer: "My standing and the value of my work are fixed by the operation of the market; and you are no more in a position to fix my price at four and threepence than I am to fix it at 400 and threepence" (*Collected Letters*, vol. I, p. 144). In an exchange lasting eight months, Shaw and Swan et al. illustrated competing views of the literary market, with Swan claiming to determine fees based upon their personal judgment of a particular writer's worth, and Shaw insisting that their judgment was not independent of the same market forces controlling his own worth and other publishers' pricing practices. It does not appear that Shaw "won" in this exchange, but he secured the satisfaction of delivering "a couple of essays on P[olitical] E[conomy]" (*Collected Letters*, vol. I, p. 144) to publishers who were fighting to keep the upper hand in negotiations with authors. The 1884 forming of the Society of Authors, which Shaw joined in 1887, signaled the beginning of a shift in the balance of power that would eventually favor the author during publishing negotiations.

By 1889, Shaw the Fabian was relishing the prospect of publishing *Fabian Essays*, approaching many of the same publishers who had rejected his fiction and noting privately, "There is nothing like [the Essays] in the market & it is *commercially unproducible*" (*Collected Letters*, vol. I, p. 225). The volume would appeal by virtue of its uniqueness, while retaining its Fabian difference from commercial best-sellers. The *Essays* were originally to have been undertaken by Unwin Brothers' firm at Chilworth, which, since 1889, had been involved in a union wage dispute. When chairman Edward Unwin refused to permit the secretary of the London Society of Compositors to attend a conference in 1889 to discuss fair wages, Shaw withdrew the *Essays* and redirected the printing job to Arthur Bonner's "fair house" (*Collected Letters*, vol. I, p. 283). Significantly, Shaw supervised all facets of production, paid for entirely by the Fabians. The *Essays* first appeared in December of 1889. The original 1,000 copies, distributed from Edward Pease's flat, "went up like smoke" and the volume proved a surprisingly steady seller. Later, in September of 1890, the Fabians published a "cheap" (six shilling) edition with the Walter Scott Publishing Co., using the plates they purchased from Bonner.

By September of 1890, Shaw was writing to Will H. Dircks, editor and reader of the Walter Scott Publishing Co., who had offered to increase the royalty rate on the essays by a halfpenny. Shaw retorted that the increase had been owing the Fabians all along. Shaw further rejected Dircks's presumption that the Fabians would agree to a two-shilling cloth edition, suggesting instead, "We might not object to allowing you to print a half crown edition on large paper, provided you gave us sixpence a copy or so" (*Collected Letters*, vol. I, p. 260). (During Shaw's absence, a split Fabian executive committee accepted Dirck's proposal for a two shilling cloth edition, provoking Shaw to write to Pease, "Ass that I was to trust my copyright to a council of pigeons!" [*Collected Letters*, vol. I, p. 265].)

When Shaw completed the financial analysis in his letter to Dircks, he turned to an aesthetic critique, blasting Scott's cover design and rejecting the handbill "with disdain." Typeface, type size, and choice of reviewers' extracts all called forth Shaw's mock rage, topped by a threat that, should Scott even consider redesigning the cover of his novel, *Cashel Byron*, to include a design "of some pugilistic kind . . . without first submitting the cover to me, I will have your heart's blood" (*Collected Letters*, vol. I, p. 260). The pugilist figure did appear on the cover of the novel, presumably with Shaw's approval (see Figure 3a). With the publication of *Fabian Essays*, Shaw began to exercise control over the design, printing, and publishing of his books in a manner consistent with his Fabian principles, which included using union (or equivalently paying) printers, protecting his

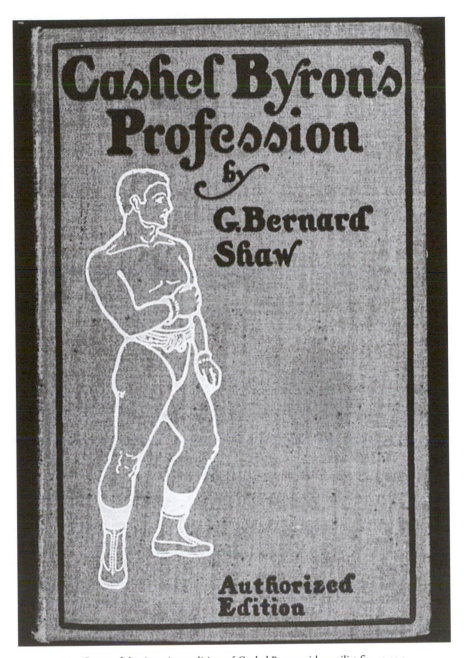

3a   Cover of the American edition of *Cashel Byron* with pugilist figure as a
marketing device

copyright as a property right, maximizing his royalties by stimulating competition, and exercising control over book production, from the setting of plates to the setting of prices.

The success of the *Essays* boosted Shaw's career as an (unpaid) lecturer, whose appearances on the platform had, until this time, been limited primarily to Sundays. By September of 1890, Shaw records in a letter, "[T]hirteen lectures within thirteen days" (*Collected Letters*, vol. I, p. 262), and notes one month later, "My addresses were magnificent – most of them; but they needed to be multiplied by dozens to be of much use" (*Collected Letters*, vol. I, p. 267). Shaw's devotion to Fabian public speaking both in London and in the provinces coincided with a near tripling of London Fabian memberships (from 300 to nearly 900) between the years 1890 and 1899. Provincial memberships increased rapidly from 1890 to 1893, peaking at about 1,500 (McBriar, *Fabian Socialism*, pp. 165–66). In retrospect, however, Shaw judged his oratory harshly, telling Lena Ashwell, "My career as a public speaker was not only futile politically . . . It was sometimes disgraceful and degrading" (quoted in Holroyd, *Bernard Shaw*, p. 196). Public speaking, the contingent, embodied performance of political conviction to a randomly gathered audience, later embarrassed a Shaw who had become adept at professionalizing his political and artistic efforts.

Ibsen: artform meets platform

In his next publication, *The Quintessence of Ibsenism* (London, Walter Scott Publishing Company, 1891), Shaw reconciled his political and aesthetic principles, finding in Ibsen a compelling critic of Victorian cant and a symbol for his own iconoclasm and that of his fellow Secularists, Richard Aveling, Eleanor Marx, and others. Shaw's iconoclasm – a cheerful rejection of dogmatism in favor of skepticism – was illustrated by his claim, "I never gave up an old belief without feeling inclined to give three cheers and jump into the air" (*Collected Letters*, vol. I, p. 302). It was roughly synonymous with "freethinking" and evolutionary in its progress. The "freethinking will" could grow and develop within an individual's world view, just as Fabian socialism would grow and spread throughout English society. But freethinking was not compatible with all forms of socialism, a strategic point Shaw made before the Fabian Society, where he embraced Ibsen as a freethinking Fabian socialist and an enemy of idealist socialism.

The Quintessence began as Shaw's contribution to the Fabian lecture series, "Socialism in Contemporary Literature," proposed in the late spring of 1890. Shaw selected Ibsen as his subject and spent two months writing a lecture that eventually raised a storm of controversy (Holroyd, *Bernard Shaw*, p. 197). For the most part, the published essay expands upon the lecture, but Shaw deleted several fragments of the original lecture from the published book. These fragments, printed in J. L. Wisenthal's *Shaw and Ibsen*,[12] reveal the particular political context within which Shaw constructed Ibsen as an anti-idealist. "With Ibsen's thesis in one's mind," wrote Shaw in an excised fragment, "it is impossible to think without concern of the appalling adaptibility [*sic*] of Socialism to idealist purposes . . . and [a] consequent number of members whose entire devotion to the ideal of Socialism enables them to enlist under the red flag as revolutionary socialists without meaning anything whatever by the word. I know that many of my colleagues believe that we shall never enlist enthusiasm for our cause unless we, like the gentleman in [Ibsen's] Pillars of Society, hold up the banner of the ideal" (quoted in Wisenthal, *Shaw and Ibsen*, p. 89). Shaw continues, "Socialism means practically the nationalization of land and capital, and nothing else. Yet we are constantly told by our own members that we lay too much stress on the economic side of socialism . . . The idealist Socialist always rebels against a reduction of socialism to practice . . ." (Wisenthal, *Shaw and Ibsen*, p. 90). The lecture provided the political occasion for Shaw's frontal attack on what he called the "idealist socialism" of the Marxists, an attack that used Ibsen's plays as a powerful aesthetic springboard. But in revising and expanding the two-hour lecture for the first published edition of 1891, Shaw would relegate the intra-socialist quarrel to a submerged, simmering text, lending subterranean intensity to his defense of Ibsen as a debunker of the ideal. Of the several lecture segments omitted from the published version, the longest pointedly condemns the anarchist Social Democratic Federation and the Socialist League, calling down – by name – those Shaw felt had sacrificed the practice of socialism for the satisfaction of proclaiming its ideals. In revising his lecture for publication, Shaw strategically avoided exposing socialist divisions, bending his energies instead on expanding his literary analysis to give his work the heft of an extended and current critical analysis of Ibsen's plays. With the significant omission of his pointed attack on the SDF and the Socialist League, Shaw's lecture provided the majority of the material for the 1891 published edition. The new material – an essay entitled "The Two Pioneers" comparing Shelley and Ibsen, an analysis of *Emperor and Galilean* and *Hedda Gabler*, as well as expanded analyses and descriptions of other individual plays – concentrated solely on his literary and philosophical analysis of Ibsen. The layering of art and politics accomplished in

Shaw's *Quintessence* foreshadowed the later Prefaces written to lengthen and mediate the reader's introduction to his published plays.

Five months after reading his lecture before the Fabian Society, Shaw wrote to French socialist Jules Magny, "I hope soon to get it into print. When Ibsen's new play appears, I shall complete my paper by an analysis of it, and then set to in earnest to get it published" (*Collected Letters*, vol. I, p. 277). Shaw recognized the potential of his lecture – widely reported in London newspapers as well as European capitals, which also covered Ibsen's responses to reports of the lecture – to attract a readership, writing in the Preface to his 1891 edition: "I had laid [the lecture] aside as a *piece d'occasion* which had served its turn, when the production of *Rosmersholm* at the Vaudeville Theatre . . . the inauguration of the Independent Theatre by Mr. J.T. Grein . . . and the sensation created by the experiment of Elizabeth Robins and Marion Lea with *Hedda Gabler*, started a frantic newspaper controversy, in which I could see no sign of any of the disputants having . . . ma[d]e up his mind definitely as to what Ibsen's plays meant, and to defend his view face to face . . . And I came to the conclusion that my explanation might as well be placed in the field until a better could be found" (Wisenthal, *Shaw and Ibsen*, p. 104). Controversy created readers, and it was no doubt the wave of public interest in "Ibsenism" together with a heated response to his lecture, that prompted Shaw to try his fortunes by expanding it into a short, book-length monograph eventually titled, *The Quintessence of Ibsenism*.

Shaw appears to have intended all along to offer the first edition of *The Quintessence* to Walter Scott for publication, in spite of goading Fisher Unwin in March of 1891 to make an extravagant counter-bid: "I have . . . attacked the Ibsen essay . . . Scott is immensely on to it . . . I suppose you are not particularly sweet on it. If you are, send me by return of post a cheque for £5,000, with an agreement securing me a $66\frac{2}{3}$% royalty, not to commence until the sixteenth copy" (*Collected Letters*, vol. I, p. 286). Three weeks later Shaw advised Unwin in a statement balancing gentlemanly honor with free market socialism, "I am in a certain degree bound to Scott, *provided he offers me no worse terms than anyone else* [my emphasis]: partly because he has behaved handsomely to Ibsen . . . and partly because he published Cashel Byron . . . (The shilling edition of the Essays [i.e. the *Fabian Essays*] – 20,000 of them all sold at one volley – must have recouped him a bit)" (*Collected Letters*, vol. I, p. 293). Scott published 2,100 copies of the book in September of 1891 at a price of two shillings, six pence.[13] Two pirated US editions – a common occurrence during this period – were issued in 1891 and 1894.[14] All told, *The Quintessence* sold 2,000 copies between 1891 and 1897.

Play publishing begins: *Widowers' Houses*

During the next three years, from 1891–94, Shaw became generally known as a public figure in London (*Collected Letters*, vol. I, p. 107), publishing seven distinct political tracts, and, in May of 1893, a small run (500) of his first published play, *Widowers' Houses*, brought out by Henry and Company as the first in the newly established "Independent Theatre Series" edited by J. T. Grein.

Begun in 1884 as a William Archer–G. B. Shaw collaboration, what was originally titled *Rheingold* proceeded from a series of "dialogues" for which William Archer provided the outline and Shaw the language, to a Shaw-only project, picked up again in 1892 and completed as *Widowers' Houses*. On November 22, 1892, two weeks before its opening date, Shaw wrote to John Lane proposing a "limited edition at a high price" and advising that if the play is to be printed, "it will need all the send-off it will get from the criticism and discussion of the performance." As always, Shaw had given the edition some thought, proposing photographs of the cast in costume and a largish (quarto) page, both designed to justify an *édition de luxe* (*Collected Letters*, vol. I, p. 370). Lane did not take up Shaw's invitation, although Shaw reported to prospective publisher Alfred T. Nutt one month later that he had received three offers for its publication. He repeated the terms offered by Henry and Company (a half-crown edition with a sixpenny royalty) in hopes Nutt would surpass them. Admitting himself somewhat beholden to Grein to accept Henry's offer, he nevertheless tempted Nutt to surpass these terms, noting more than 130 press cuttings (several of them his own) devoted to the play: "[I]t is the value of the curiosity that is now in the market," wrote Shaw candidly (*Collected Letters*, vol. I, p. 373).

Two lessons learned from his earlier experiences as a published author set his strategy for attempting to secure a publisher: (1) the play's "value" was of two kinds, intrinsic or literary and extrinsic or market-determined. These two kinds of value did not necessarily coincide, but in the absence of market value, determined by the public's curiosity and interest in a piece, its intrinsic or literary value was moot, particularly if one wrote plays for the purpose of becoming recognized and rewarded as a professional playwright. (2) The public's curiosity was not entirely self-generating. Book sales depended in part upon an author's reputation at the time of publishing and in part upon a publisher's willingness to advertise an author's work. Shaw agreed to publish with Henry and Company, later complaining bitterly that the firm "never advertized it even once; and the sale . . . was 150 copies!" (*Collected Letters*, vol. I, p. 424).

The arrangement began and ended unhappily for Shaw. With a keenness fed by years of frustrated dealings with capitalist publishers, Shaw drew up a contract for the publication so formidable that Henry and Company found it necessary to advise him, "[W]e do not think such an elaborate agreement necessary, especially as we do not expect the sale . . . to recoup us for our outlay, and as we are publishing your work chiefly to oblige our Mr. Grein" (quoted in Laurence, *Bibliography*, vol. I, p. 23). The publisher's subsequent refusal to advertise the play added to Shaw's disgust. He prepared on his own an advertising sheet, and wrote a letter to be sent by the publisher to press correspondents. But sales appear not to have exceeded two or three hundred copies. Of course, Shaw may not have expected great sales from the play, subtitled "An Original Didactic Realistic Play in Three Acts," suited to the coterie audiences of the Independent Theatre Society, but, in Shaw's words, "too experimental" to be put on elsewhere (*Collected Letters*, vol. I, p. 372).

The hazards of publication

For five years following the disappointing publication of *Widowers' Houses*, Shaw wrote and produced plays at a prodigious rate, but withheld them from publication. Focusing on playwriting and production represented an economy of effort as well as a recognition of the vexed status of copyright in England and the US. There were, in fact, disincentives at this period for dramatic authors to publish their playscripts. As J. R. Stephens has demonstrated, England and the US had distinct, mutually exclusive, and mutually discouraging laws governing dramatic copyright. English publication of a script meant, in effect, forfeiting the British playwright's US rights; US publication effectively deprived American authors of British copyright protection. Wilson Barrett warned playwright Henry Arthur Jones in 1879, "Are you aware that by printing your plays and publishing them, you forfeit your American rights? A play kept in MS or printed in slip as MS for use of actors only is to a certain extent protected in the United States" (quoted in Stephens, *The Profession of the Playwright*, p. 104). British law treated US stage performance as "publication"; therefore, when a British play was pirated in a US city in advance of performance in Britain, the author forfeited his or her British copyright protection (p. 104). Shaw was typical of British playwrights in expressing uncertainty about the "international" situation regarding copyright at this time. He asked T. Fisher Unwin in 1895, "[D]o I forfeit my American stageright if publication precedes performance? If I could secure both copyrights and stagerights intact here and in America, I should be strongly tempted to try a volume of dramas" (*Collected Letters*, vol. I, p. 574). Such uncertainty would have discouraged publication, given the long-established practice of piracy on both sides of the Atlantic. In an 1896 letter attempting to interest Grant Richards in publishing what became the two-volume *Plays Pleasant and Unpleasant*, Shaw noted that two of the plays had not yet been performed, adding "[I]t would be better to wait until after their production before printing them" (*Collected Letters*, vol. I, p. 698). Shaw coined the term "stagerighting" to describe what became his and others' common practice of staging at least one (typically hasty and low-budget) British production of a play to secure its copyright. The point of stagerighting was to prohibit the first performance of a British play occurring in the US, which would nullify its copyright protection in Britain. Shaw had the belief (eventually proved true by *Man and Superman*) that his stage reception in the US was more favorable than in England, and that he therefore had to secure US production and publication rights for his works quickly and efficiently.

Shaw wrote all three of what came to be called the "unpleasant" plays – *Widowers' Houses* (1892), The Philanderer (1893), and *Mrs. Warren's Profession* (1893) – for the Independent Theatre Society, but only the first of these actually premiered at J. T. Grein's theatre. In each of these early plays, Shaw worked toward adapting dramatic conventions to his critique of modern capitalism, and in each the critique became more deeply submerged. *Widowers' Houses*, showing "the rich suburban villa standing on the rents of the foul rookery," was designed to please the audience artistically while inducing them "to vote on the Progressive side at the next County Council election in London."[15] Whether or not it succeeded at the polls, the play failed among critics, including William Archer, and ran for only two performances. But the popular press's general condemnation of the piece was a powerful form of advertising and indicated that the play had hit a nerve. Shaw wrote on. *The Philanderer*, Shaw's second play, was to be a frontal attack on capitalist marriage and divorce customs that would incorporate the emerging figure of "The New Woman" and her opposite "The Womanly Woman" in a parody of Ibsenite progressives. J. T. Grein would not even consider the piece for the Independent Theatre, calling it "excessively verbose." Shaw himself had intended that it be "unspeakably improper," with the understanding that such impropriety would stimulate interest, attention, and even perhaps reform. He hoped for commercial success, telling Harley Granville Barker, "When I work [*The Philanderer*] up with a little extra horse play, it will go like mad" (quoted in Holroyd, *Bernard Shaw*, p. 288). But he recognized that he was still learning the art of playwriting: "I've all but finished another play," he wrote Archer chidingly in May of 1893, "a step nearer to something more than talk about what plays ought to be" (*Collected Letters*, vol. I, p. 395). Shaw periodically urged Archer to write plays rather than talk about what they should be. One year later, he took up dramatic criticism for the *Saturday Review*, but did so to support his efforts as a playwright. Optimistic and determined, Shaw swallowed the failure of his second play and six weeks later was again playwriting, returning this time to the didactic mode of his first play, cleansed of the autobiographical references he came to despise in *The Philanderer*, and even more defiantly outrageous in his choice of subject: prostitution. He originally subtitled *Mrs. Warren's Profession* "A Tragic variation on the theme of 'Cashel Byron's Profession,'" using the socially disreputable profession as a metaphor for the way in which society actually conducts its business (Holroyd, *Bernard Shaw*, p. 290). In *Mrs. Warren's Profession*, Shaw directed his corrective pen toward the fiction of "clean" moneymaking and exposed, through the metaphor of prostitution, capitalism's coupling of gender, money, sex, and freedom disguised by middle-class "family values." When *Mrs. Warren's Profession* was not only refused a license by the Lord Chamberlain but also refused production by J. T. Grein who found it "unfit for women's ears," Shaw backed off from thesis drama and began to write plays with a chance of being produced – romantic comedies of the "private imagination" (Holroyd, *Bernard Shaw*, p. 297).

Shaw wrote his first three plays through his deep engagement with socialism and the theatre. But how he wrote them expressed his determination to gauge the public's interest and to gain if not popularity, at least notoriety, for himself. Later, perhaps, they would be published and purchased by readers already familiar with the phenomenon of G. B. Shaw. Notoriety had to precede publication, since the growing English book-buying public was not at this time inclined to purchase playtexts as mid-priced "books" but as inexpensive mementoes of performances.

On November 26, 1893, Shaw began a "romantic" play for Florence Farr that was to become *Arms and the Man*. When it opened on April 21, 1894, it proved a success, and Shaw's career as a dramatist began in earnest: "[*Arms and the Man*] has produced reputation, discussion, advertisement; it has brought me enough money to live on for six months, during which I will write two more plays" (*Collected Letters*, p. 458). To be a dramatist meant to be produced, to be applauded, to be paid, and, if he had his way, to be published.

The next three years would be crucial in establishing Shaw's future as a published author. In July of 1894, Shaw announced (somewhat prematurely, as it turned out) that he was surrendering journalism for playwriting, dropping his *World* columns at the end of the season (*Collected Letters*, vol. I, p. 448). By 1895, Shaw was hoping to follow the example of John Ruskin, who had acted as his own publisher, binder, and distributor. He described his plans to London bookseller Frederick H. Evans, complaining that publishers "combine commercial rascality with artistic touchiness and pettishness, without being either good business men or fine judges of literature." Authors and booksellers can carry on the business of bringing good books into the world without parasitic intermediaries. The strength of the author's not the publisher's name would determine the success or failure of a book. Pricing, typically determined by publishers, could more accurately be set by authors, as authors know their book-buying public. "My public is small and select," Shaw wrote; "if people will go past half a crown net for a book they will go . . . to six shillings gross: that is, four and sixpence net" (*Collected Letters*, vol. I, p. 543). Shaw's description of the "net" and "gross" prices of a book is a reference to the Net Book Agreement, first proposed in 1890 by Frederick Macmillan, by which new books would be divided into two categories, net books, to be sold at the published price without discount, and subject books, to be sold subject to discount at each bookseller's discretion. Publishers could choose whether to publish net books, and authors could make their own terms with regard to net publishing. By 1899, the recently formed Publishers' Association and the Associated Booksellers agreed on a joint scheme for adopting the net plan.[16] Books under six shillings (what came to be the typical price for Shaw's early volumes) did not fall under the Agreement. The spread of free libraries justified, in Shaw's mind, setting his prices above the "popular" level – i.e. presumably the two shillings six pence price of *Quintessence* and *Widowers' Houses*, published several years earlier. But Shaw did not yet have sufficient capital to afford paying outright for publishing services, and by March of that year, he told Ellen Terry he was "being pressed to publish" his plays, by which he meant in the traditional fashion, with the publisher assuming the costs and agreeing to a copyright fee. The pressure came from a young member of the profession who would bring out a total of six titles by Shaw before undergoing his first bankruptcy proceedings in April of 1905.

Plays Pleasant and Unpleasant

Grant Richards, son of Oxford University classics scholar Franklin Thomas Grant Richards, followed Shaw home after the theatre one evening in November of 1896 in an attempt to secure an agreement to publish Shaw's first collection of plays. Richards's publishing house would not open until

January of 1897, but he was soliciting in advance the work of carefully selected writers to launch his new enterprise. Shaw responded with a challenge: "As far as I have been able to ascertain . . . the public does not read plays, or at least did not a very few years ago. Have you any reason to suppose that it has changed its habits?" But he continued to propose conditions for such a venture, one of which was simultaneous publication in America (*Collected Letters*, vol. I, p. 698). With several stage successes behind him, and armed with a critical mass of publishable pages, Shaw agreed to Richards's offer. The attention to detail he brought to the volumes made publishing history.

Shaw had written eight plays by this time, the first six of which he initially proposed to Richards as a one-volume, piebald publication to be called "Plays Pleasant and Unpleasant," with the unpleasant plays printed in an ugly type style on light brown paper and the pleasant ones on white paper in Kelmscott style. Shaw felt sure a piebald volume would "make a sensation." In May of 1897, Shaw announced that he had accepted Grant Richards's offer to publish his plays, feeling compelled to add: "I am not a disappointed dramatist . . . But in the present condition of the theatre it is evident that a dramatist like Ibsen, who . . . throws himself on the reading public, is taking the only course in which any serious advance is possible, especially if his dramas demand much technical skill from the actors" (*Collected Letters*, vol. I, p. 754). In striking the high-art pose, Shaw appeared to be choosing publication over the vagaries of production, when in fact, he remained committed to the initial production of his new plays and to revivals of his published plays over the next few decades. In refusing to be described as "disappointed," Shaw was addressing the perception that publication of a play signaled its exhaustion or failure on the professional stage, a perception linked to the practice described earlier of withholding publication of a play until after a successful stage run in order to protect the author's copyright. Shaw's mention of Ibsen, with whom he had long felt sympathetic, was intended to substitute for any suspicions of dramatic failure or staleness a militant assertion of artistic integrity in the face of "the present condition of the theatre," including its implied lack of skilled actors.

The proposed project changed over several months of discussions between Shaw and Richards. By May of 1897, *Plays Pleasant and Unpleasant* had become a two-volume publication with volume one, "Unpleasant," containing a reprint of *Widowers' Houses*, *The Philanderer*, and *Mrs. Warren's Profession*, and volume two, "Pleasant," containing *You Never Can Tell*, *Arms and the Man*, *Candida*, and *The Man of Destiny*. While producing these two volumes with Grant Richards, Shaw put into action a publishing strategy that would last many years, centered on union-friendly printers, simultaneous US publication, William Morris aesthetics, and mid-level pricing.[17] After some discussion with Richards, during which Shaw referred to his preference for a "union house" and subsequently broadened this requirement to a fair paying house, Richards proposed R. & R. Clark, Ltd. as the printer of the two volumes. Shaw heartily agreed, calling Clark a "first-rate house" and enclosing a letter "as your certificate of compliance with my Fair Wages Clause" (*Collected Letters*, vol. I, p. 766). Shaw used the firm for the next fifty years, writing in a centennial tribute, "[E]ver since it printed my first plays, Pleasant and Unpleasant, in 1898 [R. & R. Clark] has been as natural a part of my workshop as the pen in my hand."[18] Shaw next agreed that Clark's US counterpart would be the Chicago firm of Herbert S. Stone and his partner, Hannibal I. Kimbell, who had been the US publishers of *Widowers' Houses* in their founding year of 1893. When Stone and Kimbell separated in 1896, Stone continued to publish Shaw as Herbert S. Stone & Company, until 1904.

The pricing and aesthetics of the two volumes remained to be worked out. In pricing, Richards prevailed, convincing Shaw that the author's preferred price – three shillings per volume and six for the set – was unwise. Shaw initially held the view that books should be priced cheaply to sell more copies, even if this required choosing a cheaper paper. This had been his strategy with his Fabian publications, designed to be read by the largest possible number of readers. Richards's view was that the volumes should be beautiful and five shillings each, sold separately. The Fabian Shaw strenuously objected, offering the (dubious) example of a common reader who would pay six shillings only for a book of sufficient length to occupy him for several Sundays. Plays, filling less reading time, could not sustain a price equal to that of novels. In addition to length, Shaw doubted his reputation justified a ten shilling price, noting that Ibsen's plays sold at three and sixpence per volume of three plays and that the first issue by Heinemann of a new play was priced at five shillings (*Collected Letters*, vol. I, p. 808). At some point, however, Shaw relented. Richards added in his memoirs, "I still believe I was right," and noted with satisfaction that by June of 1900, Shaw was advocating raising the price of each volume to six shillings, to ensure a profit of one and fourpence instead of a shilling (*Author Hunting*, pp. 113, 131).

But in aesthetics Shaw prevailed, riding – in modest fashion – the wave of the "Morris Revolution" announced by socialist William Morris, and his colleagues, printer Emery Walker and binder Thomas James Cobden-Sanderson, in Edinburgh at an 1889 meeting of the National Association for the Advancement of Art, and later published in *Arts and Crafts Essays*

printed in Edinburgh in 1893. Morris revived book design on the principles
established in the *Essays* when he founded the Kelmscott Press in 1890.
The purpose of the revolution was to recover bookmaking as an art and
craft through a knowledge of the history of papermaking, printing, illustration, and binding. Emery Walker recommended spacing words evenly,
filling the rectangle of the page with deeply black print, and selecting paper
with care. William Morris had the financial and artistic resources to put the
principles of the revolution into practice, turning his Hammersmith house
into the Kelmscott Press in 1890, commissioning his own private typeface
and his own paper, a facsimile of the Bolognese paper of *c.* 1473.[19] Shaw's
acquaintance with the makers of the printing revolution dated from his pre-
Fabian days, when he attended meetings of the Social Democratic Federation, from which Morris, Walker, and others withdrew in 1885 to form the
Socialist League. His membership in the Fabian Society eventually settled
the difference between Shaw's "municipal socialism" and their "idealist
socialism," but he insisted on printing his books in sympathy with Morris's
principles to the extent that he could afford to do so. In fact, his
contribution to publishing history at this time was to demonstrate the
feasibility of introducing elements of the "Kelmscott style" into the printing
of affordable books, including plays, whose fractured lines of dialogue
necessarily broke the solid-looking rectangle of black print prized by
Morris and his school. Shaw, that is, introduced a performative print style
into play publishing that called attention to the singularity of his plays by
the material appearance of type, paper, and white space on the printed
page. The "Shaw book" contributed to Shaw's self-fashioning by establishing an instantly recognizable cover and print style. So much the better if
his books gestured – modestly – toward the elegance of Morris's masterpieces.

In his earliest correspondence with Richards, Shaw suggested that Walter
Scott's volumes of Ibsen's plays be used as a model for setting three plays to
a volume (see Figure 3b). The point lay both in the Ibsen example and in
Scott's reputation as a quality publisher. But Shaw would not settle merely
for adopting an existing template. He pushed for a closer approximation to
the Morris/Walker design, faulting the edition's setting of letterpress on the
page. His objection presumably lay in the lack of uniform spacing,
disproportionate margins, and faintness of print. "Otherwise," he wrote,
"it is not so bad" (*Collected Letters*, vol. I, p. 767). As the volumes moved
into production, Shaw insisted upon his own system of type and typesetting. He eliminated apostrophes wherever possible, encouraged tightly
knit spacing within a word, and even spacing between words. This move,
inspired by Morris, was in part a corrective to a nineteenth-century practice

LADY INGER OF ÖSTRÅT.

DRAMA IN FIVE ACTS.

———••———

Act First.

(*A room at Östråt. Through an open door in the back, the Banquet Hall is seen in faint moonlight, which shines fitfully through a deep bow-window in the opposite wall. To the right, an entrance-door; further forward, a curtained window. On the left, a door leading to the inner rooms; further forward a large open fireplace, which casts a glow over the room. It is a stormy evening.*)

(BIÖRN *and* FINN *are sitting by the fireplace. The latter is occupied in polishing a helmet. Several pieces of armour lie near them, along with a sword and shield.*)

FINN (*after a pause*).   Who was Knut[1] Alfson?

BIÖRN.   My Lady says he was the last of Norway's knighthood.

FINN.   And the Danes killed him at Oslo-fiord?

BIÖRN.   Ask any child of five, if you know not that.

FINN.   So Knut Alfson was the last of our knighthood?   And now he's dead and gone!   (*Holds up the helmet.*)   Well then, hang thou scoured and bright in

[1] Pronounce *Knoot.*

3b   A page from Walter Scott's 1890 edition of Ibsen's *Prose Dramas*. Shaw considered this an imperfect model for his *Plays Pleasant and Unpleasant*

Act III   The Devil's Disciple   59

factory !! [*He stares at him for a moment, and then adds, with grim intensity*] I am glad you take that view of them.

SWINDON [*puzzled*] Do I understand that in your opinion —

BURGOYNE. I do not express my opinion. I never stoop to that habit of profane language which unfortunately coarsens our profession. If I did, sir, perhaps I should be able to express my opinion of the news from Springtown —the news which you [*severely*] have apparently not heard. How soon do you get news from your supports here ? — in the course of a month, eh ?

SWINDON [*turning sulky*] I suppose the reports have been taken to you, sir, instead of to me. Is there anything serious ?

BURGOYNE [*taking a report from his pocket and holding it up*] Springtown's in the hands of the rebels. [*He throws the report on the table*].

SWINDON [*aghast*] Since yesterday !

BURGOYNE. Since two o'clock this morning. Perhaps we shall be in their hands before two o'clock to-morrow morning. Have you thought of that ?

SWINDON [*confidently*] As to that, General, the British soldier will give a good account of himself.

BURGOYNE [*bitterly*] And therefore, I suppose, sir, the British officer need not know his business : the British soldier will get him out of all his blunders with the bayonet. In future, sir, I must ask you to be a little less generous with the blood of your men, and a little more generous with your own brains.

SWINDON. I am sorry I cannot pretend to your intellectual eminence, sir. I can only do my best, and rely on the devotion of my countrymen.

BURGOYNE [*suddenly becoming suavely sarcastic*] May I ask are you writing a melodrama, Major Swindon ?

SWINDON [*flushing*] No, sir.

BURGOYNE. What a pity ! What a pity ! [*Dropping his sarcastic tone and facing him suddenly and seriously*] Do you

3c   A sample of dialogue from an original edition of *Three Plays for Puritans*, set in Caslon long primer solid

by which compositors had permitted excessively wide spacing between words, particularly after full stops and other marks of punctuation, to minimize their typesetting efforts and maximize their fees (McLean, *Modern Book Design*, p. 34). Shaw called for eliminating "mutton quads," a type body used to create blank spaces at the beginning of paragraphs and sometimes following a full stop. It was especially important to eliminate extra spacing in printing his plays, because he used spaces in lieu of italics for emphasis, italics being the type style he selected for his infamously long stage directions. Shaw complained of ink that was not black enough and not applied evenly. And he insisted on "Morris Margins," broad margins below and at the sides of the page with narrow ones above and at the inside. These he shrewdly characterized as practical rather than "artistic" preferences, having dismissed imitation "artistic printing" (e.g. Joseph Dent's Everyman Library series with pseudo-Kelmscott title and end pages) as unnecessary and beside the point (*Collected Letters*, vol. I, p. 550). Unable to afford a rigid adherence to Morris's methods, Shaw signaled approval of his revolutionary principles while applying them, in Fabian fashion, to a practical and affordable printing strategy.

Morris's *Roots of the Mountains* had been printed in Caslon Old Face at the Chiswick Press in 1892. Shaw's pages were hand-set (although by the late 1880s, machine composition was beginning to overtake hand-setting) in typefounder's Caslon, long primer solid (see Figure 3c). Determined to create a visual signature for his works, Shaw retained this typographical style until the late 1920s, when he assented, but only after consulting Emery Walker, to a machine justified page set in Monotype Caslon. Shaw succeeded in creating a visual signature for his works. The title page of *Plays Pleasant and Unpleasant* (see Figure 3d) was striking in its off-center placement and use of bold capitals. Shaw tried variations, such as all lower case, before settling on 24-point Caslon, upper and lower case, breaking words to achieve close spacing, and ending with short lines that were neither spaced out nor centered. Shaw designed his title page as a no-nonsense replica of his text style that became, together with the gray-green binding of his books, an immediate identifier of works by G. B. Shaw.

Yet, when all was said and done, sales were less than brisk. Richards brought out *Plays Pleasant and Unpleasant* in a first edition of 1,240 sets at five shillings per volume and sold 756 sets in six months. In the US during the same period, 734 sets were sold. Shaw had not expected great sales, but Richards was apparently disappointed. Judging from Shaw's letter of May 29, 1899, the heavily indebted Richards was having regrets and so, in fact, was Shaw, who was threatening to move to "commission publishing" as he would reluctantly do in 1903, to avoid becoming implicated in Richards's

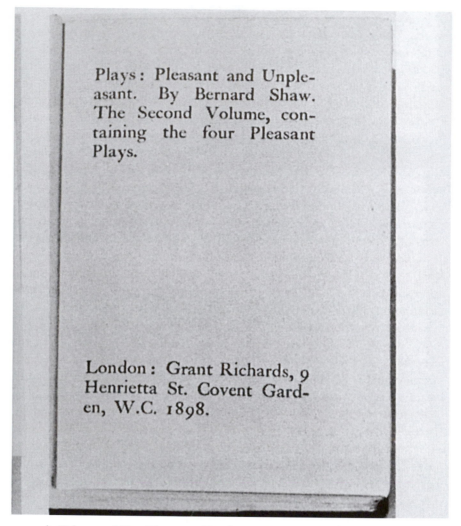

Plays: Pleasant and Unpleasant. By Bernard Shaw. The Second Volume, containing the four Pleasant Plays.

London: Grant Richards, 9 Henrietta St. Covent Garden, W.C. 1898.

3d   Title page of *Plays Pleasant and Unpleasant*. First example of Shaw's off-center placement. Set by R. and R. Clark, Edinburgh

financial difficulties: "I propose to take the responsibility [for producing my books] on myself in future . . . the blame and loss will be mine . . . [S]end me an exact account of the whole transaction, and let me readjust it on a commission basis as from the beginning. In this way I will make good all your loss; and you can sell the remainder of the edition for me on commission" (*Collected Letters*, vol. II, p. 91). This does not appear to have happened, although one year later Shaw repeated his offer to publish with Richards on commission without making the fact publicly known: "And now, what about *Three Plays for Puritans*? . . . You have not done so amazingly well with *Plays P. and Unpl* (an edition of 1200 in two years) as to feel certain that this book is going to be a treasure. I offer to pay for it (instead of Clark), and hold you harmless. The public and the press won't know . . . I want to know definitely and at once, because if it is to be commission, I must set about the printing at once; and if it is to be as before, I must draw up an agreement" (*Collected Letters*, vol. II, pp. 163–64). Their arrangements remained "as before," but Richards's losses were quickly catching up with him. The 1902 *Mrs. Warren's Profession*, issued as a separate impression with a new preface, was the last of Richards's Shaw publications. By 1904, Shaw's relations with the now virtually bankrupt Richards had deteriorated. In a letter written on December 31 of that year, an exasperated Shaw informed Richards that, due to the publisher's failure to keep his plays in print, he was forced to join other author creditors to have Richards adjudicated a bankrupt. This episode concluded Shaw's reliance on conventional publishing methods. His next play, *Man and Superman*, was, he believed, too long to serve as an acting play, at least for the contemporary stage. It was, above all, a "book," a sustained, philosophical comedy of sufficient length, breadth, and controversy to serve as Shaw's first commission publication.

Man and Superman and commission publishing

It was one thing to threaten Grant Richards with commission publishing, but quite another thing to undertake it. Commission publishing required two things: an author with a reputation to guarantee a profitable level of sales and sufficient capital to advance the costs of composition, machining, paper, and binding. Shaw had been talking for years about publishing in this fashion, but had not, before this time, taken the risks implicit in such a plan. Publishers' fears of the controversial subjects addressed by the new play forced Shaw's hand and the healthy profits of £3,000 or more earned from the US run of *Devil's Disciple* must have bolstered his courage (*Collected Letters*, vol. II, p. 30). When *Man and Superman* failed to bring an offer from British or American publishers, Shaw took the decisive step in the summer of 1903 and commissioned Archibald Constable & Co. to serve as the distributing agent for his works. Shaw liked to do business with politically sympathetic firms or at least with firms recommended by his political/artistic allies. At Shaw's request, the photographer Frederick H. Evans had suggested the firm of Constable. A subsequent agreement, executed in a few scribbled lines on a single sheet of paper (a radical shift from Shaw's ultra-legal contract for Henry & Co.) lasted from 1903 until his death. Clark's of Edinburgh, as always, set the edition. Eager to publish simultaneously on both sides of the Atlantic, refusing to use Stone who (Shaw believed) had failed to market his works aggressively, and without a willing US substitute, Shaw found himself forced to act on a commission basis. He sent the edition already set and printed by Clark's of Edinburgh to William Dana Orcutt of the University Press, Cambridge, Massachusetts, with instructions to set it following Clark's example. The results occasioned one of Shaw's more thorough lessons on the economics and aesthetics of book publishing, including a reference to "Morris Margins": "Your margins are very far from the Mazarin Bible. Your top margin is a full inch – *much* too wide . . . and the lower only $1\frac{1}{4}''$ . . . Try $\frac{1}{2}''$ for the top margin . . . measuring from the top line of the text . . . The inner margins are monstrous – $\frac{3}{4}''$ each . . . The rule here is simple: the book, when open, should look as if there were no division (down the middle) at all" (*Collected Letters*, vol. II, pp. 353–54).

After securing US copyright, Shaw planned to wait until sufficient interest would be wakened in the US to come to an arrangement with an American publisher and order an edition to be printed at once. Shaw claimed to have spent £70 cash (*Collected Letters*, vol. II, p. 367; Laurence lists £60, *Bibliography*, vol. I, p. 54) securing the American "electros," or printed plates, which made him "master of the (publishing) situation" in the US. But it wasn't until 1904, when he formalized a printing agreement with Brentano's, the US firm recommended to him by James Huneker, that had for several years been publishing pirated editions of his works, that Shaw could ensure the commission publishing of this and later works in the US. Brentano's took over the stereos of *Man and Superman* after agreeing to pay Shaw a royalty of 25 percent on sales, an agreement that remained in effect until 1933 (*Collected Letters*, vol. II, p. 420). Assuming ownership of his plates gave Shaw leverage to secure a slightly more favorable copyright, one of the greatest advantages of his commission arrangement. The rest of the terms of the agreement would likely have matched those regularly insisted upon by Shaw and described to Methuen & Co. in a letter soliciting their interest in *Man and Superman*: an exact counting of copies (thirteen copies being counted as such and not, following the usual custom of the time, as twelve); inclusion of a "fair wages" clause (which Shaw attempted to pass off as political expediency for the "defence of parliamentary authors against hostile electioneering agents"); a limited, five-year license to publish; and simultaneous cross-Atlantic publication (*Collected Letters*, vol. II, pp. 310–11). Methuen respectfully declined. In the case of *Man and Superman*, commission publishing raised Shaw's royalties from 20 to 25 per cent; retained the "fair wages" provision and the requirement for simultaneous publication in England and the US; and put Shaw in control of selecting a printer, binder, and distributor. Four years later, Shaw told an old friend that the "blazing" American success of *Man and Superman* – on the stage rather than the page – had largely been responsible for raising his writing income to £13,000 for a single year (*Collected Letters*, vol. II, p. 792). As a published book, it received initially very different treatment, having been briefly removed from the open shelves of the New York Public Library in 1905. In the US, production rather than publication initially brought Shaw's *succès de scandale* before large numbers of theatregoers. But Shaw was satisfied that his commission experiment was working to his advantage. In a letter to Grant Richards dated March 20, 1904, he took care to point out the relative benefits of publishing on commission, noting that at a customary US price of $1.25 and a British price of six shillings, Constable sold 2,707 copies of *Man and Superman* in the first six months following publication, with a net author's profit of £148 2s 10d. Over an eighteen month period, Grant Richards had sold only 1,421 copies of *Three Plays for Puritans* for a net author's profit well under £100.

Conclusion: "Modern Drama" and the printed play

By 1903, Shaw had worked through a printing, pricing, and publishing strategy that agreed with his Fabian principles while claiming for the mid-priced printed drama an aesthetic and economic status previously reserved largely for novels and poetry. Both Shaw's Prefaces and his stage directions, inserted for the benefit of the reader rather than the playgoer, looked and functioned like glosses to the printed text, giving them the appearance and the "value" of novels. As mentioned earlier, Shaw believed that readers equated the value of a printed work in part with the length of time it would take them to read the work. Prefaces added length as well as literary and political interest to his playscripts, ensuring readers their "money's worth" with an entertainment of novelistic scope, political topicality, and comic levity. Shaw also believed that the sale of his work rested on a small but growing public's acquaintance with his (public) self. Consequently, he titled his published Preface in *Plays Pleasant and Unpleasant* "Mainly about Myself," an essay intended to enlarge his market share by increasing the public's knowledge of his opinions, his history, and his checkered fortunes as a published author. But while Shaw actually disclosed very little about "himself," he gave a professional's behind-the-scenes account of the development and difficulties of dramatic authorship imposed by several business and institutional practices, chief among them the office of the Lord

Chamberlain. Offering insider knowledge about the controversies within the playwriting profession, Shaw rewarded his readers with "investigative" discoveries counterpointed by Fabian polemic.

In this two-volume collection, the longest preface accompanied the most controversial play, *Mrs. Warren's Profession*, suggesting Shaw used Prefaces not only to engage and reward the reader but also to mediate the reader's reception of the drama. The Prefaces, that is, served as conditioning rooms through which readers were invited to pass on their way to the plays. This practice continued in his next collection, *Three Plays for Puritans* (Grant Richards, 1901), whose general Preface, running half again as long as the general Preface to *Plays Pleasant and Unpleasant*, focused once more on insider knowledge of the conditions of the English theatre, while rehearsing the arguments made by the three plays in the volume. But in this volume, Shaw resorted to using "notes," and placed these at the end of the playtext rather than at its front. The material in these notes takes several forms, reprints of Shaw's own criticism published elsewhere, historical explanation of the play's characters or events, and responses to other critics' comments about the play. They again show Shaw's eagerness to exploit the print medium to condition the reader's reception of the play both before and after reading it. *Man and Superman*, with its thirty-two-page Epistle Dedicatory, Preface to "The Revolutionist's Handbook," text of the "Handbook," and "Maxims for Revolutionists" is perhaps the most complex and self-referring example of Shaw's glossing, prompted, again, by critics' disapproval of the play's controversial content and by Shaw's ambitions for his "comic philosophy." It would appear that, between 1883 and 1903, the more controversial the play, the greater the number of narrative layers Shaw was likely to give it, layers that functioned to ward off misreadings, to build up ironical and complex readings, and to give the work the material weight and protective coloration of a novel.

Shaw's contribution to the construction of Modern Drama during this period was to extend it from the stage, where it had the status of a scarce commodity performed for short runs in small, coterie theatres by select actors before select audiences, to the page, where it assumed the distinctive look of a mid-priced "book," printed reverently in accord with revisionist bookmaking conventions, lengthened and decorated by prefaces, conclusions, production photographs, and stage directions, and priced to sell to a growing market of book-buying consumers. In taking play publication seriously, Shaw proved a shrewd forecaster of a growing interest in drama as a literary genre. By 1910, professional critics, amateur enthusiasts, and academics were fashioning the canon of "modern drama" as a focus of national and international dramatic writing. In England and the US, dozens of anthologies, histories, and full-length critcial studies of "modern," "new," "continental," and "changing" drama began to appear, the vast majority of which included Shaw as one of the noteworthy writers for the modern stage. Over the first two decades of the twentieth century, Modern Drama assumed its identity as a continental canon (translated into English), comprised almost exclusively of Western male writers praised for avoiding specifically political, historical references and for aiming instead at the "universal" concerns of modernity, concerns such as the nature of human consciousness and the value of individual expression. The translated and published continental canon of Modern Drama – plays by Ibsen, Strindberg, Shaw, Chekhov, Brieux, etc. – became a subject of organized reading and discussion in university classrooms and among societies of drama enthusiasts. These plays were performed as modern "classics" in professional and university theatres.

Shaw's attempts to provoke and profit from a "play-reading habit" among large numbers of middle-class readers coincided with widespread efforts in England and the US to regulate and professionalize the production of literature. The vexed state of dramatic copyright delayed and complicated the publication of drama as mid-priced "books" suitable for reading pleasure. In addition to calling for expanded copyright protection for both performed and printed texts, playwrights like Shaw and Henry Arthur Jones strove to entice a book-buying public to purchase printed drama for reading pleasure. Shaw developed an elaborate system of enticements, adapting Morris's publishing "revolution" to give his books a distinctive and uniform appearance, and creating multiple glosses to engage readers in a continuous performing of their interpretive strategies. Shaw did not single-handedly reform the practice of drama production and reception, nor did he grow wealthy from the publication of his plays during the period I have examined. But he correctly anticipated and may well have encouraged by his example the production of plays as mid-priced books aimed at a growing market of literate, middle-class readers.

NOTES

1 By the "performing canon" of Modern Drama, I mean those plays selected to be performed at theatres devoted to the new drama, e.g. J. T. Grein's Independent Theatre Society. By a "reading canon" of Modern Drama, I mean a subset of printed dramas limited to (almost exclusively) male European playwrights that began to appear in histories and anthologies of "Modern Drama" c. 1910 and later in the US and England. These anthologies and histories of Modern Drama, typically containing works by Henrik Ibsen, August Strindberg, Eugene Brieux,

Maurice Maeterlinck, etc., were directed to the mature student reader, the adult drama enthusiast, and the amateur performer. Barrett H. Clark's *The Continental Drama of To-day: Outlines for Its Study; Suggestions, Questions, Biographies, and Bibliographies for Use in Connection with the Study of the More Important Plays* (New York: Henry Holt and Co., 1914), or J. W. Marriott's *Modern Drama* (London: Thomas Nelson and Sons, Ltd., n.d. but post-1928) are typical of literate interest in the new drama on both sides of the Atlantic.

2 An avid reader of Shakespeare, Shelley, and other earlier dramatists, Shaw did not present himself as the first of the literary playwrights but rather recognized the changing social and economic conditions of the playwriting profession at the end of the nineteenth and beginning of the twentieth centuries. Placing himself squarely on the side of the "author" (rather than the actor manager or the publisher) as the primary producer of written drama, Shaw set out not to remake drama as art – as if it were not art already – but to change the material conditions under which the playwright wrote and copyrighted, the publisher printed, and the buyer read "literary" dramas.

3 J. R. Stephens, *The Profession of the Playwright: British Theatre 1800–1900* (Cambridge: Cambridge University Press, 1992), see esp. chapter 4.

4 Quoted in Michael Holroyd, *Bernard Shaw: A Biography Vol. 1* (New York: Random House, 1988), p. 119.

5 *Bernard Shaw: Collected Letters*, ed. Dan H. Laurence, 4 vols. (New York: Dodd, Mead, 1965), vol. I, p. 229.

6 Simon Eliot describes this market in *Some Patterns and Trends in British Publishing 1800–1919*, Occasional Papers 8 (London: The Bibliographical Society, 1994), pp. 13 ff.

7 It is difficult to know what prompted Shaw to believe that the French at this time had a play-reading habit. His source of information may have been Augustin Hamon, French socialist-anarchist author and editor, who became Shaw's French translator in 1904. In any case, I can find no verification of the French public's "play-reading" habit, although F. W. J. Hemmings refers in his book, *The Theatre Industry in Nineteenth-Century France* (Cambridge: Cambridge University Press, 1993), to the early nineteenth-century custom of spectators buying playtexts to help them follow the performance of classics at the Comédie-Française (p. 43). But Shaw seems to be referring to a large-scale purchase of published playtexts at the close of the nineteenth century.

8 The Appendix to Shaw's novel takes the form of a humorous Letter to the Author written by the novel's hero, Mr. Sidney Trefusis, in which he objects that the author has fictionalized his (Trefusis's) life and thereby invited self-indulgent readers of fiction (chiefly female) to conclude that the novel is a satire of socialism: "Actions described in novels are judged by a romantic system of morals as fictitious as the actions themselves." The Appendix acts as a kind of dialogic commentary on the conventions of fiction and the relation of fiction to social fact. A typical Shavian blend of overstatment, irony, and moral judgement, it prefigures the self-referring dialogue of John Tanner in *Man and Superman*.

9 See *Collected Letters*, vol. I, p. 18; and Mark Bevir, "The Marxism of George Bernard Shaw 1883–1889," *History of Political Thought* 13, (1992), p. 302.

10 For a history of the Fabian Society, see A. M. McBriar, *Fabian Socialism and English Politics 1884–1918* (Cambridge: Cambridge University Press, 1962), esp. chapter 1.

11 For a description of the socialism implicit in Shaw's early novels, see Tracy C. Davis, *George Bernard Shaw and the Socialist Theatre* (Westport, CT: Greenwood Press, 1994), esp. chapter 1.

12 J. L. Wisenthal (ed.), *Shaw and Ibsen: Bernard Shaw's The Quintessence of Ibsenism and Related Writings* (Toronto: University of Toronto Press, 1979).

13 Publication information for all of Shaw's works is taken from Dan H. Laurence (ed.), *Bernard Shaw: A Bibliography*, 2 vols. (Oxford: Clarendon Press, 1983), vol. I, p. 17.

14 This was not the first time Shaw's work had been pirated in the US. *Cashel Byron's Profession* had been through two pirated US editions by the end of 1886, and *An Unsocial Socialist* appeared in an unauthorized US edition in 1900.

15 From the original preface to *Widowers' Houses*, in *The Bodley Head Bernard Shaw: Collected Plays with their Prefaces*, ed. Dan H. Laurence, 7 vols. (London: Max Reinhardt, The Bodley Head, 1970–74), vol. I, p. 46.

16 For further information on the Net Book Agreement and other practices, see Charles Morgan's *The House of Macmillan (1843–1943)* (London: Macmillan & Co. Ltd, 1943), esp. pp. 170 ff.

17 The details of Shaw's negotiations with Richards are taken both from Shaw's *Collected Letters* and from Richards's memoirs, *Author Hunting* (London: The Unicorn Press, 1934, rpt. 1960), esp. chapter 13.

18 From Shaw's letter dated November 13, 1946, reproduced in James Shand, "Author and Printer: G.B.S. and R. & R.C.: 1898–1948," in Robert Harling (ed.), *Alphabet and Image: A Quarterly of Typography and Graphic Arts*, Volume II: Original Issues 5–8 (New York: Arno Press, 1975), no. 8, p. 8.

19 Ruari McLean, *Modern Book Design from William Morris to the Present Day* (New Jersey: Essential Books, 1959), pp. 8–11.

FURTHER READING

In addition to the works already cited in the notes, the following can provide more information on play publication: Brian Corman's "What Is the Canon of English Drama, 1660–1737?" *Eighteenth-Century Studies* 27:2 (1992/93), pp. 307–22, describes the relationship between performance and publication in an earlier century, as does Shirley Strum Kenny's "The Publication of Plays," in Robert D. Hume (ed.), *The London Theatre World 1660–1800*, Carbondale: Southern Illinois University Press, 1980, pp. 309–36. Valuable background works on publishing and authorship include: Roger Chartier, "Texts, Printing, Readings," in Lynn Hunt (ed.), *The New Cultural History*, Berkeley and Los Angeles: University of California Press, 1989, pp. 154–75; Gaye Tuchman and Nina E. Fortin, *Edging Women Out: Victorian Novelists, Publishers, and Social Change*, New Haven: Yale University Press, 1989; and Michael Warner, "Professionalization and the Rewards of Literature: 1875–1900," *Criticism* 27:1 (1985), pp. 1–28. Henry Arthur Jones's appeals for play publication are worth consulting. See especially "A Plea for the Printed Drama," *The Theatre*, October, 6, 1906, pp. viii, 269–71. Shaw biographer

Archibald Henderson devoted a chapter of his book, *The Changing Drama*, New York: Henry Holt and Company, 1914, to "The Printed Play, A New Technic," in which he casts Shaw as a pioneer of "new drama" play publishing. Henderson describes play publishing, in its turn, as a means of raising the standards of drama to the highest literary levels. His comments on play publication are less an attempt at historical understanding than they are a means to promote Shaw as a man of genius. The construction of Modern Drama as a reading and performing canon that excluded works by women is addressed in the Introduction to Katherine E. Kelly's *Modern Drama by Women 1880s–1930s: An International Anthology*, London: Routledge, 1996.

3

CHARLES A. BERST

New theatres for old

"Bestial, cynical, disgusting, poisonous, sickly, delirious, indecent, loath-some, fetid, literary carrion, crapulous stuff": in short, they did not much care for the play.

Nor for its admirers: "Lovers of prurience and dabblers in impropriety" . . . "Ninety-seven percent of the people who go to see Ghosts are nasty-minded people who find the discussion of nasty subjects to their taste in exact proportion to their nastiness" . . . "The unwomanly woman, the unsexed females . . . Educated and muck-ferreting dogs . . . Effeminate men and male women . . . Outside a silly clique, there is not the slightest interest in the Scandinavian humbug or all his works" (Works, vol. XIX, p. 17).[1]

The target was Henrik Ibsen's *Ghosts*. The year was 1891, and these snippets from press reports appear in Bernard Shaw's *The Quintessence of Ibsenism*, published in September. Historic revolutions in industry, society, politics, science, trade, and economics in nineteenth-century England had scarcely been matched by important events in its theatre until this occasion. But now, against all expectations, a Norwegian, a Scotsman, a Dutchman, and an Irishman jolted Victorian conventions, morals, and ideals, jump-starting a thrust toward modern drama.

To the credit of England's honor and virtue, none of these troublemakers was English. But one was too nearly so for comfort. William Archer, a Scotsman and major drama critic, was the primary English translator of Ibsen's plays and a friend of Shaw, which should have warned the wary. A performance of his translation of Ibsen's *A Doll's House* had scandalized London in 1889 when its heroine violated the heart and hearth of Victorian society by actually *walking out* on her husband and children – merely to do her "duty" towards herself!

Shocking as that was, however, it only prefaced the forthcoming torpedo. In 1890 Shaw, renowned as a music critic and Fabian socialist, delivered a talk on Ibsen for a summer session of the Fabian Society. He shelved his notes afterwards, but as luck would have it productions of Ibsen's

Rosmersholm, *Hedda Gabler*, and *Ghosts* caught London's attention the next winter and spring. The first two were grim enough, but *Ghosts*, which inaugurated the Independent Theatre managed by J. T. Grein, a Dutchman, was unspeakable. So the press screamed. Here Ibsen had answered critics of *A Doll's House* with a heroine whose dutiful return to her husband leads to debauchery, a bastard daughter, a syphilitic son, near incest, and likely prostitution. Delighted by the outraged response, Shaw promptly expanded his talk into *The Quintessence*.

Since then his book has been a classic point of reference in Ibsen studies. Often begrudgingly. Ibsen scholars complain that Shaw exaggerates the Norwegian's role as a radical social thinker, neglecting his greatness as a dramatic poet. A favorite critique among them is that Shaw's volume should have been called *The Quintessence of Shavianism* – a clever quip, as far as it goes, which is not very far.

Many overlook Shaw's point at the start of *The Quintessence* that his book "is not a critical essay on the poetic beauties of Ibsen, but simply an exposition of Ibsenism," one showing "the existence of a discoverable and perfectly definite thesis in a poet's work" (*Works*, vol. XIX, p. 14). They also fail to notice that his claims in it for Ibsen's originality and power as a moral pioneer were borne out in the hysterical press reactions to *Ghosts*: excepting Shaw, few Victorians mentioned "poetic beauties." Then too, Ibsen scholars show little awareness of striking similarities between Shaw and their playwright. For example, while Shaw's youthful second novel, *The Irrational Knot* (1880), and *Ghosts* (1881) have quite different plots, a multitude of their social issues and their very unorthodox treatments of those issues are remarkably parallel, though neither author knew the other's works at the time.

And perhaps most telling of all, Shaw's perception of Ibsen's social radicalism closely matches sentiments Ibsen expressed in personal letters, where he repeatedly places himself in a bold vanguard: "I stand like a solitary sharpshooter at the outpost, acting entirely on my own"; "that man is right who has allied himself most closely with the future"; "My book belongs to the future"; "In these times every piece of creative writing should attempt to move the frontier markers."[2] Then too, such sentiments spring from his plays. In *An Enemy of the People* (1882), for example, Dr. Stockmann is nearly Ibsen's double: "Our entire community rests on a muckheap of lies . . . the stupid are in a fearsomely overpowerful majority . . . The right is with me, and the other few, the solitary individuals . . . holding their positions like outposts, so far in the vanguard . . . We fighters on the frontiers . . . I'll sharpen my pen into a stiletto and skewer them; I'll dip it in venom and gall; I'll sling my inkstand right at their skulls!"[3]

With *Ghosts* and the fury it provoked as touchstones, *The Quintessence* moves into Ibsenism: "every step of progress means a duty repudiated, and a scripture torn up ... duty is the primal curse from which we must redeem ourselves" (*Works*, vol. XIX, pp. 20, 26). Reformers must repudiate duty as an idol of the *status quo*. Duty to a theologically constructed God or to society's assertions of its authority equals slavery; one's duty should be to oneself. Social progress relies on the boldness of individual wills (the soul or spirit of man) seeking freedom and self-expression.

For Shaw, moral pioneers such as Ibsen represent the spirit of mankind growing through the ages by daring to face facts as opposed to cowardly souls who conceal facts, such as death and sexual instinct, behind claims of the immortality of the soul and conventions of marriage. He postulates a typical community of a thousand persons: 700 will be Philistines, 299 will be idealists, one will be a realist. Easygoing Philistines generally accept things as they are. Idealists, however, suppress their terror of truth about themselves, their failures, and human nature by masking them and forcing the masks upon society as ideals. The one-in-a-thousand realist, in contrast, sees through this deception. With self-respect and faith in his independent will, he confronts realities, and must consequently bear the rancor of idealists. So it is with Ibsen, who particularly exposes the Victorian ideal of the Womanly Woman as an abomination, an idol through which society demands the self-sacrifice of women to preordained roles as wives and mothers. Women must emancipate themselves from such enslavement; theirs must be the path of the moral pioneer who "repudiates duties, tramples on ideals, profanes what was sacred, sanctifies what was infamous" (*Works*, vol. XIX, p. 45).

Shaw then views Ibsen's plays from *Brand* (1866) through *Hedda Gabler* (1890), emphasizing their diverse critiques of idealism. He concludes that in so far as morality represents current ideals, Ibsen is immoral because he shows that morality is relative to different circumstances and to points of view that should not be fixed by law but developed according to one's living will. Not surprisingly, in drama such relativism makes sophisticated demands on actors, audiences, and critics who have been bred on melodrama and ideals.

A league ahead of later critics who stress Ibsen's dramatic poetry above his social thought, Shaw perceives that original social views can vitally inform dramatic poetry and vice versa, and while historical progress may date ideas in drama, energies wrought by ideas can give plays enduring life (a point that helps explain why Ibsen's social dramas remain popular). Besides, Shaw had first been attracted to Ibsen not by Ibsen's social dramas but by William Archer reading *Peer Gynt*, from his early poetic period, whereupon "the magic of the great poet opened my eyes in a flash to the importance of the social philosopher" (*Works*, vol. II, p. xxii). Contrary to contemporary critics and anticipating modern ones, Shaw admired Ibsen's symbolic and psychological plays later in the nineties, and concluded his 1913 edition of *The Quintessence* with new chapters on Ibsen's dramatic innovations, emphasizing the discussion element in his plays, his disuse of old stage tricks in favor of ambiguous characters and circumstances that move audiences to confront themselves, and, finally, his combination of art and spiritual revelation.

Thus Shaw caught the quintessence of his subject more adeptly than most of his contemporaries and more aptly than many subsequent critics. While his extroverted flair and comedic talents contrasted with Ibsen's introverted depths, leading him to mine from those depths what most appealed to him, similarly unorthodox moral convictions and social insights linked the two. Even their art, seemingly so diverse in mood, developed through similar tastes for paradox, irony, and allegory. In this sense *The Quintessence* grasped much of the quintessence of both and was a critical harbinger of fresh perspectives, depths, and freedoms soon to flourish in twentieth century drama.

Ibsen became a crucial influence on Shaw quite late in his self-education. During the 1880s, Shaw had spent years in the Reading Room of the British Museum, pouring over social studies, the arts, and modern thought, besides writing five novels and anonymous reviews of music, literature, and art. William Archer first noticed him there studying both Wagner's orchestral score for *Tristan and Isolde* and Marx's *Capital* (in French). Wagner impressed him aesthetically, Marx influenced him socially, and later Ibsen helped link his aesthetics and social views. Meanwhile, his diligent study increased his effectiveness as a socialist spokesman and made him one of the best music critics in history – achievements contributing to *The Quintessence*, which turned him toward playwriting.

These capacities led to his tenure as theatre critic for *The Saturday Review* from 1895 to 1898. A telling perspective on his thousand pages of drama reviews appears in his preface to their reprinting in 1906, where he explains that the reviews were "not a series of judgments aiming at impartiality, but a siege laid to the theatre of the XIXth Century by an author who had to cut his own way into it at the point of the pen, and throw some of its defenders into the moat . . . I postulated as desirable a certain kind of play in which I was destined ten years later to make my mark as a playwright (as I very well foreknew in the depth of my own unconsciousness); and I brought everybody, authors, actors, managers, to the one test: were they coming my way or staying in the old grooves?" (*Our Theatres*, I, p. vii).[4]

What were drama's old grooves? For the first half of the century, mostly melodramas, farces, burlesques, and extravaganzas pitched to raucous lower-class audiences. In the 1840s, however, social tides began to alter matters. Young Queen Victoria happened to be stage struck, and later her son, the popular Prince of Wales, was smitten by the celebrated beauty, Lillie Langtry, the first society woman to appear on stage. So royalty started to mix with actors, actors with high society, theatre with fashion, and fashion made theatregoing respectable for the burgeoning middle classes. To these ingredients, add handy railway access from London's suburbs, the 1843 repeal of Patent Acts which had given Covent Garden and Drury Lane a privileged grip on London theatre, an 1856 law girding dramatic copyrights, plus drama critics superior to their counterparts earlier in the century, then sift lower-class rowdies into music halls, and one has a recipe for success. Accordingly, from 1851 to 1899 London's theatres proliferated from nineteen to sixty-one and became ever more luxurious in decor, seating, lighting, and elaborate stage machinery.

The tastes of audiences, however, hung back. Many were ready for shifts beyond melodrama and farce to the domestic realism of Tom Robertson's plays in the 1860s, the wit of W. S. Gilbert in the 70s and 80s, Henry Arthur Jones's earnestly idealistic dramas and Arthur Wing Pinero's variously amusing, sentimental, or cautiously adventuresome social plays from the 1880s onward. Still, these succeeded by observing Victorian propriety, perhaps tweaking it a bit now and then, but usually just to tickle patrons or to make them thrill at their own liberality. Propriety girded the status of the middle class. In *On Liberty* (1859), John Stuart Mill diagnosed England's young democracy as "collective mediocrity," but why berate success? Darwin's survival of the fittest validated the middle classes; otherwise Darwin and Marx and social or philosophical or religious challenges could upset apple carts. Against these, a bulwark of morals, constancy, and ideals – a solid *status quo* – provided comfort, reliability, safety, sanction. And, naturally, theatre catering to such sensations or offering an escape from insecurities was *right*, sensible, satisfying.

Given these affirming grooves, what was Shaw's way? *The Quintessence* provides a major key as it exposes and counters Victorian conventions, moralities, and ideals. Its definition of phlegmatic Philistines and idolatrous idealists capsulizes the typical Victorian audience. Against these stood Shaw the realist, attended by the revolutionary spirits of Wagner, Marx, and Ibsen, but he was his own man because he was also Promethean, an instinctive culture hero with a spiritual sense of mission on the one hand, and, balancing it on the other, a lively sense of humor. His 1906 preface to his drama reviews presents his credentials:

> Only the ablest critics believe that the theatre is really important: in my time none of them would claim for it, as I claimed for it, that it is as important as the Church was in the Middle Ages ... The apostolic succession from Aeschylus to myself is as serious and continuously inspired as that younger institution, the apostolic succession of the Christian Church.
>
> (*Our Theatres*, I, p. viii)

As ancient Greek drama evolved from religious rituals, so did drama's rebirth in the Middle Ages, and as a successor to this tradition Shaw gives it his particular twist:

> Unfortunately this Christian Church ... has become the Church where you must not laugh; and so it is giving way to that older and greater Church to which I belong: the Church where the oftener you laugh the better, because by laughter only can you destroy evil without malice, and affirm good fellowship without mawkishness ... [The theatre should take] itself seriously as a factory of thought, a prompter of conscience, an elucidator of social conduct, an armory against despair and dullness, and a temple of the Ascent of Man. I took it seriously in that way. (*Our Theatres*, I, pp. viii–ix)

The serious ends of laughter and the emphasis on the theatre's potential as a temple of the Ascent of Man are Shaw's most distinctive contribution to the discussion of the historic link between religion and the stage. The laughter in his "older and greater Church" is akin to the laughter evoked by satyr plays which followed tragedies in Greek drama festivals, pricking their bleak bubbles (hence the term "satire"). A theatre stimulating thought, conscience, social awareness, could become a temple for mankind's spiritual growth. Ultimately, "The claim of art to our respect must stand or fall with the validity of its pretension to cultivate and refine our senses and faculties ... this is why art has won the privileges of religion" (*Works*, vol. XIX, pp. 328–29).

Other than for brief comments such as "The theatre is really the weekday church" (*Our Theatres*, I, p. 277), however, Shaw seldom had the occasion or space in his reviews to write about linking the temporal and the spiritual. So he promoted the goals of both through a temporal voice or role. For instance, in describing himself as a music critic he is less an evangelist in his zeal than a partisan passionate for reform:

> I am as much a politician at a first-night or a press-view as I am on the hustings ... I am always electioneering. At the Opera I desire certain reforms; and, in order to get them, I make every notable performance an

example of the want of them . . . Never in my life have I penned an impartial criticism; and I hope I never may . . . I know that the critic who accepts existing circumstances loses from that moment all his dynamic quality. He stops the clock. (*Works*, vol. XXVII, pp. 135–36)

Energizing this passage is Shaw's forceful sense of an agenda, dedication, a touch of ruthlessness, and candor about them all, while his admission that he uses performances for ends greater than themselves flips a Machiavellian deception into a critical virtue.

Similarly agenda-oriented legerdemain occurs when he discusses Shakespeare. While most Victorian audiences preferred theatrical fare that appealed to their relatively middlebrow tastes, some with more pretensions also adored Shakespeare, most famously served up in versions edited by London's leading actor-manager Henry Irving for his mechanized stage in the Lyceum Theatre. As this adulation involved idealism or, as *The Quintessence* would say, idolatry, Shaw dubbed it "bardolatry," and went after its idol as any pioneering realist should. In a 1931 retrospective he explained: "Until then Shakespear had been conventionally ranked as a giant among psychologists and philosophers. Ibsen dwarfed him so absurdly in those aspects that it became impossible for the moment to take him seriously as an intellectual force . . . If my head had not been full of Ibsen and Wagner in the nineties I should have been kinder and more reasonable in my demands. Also, perhaps, less amusing" (*Our Theatres*, I, pp. ix–x).

"Amusing" reflects a quality of many Shaw reviews that has often been simply assumed or overlooked, though Shaw includes laughter in drama's link with religion. Time and again his reviews take delight in apt expression, felicitous turns of phrase, rhetorical waves, pugilistic episodes, ironic twists, surprises, exaggeration, overstatement, microscopic and panoramic shifts, colorful metaphors, wide-ranging allusions, ascending climaxes, and swift anticlimaxes.

Shaw's notorious 1896 critique of *Cymbeline*, titled "Blaming the Bard," offers a good example. A stormy paragraph calls the play stagey trash, "vulgar, foolish, offensive, indecent, and exasperating beyond all tolerance," then in great waves of scorn Shaw declares Shakespeare a pretentiously platitudinous pilferer of other men's stories and ideas, less subtle than a polytechnic debating club, like transcendently platitudinous grandmothers, and avers that "With the single exception of Homer, there is no eminent writer, not even Sir Walter Scott, whom I can despise so entirely as I despise Shakespear when I measure my mind against his," then caps this with "my impatience with him occasionally reaches such a pitch, that it

4 Arguing with Shakespeare: Canadian puppeteer Ronnie Burkett's view of
William Shakespeare and George Bernard Shaw in the Shaw Festival's 1989 production
of *Shakes versus Shav*

would positively be a relief to me to dig him up and throw stones at him," then deflates with self-irony: "To read Cymbeline and to think of Goethe, of Wagner, of Ibsen, is, for me, to imperil the habit of studied moderation of statement which years of public responsibility as a journalist have made almost second nature in me" (*Our Theatres*, II, p. 205).

For the uninitiated, what follows may come as a surprise: "But I am bound to add that I pity the man who cannot enjoy Shakespear"; whereupon Shaw brings forth Shakespeare's "enormous power over language . . . his miracles of expression; his sense of idiosyncratic character," and the vital energy of his genius, through all of which "the imaginary scenes and people he has created become more real to us than our actual life" – a reality which, Shaw admits, captivates him. Thus he sees in Rosalind's forthright pursuit of a man in *As You Like It* "a piece of natural history which has kept Shakespeare's heroines alive" (*Our Theatres*, II, pp. 282–83). And with "deviltry, humor, and character," Richard III is "the prince of Punches: he delights Man by provoking God," while Petruchio in *The Taming of the Shrew* is a masterful portrait of an ambitious, selfish, healthily good-humored man – a realistic portrait in contrast to Katherine's disgusting servility to him in the last scene (*Our Theatres*, II, p. 299; III, pp. 252–53).

This last sentiment and Shavian characteristics in Rosalind, Richard, and Petruchio suggest that Shaw uses Shakespeare to further his own dramatic agenda. His examples of lesser characterizations work that way as well. He finds Othello's role "pure melodrama. There is not a touch of character in it that goes below the skin; and the fitful attempts to make Iago something better than a melodramatic villain only make a hopeless mess of him and his motives" (*Our Theatres*, III, p. 154). Then too, "There is not a single sentence uttered by Shakespear's Julius Caesar that is, I will not say worthy of him, but even worthy of an average Tammany boss" (*Our Theatres*, III, p. 314). Each of these three is quite unShavian.

In a review of *Much Ado About Nothing*, Shaw provides the best key to his reservations: *paraphrase* Shakespeare. Paraphrase every idea of Benedick and Beatrice, and see how little you have. In comparison, "Paraphrase Goethe, Wagner, or Ibsen in the same way, and you will find original observation, subtle thought, wide comprehension, far-reaching intuition, and serious psychological study." But then,

> Give Shakespear a fairer chance in the comparison by paraphrasing even his best and maturest work, and you will still get nothing more than the platitudes of proverbial philosophy, with a very occasional curiosity in the shape of a rudiment of some modern idea, not followed up. Not until the

Shakespearean music is added by replacing the paraphrase with the original lines does the enchantment begin. Then you are in another world at once.

(Our Theatres, III, p. 339)

The test is worth a try. Othello? Lear? Hamlet? Or how about Jaques in As You Like It, "who spends his time, like Hamlet, in vainly emulating the wisdom of Sancho Panza"? Shaw notes how Jaques's famous Seven Ages of Man speech becomes especially paltry as Shakespeare lets the great metaphor of "all the world's a stage" slip into a literary toy "silly in its conceit and common in its ideas" (Our Theatres, II, pp. 280–81). – But ahh . . . the enchantment.

Thus Shaw's ambivalence about Shakespeare: on the one hand, keen disappointment and frustration with his mediocrity as an original or deep thinker; on the other hand, enticement by the vividness of his characters and scenes, admiration for his immense power over language, and enchantment with his musical expression. In An Essay on Criticism, Alexander Pope advanced a poetic gauge more flattering to Shakespeare: "True wit is Nature to advantage dressed, / What oft was thought, but ne'er so well expressed" (lines 297–98). Shaw would disagree: for him, true wit springs foremost from what is true, and what is true is often not commonly thought.

If one dares to besmirch the Bard, what about the Bard's dramatic contemporaries? Shaw has little patience with any bloating of their reputations: "Marlowe's blank verse has charm of color and movement," but when he's exhausted from raving he becomes "childish in thought, vulgar and wooden in humor, and stupid in his attempts at invention . . . Nature can produce no murderer cruel enough for Webster, nor any hero bully enough for Chapman . . . Greene was really amusing, Marston spirited and silly-clever, Cyril Tourneur able to string together lines," while Jonson and Beaumont and Fletcher had passable talents, but there is "much variety in a dustheap," and without Shakespeare's light "they would now be as invisible as they are insufferable" (Our Theatres, II, pp. 190–92).

So much for dramatic luminaries of the seventeenth century. What about the eighteenth? The Lyceum's revival of Sheridan's School for Scandal (1777) prompted Shaw to consider various tests of time a drama must survive before being dubbed "Immortal": "Everything has its own rate of change. Fashions change more quickly than manners, manners more quickly than morals, morals more quickly than passions, and, in general, the conscious, reasonable, intellectual life more quickly than the instinctive, wilful, affectionate one. The dramatist who deals with the irony and humor of the relatively durable sides of life, or with their pity and terror, is the one whose comedies and tragedies will last longest" (Our Theatres, II, p. 175).

If Ibsen was a century ahead of his time with *A Doll's House*, Shaw may be even more ahead of our time in finding *The School for Scandal* morally dated by its climax when Lady Teazle, caught in a man's rooms, "pleads for sympathy and forgiveness as an innocent young creature misled and seduced by a villain," and does so "without the least misgiving on the part of the dramatist as to the entire approval and sympathy of the audience." Shaw objects that were a man to do this under like circumstances we would consider him a cad: "so The School for Scandal dates on the Woman Question almost as badly as The Taming of the Shrew" (*Our Theatres*, II, pp. 177–79).

This twist on the Woman Question delivers a surprise of the sort that often gives drama to Shaw's reviews: he takes original shots that strike key issues sharply, or if they miss a bull's eye are unsettling enough to spur contention and drive home allied points. Such shots are a good part of his mode with Shakespeare, and a variant occurs in his review of a revival of Wilkie Collins's *New Magdalen*. To a theatre manager's claim that twenty years ago the play's realism influenced the so-called "new movement" in drama, Shaw responds by detailing its artificial idealism, concluding: "to do all this was not to anticipate 'the new movement,' but to provoke it" (*Our Theatres*, I, p. 243).

When a revival of Robertson's *Caste* moved the clock back ten more years, however, Shaw flexed another way: in a style that momentarily plunges his review into drama, he reminds young modernists who scorn the play (disparaged as "cup-and-saucer drama") that in the past thirty years "a great many things have happened, some of which have changed our minds and morals more than many of the famous Revolutions and Reformations," yet *Caste* survives as a dramatic landmark: "After years of sham heroics and superhuman balderdash, Caste delighted everyone by its freshness, its nature, its humanity. You will shriek and snort . . . 'Nature! Freshness! . . . In Heaven's name [if you are not too modern to have heard of Heaven], where is there a touch of nature in Caste?' I reply, 'In the windows, in the doors, in the walls, in the carpet, in the ceiling, in the kettle, in the fireplace, in the ham, in the tea . . . the quiet, unpumped, everyday utterance: in short, the commonplaces that are now spurned because they are common-places, and were then inexpressibly welcome because they were the most unexpected of novelties'" (*Our Theatres*, III, pp. 173–75).

Unfortunately, the memory of young modernists often goes back less than ten years, and their modernism about four. How did some sort of New Drama, other than Ibsen's, reflect the great changes of minds and morals in the thirty years since Robertson staged a fresh sense of realism? Put to this question in the 1890s were plays by Pinero, Jones, and Oscar Wilde, the major commercial talents appearing in mainline theatres (no Shaw play had yet scored a London success). If today's playgoers recognize only Wilde, little matter: the others' efforts proved perishable.

Pinero's early farces are infrequently revived, and plays on which he built a serious reputation have fared even less well. When his *The Second Mrs. Tanqueray* appeared in 1893, William Archer hailed it as courageously virile, an astonishing dramatic advance both philosophically and technically. Two years later, however, Shaw observes that Pinero just took a woman-with-a-past melodrama and gave it "an air of novel, profound, and original thought," conquering the public "by the exquisite flattery of giving them plays that they really liked, whilst persuading them that such appreciation was only possible from persons of great culture and acuteness." The result? Humbuggery, which Pinero managed less well in *The Notorious Mrs. Ebbsmith*, where he has Mrs. Ebbsmith pitch a Bible into a glowing stove, then suddenly scream and pull it out: "The Church is saved; and the curtain descends amid thunders of applause" (*Our Theatres*, I, pp. 63, 66).

When Pinero staged Philistine characters in *The Benefit of the Doubt* and nostalgic theatre history in *Trelawny of the "Wells,"* Shaw approved and even felt touched, seeing these as grounds Pinero understood. Still, he much preferred Henry Arthur Jones, to whom time has been even less charitable, and who had once converted Ibsen's *Doll's House* into the melodrama of a kind, wise, noble husband whose errant wife repents her irresponsible ways. Melodramatic echoes continued in his plays and he declared himself no Ibsenist, a fact evident in his Victorian underpinnings. Whence, then, Shaw's preference for him? Shaw's contrast of the two in March 1897 suggests an answer: "If [Pinero] observes life, he does so as a gentleman observes the picturesqueness of a gipsy. He presents his figures coolly, clearly, and just as the originals like to conceive themselves . . . Mr. Jones, on the other hand, works passionately from the real. By throwing himself sympathetically into his figures he gives them the stir of life; but he also often raises their energy to the intensity of his own" (*Our Theatres*, III, p. 97).

Subsequently, Shaw likens Pinero to Thackeray, and Jones to Dickens – the one a gentleman, an insider whose views of life are circumscribed by the parochial boundaries of fashionable society, the other an outsider whose unbounded views can more clearly engage and appraise life both inside and outside "Society" (*Our Theatres*, III, pp. 222–23). In effect, Shaw creates a dialectic between aesthetic camps in which almost everything related to Pinero's playwriting involves genteel limitations and much related to Jones's relates to – Shaw's. Like Ibsen, and like his portrayal of

Jones, Shaw had long considered himself an outsider. So in this portion of his campaign for more original theatre Pinero is the loser.

Impressive sidelights early in the campaign came from Henry James and Oscar Wilde. Unlike Pinero and Jones, here were truly major talents, but as neither jibed with Shaw's agenda for New Drama his joint review of a play by each – *Guy Domville* and *An Ideal Husband* – has unique interest. The review is remarkably open to their different qualities, and to their differences from himself as both critic and playwright. Yet Shaw's definition of these qualities reveals common grounds of sophistication and sensitivity:

> There is no reason why life as we find it in Mr. James's novels – life, that is, in which passion is subordinate to intellect and to fastidious artistic taste – should not be represented on the stage. If it is real to Mr. James, it must be real to others; and why should not these others have their drama instead of being banished from the theatre (to the theatre's great loss) by the monotony and vulgarity of drama in which passion is everything, intellect nothing, and art only brought in by the incidental outrages upon it. As it happens, I am not myself in Mr. James's camp: in all the life that has energy enough to be interesting to me, subjective volition, passion, will, make intellect the merest tool. But there is in the centre of that cyclone a certain calm spot where cultivated ladies and gentlemen live on independent incomes or by pleasant artistic occupations. It is there that Mr. James's art touches life, selecting whatever is graceful, exquisite, or dignified in its serenity.

James's spoiled, idle society is certainly not Shaw's. Still, Shaw gives space to its intellect, fastidious taste, and serenity over the brainless, vulgar passions of Victorian melodrama and its insipid sentimental offspring. Rather than either, however, his agenda seeks drama in which passion, will, action, and intellect interrelate as they should in life (where intellect, though perhaps a "mere" tool, is essential to the rest). Thus the vigor of dialogue in Shaw's plays. Yet James's style tantalizes: "Line after line comes with such a delicate turn and fall that I unhesitatingly challenge any of our popular dramatists to write a scene in verse with half the beauty of Mr. James's prose" (*Our Theatres*, I, pp. 6–8).

Shifting to *An Ideal Husband*, Shaw takes a very different tack, joshing critics who "laugh angrily" at Wilde's epigrams, then protest "that the trick is obvious, and that such epigrams can be turned out by the score by any one lightminded enough to condescend to such frivolity." Or so they whimper: "The fact that his plays, though apparently lucrative, remain unique under these circumstances, says much for the self-denial of our scribes." Anticipating volumes of modern literary theory, Shaw diagnoses the Wilde phenomenon in two sentences: "In a certain sense Mr. Wilde is to me our only thorough playwright. He plays with everything: with wit, with philosophy, with drama, with actors and audience, with the whole theatre" (*Our Theatres*, I, pp. 9–10).

After this, Shaw's reaction to *The Importance of Being Earnest* six weeks later comes as a surprise: "It amused me, of course; but unless comedy touches me as well as amuses me, it leaves me with a sense of having wasted my evening. I go to the theatre to be moved to laughter, not to be tickled or bustled into it" (*Our Theatres*, I, p. 44). Shaw's discontent springs from the play's "stock mechanical fun," its inhuman characters and action. Gwendolen's cup of tea is poison for him: his own comedies, in contrast, reveal a taste for organic, character-oriented humor. Then too, *Earnest*'s stagey contrivances resemble French dramatic mechanisms Shaw derided as "Sardoodledom" after the "well-made" plays of Victorien Sardou. At one point he declares, "To laugh without sympathy is a ruinous abuse of a noble function," and later he decries the delusion "that an audience can be interested in incidents and situations without believing in or caring for the people to whom these incidents and situations occur" (*Our Theatres*, II, pp. 124, 214). Yet alas, audiences did like *Earnest* and Gilbert and Sullivan as well as less clever French and English farces, melodramas, and stage spectaculars, all infected with such qualities.

In his crusade for a New Drama to transcend these trivialities Shaw had some committed colleagues, but they were not all of one mind. Among critical forebears, he saw the mid-century philosopher-critic-dramatist George Henry Lewes (the companion of novelist George Eliot) as a forerunner. In describing "Lewes's variety of culture, flexibility, and fun" as well as "his free use of vulgarity and impudence whenever they happened to be the proper tools for his job" and his "rare gift of integrity as a critic" (*Our Theatres*, II, p. 169), Shaw might almost be sketching himself. The integrity of critics could not be assumed. Their pay was low, some editors were cowardly, some managers sent tickets selectively, threatened legal action, or could intimidate those who, like Shaw, were also playwrights in need of theatrical friends. Yet Shaw observed, "the respect inspired by a good criticism is permanent, whilst the irritation it causes is temporary." Fundamentally, "The cardinal guarantee for a critic's integrity is simply the force of the critical instinct itself . . . I spare no effort to mitigate its inhumanity, [but if] my own father were an actor-manager, and his life depended on his getting favorable notices of his performance, I should orphan myself without an instant's hesitation if he acted badly" (*Our Theatres*, I, pp. 259–60).

Critics who most interested Shaw were those who, like Lewes, had experience as dramatists or translators. Thus he favors "the genuine excitement of Mr. Clement Scott, or the almost Calvinistic seriousness of

Mr. William Archer, [over] the gaily easy what-does-it-matterness of Mr. [Arthur Bingham] Walkley" (*Our Theatres*, I, p. 262). Scott had first attracted a vast body of readers and championed Robertson's naturalism in the early 1860s, yet by 1891 Shaw used his hysterical assault on Ibsen for fodder in *The Quintessence*. As a translator of Ibsen, Archer was obviously closer to Shaw's camp. Yet even he was not exactly in it. "For him," Shaw remarked, "there is illusion in the theatre: for me there is none . . . for me the play is not the thing, but its thought, its purpose, its feeling, and its execution" (*Our Theatres*, I, p. 95).

Though Shaw commented that "An actor of the same standing in the theatres as I have in journalism would drop dead with indignation if he were offered my salary" (*Our Theatres*, III, p. 120), he saw a consolation: "Some day they will reprint my articles; and then what will all your puffs and long runs and photographs and papered houses and cheap successes avail you, O lovely leading ladies and well-tailored actor-managers? The twentieth century, if it concerns itself about either of us, will see you as I see you" (*Our Theatres*, II, pp. 168–69). In most cases, so it has. Even his preference for international superstar Eleonora Duse's skill at playing diverse roles, over Sarah Bernardt's playing herself in all roles, informs *The Encyclopedia Britannica*. As some of Duse's greatest successes were in Ibsen's plays, she personified an evolution beyond hackneyed character types which lingered in late Victorian drama, prompting Shaw to deplore the stage lover as "always the same sort of young man," and declare, "We would all, I believe, willingly push the stage old man into the grave upon whose brink he has been cackling and doddering as long as we can remember him" (*Our Theatres*, III, pp. 260, 324).

Since New Drama involved relatively fresh and complex ways of looking at life, its distinctive, often ambiguous roles escalated an age-old theatrical issue: whose view of a play should prevail, the author's or the performers'? Countering the powerful actor-managers who adapted plays, especially Shakespeare's, to suit their tastes and egos, Shaw usually champions fidelity to scripts: "The history of the Lyceum, with its twenty years' steady cultivation of the actor as a personal force, and its utter neglect of the drama, is the history of the English stage during that period . . . And now I, being a dramatist and not an actor, want to know when the drama is to have its turn" (*Our Theatres*, III, p. 41). Yet he also admits that the issue rests with the relative quality of the script and the players. As Shylock, for example, Henry Irving "simply played in flat contradiction of the lines, and positively acted Shakespear off the stage," a fascinating feat, but "Shakespear at his highest pitch cannot be set aside by any mortal actor, however gifted." On the other hand, Irving as Iachimo, the melodramatic villain of

Shakespeare's deplorable *Cymbeline*, delighted Shaw as "a new and independent creation . . . unbroken in its life-current from end to end" (*Our
Theatres*, II, pp. 208–9).

Similarly, Pinero's artificial Mrs. Ebbsmith set Mrs. Patrick Campbell
free to do what she pleased with the role, "the result being an irresistible
projection of that lady's personal genius" (*Our Theatres*, I, p. 64); whereas
Ellen Terry, her refined talents wasted under Henry Irving's management,
poured her enchantments into an insipid part, overcoming a "transcendently idiotic speech" only by ravishing the audience "with an expression
that meant 'Dont blame me: *I* didnt write it'" (*Our Theatres*, III, p. 399).
And in contrast to Irving's reinventing the Bard, Johnston Forbes-Robert-
son's great *Hamlet* at the Lyceum was remarkable for its minimal cuts and
for his playing "as Shakespear should be played, on the line and to the line,
with the utterance and acting simultaneous, inseparable and in fact
identical" (*Our Theatres*, III, p. 217).

Such critiques reflect on Shaw's own playwriting. A source of his
remarkable character descriptions surfaces: "One facility offered to the
stage by Dickens is a description of the persons of the drama so vivid and
precise that no actor with the faintest sense of character could mistake the
sort of figure he has to represent" (*Our Theatres*, II, p. 141); and a citing of
Titian's "Assumption of the Virgin" for its triumphantly beautiful "union of
the flesh and the spirit" clarifies the painting's symbolic role in *Candida*
(*Our Theatres*, I, p. 80).

Shaw's critical objections to Shakespeare's Caesar preceded his own
Caesar by just a few months, yet it took twenty years for his put-down of
Othello's melodrama to surface in *Heartbreak House*, where the Moor's
story-telling titillates Ellie's romantic dreams. Meanwhile, Eliza Doolittle
could have developed in part from poor diction Shaw faults in Mrs.
Campbell, for whom he created the role (*Our Theatres*, I, pp. 142–43; II,
pp. 40–41). And seeds of *Passion, Poison and Petrifaction*, and *The
Doctor's Dilemma* appear in Shaw's amusement at unintentional comedy
provoked by a vegetarian teetotaler who stuffs his wife as if she were an
elephant and would rather she die than drink alcohol, then considerately
drops dead himself when she is about to elope with an incompetent doctor
(*Our Theatres*, III, pp. 241–44).

More profoundly linking the critic and playwright in Shaw are critical
views that inform his creative talent. For example, the fact that his dramas
are less overtly socialistic than one might expect relates to his disdain for
melodrama. Stabbing a melodramatic beast, and anticipating its opposite
in his *Androcles and the Lion* fifteen years later, he ironically praises
Wilson Barrett's immensely popular *Sign of the Cross* for the "irony" of its

"terrible contrast between the Romans ('Pagans, I regret to say,' as Mr. Pecksniff remarked of the sirens), with their straightforward sensuality, and the strange, perverted voluptuousness of the Christians, with their shuddering exaltations of longing for the whip, the rack, the stake, and the lions" (*Our Theatres*, II, p. 13). Socialist drama can be similarly nonsensical: "we are coming fast to a melodramatic formula in which the villain shall be a bad employer and the hero a Socialist; but that formula is no truer to life than the old one in which the villain was a lawyer and the hero a Jack Tar" (*Our Theatres*, II, p. 202). Then too, Shakespeare slips into producing simplistic villains. In contrast, "The average normal man is covetous, lazy, selfish; but he is not malevolent, nor capable of saying to himself, 'Evil: be thou my good.' He only does wrong as a means to an end, which he always represents to himself as the right end" (*Our Theatres*, II, p. 4).

In such ways, Shaw's reviews, for all their "electioneering," reflect the ambiguous qualities of his dramas. Paradoxically, his straightforwardness as a realist leads to dramatic relativities, ironies, contradictions, circularities, and layerings, because these are the stuff of life, and if criticism as well as drama wishes to engage life honestly, it must, perforce, engage these. For example, Shaw's critical rendering of Sir Augustus Harris, the impresario who had controlled London opera during his years as a music critic, evokes the mixed nature of most "villainy" in life. After Harris's death, Shaw reports, someone shocked him by remarking that his "old enemy" was gone, a view as unlifelike as the funeral eulogy declaring Harris "honest, honorable, straightforward." Countering both views, he depicts a manager who tried to intimidate critics yet became personally friendly; who cornered the market, exploited singers, and fought for "Italian fatuities against the German reforms," yet under whom the Opera flourished and the public received gorgeous value for its money; all told, a creature like "captains of industry" (a cultured anticipation of Boss Mangan of *Heartbreak House*), more conniving and fortunate than great (*Our Theatres*, II, pp. 182–89).

The ambiguity of this depiction corresponds to the mode and direction of most of Shaw's reviews as they forward the New Drama by thrusting beyond melodrama, sentimentality, stereotypes, and worn-out conventions of the Victorian stage. Advancing perspectives intelligent and sensitive to life as it is rather than life as many would like it to be, they stir up greater theatrical aspirations, new freedoms, more sophistication. From the earliest ones onward, Shaw's drumbeat is persistent: "The real history of the drama for the last ten years is not the history of the prosperous enterprises of Mr. Hare, Mr. Irving, and the established West-end theatres, but of the forlorn hopes . . . of the Impossiblists . . . I always make friends with able desperadoes, knowing that they will seize the citadel when the present garrison retires" (*Our Theatres*, I, pp. 20–21). The Impossiblists braved censure, neglect, and small receipts, in order to perform plays by Ibsen or Shaw, or authentic stagings of Shakespeare. Their primary venues were the Independent Theatre (founded in 1891), the New Century Theatre (1897), or the Elizabethan Stage Society (1894), which rented halls or courtyards.

Were they successful? Not very, but greatly. After three years, Shaw observes that "English theatre took not the smallest notice" of Ibsen's seventieth birthday; and the Elizabethan Stage Society "has issued a balance sheet which is a very genuine tragedy" (*Our Theatres*, III, pp. 359, 380). During those years, however, he chronicles a tectonic shift in taste. In 1895: "a modern manager need not produce The Wild Duck; but he must be very careful not to produce a play which will seem insipid and old-fashioned to playgoers who have seen The Wild Duck" (*Our Theatres*, I, p. 174). In 1896: ten years ago one of Sydney Grundy's plays would have seemed insanely radical, but after Ibsen and Nietzsche "it is rather too crude, parochial, and old-fashioned" (*Our Theatres*, II, p. 166). And in 1897: "Ibsen's plays are at this moment the head of the dramatic body . . . When any person objects to an Ibsen play because it does not hold the mirror up to his own mind, I can only remind him that a horse might make exactly the same objection" (*Our Theatres*, III, pp. 30–31).

Although Ibsen's plays never achieved long runs they were news, had memorable productions, and attracted arbiters of taste who saw contemporary English dramatists as second- or third-rate by comparison. But where did this put Shaw as a playwright? Shortly before retiring as a critic, he reports statistics by William Archer on the number of weeks British playwrights' works held the stage during the past five years. From first to fifth came Jones, Shakespeare, Pinero, Grundy, Carton. And *Shaw*? At the very bottom. Furthermore, four socially adventuresome plays by Jones and Pinero were their least successful (*Our Theatres*, III, pp. 354–57). So after Ibsen, whither New Drama?

Few prospects seemed promising, and at the end of the 1897–98 theatre season, Shaw, overworked, suffered a physical breakdown, an incapacitating foot operation, marriage to a wealthy Irishwoman, physical accidents, and a prolonged recuperation in the country, all forcing him to give up Fabian committee work, lecturing, political activities, freedoms of bachelorhood, and theatre reviewing. Down as he was, however, he was hardly out. Rather, freed from public activities and the weekly grind of reviewing, he pursued subjects more engaging than mediocre Victorian drama. His overload had included editing his first seven plays for publication, then starting *Caesar and Cleopatra* and *The Perfect Wagnerite*, his landmark book on Wagner's *Der Ring des Nibelungen*. So on his honeymoon he had worthwhile things to do.

The Perfect Wagnerite fittingly climaxed Shaw's reviewing career. Since Wagner wrote the books as well as the music for his operas, the *Ring* cycle called upon Shaw's expertise in both arts. Moreover, *The Ring*, like Ibsen's plays, incorporated radical social views, calling up shades of Shaw as a young man studying *Tristan* and *Capital* side-by-side.

Having used allegory in his own plays, Shaw argues that Wagner's persuasions as a social agitator and poet led him to render *The Ring* as an allegory of riches, power, and the defeat of an obsolete establishment. This interpretation – recently staged at Bayreuth – sees Alberic's greed and exploitation of fellow dwarfs as predatory capitalism; the two toiling, stupid, money-worshipping giants as the common run of humanity; and Wotan and other gods as intellectual, moral, talented people who devise and administer states and churches. Fearless and instinctively Protestant, the hero Siegfried is a youthful agent of change as he overcomes Wotan, whose authority has become increasingly dated, devious, and cruel.

In tandem with this interpretation, one can also see a version of Shaw's social distinctions in *The Quintessence*, with the dwarf and the giants as Philistines, Wotan and his godly crew as idealists, and Siegfried as the realist. Yet now Shaw's sense of ambiguity and Wagner's allegory appear to have matured his outlook: he sympathizes with Wotan as a figure bound to uphold his godly position and laws while covertly desiring the higher and fuller life his overthrow would bring.

Toward the end of his essay, Shaw's focus on *The Ring*'s music, dramatic qualities, and staging reveals his virtuosity as the best music and drama critic of his day. He discusses Wagner's use of musical themes for objects and characters, from the simple Valhalla theme to the complex richness of the ring and Wotan themes, a richness textured variously through different dramatic contexts. He observes that "the dramatic play of the ideas is reflected in the contrapuntal play of the themes," interrelating thought and diverse emotions, while musical and dramatic flexibility transcend the timeworn metrics of most musical theatre. With apt strokes he then defines and compares gothic, baroque, rococo, and romantic music, finally emphasizing Wagner's greatest distinction: beyond his major forebears, "Wagner was the literary musician par excellence . . . he produced his own dramatic poems, thus giving dramatic integrity to opera, and making symphony articulate" (*Works*, vol. XIX, pp. 266–80).

While Shaw's decade of reviewing ended in May 1898, capped by *The Perfect Wagnerite* that December, his publication of *Plays Pleasant and*

Unpleasant in April signaled a new beginning for him, less as a playwright – in his spare time he was already penning plays at a fairly regular clip – than as a writer of prefaces. Before 1898 he had produced just four prefaces; subsequently, he wrote nearly a hundred, not just on his dramas but also on a great assortment of personal, political, social, and cultural subjects. In prefacing *Three Plays for Puritans* (1900), he declares, "The reason most playwrights do not publish their plays with prefaces is that they cannot write them, the business of intellectually conscious philosopher and skilled critic being no necessary part of their craft . . . I write prefaces as Dryden did, and treatises as Wagner, because I *can*; and I would give half a dozen of Shakespear's plays for one of the prefaces he ought to have written" (*Works*, vol. IX, pp. xxiii–xxv).

How about half a dozen of Shaw's prefaces for another good play? Though some are powerful and most are pithy, many ramble. Two are twice as long as the plays they precede. Still, Shaw has a good rationale for them: they give readers his viewpoint on subjects too large for staging; and, like his stage directions, they also give actors and directors information useful for interpreting the plays. As with Ibsen and Wagner, quintessences and perfection in thoughtful art may not be easily grasped at first; so artist-critics who can clarify difficult matters might well do so.

Thus Shaw the critic-artist sets out as a Promethean culture hero to replace stale, mediocre theatre with drama at the cutting edge of consciousness, because drama and life cross-circulate: "Public and private life become daily more theatrical: the modern [leader] is nothing if not an effective actor; all newspapers are now edited histrionically; and the records of our law courts shew that the stage is affecting personal conduct to an unprecedented extent . . . The truth is that dramatic invention is the first effort of man to become intellectually conscious" (*Works*, vol. VIII, p. xiii).

NOTES

1 Here and later, *Works* refers to the first collected edition of *The Works of Bernard Shaw* (London, 1930–38). The American Ayot St. Lawrence edition has similar pagination.

2 To Olaf Skavlan (January 24, 1882); to Georg Brandes (January 3, 1882); to Frederik Hegel (March 16, 1882); to Leopold von Sacher-Masoch (December 12, 1882), in *Ibsen: Letters and Speeches*, ed. Evert Sprinchorn (New York, 1964), pp. 202, 199, 206, 214. Selections from many such sentiments.

3 Ibsen, *An Enemy of the People*, in Henrik Ibsen, *The Complete Major Prose Plays*, trans. Rolf Fjelde (New York, 1978), pp. 353–57, 383.

4 *Our Theatres in the Nineties*, Volumes XXIII, XXIV and XXV in *The Works of Bernard Shaw*, but also sub-numbered there as a set: I, II, and III. For a clear sense of sequence, the latter numbering will be used in citations.

FURTHER READING

Fromm, Harold, *Bernard Shaw and the Theater in the Nineties: A Study of Shaw's Dramatic Criticism*, Lawrence: University of Kansas Press, 1967.

Jenkins, Anthony, *The Making of Victorian Drama*, Cambridge: Cambridge University Press, 1991.

Kaye, Julian B., *Bernard Shaw and the Nineteenth-Century Tradition*, Norman: University of Oklahoma Press, 1958.

Meisel, Martin, *Shaw and the Nineteenth Century Theater*, Princeton: Princeton University Press, 1963.

Shaw, Bernard, *Ellen Terry and Bernard Shaw: A Correspondence*, ed. Christopher St. John, New York: Putnam's, 1932.

Turco, Alfred, Jr., *Shaw's Moral Vision: The Self and Salvation*, Ithaca: Cornell University Press, 1976.

Wisenthal, J. L. (ed.), *Shaw and Ibsen: Bernard Shaw's The Quintessence of Ibsenism and Related Writings*, Toronto: University of Toronto Press, 1979.

4

KERRY POWELL

New Women, new plays, and Shaw in the 1890s

In a moment of crisis in the 1890s masculine control of the theatre as an institution was shaken by the efforts of insurgent women and a few male sympathizers. Bernard Shaw, writing about the London theatre of 1894 – the *annus mirabilis* of the New Woman – described the importance of that revolt with a clearsightedness unusual, perhaps unique, among men of the theatre. Shaw declares in the preface he wrote for William Archer's *Theatrical "World" of 1894*, assessing developments of that year in the London stage:

> We cannot but see that the time is ripe for the advent of the actress-manageress, and that we are on the verge of something like a struggle between the sexes for the dominion of the London theatres, a struggle which failing an honourable treaty, or the break-up of the actor-manager system by the competition of new forms of theatrical enterprise, must in the long run end disastrously for the side which is furthest behind the times. And that side is at present the men's side.[1]

What is striking here is Shaw's recognition as a male commentator that the theatre was on the threshold of apocalypse, one that would be wrought by the efforts of newly assertive women of the stage. It would be the manifestation in the London theatre of the changes being wrought by the New Woman. But Shaw's enthusiasm for those changes was not nearly as unqualified as his remarks about a "struggle between the sexes" would suggest, or as one might infer from his praise of the "unwomanly woman" in *The Quintessence of Ibsenism* (1891).

For many, including Shaw himself at times, the New Woman created intellectual panic in her function as what Carroll Smith-Rosenberg has called "a condensed symbol of disorder and rebellion."[2] She was not so much a person, or even group of people, as a constructed category which expressed metonymically some of the historic challenges being brought to bear in the 1890s on traditional ideas of woman, in particular, and gender as whole. Individuals did not often identify themselves as New Women;

and when they were so identified by others, the term seems usually to have been freighted with disparaging meanings, although these meanings were different, or contradictory, even while cohering as a symbol of "disorder and rebellion." As Ann Ardis has pointed out, the term "New Woman" was a way of naming, and thus controlling, a range of ongoing disruptions in the social understanding of gender.[3] That is why the New Woman seemed to be, and in one sense actually was, more an element of discourse than a real person or group of people. Commentators in the 1890s often noted this fact, labeling the New Woman a "figment of the journalistic imagination" and "a product oftener met with in the novels of the day than in ordinary life."[4]

On the whole the New Woman was treated with contempt or fear because in various incarnations, whether in discourse or in "real" life, she reopened for discussion some deeply held assumptions about what it meant to be a man or woman. One version of the New Woman defied traditional codes of female beauty, smoking cigarettes and dressing in a simple and "manly" fashion which seemed to complement her discontented mouth and a nose "too large for feminine beauty" but indicative of intelligence.[5] New Women were often perceived to be masculine in other ways too, sometimes devoting themselves to a profession or business in preference to the bearing and bringing up of children. This abrogation of a woman's supposed highest duty was perhaps the chief illustration of what one writer described as the New Woman's "restlessness and discontent with the existing order of things." Sometimes the New Woman was perceived to be freer in her dealings with men than custom allowed, and at other times a cold and "apparently sexless" creature who rejected out of hand all relations with men.[6] In these varied forms the New Woman was consistently a symbol of upheaval, threatening to dissolve the boundaries of gender and disrupt the maternal activites which nature was thought to have ordained for women. "The day of our acquiescence is over," as Sarah Grand announced on behalf of all women in "The New Aspect of the Woman Question," published in 1894.[7]

Shaw's own response to the New Woman makes clear with what mixed feelings even a sympathetic and progressive man could regard her. For example, *The Philanderer* (written in 1893, but not publicly produced until 1907), presents a coterie of women who belong to an Ibsen Club, dress in trousers, smoke, call each other by their surnames, and in general cultivate a masculine aura which makes them as much the object of ridicule as the "advanced" women lampooned in popular plays of the time such as Sydney Grundy's *The New Woman* (1894). So pronounced was this trend toward caricature of progressive women on stage that the theatrical newspaper the

Era took notice of it by asking "Why hasn't the New Woman a word to say for herself on the stage?" Noting that male dramatists "carciature the poor thing to their hearts' content," the newspaper suggested tongue-in-cheek that women should begin writing plays in response to the ridicule of New Women in plays by men.[8] While expressing sympathy for women in the impending "struggle between the sexes" for control of the theatre, Shaw actually contributed to the pattern of ridicule and caricature that the *Era* noticed as prevalent in plays about New Women in the mid-1890s – a pattern that it believed would be reversed only when women began writing plays of their own.

On the other hand Shaw's *Philanderer* refers to marriage as a degrading arrangement by which a woman sells herself, a declaration of which many New Women of the 1890s would have approved if the play had found a producer at the time. Similarly *Mrs. Warren's Profession*, written in 1893–94 but banned by the Lord Chamberlain, would have pleased some New Women with its straightforward linkage of prostitution and marriage, but its representation of Vivie Warren surely would have been problematic. Not only is she a caricature of the New Woman with her manly dress, bone-crushing handshake, and predilection for cigars and whisky, but her uncritical focus on working and making money in a capitalist and sexist economy makes her no more appealing than her notorious mother, an underworld entrepreneur who owns a chain of brothels but has thought long and hard about what she does, and why. What is wrong with Vivie Warren, for Shaw, is her coldness and calculation, her immersion in the practical side of life, her estrangement from what he would eventually call the Life Force. Vivie Warren is a strong woman, to be sure, but for Shaw a woman's strength is misdirected and grotesque unless fundamentally sexual, seeking out and compelling a superior man to mate with her and produce "supermen." Like many men of the 1890s, therefore, Shaw could be enthusiastic about the New Woman when he could imagine her disruptions being confined to the realm of the domestic and sexual. Ann Whitefield in pursuit of Jack Tanner in *Man and Superman*, not the strong female accountant of *Mrs. Warren's Profession*, represents the kind of woman's strength that most appealed to Shaw. Similarly the title character of *Candida* – written in 1894 and pre-eminently "THE Mother Play," as Shaw put it – is a woman of strength and intelligence who has no impact outside the household and makes the young working woman Proserpine Garnett her ineffectual comic foil.[9]

Shaw's attitude toward the pre-eminent New Woman of the theatrical world – Elizabeth Robins, a transplanted American – was for the most part adversarial, although he believed her work as an actress and producer to be of the highest importance. To Shaw, what distinguished Elizabeth Robins was her performances in plays by Henrik Ibsen of which she was also the producer – beginning with the epoch-making *Hedda Gabler* and *A Doll's House* (both 1891) and continuing with *The Master Builder* in 1893 and a subscription series of plays by Ibsen in the same year. None of these plays was financially successful, or likely to be, which explains in part the reluctance of mainstream theatres and their actor-managers to produce them. Indeed Robins sold her father's wedding gift to help pay the costs of *Hedda Gabler*, which she co-produced with Marion Lea, another American actress in London, and in which she played the titled role with electrifying results. On the basis of these independent productions staged by women – Elizabeth Robins, Janet Achurch, Eleanor Calhoun, Marion Lea, Florence Farr, and a few others – Shaw detected by 1894 the signs of a gender war in the theatre, the first shots having been fired by women, and for good cause. "A glance at our theatres will show," writes Shaw in his preface to *The Theatrical "World" of 1894*, "that the highest artistic career is practically closed to the leading lady." Thus actresses in the employment of actor-managers, even the most succesful like Ellen Terry and Kate Rorke, merely "support" the manager and give up any of the few good women's parts that come along, from Ibsen or others. Shaw points to Elizabeth Robins, "the creator of Hedda Gabler and Hilda Wangel," and to Janet Achurch, "virtually actress-manager" of the first English production of *A Doll's House*, as the omens of revolutionary change.[10]

Shaw perceived the work of Robins and other actresses, particularly their performances of Ibsen, as contesting in the theatre the same masculine authority which was under attack by New Women elsewhere. Critics less sympathetic than Shaw also saw Ibsenite women as engaged in a "struggle between the sexes," but reviled them with the same kind of excessive language which conservatives used against New Women in other contexts. One reviewer, for example, described women in the audience of Madge Kendal's production of Ibsen's *The Pillars of Society* (1889) as monstrous distortions of nature, "masculine women," disruptive and with a propensity to violence.[11] In *Degeneration* (1895) Max Nordau can make sense of the women in Ibsen's plays only by seeing them as insane – "raving so wildly as to require strait-jackets" – the casualties of an epidemic of mental and physical "degeneration" undermining the foundations of the social order. For the enactment of such characters Nordau imagines a fantastic, feminized theatre with an audience of hysterics, nymphomaniacs, and prostitutes who recognized their own lawless selves glorified in a Nora Helmer or Mrs. Alving. The theatre of Nordau's nightmare thus becomes a madhouse in which an audience of lunatic New Women applauds "their own portrait" in representations of women mad like themselves.[12]

Elizabeth Robins would not have recognized herself in these wild attacks against New Women in the theatre, but neither would she have seen herself, initially at least, in Shaw's more sympathetic portrait of a heroic actress-producer making war against a male-dominated London stage. As Robins herself remarked in a lecture to the Royal Society of Arts in 1928, her first attraction to Ibsen had nothing to do with New Women but everything to do with the art of acting. "How could we find fault," she asked, "with a state of society that had given us Nora, Hedda, and Thea?"[13] Elizabeth Robins's disillusionment, and her subsequent politicization as a New Woman of the theatre, came in the wake of her landmark production of *Hedda Gabler* at the Vaudeville Theatre in 1891. Any hope that the impact of *Hedda Gabler* would provide Robins, or any actress, with meaningful opportunities in the usual West End venues was soon disappointed. Robins notes in an unpublished memoir, "Heights and Depths," that parts were offered to her and her coproducer Marion Lea, but alas, "not such parts as we had in mind – but pretty little dears however much they were called heroines or 'leading parts.'"[14] In notes written and typed at the end of the manuscript of *Whither and How*, Robins added these comments:

> Marion Lea and I had started out to do something that hadn't ever been tried before, never realising the peril of this, a peril the more should the first steps show marked success . . . Offers of engagements under regular managers began to flow in. The first on record I refused to go further with, because I knew to what a blind alley it would lead. All the theatres then were either frankly commercial like the Adelphi, or commercial in disguise, & without exception were under the management of men . . . Men who wrote plays for women had long been seeing that they simply had little or no chance of being acted.[15]

Recognizing her dilemma as an actress, Robins recollects that "a help-lessness and depression fell upon me, for I saw what I was facing." All she had really gotten from the spectacular achievement of *Hedda Gabler* had been personal and transitory, for what she called the "rational Theatre" of her hopes was no nearer now than it had been before. This failure, and her reaction to it, completed the transformation of Elizabeth Robins into a New Woman.

Other voices for theatrical reform were audible, or soon would be, but none of them, not even Shaw's, addressed the issue in the same way as Elizabeth Robins. Matthew Arnold, for example, had pleaded for a subsidized and "irresistible" national theatre of literary merit, and Henry

James espoused a similar project in *The Tragic Muse*. Shaw himself, William Archer and J. T. Grein pursued in print and action their own hopes for a serious and artistic English drama for which the West End venues had shown little or no sympathy. Robins's "Theatre of the Future," as she would eventually call it, deserves not only to be redeemed from oblivion, but distinguished from these and other men's proposals for theatrical reform.[16] Robins's analysis was marked by her insight that inequities of gender conspired with self-interested economic motives to weaken the theatre as an artistic institution. Reform would come about through the efforts of women playwrights and managers, along with their male sympathizers, who would inaugurate a noncommercial theatre – an "association of workers" not owned by any individual – in which self-interest played no part and drama was more than a commodity. "Lifting higher the standard of dramatic work," writes Robins in an unpublished memoir, "we should help actors, the stage – the world."[17]

In thus linking the theatre, sexual justice, and social regeneration, Robins anticipated in more conciliatory tones the American anarchist Emma Goldman, who believed the drama had power to show that "society has gone beyond the stage of patching up" and that the human race "must throw off the dead weight of the past." Goldman, although an amateur, worked with an experimental theatre group at the turn of the century and was a fervent admirer of Ibsen for what she saw as his revolutionary opposition to every social arrangement that impinged upon personal liberty and spontaneity, including the "bondage of duty" from which he frees Nora Alving at the end of *A Dolls's House*. Plays – at least plays like Ibsen's – would be the "dynamite which . . . shakes the social pillars, and prepares men and women for reconstruction." But what role could women play in this campaign when, as Goldman writes in *The Social Significance of Modern Drama* (1914), the writing of plays remained "so far the stronghold exclusively of men" and no country, at least until the advent of the young Githa Sowerby, had produced a single woman dramatist of note? Robins's own work in the theatre escapes notice in *The Social Significance of Modern Drama*, but Goldman devotes considerable space to Shaw, whom she criticizes for writing plays shaped too rigidly by his moderate Fabian political views. Nor is Goldman impressed with Shaw's portrait of a New Woman in *Mrs. Warren's Profession*; for Vivie Warren, remote from the grim circumstances that shaped her notorious mother, must in the end be classified with the "bigots and inexperienced girls."[18]

Robins herself had given up on Shaw very early in her quest to change the face of late Victorian theatre and society. She gave up on Oscar Wilde eventually, too, despite her many exhortations that he help organize and

5 Sacrificing companionship for a male profession: Jan Alexandra Smith as Vivie Warren
in the Shaw Festival's 1997 production of *Mrs. Warren's Profession*

write for the "Theatre of the Future."[19] Robins's vision depended upon
redressing the grievances of women in the theatre and the world at large,
yet men themselves rarely wrote, and still more rarely produced, what
Robins called "women's plays." Like Vida Levering, the heroine of her own
play *Votes for Women!*, Robins had to face the realization that "winning
over the men" – even the best and brightest men, even Shaw or Wilde – was
not enough. The struggle for theatrical reform was basically, from her
perspective, a woman's cause, and some battles concerning women, as Vida
Levering says in the play, "must be fought by women alone."[20]

Shaw was more hopeful than Elizabeth Robins herself by the mid-1890s in
forecasting an apocalypse of the theatre being brought about by oppressed
and rebellious actresses. But at the same time, and without exactly saying
so, Shaw found it much easier to imagine actresses contesting the authority
of actor-managers than writing plays themselves. On this point he was in
substantial agreement with a long, often unspoken Victorian tradition
which deemed the writing of drama to require a cast of mind recognized as
masculine. An example of the Victorian tendency to define playwriting so
as to exclude women, implicitly at least, appears in Frank Archer's *How To
Write a Good Play* (1892). "Play-making may not be one of the exact

sciences," the author concedes, "but it is more nearly allied to them than appears at first sight. It can fairly be described as a sort of *sympathy in mathematics*." The playwright, by this analysis, is a sort of architect whose "constructive ability" arises out of an analytical mind that the Victorians rarely associated with women.[21] This prejudice also finds expression in a theatrical story by Henry James, "Nona Vincent," in which a male playwright discovers with satisfaction that his craft relies upon qualities of "line and law" that Victorians usually considered to be masculine. The "dramatic form," observes dramatist Allan Wayworth in the story by James, "had the high dignity of the exact sciences, it was mathematical and architectural. It was full of the refreshment of calculation and construction." Women, with their abundant reserves of emotion, must be called on for the "vulgar" necessity of acting Wayworth's first play, but only he – a man – could actually write it.[22] If a woman wrote a good play, as critic William Archer believed was the case with Constance Fletcher's *Mrs. Lessingham* in 1894, the fact could be explained by the woman playwright's masculine style. "I fancy," Archer comments in his review of the play, "it would be a very keen critic who should detect a feminine hand in the workmanship."[23] Similarly, in the play *Our Flat* (1888), the success of a woman playwright's drama is explained on the grounds that, as one character says, it is "impossible to tell it's a woman's work."[24] And the author of "Women as Dramatists" (1894) explains the success of Joanna Baillie's writing for the pre-Victorian stage on the basis of the supposed "masculine strength and vigour" of her prose.[25]

Elizabeth Robins herself was keenly conscious of this deep-seated prejudice against women writing for the stage. "There was a widespread conviction," Robins recalls in *Theatre and Friendship*, "that no woman can write a good full-length play." Indeed, when she mentioned to Henry James the possibility of writing one herself, he reacted "with a start, and a look of horror."[26] Even William Archer, her secret collaborator in the epochal production of *Hedda Gabler*, found it incredible that Robins could write good drama: "To tell you the truth I don't think you have the power of concentration required for playwriting. Certainly you could find a novel far easier than a play."[27] When Robins herself approached Herbert Beerbohm Tree about writing a play for the Haymarket, he was similarly incredulous, telling her in a hastily scrawled note that he had "never . . . read a good play from a woman's hand."[28] Nevertheless, if the "Theatre of the Future" was ever to be realized, it seemed clear to Robins that women would not only have to stage their own productions of plays, but write them too.

Robins, for her part, persuaded John Hare to produce Constance Fletcher's *Mrs. Lessingham* at the Garrick Theatre in 1894, playing the lead role while also rewriting the play in collaboration with the author and Hare. Although Shaw was contempuous of *Mrs. Lessingham*, it is nonetheless remarkable for its sympathetic portrayal of a married woman who elopes with her lover and later comes into conflict with the more conventional heroine to whom the leading man is engaged.[29] An unconventional play by Robins herself, called *The Mirkwater*, concerns Felicia Vincent, who assists in the suicide of her sister, a young woman stricken with breast cancer who "dominated every one she came near."[30] *The Mirkwater* was never produced or published, nor was another play by Robins, *The Silver Lotus*, written in about the middle of the decade. *The Silver Lotus* focuses on a young mother driven to alcoholism by the death of her children and the shallow grief of her husband. However, "what the world wants from her," Shaw wrote of Elizabeth Robins in 1896, was not writing at all but "acting" – or rather, acting of a particular kind, in plays by Ibsen, for example, and not in "that confounded Mrs. Lessingham business."[31]

Shaw would continue to complain in this vein to Robins herself, characterizing her as "an actress neglecting that everyday work at her profession which is the foundation of all real character and power."[32] But Robins's infrequent appearances on stage after 1894 were really the outcome of her "hopelessness and depression" caused by the lack of suitable, challenging female roles. One way to deal with the problem was to write plays herself, which Robins first began to do, in collaboration with Florence Bell, when she adapted a story by Elin Ameen under the title *Alan's Wife*, staged by the Independent Theatre in 1893. In writing *Alan's Wife* she provided herself with the kind of role she desired but rarely found in the regular theatres, a woman of depth and power, in this case a working-class heroine who celebrates her murder of her sick child as the strongest and most courageous action of her life. Beerbohm Tree turned down the chance to produce it at the prestigious Haymarket Theatre, finding it "too horrible, too gruesome" when Robins read him a scenario of it.[33]

Even Shaw was made uncomfortable by *Alan's Wife*, so remote from the drawing-room comedy in which his own reforming impulse was finding expression. The howling strength of the heroine struck him as manic and "most horribly common," and further to discredit the play he ascribed to its heroine an implausible repentance which in fact never actually occurs. Then, as he would often do with women playwrights, Shaw proceeded to "rewrite" the play to his own specifications. "If I were to treat the subject," he says in a letter to William Archer, "I should represent Jean as a rational being in society as it exists at present; and I should shew her killing the child with cool and successful precautions against being found out." The heroine would then proceed to live a normal life among her neighbors, and even marry the parson. Shaw's imaginary rewrite of *Alan's Wife* thus purges it of what were to his mind the emotional excesses associated with sensational woman novelists and popular melodrama. The title role, according to Shaw, "uncorks the eye of the emotional actress" at the cost of spoiling a play about an unconventional and independent woman. "When I think of that wasted opportunity," Shaw says, "I feel more than ever contemptuous of this skulking author who writes like a female apprentice of [Robert] Buchanan."[34]

Soon thereafter Shaw again ventured to "rewrite" another fledgling woman playwright. Janet Achurch, the actress who helped produce and starred in the original London production of *A Doll's House* in 1889, suggested that Shaw consider dramatizing *Yvette*, a story by Guy de Maupassant. Achurch summarized it for Shaw in conversation with the result that both of them set out in 1893 to write plays about a woman who becomes rich managing houses of prostitution. In a letter written at the end of 1893 Shaw refers to the leading role in Janet Achurch's version, entitled *Mrs. Daintree's Daughter*, as "the original" of the title character of his own *Mrs. Warren's Profession*.[35] Although he encouraged Achurch to write *Mrs. Daintree's Daughter*, Shaw severely attacked the completed play after learning that she had tried to interest Lewis Waller in staging it. "I am not surprised about Mrs. Daintry," Shaw writes in early 1895; "the ending is not the sort of thing for his audience" – the "smart clientele" of the Haymarket Theatre where Waller was temporarily actor-manager. What was wrong with *Mrs. Daintree's Daughter*, for Shaw, was also what had marred Elizabeth Robins's writing in *Alan's Wife*, namely a surrender to an excessive pathos which was incompatible with "really good drama." Indeed Janet Achurch's play wasn't drama at all, as far as Shaw was concerned: "You know," he wrote in summing up the matter for her, "I told you that you hadn't written your play." What Achurch had written instead was a spectacle of emotional excess – not a play, but something "for a Bernhardt to star in."[36] Shaw claimed elsewhere that Sarah Bernhardt used her spectacular talent to the detriment of "really good drama," and in particular to the detriment of the script of a play: that she usurped the character fashioned by the author in order to stage *herself* and, as herself, overwhelm the audience. "She does not enter into the leading character: she substitutes herself for it," he explained.[37] Shaw, who had declared sympathy with women in the "struggle between the sexes," thus finds himself locked in struggle with Bernhardt and other upstart women of the theatre such as Janet Achurch and Elizabeth Robins for control of the dramatic text itself. Now he was on "the men's side," as he called it, resisting women as playwrights and insisting on the subjection of actresses to the authority of the (male-authored) script.[38]

Thus the New Woman movement as it touched the theatre depended to a large degree on the ability of women to write plays, but repeatedly Shaw discredited the efforts of women as playwrights. His reactions in the aggregate suggest a skepticism that women could write good drama at all, although he stopped short of the sweeping assertions that Victorian men often made about women's lack of capacity for playwriting. For Shaw, women got it all wrong when they wrote for the theatre – echoing his comment to Janet Achurch when Dorothy Leighton's *Thyrza Fleming* was produced by the Independent Theatre in 1894, Shaw's review included the dismissive remark that "she has not written the play at all."[39] He went on to propose, as usual, a rewrite of the woman's play – arguing that *Thyrza Fleming* needed more "feeling" to qualify as "true . . . drama," despite the fact that earlier he had diagnosed *Alan's Wife* and *Mrs. Daintree's Daughter* as not "really good drama" because of an excessive amount of feeling in those plays by women. The rationale may shift, therefore, but for Shaw these New Women's attempts to write plays were inappropriate, even ludicrous, and the scripts they produced were not really plays at all.

In the same year that her play *Thyrza Fleming* was produced by the Independent Theatre, Dorothy Leighton introduced a fictional woman dramatist in a long-forgotten novel entitled *Disillusion* (1894). Leighton's fictional heroine Linda Grey is loath to make known her authorship of a hit play, for although an ardent feminist, "her shy, reserved nature shrank from any approach to notoriety."[40] The credit goes to the New Woman's male collaborator, just as in the play *Our Flat* (1889) a woman playwright allows all acclaim for her hit play to fall to her husband, who wrote none of it himself.[41] These representations by, and of, women writers for the stage suggest that Virginia Woolf was correct in her assessment that women were socially conditioned not to write plays; or if they wrote them, to deny authorship. Women who aspired to become playwrights did not always realize the extent of the bias against them until it was pointed out. At the close of the Victorian period Cicely Hamilton, another New Woman of the theatre, "most of all . . . desired to write a good play," but learned from a manager, when her first one-act piece was about to be produced, that "it was advisable to conceal the sex of its author until after the notices were out, as plays which were known to be written by women were apt to get a bad press."[42] This point is not lost on the heroine of *Our Flat*, an aspiring woman playwright who signs her first play with her husband's name, withholding her own identity as author "till the agreement is signed."[43] In "real" life Florence Bell and Elizabeth Robins disguised their authorship of *Alan's Wife* from Beerbohm Tree, who they hoped would produce it, being well aware of his view that "women can't write."[44] Tree declined to produce *Alan's Wife* anyway, and yet the hopes of these New Women for reforming the London stage hinged to a considerable extent on plays written as well as acted and produced by women. Shaw, belittling women's attempts to become playwrights, denying they had written "real" plays at all, contributed to the subjection of women in the theatre even while he proclaimed himself their ally in the "battle between the sexes for control of the London stage."

"In order to realize what a terrible person the New Woman is," Shaw wrote in 1897, it is necessary to have read "that ruthlessly orthodox book, *The Heavenly Twins*." Shaw describes Sarah Grand, the author, as a "New Woman," but one who "will connive at no triflings with 'purity' in its sense of monogamy." In one strand of the book's complicated plot a New Woman bride named Evadne discovers that her husband has had sexual relationships before their marriage, making him a "moral leper" with whom she can have no intimacy, physical or emotional. Their marriage is never consummated because the New Woman has taken to heart an underlying premise of the Victorian double standard – namely, that the "angel in the house" is required to save the male from his own depravity, feminizing him, requiring from him a purity as absolute as her own. *The Heavenly Twins* was, as Shaw himself wrote, an "instant and huge success," and more than any other New Woman text it created an awareness of what seemed to many men, including Shaw, the most problematic demand of the developing women's movement.[45] Sarah Grand expressed that demand in her own voice in a magazine article that appeared shortly after the publication of *The Heavenly Twins*. "Man morally is in his infancy," she wrote in 1894. "There have been times when there was a doubt as to whether he was to be raised or woman was to be lowered, but we have turned that corner at last; and now woman holds out a strong hand to the child-man and insists . . . upon helping him up."[46]

But this demand for male purity was a controversial aspect of the New Woman movement, and one which made many men uncomfortable – not just Shaw. It made some "advanced" women uncomfortable too, and male playwrights sometimes turned this disharmony within the ranks of progressive women into ridicule. For example, in Sydney Grundy's *The New Woman* two women stake out opposite positions – Enid Bethune arguing that men should be better, Victoria Vivash that women should be worse:

Victoria: I want to be allowed to do as *men* do.

Enid: Then you ought to ashamed of yourself; there!

Victoria: I only say, I ought to be allowed.

Enid: And I say that a man, reeking with infamy, ought not to be allowed to marry a pure girl –

Victoria: Certainly not! She ought to reek with infamy as well.[47]

The target of Grundy's humor is not only the New Woman who would claim some of the liberties traditionally belonging to men, but also the one who would raise men to the standard of purity usually reserved for women. The latter type of New Woman is also the satirical target of an unpublished play by Charles Rogers called *The Future Woman* (1896) in which the husband Jenkins agrees never to "go astray" again and to become a model husband, but only when his wife agrees to give up the "Society for the Advancement of Woman's Rights."[48] Similarly, in their play *Husband and Wife* (1891), F. C. Philips and Percy Fendall make sport of the feminist Mrs. Greenthorne, founder of the "Married Women's League" which, she explains, "we started for the amelioration of men's morals . . . to elevate the standard of husbands to a degree of refinement and purity."[49] On other occasions New Women were represented as daunting adherents of an "ascetic ideal," as Rhoda Nunn calls it in George Gissing's novel *The Odd Women* (1893) – "propagating a new religion, purifying the earth." So when she hears that the man she loves is a man with a past, Rhoda Nunn scorns the idea of marriage with him, preferring to become one of the unmated "odd women" of the book's title.[50] The austerity with which Gissing invests the aptly named Rhoda Nunn has much in common with Shaw's own portrait of an Ibsenite New Woman in *The Philanderer*, written in 1893, the year *The Odd Women* was published. Grace Tranfield refuses to marry Leonard Charteris – surely a self-portrait of the author to some extent – because of a libertine career which has made him unable to respect even a woman he loves.

Shaw was thus involved in this aspect of the New Woman question as part of a nervous male reaction to "this new-fangled folly that a man's life must be immaculate," as one popular but long-forgotten play put it.[51] Shaw's reaction to "this new-fangled folly" in *The Philanderer* may seem comparatively thoughtful and restrained, especially if compared, say, to Oscar Wilde's *An Ideal Husband* (1895), whose self-consciously feminist heroine not only gives up the idea that her politician husband should be an "ideal" man, but in the end takes part in the cover-up to shield him from the consequences of his own crime. Like Wilde and many other men, however, Shaw found it difficult to sympathize with the New Woman's advocacy of a higher standard of conduct, of "purity" even, where men

6 Parodying the "New Woman": Shauna Black as Sylvia Craven shocks Simon Bradbury as Leonard Charteris in the Shaw Festival's 1995 production of *The Philanderer*

were concerned. He confesses, indeed, that "I am a man; and Madame Sarah Grand's solution fills me with dismay." Shaw, despite his own hesitancy over sex, is nostalgic for a double standard which provides for two types of women:

> What I should like, of course, would be the maintenance of two distinct classes of women, the one polyandrous and disreputable and the other monogamous and reputable. I could then have my fill of polygamy among the polyandrous ones with the certainty that I could hand them over to the police if they annoyed me after I had become tired of them, at which date I could marry one of the monogamous ones and live happily ever afterwards.

Shaw then reflects that if a woman were to say anything of the kind about men "I should be shocked" – a realization, he says, which forces him to reconsider his position. Should he accept for himself the "asceticism" that he has always demanded of so-called respectable women, or on the other hand live freely, polygamously, and extend the same right to women? Shaw poses the question, but does not answer it. "Space presses," he concludes abruptly, "and this is not dramatic criticism" – for his ruminations on the "asceticism" of Sarah Grand and the New Woman, or rather *some* New Women, had distracted him from the business at hand, a review of a play called *Nelson's Enchantress* (1897) by Risden Home.

But was it really a distraction? That forgotten play by Risden Home, and the meandering review of it, allows us to reconstruct Shaw's confused response to the developing identity of the New Woman in the 1890s. Sarah Grand is mentioned in this review only because her demand that men as well as women be "certified pure" contrasts starkly with the message of *Nelson's Enchantress* – a play by "another New Woman," according to Shaw, but one extremely different from the author of *The Heavenly Twins*. This play by the daughter of an admiral would scandalize not only "the conventional male dramatist" but also the type of New Woman exemplified by Sarah Grand.[52] Its sympathethic heroine starts out as one man's mistress, marries another, and ends up in love with the naval hero Nelson himself. And what, asks Shaw, is the woman playwright's verdict on this notorious "polyandrist," Lady Hamilton?

> Simply that what the conventional male dramatist would call her "impurity" was an entirely respectable, lovable, natural feature of her character, insepar- ably bound up with the qualities which made her the favorite friend of England's favorite hero. There is no apology made for this view, no conscious- ness betrayed at any point that there is, or ever was, a general assumption that it is an improper view.

For Shaw – "for my part, I am a man" – Risden Home is the most appealing kind of New Woman, one who makes it a priority to loosen the traditional restraints on the sexual behavior of women, leaving the time-honored liberties of men undisturbed.

But Shaw finds that, like so many other would-be women playwrights, Risden Home "does not rise to the occasion" and her play is not "genuinely dramatic." Why not? In her play, Shaw believes, the rough-edged, unscru- pulous, uncultured Nelson is made out to be too good: "Though she deals with Lady Hamilton like a New Woman, she deals with Nelson like a Married one, taking care that he shall not set a bad example to husbands." England's idol is contaminated by what Shaw's fellow dramatist of the mid- 1890s, Sydney Grundy, termed "this new-fangled folly that a man's life must be immaculate." On the other hand, as we have seen, the idea of polyandrous women had its appeal for Shaw, particularly if they were beautiful like Lady Hamilton or Mrs. Patrick Campbell, the actress who impersonated her at the Avenue Theatre and whom Shaw tried his best (at least on paper) to seduce. But Shaw hesitated and sometimes mocked and resented the New Woman whenever he began to suspect that her project of regenerating the world meant, as he put it, "purification" of the male sex.[53]

This conflict among New Women and their sympathizers – whether to achieve sexual equality through raising the man or lowering the woman – also concerned Shaw in his review of *Thyrza Fleming*. Here, again, he cites

Sarah Grand disparagingly as the exemplar of an ascetic feminism which demanded "purity" of the male no less than the female. Shaw interprets Dorothy Leighton's play for the Independent Theatre Society as a bold counterblast to the radical feminism of Grand's novel *The Heavenly Twins* and its story of a woman who "married a gentleman 'with a past'; discovered it on her wedding day; and promptly went home, treating him exactly as he would have been conventionally expected to treat her under like circumstances." By contrast, the fastidious New Woman who leaves her husband in *Thyrza Fleming* learns, as Shaw puts it, "what a frightful mistake it is for a woman to take such a step."[54] A woman's business, as Dorothy Leighton's heroine realizes by the end of Act III, is to transcend her own "isolated notions of morality" and realize that men "can't be flogged into perfection."[55] This is the realization, of course, that eludes Shaw's own New Woman in *The Philanderer*, Grace Tranfield, who suppresses her love for Leonard Charteris because he is a man with a sexual past. Sarah Grand, like Grace Tranfield, insisted that men, no less than women, had an ideal to live up to. Although morally in their infancy, men could in fact be brought to perfection – or flogged into it, if necessary, by the "strong hand" of the New Woman. "To bring this about is the whole aim and object of the present struggle," Sarah Grand wrote in her essay on the New Woman, "and with the discovery of the means lies the solution of the Woman Question."[56]

Shaw would return to these issues when he wrote *You Never Can Tell* in 1895–96, a play which appears to echo *The Heavenly Twins* in certain respects and contradict it in others. The twins of Grand's title are two madcap children named Angelica and Diavolo whose mischief is in itself a challenge to Victorian authority. But Grand, by representing the twins as similar in intellectual power and in their turn for devilish behavior, creates an androgynous pair who, despite their names, show the falseness of the Victorian classification of woman as angel and man as lower, to be sure, yet intellectually her superior. Indeed Angelica in Grand's novel turns out to be stronger and smarter than her brother as they grow older, but her potential is smothered in an early marriage while Diavolo is sent off to be educated at Sandhurst and enjoys the prospect of a fine career. Shaw, in *You Never Can Tell*, creates in Dolly and Philip Clandon a set of twins whose irrepressible behavior recalls unmistakably the "heavenly twins" of Sarah Grand. Instead of making the case for the New Woman, however, Shaw's characters make fun of their mother, Mrs. Lanfrey Clandon, a long-time advocate of woman's rights and author of many books on that and related subjects. "No household is complete without her works," says Philip, who then expresses his urgent desire "to get away from them." He concedes that his emancipated mother's writings may "improve your mind" – but, interjects his sister Dolly, "not till weve gone, please." Their mother may be the well-known author of *Twentieth Century Women*, but the twins perceive her ideas as old-fashioned – and so they are, at least in the world of *You Never Can Tell* where socialism (as the solicitor M'Comas explains in Act II) has made the women's rights movement obsolete.

Shaw's irreverent twins, therefore, evoke the atmosphere but mock the content of Sarah Grand's "heavenly twins." They mock feminism instead of illustrating the need for it, and rather than attacking Victorian patriarchy they are in search of a patriarch – searching, that is, for their "lost" father. "My knowledge of human nature leads me to believe that we had a father," says Philip, teasing his mother, "and that you probably know who he was." Mrs. Clandon would say, perhaps, that she knows him all too well. Like a character in a novel by Sarah Grand, she left her husband years ago because of his flawed character. "I discovered his temper," as she explains to her friend M'Comas, "and his – [*she shivers*] the rest of his common humanity." This intolerance for the moral fallibility of the male is what distinguished Sarah Grand in particular and the New Woman movement in general for Shaw, who became uneasy, even resentful or confused, whenever he thought about it. A corollary of Mrs. Clandon's austere morality is her own lack of passion, for "though I am a married woman, I have never been in love; I have never had a love affair." Even her dress, although not masculine, rules out "*all attempt at sex attraction.*" Shaw pointedly contrasts Mrs. Clandon with her daughter Gloria, a New Woman who is "*all passion*" and who in the end rejects her mother's emphasis on intellectual qualities for women and a high moral and sexual standard for men. Thus Gloria Clandon, following her mother's lead, means at first to walk away from her love for Valentine when she learns of his past sexual escapades. In the end, however, Gloria succumbs to Valentine's argument that a man must experience love many times to find out who is really worthy of it. And Gloria is worthy of it not because of her New Woman's intellect – for intellect, Valentine declares, is a "masculine speciality" – and not because of her austere morality. Gloria is worthy of Valentine because of her sexual magnetism, her ability to "stir" the depths of him, to make him adore her as the agent of biological forces beyond the control of either of them. "Let's call it chemistry . . . the most irresistible of all natural forces," Valentine explains.[57] Gloria's strength, being purely sexual, has nothing to do with the intellectual and political development of women or with the moral amelioration of men.

In an article written a few years before the rediscovery of Sarah Grand by feminist critics, Stanley Weintraub argues that *The Heavenly Twins* provided Shaw with inspiration for *You Never Can Tell*, focusing on similarities between Philip and Dolly Clandon and the twins in Grand's novel and on Shaw's having credited Grand with "a touch of genius." There can be no doubt that Grand's novel was an important influence on Shaw's play, but I argue that Shaw's "borrowings" as such are comparatively insignificant and indeed are enlisted to help express his revulsion against what *The Heavenly Twins* represented in the 1890s – "a *reductio ad absurdum* of our whole moral system," as Shaw complained in a review written in 1896. Sarah Grand, he writes, demands that "the man shall come to the woman exactly as moral as he insists that she shall come to him. And, of course, not a soul dares deny that claim."[58] *You Never Can Tell* was written, in part, to supply that deficiency – to provide a resounding denial of Sarah Grand's "claims" of the intellectual equality of the sexes and her insistence upon male (as well as female) rectitude.

From another perspective, however, *You Never Can Tell* rewrites another play by a woman, one much more successful, or rather more popular than Dorothy Leighton's, even though we have lost all memory of it today. *A Mother of Three*, by Clotilde Graves, an actress known for her masculine dress and manner, opened at the Comedy Theatre in April 1896 to favorable reviews and enthusiastic crowds. Shaw himself reviewed it, expressing admiration for the "fun" in it, but regretting the lack of "philosophy" with which Clo Graves wrote the piece. Once again, a woman dramatist had started with a good idea but, Shaw believed, got it all wrong in the execution, for in *A Mother of Three* Clo Graves wastes on farce "a talent which evidently has a rare intensity of emotional force behind it."[59] Shaw saw *A Mother of Three* on April 8, 1896, just when he was working on the second act of *You Never Can Tell*, uncertain about how to develop the action of his own play.[60]

Much of the material in *You Never Can Tell* that is not traceable to Sarah Grand seems modeled on Clo Graves's forgotten comedy, even as it undercuts *A Mother of Three* in other respects. Both plays deal with a woman bringing up her three children on her own, apart from the father who in both plays has been absent for precisely eighteen years. In both plays, moreover, the three children find their social standing called into question because they are unable to produce a father – that "certificate of respectability," as one of the daughters says in *A Mother of Three*; that "indispensable part of your social equipment," as Shaw writes in *You Never Can Tell*.[61] Both Shaw and Graves return the long-absent father to his family – but the similarities end precisely there. In *You Never Can Tell* Mrs. Clandon left Fergus Crampton eighteen years ago because of his moral shortcomings. In *A Mother of Three*, by contrast, Mrs. Murgatroyd's husband abandoned her eighteen years ago for reasons of his own, and his own belated moral awakening brings him home again. "Conscience tore at me," explains Professor Murgatroyd, realizing that a man has a responsibility, neglected in his case, to be "actively engaged in assisting his better half in the discharge of her domestic duties."[62]

Even though Shaw could find no seriousness or "philosophy" in *A Mother of Three*, Clo Graves's farcical comedy, far from being empty of thought, agrees ultimately with the New Woman posture of Sarah Grand, that there should be only one standard, and a high one at that, for both men and women. What is required is a "feminizing" of the male like that produced by the transformation of Professor Murgatroyd, as well as a "masculinizing" of the woman – represented in *A Mother of Three* in a comic vein by Mrs. Murgatroyd's cross-dressing as a male, and, more to the point, by her success as provider and head of the family during her husband's eighteen-year absence. "The void you left behind was very great," Mrs. Murgatroyd tells her reappearing spouse, "but I tried my best to fill it – and though I was very young and inexperienced at first, I haven't done so very badly."[63] What Shaw took to be a brainless farce was instead a deeply thoughtful as well as funny play in which the Victorian sense of "male" and "female" was refigured entirely. In rejecting Clo Graves's credentials as a playwright, then rewriting her farcical comedy as *You Never Can Tell*, Shaw was actually resisting that aspect of the "philosophy" of the New Woman which made him most uncomfortable – that part which challenged the polarization of male and female and dared to require modification in the behavior of men.

Looking at Shaw in this way makes him something less than "woman's champion," the phrase by which Margot Peters expressed her first, but not final opinion of him.[64] His relationship with Elizabeth Robins, the most important New Woman in the London theatre of the 1890s, helps explain what Peters refers to as Shaw's "ambiguous attitudes" on issues of gender. On one hand he looks to Robins as a moving force behind the emerging "struggle between the sexes for control of the London stage," declaring his sympathy with her and other Ibsenite actresses such as Janet Achurch, Florence Farr, and Marion Lea. "I take my hat off to them," he declares in a review of 1894, for in their defeated hopes for a new kind of theatre lay the "real history" of the drama of the 1890s.[65] At the same time, however, Shaw resisted a cornerstone of Robins's agenda for reform of the theatre – the necessity, as she saw it, for women to write plays of a type that male dramatists would not, or could not, produce. Shaw's repeated assertions that women "Impossibilists" were not writing good drama, or even plays at all, were founded on the Victorian wisdom that playwriting required the kind of intellectual power that, as Valentine remarks in *You Never Can Tell*, is a "masculine speciality."

In resisting women playwrights, therefore, Shaw set himself against a main current of the New Woman movement as it existed in the theatre. He became part of the problem that Elizabeth Robins, who was about to give up on the stage in the mid-1890s, felt she could never overcome. But Shaw's experience with Robins also illustrates a second area in which he found himself at times troubled by, at times in conflict with, what he called the "terrible" New Woman. Robins's rejection of Shaw's gallantries – she threatened to shoot him during an interview that he conducted with her in 1893 – became a sore point that vexed their relationship for many years to come. Shaw reacted in a tone of comic indignation in a letter of February 5, 1893: "I have interviewed beautiful women before; but none of them were ever so noble as to threaten to shoot me."[66] A few months later he wrote to Robins again, confessing "being in love with you in a poetic and not in the least ignoble way," mocking her once again for having terrified him with a pistol and complaining that on another occasion she flung him out of a cab into the mud.[67] What came between them was was what came between Shaw and the New Woman more generally, whether inside or outside the theatre – her emphasis upon a high moral standard for men as well as women. This angle of attack upon the double standard for men and women had been displayed most famously in Sarah Grand's *The Heavenly Twins*; and as Shaw had written, "For my part, I am a man; and Madame Grand's solution fills me with dismay."

Elizabeth Robins was the Sarah Grand of the theatre as far as Shaw was concerned, and many of his subsequent references to Robins are colored by that perception. A letter that he wrote to Robins in 1899 contains a sneering reference to her as "St. Elizabeth," and in a letter to William Archer he expresses frustration that Robins could not conceive his "anti-ethical, anti-virtuous view of life" as anything but blackguardism.[68] Shaw's biographers have generally accepted his interpretation of Robins's behavior toward him as symptomatic of her being "squeamish" about men in general.[69] She felt convinced, offers Michael Holroyd in the mocking tone of Shaw himself, that "all men were potential rapists."[70] Such caricatures ignore the fact that Robins's objections to Shaw were in response to his unwanted advances. If Shaw could have rewritten the life of Elizabeth Robins, and not just her play *Alan's Wife*, she would have been more like Proserpine Garnett in *Candida*, the "new" working woman enthralled by the golden-tongued hero of the play, the Rev. James Morell. Prossy's name, as Ellen Gainor points out, recalls the myth of Proserpine and her rape by Pluto – but in Shaw's play Prossy and many other women are magnetized by Morell, and so the guilt of rape or sexual aggression is transformed into Proserpine's undeclared but ardent attraction to him.[71] It was sexual attraction that Shaw hoped for from Elizabeth Robins despite the emphatic "no" with which she responded to his overtures. From this perspective women desire or even invite the men who harass them, even if their real feelings are covered by an outward show of reluctance. Proserpine Garnett could have "taught" Robins this, but only Gloria Clandon in *You Never Can Tell* could have modeled a complete new narrative for Robins's life – the story of a high-minded New Woman who gives up her feminism when her own surging womanliness makes it impossible for her to resist any longer the call of sex.

NOTES

1   Bernard Shaw, preface to William Archer, *The Theatrical "World" of 1894* (London: Scott, 1895), pp. xxix–xxx. Lyn Picket has proposed 1894 as the "*annus mirabilis* of the New Woman," based on the large number of women who were writing oppositional fiction and polemics at the time (*The Improper Feminine: The Women's Sensation Novel and the New Woman Writing* [London: Routledge, 1992], p. 137). This essay will show that Pickett's identification of 1894 as the heyday of the New Woman is at least roughly applicable to the theatre as well. Thus it is no accident, I believe, that Shaw's announcement of a gender crisis in the theatre appears in a review of events on the London stage of 1894. I have also discussed this gender crisis in *Women and Victorian Theatre*, forthcoming from Cambridge University Press, which I have drawn on to some extent in writing this chapter.

2   Carroll Smith-Rosenberg, *Disorderly Conduct: Visions of Gender in Victorian America* (New York: Oxford University Press), p. 247.

3   Ann Ardis, *New Women, New Novels: Feminism and Early Modernism* (New Brunswick, NJ: Rutgers University Press, 1990), pp. 10–28. I am greatly indebted to Ardis's book for the conceptualization of the New Woman that I offer in the first section of this chapter.

4   *Athenaeum*, March 23, 1895, p. 375; Mrs. Morgan-Dockrell, "Is the New Woman a Myth?", *Humanitarian* 8 (1896), pp. 339–50 (quoted by Ardis, *New Women, New Novels*, pp. 13–14).

5   H.S. Scott and E. Hall, "Character Note: The New Woman," *Cornhill* 70 (1894), pp. 365–68.

6   H. M. Stutfield, "'Tommyrotics'," *Blackwood's* 157 (1895), pp. 833–45; and Stutfield, "The Psychology of Feminism," *Blackwood's* 161 (1897), pp. 104–117.

7   Sarah Grand (Frances Elizabeth Macfall), "The New Aspect of the Woman Question," *North American Review* 158 (1894), pp. 170–76.

8   *Era*, June 10, 1894, p. 10.

9   *Bernard Shaw: Collected Letters*, ed. Dan H. Laurence, 4 vols. (New York: Dodd, Mead, 1965), vol. I, p. 641. Barbara Bellow Watson argues that although Shaw in *Candida* wrote *A Doll's House* backwards, the choice to remain with

her family is at least Candida's own. Likewise in *Man and Superman*, first produced in 1905, Watson finds a reversal of gender roles with Ann Whitefield as the sexual aggressor and Tanner as her prey ("The New Woman and the New Comedy," in Rodelle Weintraub (ed.), *Fabian Feminist: Bernard Shaw and Woman* [University Park: Pennsylvania State University Press, 1977], pp. 114–29.) Watson's *A Shavian Guide to the Intelligent Woman* (London: Chatto, 1964) also emphasizes Shaw's creation of strong, "unladylike" women in his plays. Such arguments are true on one side, but lose sight of the fact that these heroines are limited in the exercise of their power to the realms of home, sex, and private feeling, and in this respect are characteristically Victorian.

10 Shaw's own practice was less consistent in this regard than that of the women he referred to as "Impossibilists." He was sensitive at an early date to the requirements of the West End stage; for example, *You Never Can Tell* was an attempt, he said, to temper his playwriting "by some consideration for the requirements of managers in search of fashionable comedies for West End theatres" ("Preface" [1898], in *Complete Plays with Prefaces* [New York: Dodd, Mead, 1962], vol. III, p. 113).

11 *Playgoer*, August 1889, p. 1.

12 Max Nordau, *Degeneration* (New York: Appleton, 1895), pp. 405, 412–13.

13 Elizabeth Robins, *Ibsen and the Actress* (London: Woolf, 1928), p. 32. Robins eventually became prominent in the women's suffrage movement, which formed the basis of her best-known drama, *Votes for Women!* (1907). But some of her friends and allies – such as Florence Bell, co-author of *Alan's Wife*, and Mary Augusta Ward, the novelist and dramatist who wrote *Eleanor* (1902), an unconventional "woman's play" which provided Robins with her last professional stage role – were vehement "Anti's" even though they matched the profile of the New Woman in many respects. Indeed, as Angela John points out, Robins admired Mrs. Ward as a "social activist" (Angela John, *Elizabeth Robins: Staging a Life, 1862–1952* [London: Routledge, 1995], p. 94). Even Emma Goldman, a revolutionary anarchist and sexual heretic, regarded the suffragists as making "bombastic and impossible claims," and was herself branded by many feminists as "a man's woman and not one of us" (quoted from Harry Carlson's introduction to Emma Goldman, *The Social Significance of Modern Drama* [1914; rpt. New York: Applause, 1987], p. vi). Thus Shaw's own advocacy of women's suffrage does not necessarily align him with New Women, some of whom were indifferent toward the issue, or even opposed.

14 Robins, "Heights and Depths," MS. Fales Library, New York University.

15 Robins, *Whither and How*, handwritten and typed notes under the title "Odd Bits" at the end of the manuscript (MS. Fales Library, New York University).

16 Even recent histories such as John Elsom and Nicholas Tomalin's *The History of the National Theatre* (London: Cape, 1978) make no mention of Robins's crucial role in envisioning a noncommercial national theatre. The contributions of other women such as Eleanor Calhoun are ignored as well. Discrimination against women in the Victorian theatre was what made it obvious to New Women actresses that the English drama needed a new, more equitable institutional framework.

17 Robins, *Whither and How*, chapter 2, p. 11.

18 Emma Goldman, *The Social Significance of Modern Drama*, pp. 2–3, 101, 130.

Nevertheless Goldman wrote that *Mrs. Warren's Profession* "goes to the bottom of our evils," and found *Major Barbara* to be "one of the most revolutionary of plays" (pp. 102, 107) because in writing it Shaw forgot about his narrow and dogmatic politics.

19 I have discussed the Wilde–Robins connection in "Oscar Wilde, Elizabeth Robins, and the Theatre of the Future," *Modern Drama* 37 (1994), pp. 220–37.
20 Robins, *Votes for Women: A Dramatic Tract in Three Acts* (Chicago: Dramatic Publishing, 1907), pp. 122–23.
21 Frank Archer, *How To Write a Good Play* (London: French, 1892), p. 71.
22 Henry James, "Nona Vincent," *The Complete Works of Henry James*, ed. Leon Edel (London: Hart-Davis, 1963), vol. VIII, p. 157.
23 William Archer, *The Theatrical "World" of 1894*, p. 97. Shaw, on the other hand, ridiculed *Mrs. Lessingham*.
24 Mrs. Musgrave, *Our Flat*, unpaginated licensing MS. in the Lord Chamberlain's Collection, British Library.
25 "Women as Dramatists," *All the Year Round*, September 29, 1894, p. 300.
26 Robins, *Theatre and Friendship* (New York: Putnam's, 1932), pp. 144–45.
27 Letter from Archer to Robins, quoted by Joanne Gates in *Elizabeth Robins, 1862–1052: Actress, Novelist, Feminist* (Tuscaloosa: University of Alabama Press, 1994).
28 Letter from Tree to Robins, February 23, 1900, MS. Fales Library, New York University.
29 The only printed text of *Mrs. Lessingham* is an acting edition (London: Miles, 1894), "printed as manuscript."
30 Robins, *The Mirkwater*, MS. Fales Library, New York University, Act III, p. 8.
31 *Collected Letters*, vol. I, pp. 600–01.
32 *Bernard Shaw: Collected Letters*, ed. Dan H. Laurence (London: Reinhardt, 1972), vol. II, p. 76.
33 Letter from Bell to Robins (1892), MS. Fales Library, New York University.
34 *Collected Letters*, vol. I, pp. 393–95. Robert Buchanan's steamy melodramas captivated large audiences at the Adelphi Theatre in the 1890s.
35 *Ibid.* pp. 408–09.
36 *Ibid.* pp. 478–79.
37 Shaw, *Our Theatres in the Nineties* (London: Constable, 1931), vol. I, pp. 158–60. A useful interpretation of these actresses appears in John Stokes, Michael R. Booth, and Susan Bassnett, *Bernhardt, Terry, Duse: The Actress in Her Time* (Cambridge: Cambridge University Press, 1988).
38 The only known text of *Mrs. Daintree's Daughter* by Janet Achurch is in the Lord Chamberlain's Collection of the British Library. In this script the adventuress and businesswoman Leila Daintree has grown wealthy in operating a gambling den that, although she denies it, functions as a house of prostitution as well. Like Mrs. Warren in Shaw's play, this entrepreneur has labored to make life easy for the daughter – named Violet in Achurch's play, Vivie in Shaw's – whom she has had brought up in seclusion far away from herself. Absent in Achurch's play is the socialist analysis with which Shaw invests *Mrs. Warren's Profession*, where the gender problem is subsumed finally in larger economic issues. But in being less distracted than Shaw's play with the economic causes of women's behavior, *Mrs. Daintree's Daughter* focuses more steadily on the

women characters themselves and their challenge to the prevailing wisdom about what women were and should be.

39 Shaw, *Our Theatres in the Nineties*, vol. I, pp. 20–23.
40 Dorothy Leighton (Dorothy Forsyth), *Disillusion: A Story with a Preface* (London: Henry, 1894), vol. I, p. 22.
41 Mrs. Musgrave, *Our Flat*.
42 Cicely Hamilton, *Life Errant* (London: Dent, 1935), p. 60.
43 Mrs. Musgrave, *Our Flat*; performed in London at the Prince of Wales's Theatre and apparently never published.
44 Letter from Bell to Robins, possibly from November or December 1892, in the Fales Library, New York University.
45 Shaw, *Our Theatres in the Nineties*, vol. I, p. 52.
46 Sarah Grand, "The New Aspect of the Woman Question," pp. 272–73.
47 Sydney Grundy, *The New Woman: An Original Comedy in Four Acts* (London: Chiswick, 1894), Act I, p. 28.
48 Charles Rogers, *The Future Woman, or Josiah's Dream*, is quoted from the licensing MS in the British Library, Act IV, pp. 15, 17.
49 F.C. Philips and Percy Fendall, *Husband and Wife*, in F. C. Philips, *A Barrister's Courtship* (Leipzig: Tauchnitz, 1907), p. 103.
50 George Gissing, *The Odd Women* (New York: Norton, 1971), pp. 61, 87, 99.
51 Sydney Grundy, *A Bunch of Violets: A Play in Four Acts* (London: French, 1901), p. 40.
52 It is not clear who "Risden Home" – perhaps a pseudonym – really was. *Nelson's Enchantress* has been misattributed in bibliographies of the drama to "R. Horne," probably a misreading of "Risden Home." In addition, Risden Home has been misidentified as a man (see e.g. *Bernard Shaw: The Diaries, 1885–1897*, ed. Stanley Weintraub [University Park: Pennsylvania State University Press, 1986]) even though Shaw refers to her as "a lady" and a "New Woman" (*Our Theatres in the Nineties*, vol. III, pp. 52, 209).
53 Shaw's review of *Nelson's Enchantress* is cited from *Our Theatres in the Nineties*, vol. III, pp. 50–55.
54 *Ibid.* vol. I, pp. 20–23.
55 Leighton, *Thyrza Fleming*, p. 56 of the licensing MS, Lord Chamberlain's collection, British Library.
56 Grand, "The New Aspect of the Woman Question," pp. 272–73.
57 Shaw, *You Never Can Tell*, in *Complete Plays with Prefaces*, vol. VI, pp. 619–20, 673, 681, 686, 693.
58 Stanley Weintraub, "G. B. S. Borrows from Sarah Grand: *The Heavenly Twins* and *You Never Can Tell*," *Modern Drama* 14 (1971), pp. 288–97; Shaw, *Our Theatre in the Nineties*, vol. III, p. 178.
59 Shaw, *Our Theatre in the Nineties*, vol. II, pp. 101–02.
60 *Bernard Shaw: The Diaries*, nos. 1118–19, 1127.
61 Clotilde Graves, *A Mother of Three: An Original Farce in Three Acts* (London: French, n.d.), p. 18; Shaw, *You Never Can Tell*, p. 622.
62 Graves, *A Mother of Three*, p. 65.
63 *Ibid.*, p. 66.
64 Margot Peters, "The State and Future of Shaw Research: The MLA Conference Transcript. Biography," *Shaw* 2 (1982), p. 182.

65 Shaw, *Our Theatre in the Nineties*, vol. I, pp. 20–21.
66 *Collected Letters*, vol. I, p. 380.
67 *Ibid.*, p. 397.
68 *Collected Letters*, vol. II, pp. 136–39.
69 For example, Margot Peters, *Bernard Shaw and the Actresses* (New York: Doubleday, 1980), p. 86.
70 Michael Holroyd, *Bernard Shaw* (New York: Random House, 1988), vol. I, pp. 311–13. A good corrective to this very Shavian perspective is two recent biographies on Robins: Angela John, *Elizabeth Robins: Staging a Life*, and Joanne Gates, *Elizabeth Robins, 1862–1952*.
71 J. Ellen Gainor, *Shaw's Daughters: Dramatic and Narrative Construction of Gender* (Ann Arbor: University of Michigan Press, 1991), p. 26.

FURTHER READING

Ardis, Ann, *New Women, New Novels: Feminism and Early Modernism*, New Brunswick, NJ: Rutgers University Press, 1990.

Gainor, Ellen, *Shaw's Daughters: Dramatic and Narrative Constructions of Gender*, Ann Arbor: University of Michigan Press, 1991.

Gates, Joanne, *Elizabeth Robins, 1862–1952: Actress, Novelist, Feminist*, Tuscaloosa: University of Alabama Press, 1994.

Goldman, Emma, *The Social Significance of Modern Drama*, 1914; rpt. New York: Applause, 1987.

John, Angela, *Elizabeth Robins: Staging a Life, 1862–1952*, London: Routledge, 1995.

Peters, Margot, *Bernard Shaw and the Actresses*, New York: Doubleday, 1980.

Powell, Kerry, *Women and Victorian Theatre*, Cambridge: Cambridge University Press, 1997.

Stokes, John, Michael R. Booth, and Susan Bassnett, *Bernhardt, Terry, Duse: The Actress in Her Time*, Cambridge: Cambridge University Press, 1988.

Watson, Barbara Bellow, "The New Woman and the New Comedy," in Rodelle Weintraub (ed.), *Fabian Feminist: Bernard Shaw and Woman*, University Park: Pennyslvania State University Press, 1977, pp. 114–29.

2
SHAW THE DRAMATIST

5

FREDERICK J. MARKER

Shaw's early plays

Especially during the formative years leading up to his emergence as a playwright with *Widowers' Houses* (1892), the course of Shaw's career was deeply influenced by his friend and self-proclaimed mentor, William Archer. Archer, born in the same year as Shaw (1856), became one of the foremost early translators of Ibsen's dramas and, next to Shaw, their most vigorous advocate in the English theatre of the late nineteenth century. He first came across Shaw, at the age of 26, in the British Museum Reading Room, where he noticed both the pale young man with the bright red beard and "the odd combination of authors whom he used to study – for I saw him day after day poring over Karl Marx's *Das Kapital* and an orchestral score of Wagner's *Tristan und Isolde*."[1] Not long afterwards, early in 1884, Archer was hired by Edmund Yates's *World* as that newspaper's drama critic, and he soon persuaded his publisher to take on his unemployed friend as well, to serve as the paper's art critic. Some time later, Archer recalls, "the post of musical critic fell vacant, and I secured it for Shaw by the simple process of telling Yates the truth: namely, that he was at once the most competent and most brilliant writer on music then living in England."[2] Shaw himself could not have put it better in one of his prefaces.

In spite of all this serendipity, however, it was inevitable that Archer's attempt to collaborate with Shaw on the play that eventually became *Widowers' Houses* was doomed to catastrophe. The sharp difference between their attitudes to drama and dramatic construction is, after all, the difference that made Shaw a brilliant and exciting (if sometimes erratic) playwright and Archer a forgotten one. "It was my deliberate and un-accountable disregard of the rules of the art of play construction that revolted him," Shaw later observed in a genial preface written a couple of years after Archer's death in 1924 and published in a posthumous edition of three of his friend's plays. For Shaw a play had to be "a vital growth and not a mechanical construction," and hence he refused to be held hostage by Archer's quasi-Aristotelian principles. A play should need no plot, Shaw continues, because "if it has any natural life in it, it will construct itself; it will construct itself, like a flowering plant, far more wonderfully than the author can possibly construct it."[3] This is, of course, the Shaw of *Heartbreak House* speaking, not the Shaw of *The Philanderer*. Nevertheless, the growing disagreements between him and Archer over *Widowers' Houses* and other early Shavian plays bear unmistakable evidence of the new direction in which he was already trying to go in the 1890s – toward a more organic, dialectical, "musical" form of composition focused squarely on "a conflict of unsettled ideals" (to borrow an operative phrase from *The Quintessence of Ibsenism*).

Archer disagreed with much of this, not least with Shaw's ideological interpretation of Ibsenism. "Ibsen is a psychologist or he is nothing," he declares flatly in *Play-making* (1912), "a manual of craftmanship" devoted to an exposition of the clockwork mechanism of the well-made play and the supreme importance of character and psychology within that mechanism. Archer's view of drama was undividedly characterological. "Dramatic action ought to exist for the sake of character," he insists: "when the relation is reversed the play may be an ingenious toy, but scarcely a work of art." Needless to say, there was little room for the aberrations of a Shaw ("a despiser of the niceties of craftmanship") within such a tightly sealed system. "Mr. Shaw is not, primarily, either a character-drawer or a psychologist but a dealer in personified ideas," Archer declares without much discrimination. "His leading figures are, as a rule, either his mouthpieces or his butts."[4] *Candida*, not surprisingly, seems to have been his favourite Shaw play, and as his "all-too-candid mentor" (as he calls himself in a final, wistful letter to Shaw in 1924), he never tired of urging him to write more such well constructed, character-based comedies.

Widowers' Houses, however, is a play of a very different sort, "unpleasant" rather than "pleasant" in more ways than one. (In his preface to the first edition, Shaw calls it "a propagandist play . . . saturated with the vulgarity of the life it represents.") Its theme is the ruthless exploitation of the destitute and homeless by the mercantile and the upper classes alike; its avowed intention is to implicate every member of the audience in that social crime. Hence, when they sat down in 1885 to collaborate on *Rhinegold* (as Archer first titled their proposed play), it seems unlikely that either writer quite realized the full extent to which their aims and methods differed. Archer's scenario apparently called for a well-made romantic comedy of courtship and renunciation, harking back to the popular sentimental comedies of Tom Robertson. Shaw, on the other hand, was busy writing dialogue aimed at achieving what *The Quintessence of Ibsenism* later defines as "a forensic technique of recrimination, discussion, and penetration through ideals to the truth." With only two acts finished, the project collapsed after Archer withdrew from it. "The public will accept open vice, but it will have nothing to do with a moral problem" he had warned in an earlier book. "Especially it will have nothing to do with a piece to whose theme the word 'unpleasant' can be applied. This epithet is of undefined and elastic signification, but once attach it to a play and all chances for it are past."[5]

Despite such repudiations, *Widowers' Houses* was finally completed by Shaw and given two performances by J. T. Grein's struggling Independent Theatre in 1892. In his review of this event in *The World* (December 14, 1892), Archer acknowledged his participation in the earlier collaboration ("I drew out, scene by scene, the scheme of a twaddling cup-and-saucer comedy"), but he denied that any of his ideas had actually been adopted by Shaw in his final text. Both in the edition published by the Independent Theatre following its premiere and in his later preface to *Plays Unpleasant* (1898), Shaw strenuously insists that he not only made use of Archer's well-made scheme but "perversely distorted it into a grotesquely realistic exposure" of the social corruption that provides the comedy's subtext. The result is a deliberate, "revoltingly incongruous" inversion of the dramatic situation and its familiar conventions, designed to manipulate and ultimately invalidate the standard assumptions and responses of the previously complacent spectator. "Sartorius is absolutely typical in his unconscious villainy. Like my critics, he lacks conviction of sin," Shaw continues in the first edition. "Now, the didactic object of my play is to bring conviction of sin – to make the Pharisee . . . recognize that Sartorius is his own photograph."[6] Thus, behind the absurd antics of his reconstituted stereotypes – the sweet reasonableness of the rent-gouging slumlord, the foul-tempered eroticism of his daughter, the ineffectual contrition of the good-natured but spineless hero – remains the condemnation implicit in Shaw's "farfetched" Scriptural title, with its allusion to "the greater damnation" which Jesus calls down on the Pharisees and hypocrites who "devour widows' houses" (Matthew 23:14).

In the first act of *Widowers' Houses*, the situation, the tone, and even the setting all contribute to the expectation of a polite Robertsonian comedy of class-crossed lovers – or possibly even a Gilbertian farce, akin to *Engaged*, about the vicissitudes of romance in a money-mad world. Affable Harry Trench, the younger (*ergo* impecunious) son of an aristocratic family, is taking an August holiday in Germany after finishing medical school. His older and wiser companion, William de Burgh Cokane (pun no doubt intended), is a perfect specimen of the theatrical type known as the Stage Swell, with "a little tact, a little knowledge of the world, a little experience of women" to get him by. As they ponder their Continental Bradshaw over beers in the garden restaurant of a tourist hotel on the Rhine, the two travellers are joined in the garden by Blanche Sartorius, the very girl with whom Harry has flirted on their river cruise, and her wealthy and domineering father, a self-made businessman with an inaccessible air. Undaunted, Cokane suavely tackles the tycoon and pilots him off to see the sights, clearing the stage for a love scene (one of Shaw's funniest) between Blanche and the besotted young doctor. Every inch her vulgar and iron-willed father's daughter, she supplies Trench with the courage and words he needs:

> BLANCHE: (*giving him up as hopeless*) I dont think theres much danger of your making up your mind, Dr. Trench.
> TRENCH: (*stammering*) I only thought – (*He stops and looks at her piteously. She hesitates a moment, and then puts her hands into his with calculated impulsiveness. He snatches her into his arms with a cry of relief.*) Dear Blanche! I thought I should never have said it. I believe I should have stood stuttering here all day if you hadnt helped me out with it.
> BLANCHE: (*indignantly trying to break loose from him*) I didnt help you out with it.
> TRENCH: (*holding her*) I dont mean that you did it on purpose, of course. Only instinctively.
> BLANCHE: (*still a little anxious*) But you havent said anything.
> TRENCH: What more can I say than this? (*He kisses her again.*)
> BLANCHE: (*overcome by the kiss, but holding on to her point*) But Harry –
> TRENCH: (*delighted at the name*) Yes.
> BLANCHE: When shall we be married?[7]

The excerpt illustrates Shaw's technical control of comic dialogue, even as a beginner, as well as his determination from the outset to direct his plays on paper, down to the smallest movement or inflection. In terms of the action, meanwhile, the passage also pinpoints the moment at which the play starts to gravitate from romantic comedy toward something much darker. The enigmatic Sartorius readily agrees to the match (the "transaction," as he calls it) – but only on the condition that Harry will provide written guarantees from his aunt Lady Roxdale and his other aristocratic relatives that Blanche will be welcomed into the social circles that are obviously closed to her father. The bargain is struck, a letter to Trench's people is drafted, but overhanging it all is the operative secret: the real source from which Sartorius's prosperity derives ("the rental of very extensive real estate in London").

In the second act – which, in a sense, might almost mark the beginning of an entirely new play – the tone and development of the courtship comedy

7 The attack on idealism (1) Reversing the sex-roles: Elizabeth Brown as Blanche Sartorius dominates Blair Williams as Dr. Harry Trench in the Shaw Festival's 1992 production of *Widowers' Houses*

are now subverted by melodrama. (The ironic interface between melodrama and life seems fully as central to this play as the comparable interface between melodrama and history is to *The Devil's Disciple*.) From the carefree atmosphere of the hotel garden on the Rhine, we are moved to the chilly opulence of Sartorius's summer establishment in Surrey, where he conducts his affairs in a library lined with uniform rows of "smartly tooled" but obviously unread books. Lickcheese, an unctuous, melancholy rent-collector of Dickensian format, is introduced, it seems, for the express purpose of revealing the true nature of his employer's business, as the proprietor of the most notorious and run-down tenement houses in London. When the unfortunate bagman admits that he has used twenty-four shillings of his master's takings to repair a dangerous staircase in one of his squalid buildings, he is promptly sacked by the ruthless Sartorius. Lickcheese, however, takes his revenge by telling Trench – who has arrived in the meantime with the promised guarantees of Blanche's acceptance – the truth about his future father-in-law's heinous practices as a slumlord. Harry is overwhelmed, but his sophisticated companion takes the news in his stride:

> COKANE: (*looking compassionately at him*) Ah, my dear fellow, the love of money is the root of all evil.
> LICKCHEESE: Yes, sir, and we'd all like to have the tree growing in our garden.
>
> (p. 31)

The cynical humour of the wisecrack captures the growing sense of universal corruption that invades the play and ultimately engulfs it. Business is business, Harry learns, even in affairs of the heart. When he informs Blanche (while stubbornly refusing to explain himself) that they must renounce her father's money after their marriage, his sharp-tongued fiancée flies into a towering rage and breaks off their engagement.

The crucial scene in Shaw's reconstituted version of the Archer scenario is not, however, the lovers' quarrel over money but the ensuing confrontation between the naive idealist and the cunning and unscrupulous Sartorius, who blandly justifies his iron-handed treatment of his tenants as the best means "to provide additional houses for the homeless, and to lay by a little for Blanche." Charity is impractical, he reasons ("when people are very poor, you cannot help them, no matter how much you may sympathize with them"), and so his course of action is not only reasonable but inevitable: "Every man who has a heart must wish that a better state of things was practicable. But unhappily it is not." Trench's scruples turn to ashes when he is told that he, too (like Lady Roxdale and her entire social circle) lives on "tainted" money derived from investments in Sartorius's slums. "Morally beggared," he is reduced to "a living picture of disillusion." In this play, however, the disillusionment of the hero is not the process of education to something better, as it subsequently becomes in "pleasant" plays such as *Arms and the Man* and *Candida*. Harry Trench learns nothing save his own guilt and his powerlessness to change society.

In this respect, he resembles the "average homebred Englishman" described by Shaw in the preface to *Plays Unpleasant*, willing at once "to shut his eyes to the most villainous abuses" if his own welfare is threatened. And even though the wretched Harry allows himself to be persuaded by Sartorius's arguments, he is still chucked out by his angry fiancée, who refuses "to marry a fool."

The final movement of the play is a grotesque and vigorous scherzo that recapitulates the main themes in dissonant, even strident tones. Four months have passed, and Blanche and her father sit "glumly" before a winter fire in their fashionable London drawing room. The action is generated by the arrival of unexpected visitors, the first of whom is Lickcheese – a veritable Alfred Doolittle suddenly transformed from dirt and penury to the elegance of full evening dress, complete with diamond stud and silk hat of the glossiest black. (Like Doolittle's return in the last act of *Pygmalion*, this entrance is also a star turn that, by Shaw's own admission, enabled James Welch's Lickcheese to steal the show in the Independent Theatre production.) In this case, the startling transmogrification is the result of a lucrative con game, in which slums known by insiders to be scheduled for demolition are bought up and superficially renovated to make them eligible for exorbitant compensation by the expropriating authorities. Sartorius, whose rent-gouging activities have been noted by a Royal Commission inquiry, is happy enough to join Lickcheese's profitable and more "respectable" new swindle. Blanche, her thoughts still obsessed by her ex-suitor, finally discovers the truth about her father's money – and hence Harry's refusal of it – in the pages of a parliamentary report conveniently left by the playwright for her to read. Her "ladylike" revulsion is directed, however, not at her father's actions but at the socially unsavoury character of his clientele. ("Oh, I hate the poor. At least, I hate those dirty, drunken, disreputable people who live like pigs. If they must be provided for, let other people look after them.") This caricature of a strong Shavian heroine gets just the man she deserves, it seems, in Harry Trench, who is brought in by Lickcheese ("coarsened and sullen") to be convinced, as the mortgagee of Sartorius's property, to take his share of the risks and profits involved in the new speculation. Astutely, Lickcheese recognizes that a marital alliance will be the best solution for all concerned:

> I know Miss Blanche: she has her father's eye for business. Explain this job to her; and she'll make it up with Dr. Trench. Why not have a bit of romance in business when it costs nothing? (p. 61)

To further this purpose, Sartorius, Lickcheese, and Cokane (the parvenu's new "sekketerry") retire to the adjoining study, leaving the stage to Harry and Blanche for a reconciliation scene that becomes an outright travesty of the conventional conclusion to a well-made courtship comedy. Discovering her prey alone and about to kiss her portrait, Blanche launches into an angry, uninterrupted harangue that begins "shrewishly" and builds to a climax when she seizes his cheeks and twists his head around, kneels beside his chair "with her breast against his shoulder," and finally "crushes him in an ecstatic embrace," adding ("with furious tenderness"): "How dare you touch anything belonging to me?" The meaning of her tantrum is correctly diagnosed by the doctor, however, as a purely erotic display of "undisguised animal excitement." As the other conspirators join the reconciled lovers for supper, the joyful union of sex and money is consummated in Trench's salutation to his father-in-law: "I'll stand in, compensation or no compensation."

Widowers' Houses is one of Shaw's darkest and bleakest comedies, concerned more with human depravity than with the traditional comedic subject of human folly. In the original, more overtly propagandist version of the play, Shaw declared that it "deals with a burning social question, and is deliberately intended to induce people to vote on the Progressive side at the next County Council election in London." In the more finely tuned edition published in 1898, the plea for a socialist alternative to what seems an irremediable state of moral and social corruption is a more indirect one. The ongoing parody of theatrical, psychological, and moral conventions is the strategy Shaw uses – in a manner that foreshadows Brecht – to disrupt the accepted ideas of his audience and readers and to force them to take an objective critical stance to the social issues at stake. The spectator must not, in other words, be allowed to escape into an empathetic concern with what Shaw calls "the tragedy and comedy of individual character and destiny." His deconstruction of the typical pattern of courtship comedy in this play is one means of preventing that escape. Another, more recurrent means is his obliteration of what his preface to Plays Pleasant calls "the obvious conflicts of unmistakable good and unmistakable evil" which result only in "the crude drama of villain and hero." Similarly in The Quintessence of Ibsenism, the earliest version of which was published only the year before Widowers' Houses was completed, he writes: "The conflict is not between clear right and wrong: the villain is as conscientious as the hero, if not more so: in fact, the question which makes the play interesting (when it is interesting) is which is the villain and which the hero."[8] Especially on this point, his analysis of the "novelty" of Ibsen's technique strongly influenced the way in which he himself began to write plays. The method he chose was precariously balanced between the conventionality of popular theatre (which he loved and despised) and a deliberate inversion of its clichés that his detractors called – and still call – mere "paradox-making." "Take *Widowers' Houses*," he observes in a review of an unimportant play by A. W. Gattie which attempted to imitate his own method without noticing its subversion of stereotypes:

> cut out the passages which convict the audience of being just as responsible for the slums as the landlord; make the hero into a ranting Socialist instead of a perfectly commonplace young gentleman; make the heroine an angel instead of her father's daughter only one generation removed from the wash-tub; and have the successful melodrama of tomorrow.[9]

William Archer might, of course, have been happier with just such a result.

Although his first play "had not achieved a success," Shaw remarks drily in *Plays Unpleasant*, "I had provoked an uproar; and the sensation was so agreeable that I resolved to try again." Although *The Philanderer*, which was written and submitted to Grein's Independent Theatre in 1893, is often regarded by critics as a minor work, its tone and its focus on "the duel of sex" make it an interesting forerunner of such later plays as *You Never Can Tell* and *Man and Superman*. This "topical comedy" of sexual intrigue among the Ibsenites and "New Women" of the mid-nineties was widely unpopular among Shaw's friends (Archer called it "an outrage upon art and decency"), and it did not actually reach the West End stage until 1907, when it was performed during Harley Granville-Barker's epoch-making Shaw campaign at the Court Theatre (eleven Shavian productions by Barker during the three seasons of his co-management with John Vedrenne). One reason for Grein's rejection of the play in 1893 had been his feeling "that the English actors of that day could not possibly cope with the flood of dialogue – that their tongues were not glib enough to rattle it off at the lightning speed required."[10] Shaw himself shared the concern that his rhetorical, disquisitory dramaturgy was going to need a "new," anti-naturalistic style of acting to bring it off:

> In a generation that knew nothing of any sort of acting but drawing-room acting, and which considered a speech of more than twenty words impossibly long, I went back to the classical style and wrote long rhetorical speeches, like operatic arias, regarding my plays as musical performances precisely as Shakespear did . . . Yet so novel was my post-Marx post-Ibsen outlook on life that nobody suspected that my methods were as old as the stage itself. They would have seemed the merest routine to Kemble or Mrs. Siddons, but to the Victorian leading ladies they seemed to be unleadinglady-like barnstorming.[11]

This was written as "An Aside" for the autobiography of Lillah McCarthy, who emerged as a major force in the Barker enterprise at the Court in 1904–07. It was she who, to the playwright's surprise and delight, brought just the right measure of declamatory passion and authority to such strong Shavian heroines as Ann Whitefield and Doña Ana in *Man and Superman* and Jennifer Dubedat in *The Doctor's Dilemma*. Shaw had conceived the tempestuous and problematic figure of Julia Craven in *The Philanderer* in much the same vein, and hence when sudden illness prevented Lillah McCarthy from playing that part as well, the failure of the play's first major production was inevitable.

The Philanderer is, in essence, a very divided play, filled with stylistic contradictions – part anti-realistic farce, part "unpleasant" play aimed at taxing the audience for its indifference to manifestly real "crimes of society," as seen "from the point of view of a Socialist who regards the basis of that society as thoroughly rotten economically and morally."[12] No doubt the sheer verbosity of the play – "the flood of dialogue" Grein complained of – is intended by Shaw to underscore the affected and flatulent nature of its characters and of the world of "clandestine sensuality" they inhabit. But loquacious it is, all the same. The particular target of its social satire is the allegedly inhumane and immoral practice of bourgeois marriage – described in the preface as "an institution which society has outgrown but not modified, and which 'advanced' individuals are therefore forced to evade." Thus baldly stated, the subject matter might as easily have served for a problem play by Brieux (whom it pleased Shaw to refer to as the most important Western dramatist after Ibsen).[13] Shaw's own approach, however, has much closer affinity to the classical manners comedies of Wycherley and Molière, taking from the former a trace of his cynical view of sexual hypocrisy and from the latter his arch satire of preciosity (here "Ibsenism"), pomposity, and medical quackery.[14]

Leonard Charteris, the uninhibited amorist whose escapades furnish *The Philanderer* with its slender action, uses his Ibsenite pose the way Horner uses his simulated "French pox" in *The Country Wife*, as a means of gaining sexual advantage and securing an escape. (As there is not a single functioning marriage to be found in Shaw's plays, cuckoldry does not arise; the threat to Charteris's safety is matrimony, not an irate husband.) The play opens with a lovemaking scene (stringently Victorian, not a whiff of Wycherley) between Charteris and his newest conquest, the young widow Grace Tranfield; it ends on a potentially comedic note, with the betrothal of Grace's rival to another man and her own rejection of the "degrading bargain" Charteris calls marriage. Despite these vestiges of conventional romantic comedy, however, the outcome of the play remains bleak and mechanical, leaving the characters trapped in their empty intellectual "emancipation." Grace's rather bitter conclusion is also Shaw's: "They think this a happy ending, Julia, these men: our lords and masters!"

Neither melodrama nor Ibsen proves to be the means of arriving at a satisfactory resolution (in that a true resolution lies outside the scope of the play, in social reform). The first act takes place entirely in the realm of melodrama – literally so, in that it is set in the London flat of Grace's father, a drama critic named Cuthbertson whose drawing-room walls are covered with theatrical prints of nineteenth-century stage idols who look down with approval on the farcical melodrama being played out before them: the love scene; its sudden interruption by the frantically jealous Julia Craven; Grace's indignant exit; then the obligatory fight scene between the sexual duelists; and finally the unexpected return of the fathers of both the women (old, long-lost friends, it turns out, coincidentally reunited that very evening at the theatre!). It is common to mention that Cuthbertson was meant as a caricature of the noted London critic and Ibsen antagonist Clement Scott, but we are not usually told *why* this might be so. For Shaw, the falsity of the theatrical pathos and moral conventionality idealized in Scott's reviews was a mirror image of the greater falsity of the social system itself and the outmoded values and prejudices it perpetuates. Shaw points out that Scott, as the leader of the opposition to Ibsen in England, demanded the suppression of *Ghosts* on the grounds that Ibsen had urged him, as a spectator, "to laugh at honour, to disbelieve in love, to mock at virtue, to distrust friendship, and to deride fidelity."[15] The statement could as well have been made by Cuthbertson, as these same abstractions are the ethical clichés being held up for satirical scrutiny in *The Philanderer.*

From the world of melodrama, the middle acts of the play move to the world of Ibsen – or, rather, to a world of "advanced" Ibsenite thought professed by the members of the Ibsen Club.[16] Although said to be situated at 90 Cork Street ("at the other end of the Burlington Arcade"), the Ibsen Club is a fantastical state of mind, like Cloud-Cuckoo-Land in *The Birds* or, for that matter, Hell in *Man and Superman.* Here, beneath a bust of Ibsen in the club library, Charteris freely preaches and practices his previously enunciated philosophy of enlightened sexual politics: "Advanced people form charming friendships. Conventional people marry." The Old Order, represented by Cuthbertson and his friend Colonel Craven (VC Egyptian campaign, retired), naturally take umbrage, but Cuthbertson's liberated daughter Grace now embraces the philanderer's views:

> I am quite in earnest about them too, though you are not. That is why I will never marry a man I love too much. It would give him a terrible advantage over me: I should be utterly in his power. Thats what the New Woman is. Isnt she right, Mr. Philosopher? (p. 109)

Julia Craven, on the other hand, shows alarming signs of disqualifying herself from the Club by pursuing Charteris (as she had done in Act 1) around the library in a jealous rage, disempowerment clearly uppermost in her mind. The ruination of Doctor Paramore, who has diagnosed her father as mortally ill from a liver disease the doctor claims to have discovered, gives Charteris the opportunity he needs of ridding himself of Julia. Once Paramore learns that his discovery has been discredited, his reputation demolished, and his diagnosis of the Colonel thus nullified as a blunder, Charteris uses all his sophistry to persuade the self-righteous quack that proposing to Julia is the best way to make amends to the Cravens.

No time is wasted. Over afternoon tea in Percy Paramore's smart Savile Row surgery (where a photograph of Rembrandt's *School of Anatomy* now takes the place of Cuthbertson's theatre portraits), Julia reluctantly accepts Paramore's rather clinical offer of marriage – evidently because he is prepared to believe that she "is not the shallow, jealous, devilish tempered creature" everyone else thinks she is. Although the use of "word-music" – the conscious musical scoring of language in terms of rhythm, counterpoint, tempo, and sound sense ("precisely as Shakespear did") – is usually thought of as a characteristic of Shaw's later plays, there are moments in *The Philanderer* when dialogue is transformed in just this way. The most obvious instance comes in the last-act encounter between Charteris and Julia, after she has accepted Paramore. Notice how even the punctuation is used to score Charteris's speech for actor and reader alike:

> JULIA: According to you, then, I have no good in me. I am an utterly vile worthless woman. Is that it?
> CHARTERIS: Yes, if you are to be judged as you judge others. From the conventional point of view, theres nothing to be said for you, Julia, nothing. Thats why I have to find some other point of view to save my self-respect when I remember how I have loved you. Oh, what I have learnt from you! from you! who could learn nothing from me! I made a fool of you; and you brought me wisdom: I broke your heart; and you brought me joy: I made you curse your womanhood; and you revealed my manhood to me. Blessings for ever and ever on my Julia's name! (*With genuine emotion, he takes her hand to kiss it again.*)

She may both love and despise the philanderer, but she is no longer fooled by him:

> JULIA: (*snatching her hand away in disgust*) Oh, stop talking that nasty sneering stuff. (p. 136)

And moreover, she is perfectly right about "that nasty sneering stuff": in this play Shaw gives his best writing to the hypocrite – the "fraud" and "miserable little plaster saint" Julia now recognizes Charteris to be – as ironic evidence of his deceitfulness and his love of acting.

It was Bergson who called emotion the true enemy of laughter, arguing that the comic depends on "something like a momentary anesthesia of the heart" for its effect.[17] This aptly characterizes *The Philanderer* and its forced "happy ending," which retains a well-mannered insensibility to true feeling until its unexpected (and unspoken) final emotional transition. Charteris himself remains "amused and unconcerned," even after Grace denies him the satisfaction of being slapped by Julia or worse ("Never make a hero of a philanderer"). At last, the other characters then look at Julia *"with concern, and even a little awe, feeling for the first time the presence of a keen sorrow."* This fleeting glimpse of the secret in Julia's heart, so to speak, is afforded only to the *reader* of the play, much as in *Candida*. Whether playing Marchbanks or Julia Craven, however, it is with that final direction that an actor must begin the analysis of the role.

By contrast, the greater depth of passion to be felt in *Mrs. Warren's Profession*, the last and most effective of the *Plays Unpleasant*, sounds an entirely new note in Shaw's dramatic writing. In his long, argumentative Author's Apology in the Stage Society edition of the play in 1902, he still maintains staunchly "that only in the problem play is there any real drama," hence allowing "no future now for any drama without music except the drama of thought." The witty and openly sarcastic tone of G.B.S.'s voice in this seriocomic address must, however, be borne in mind when he proclaims, for example:

> The drama of pure feeling is no longer in the hands of the playwright: it has been conquered by the musician, after whose enchantments all the verbal arts seem cold and tame. Romeo and Juliet with the loveliest Juliet is dry, tedious, and rhetorical in comparison with Wagner's Tristan, even though Isolde is both fourteen stone and forty, as she often is in Germany.[18]

Assuredly, *Mrs. Warren's Profession* is an "unpleasant" play and hence also a "problem" play, in the sense that it is serious rather than frivolous in intent, is again concerned with social corruption (in this case prostitution), and is determined to fasten the blame for such vice not on the individual (the brothel madam) but on a (male, capitalistic) social system that fosters it. (In other words, as Shaw writes in the preface to *Plays Unpleasant*, "rich men without conviction are more dangerous in modern society than poor women without chastity.") This being said, however, there is nothing "cold" or "tame" about Vivie Warren's emotional confrontation with the truth about the nature of her mother's profession. The real point at issue for Shaw is that the crucial process of her disillusionment must not be allowed to degenerate into the sham sentiment of melodrama. "The drama, of course, lies in the discovery and its consequences," he explained in a letter to Golding Bright, a young journalist. "These consequences, though cruel enough, are all quite sensible and sober, no suicide nor sensational tragedy of any sort."[19]

The accusations of immorality leveled against the play by its early critics were prompted, Shaw argues in his Author's Apology, not so much by its subject as by its antimelodramatic treatment of human emotions – "the unexpectedness with which my characters behave like human beings, instead of conforming to the romantic logic of the stage," as he puts it. The actions of both Vivie and her mother are governed not by the knee-jerk motivations of romantic stage morality ("the axioms and postulates of that dreary mimanthropometry"!) but by unromantic common sense. Inevitably, perhaps, the result was that its first audiences were both bewildered and offended by its unusual point of view.

No doubt adding to the confusion was the fact that *Mrs. Warren's Profession*, like *The Philanderer*, did not actually reach the stage until after the author's reputation as a dramatist had been established by the much "pleasanter" and more popular kind of play that began with *Arms and the Man*. After completing *Mrs. Warren* in 1894, Shaw submitted it to Grein, who seems to have indicated that his Independent Theatre was preparing to perform "Mrs. Jarman's Profession," as he apparently called it.[20] To Shaw's fury, meanwhile, the censor refused to issue the required license, and public performances of the work remained banned in Britain until 1925. Already in 1902, however, the intrepid Stage Society proceeded to put on two private performances of the controversial play at the Lyric Club, with the popular comedienne Fanny Brough in the title role. Joining the chorus of reactionary outrage, Grein's unperceptive review expressed "the opinion that the representation was unnecessary and painful": "Here, as in most of G.B.S.'s work, the sublime is constantly spoilt by the ridiculous."[21] Three years later, American audiences proved similarly antagonistic when the young actor Arnold Daly brought the play to New York for the first time, as part of his ambitious two-month repertory season of Shaw. After being tried out and promptly banned in New Haven, Daly's production lasted only a single stormy night at the Garrick Theatre in New York (October 30, 1905). Afterwards, both the manager and his cast – which included the celebrated Ibsen actress Mary Shaw in the role of Kitty Warren – were arrested and jailed by the vice squad for appearing in an immoral work. "Its presentation amounts simply to offending good taste by clownish methods of telling disagreeable facts," the critic for the New York *Mirror* (November 11) agreed. The formidable William Winter was, characteristically, much harsher in his evaluation of Shaw ("a crack-brained, mischief-making English-Irish socialist") and his notions of social reform: "No right-minded, well-bred person introduces an indelicate, not to say foul, subject for conversation in a drawing-room . . . and there is no more justification for insulting people in a theatre than there would be for insulting them in a parlor."[22]

Winter might have taken his answer from Shaw, speaking (as he frequently does in this play) through Vivie: "There is nothing I despise more than the wicked convention that protects these things by forbidding a woman to mention them." On one level, at least – the only level recognized by the majority of reviewers at the time – *Mrs. Warren's Profession* attempts to paint a frank and (debatably) realistic picture of prostitution as a purely economic alternative imposed upon underprivileged women by a paternalistic society. ("The only way for a woman to provide for herself decently," Mrs. Warren claims to have learned, "is for her to be good to some man who can afford to be good to her.") There is no spokesperson and no provision in the play itself for the overthrow of such a iniquitous social system, for – in Shaw's rosy view of social ameliorism – such action must and will result from the recognition by the audience of its own guilt.

In this connection, the play functions as a quotation, so to speak, of the commonly cherished stereotypes of the "courtesan" and "fallen woman" plays that had been popular in the Victorian theatre ever since Dumas *fils* had created a sensation with *La dame aux camélias* (better known as *Camille* in the English theatre) in 1852. At the time *Mrs. Warren* was written more than forty years later, the newest hit in this hardy sub-genre was Arthur Wing Pinero's *The Second Mrs. Tanqueray* (1893). Although the suffering and delicately sensual heroine of *Camille* dies of consumption, the passionate, remorse-driven Paula Tanqueray takes her own life when she realizes, in the true Ibsen manner, that she is trapped because "the future is only the past again, entered through another gate." Before she married Aubrey Tanqueray, one of Paula's numerous social aliases was Mrs. Jarman; hence Grein's slip (if it was a slip) about Shaw's title suggests a significant connection between these two works. When we first encounter Paula Ray (as she was also known in the past) in Tanqueray's chambers in the Albany, she is "a beautiful, fresh, innocent-looking" young woman of twenty-seven "in superb evening dress." Kitty Warren, the dowdy quotation of the Mrs. Jarman persona, is by contrast "a genial and fairly presentable old blackguard of a woman" in her forties or early fifties, "formerly pretty, showily dressed in a brilliant hat and a gay blouse fitting tightly over her bust . . ." There is not a shred of Cleopatra in this sturdy old pro – no trace either of Paula's "tragic" leanings or of the tempting sexuality of the traditional stage courtesan. ("It's not work that any woman would do for pleasure, goodness knows; though to hear the pious people talk you would suppose it was a bed of roses," Kitty tells her daughter.) This, Shaw's counter-portrait proclaims, represents the unvarnished truth about the fictional Mrs. Jarmans of this world. By contrast, as he argues in a later review of the Pinero play, "Paula Tanqueray is an astonishingly well-drawn figure as stage figures go nowadays" – but no more than that, a purely theatrical construction drawn from Pinero's "own point of view in terms of the conventional systems of morals."[23]

On quite another level, meanwhile, *Mrs. Warren's Profession* is (no matter what Shaw may profess to think about it) no more a work "about" prostitution as a social crime than *Ghosts* is "about" syphilis as a communicable disease. The real dramatic tension in this early play of Shaw's arises from its inner action, which might be described as the ambiguous and inconclusive spiritual education of Vivie Warren. At the outset of the play, as she lounges in a hammock in a bucolic garden setting in Surrey, Vivie appears as an almost comedic image of the self-possessed New Woman of the age. A practical thinker with first-class honors in mathematics from Cambridge, she has (so she tells Praed, an admiring visitor and old friend of her mother's) no patience with life's frivolities:

> VIVIE: I shall set up chambers in the City, and work actuarial calculations and conveyancing. Under cover of that I shall do some law, with one eye on the Stock Exchange all the time. Ive come down here by myself to read law: not for a holiday, as my mother imagines. I hate holidays.
> PRAED: You make my blood run cold. Are you to have no romance, no beauty in your life?
> VIVIE: I dont care for either, I assure you.
> PRAED: You cant mean that.
> VIVIE: Oh yes I do. I like working and getting paid for it. When I'm tired of working, I like a comfortable chair, a cigar, a little whisky, and a novel with a good detective story in it. (p. 181)

Rather like Blanche Sartorius, however, Vivie seems not to have troubled herself about the source of the money with which her mother, whom she rarely sees and hardly knows, has paid for her expensive schooling and comfortable life style. Praed knows and is about to tell when he is interrupted by the arrival of the overbearing Mrs. Warren and her vulgar, brutish companion, Sir George Crofts. The underlying tension between mother and daughter rapidly rises to the surface until, in a confrontation between the two women later that night, Mrs. Warren is forced to reveal the sordid reality of her past life. Shaw displays a new grasp of dramaturgical technique in this scene, which moves skilfully from Vivie's initial callous denunciation of her mother ("People are always blaming their circumstances for what they are. I dont believe in circumstances") to her growing understanding of the grinding social conditions that drove their victims into prostitution ("Everybody dislikes having to work and make money; but they have to do it all the same"). The second act ends on a deceptively harmonious note of tender reconciliation ("My dear mother: you are a wonderful woman: you are stronger than all England"), visually reinforced by an idyllic view of the Surrey countryside outside, "bathed in the radiance of the harvest moon rising over Blackdown."

In a conventional melodrama (where it seems to belong) a scene such as this would mark the end of the young heroine's ordeal; in Shaw's play it is only the beginning of it. In the following act, two paired scenes in the Rectory garden the next morning dramatize the untenable nature of the alternatives which Vivie has before her. Her holiday romance with Frank Gardner, the boyishly handsome but utterly undependable son of the local vicar, has no more emotional or physical substance than the children's game of "babes in the wood" that they play together ("covered up with leaves . . . fast asleep, hand in hand, under the trees"). On this particular occasion, as Frank "nestles against her like a weary child," their fantasy is interrupted by Crofts, whose sinister unctuousness strikes an even falser note than Frank's childish cunning or his father's sham piety (for the Reverend Samuel Gardner, too, has been one of Kitty's lovers in his young days). Vivie's new-found faith in her mother's honesty is soon shattered as well by Sir George's revelation that he and Mrs. Warren still own and operate a veritable chain of brothels stretching from Brussels to Budapest. His proposal of marriage to Vivie is linked to his cynical reminder than both she and her fine schools have profited amply from this same enterprise: "It paid for your education and the dress you have on your back. Dont turn up your nose at business, Miss Vivie; where would your Newnhams and Girtons be without it?" Nor – as Sartorius also told Harry Trench in similar circumstances in *Widowers' Houses* – is there any escape from the universal moral taint: "If youre going to pick and choose your acquaintances on moral principles," Crofts reminds her, "youd better clear out of this country, unless you want to cut yourself off from all decent society." The final blow falls when the loathsome Sir George, having been rejected by Vivie and about to be driven from the garden at gunpoint by Frank, spitefully informs them that Sam Gardner, the fatuous clergyman, is Vivie's real father, making her Frank's half-sister. Whether this assertion is true or not we never learn, however, for Shaw again invokes the situation's potential for melodrama, only to dispel it. Thus, when the disillusioned

8 The attack on idealism (2) Rejecting romance: Nora McLellan as Kitty Warren refusing to listen to Norman Browning as Sir George Crofts in the Shaw Festival's 1997 production of *Mrs. Warren's Profession*

Vivie rushes from the Rectory garden in disgust, it is not to pursue some "tragic" course of action but simply to catch a train back to where she can begin again to live her own life.

In the last act of the play, which takes place two days later in a cluttered modern office in Chancery Lane, far from the mock pastoralism of Surrey gardens and cottages, Vivie's protest against the "horrible cant" and blandishments of conventional happiness is summed up in one single sentence: "Life is what it is, and I am prepared to take it as it is." She now believes neither in Praed's poetic vagaries about "the beauty and romance of life" nor in Frank's equally airy notion of "love's young dream": "If we three are to remain friends," she warns them, "I must be treated as a woman of business, permanently single (*to Frank*) and permanently un-romantic (*to Praed*)." Her third tempter, in the person of Mrs. Warren, represents a more insidious threat to her self-determination – not because Vivie regards her as "immoral," nor because the wealth she offers her daughter holds no attraction for her, but precisely because she recognizes herself and her own fiercely independent spirit in her mother. The crucial difference between them is hence not in the choice the latter has made, but in the hypocrisy with which it had been overlaid with social respectability and maternal sentiment. Vivie, the true anarchist, demands instead "all or nothing" – an uncompromising union of action and belief:

> Yes: it's better to choose your line and go through with it. If I had been you, mother, I might have done as you did: but I should not have lived one life and believed in another. You are a conventional woman at heart. That is why I am bidding you goodbye now. I am right, am I not? (p. 246)

There is one particular maxim in Jack Tanner's "Revolutionist's Handbook" (printed at the end of *Man and Superman*) that seems to crystallize the emotional struggle at the core of *Mrs. Warren*: "Youth, which is forgiven everything, forgives itself nothing: age, which forgives itself everything, is forgiven nothing." From this characteristic paradox springs Shaw's treatment of the final unfilial encounter between Kitty Warren and her daughter – a scene which no Victorian audience could possibly forgive or endure. (Grein, himself a Dutchman, was so offended by it that he rebuked Vivie not only for being "so cold of heart" but in particular for being "so un-English in her knowledge of the world."[24]) In essence, this is a play for the twentieth century, not for the nineteenth. Its open, muted ending – the image of Vivie delving into the great sheafs of paper on her desk in order to lose herself in work – is perfectly Chekhovian in the contrariness of its signals: despair and contentment, disillusionment and hope for the future. A recurrent pattern in Shaw's writing emerges for the first time in *Mrs. Warren's Profession*. As in many of his later works, the events in this early play become stages in a spiritual education – a cumulative process of disillusionment that leaves its subject decimated but stronger and more resilient, better able to bear life without illusion.

In this respect and others, *Mrs. Warren's Profession* clearly foreshadows the future direction of Shavian drama – yet it also marks the end of a distinct phase in the playwright's development. The publication of *Plays Unpleasant* and *Plays Pleasant* as companion volumes in 1898 served to highlight the contrast between his earlier preoccupation with specific social problems in his first three plays and the broader concern with human folly in general that takes over in the "pleasanter" plays which follow. With the subsequent publication two years later of the anti-romantic *Plays for Puritans*, the shift away from the earlier social realism became still more pronounced, as the scope of Shaw's subject matter broadened and the grip of Ibsenism on his writing relaxed. He himself describes his first plays, the purpose of which had been "to make people thoroughly uncomfortable," as "criticisms of a special phase, the capitalist phase, of modern organization." The difference between them and the *Plays Pleasant*, he goes on to explain in a letter, is that the latter "are not 'realistic' plays. They deal with life at large, with human nature as it presents itself through all economic and social phases."[25] Nevertheless, despite the radical changes in tone, purpose, and subject matter that occur after *Mrs. Warren's Profession*, the struggle to propound a transvaluation of values in the interest of progress remained, as it had been from the outset, the guiding force in Shaw's engaged theatre of ideas. In this sense, his early experiments form an indispensable preamble to a body of work and a theory of dramatic action based squarely on "the defiance of duty by the reformer: every step of progress means a duty repudiated and a scripture torn up."[26]

NOTES

1 Charles Archer, *William Archer: Life, Work, and Friendships* (New Haven, 1931), p. 119.
2 *Ibid.*, p. 133.
3 "How William Archer Impressed Bernard Shaw," William Archer, *Three Plays: Martha Washington, Beatriz-Juana, Lidia* (New York, 1927), pp. xxix–xxx.
4 William Archer, *Play-making: A Manual of Craftsmanship*, introduction by John Gassner (New York, 1960), pp. 249, 19, 193, 250.
5 William Archer, *English Dramatists of To-day* (London, 1882), p. 9.
6 *Widowers' Houses: A Comedy by G. Bernard Shaw, First Acted at the Independent Theatre in London*, ed. J. T. Grein (London, 1893), pp. 117–18.
7 Bernard Shaw, *Plays Pleasant and Unpleasant. The First Volume Containing Three Unpleasant Plays* (London, 1931), pp. 11–12. This volume of the Constable Standard Edition is the source for all subsequent quotations from the plays, page references to which are given in parenthesis in the text.
8 Bernard Shaw, *The Quintessence of Ibsenism*, 3rd edn. (1922) (New York, n.d.), p. 175.
9 "Daly Undaunted," *Saturday Review*, July 18, 1896: Bernard Shaw, *Our Theatres in the Nineties* (London, 1932), vol. II, p. 193.
10 J. T. Grein, *The New World of the Theatre* (London, 1924), p. 23.
11 *Shaw on Theatre*, ed. E. J. West (New York, 1959), pp. 220–21.
12 Letter of June 10, 1896: George Bernard Shaw, *Advice to a Young Critic and Other Letters*, ed. E. J. West (New York, 1955), p. 49.
13 Cf. *Three Plays by Brieux*, with a Preface by Bernard Shaw (New York, 1911), p. vii. One of the plays in this collection, *The Three Daughters of M. Dupont* (translated by St. John Hankin), chronicles the deplorable state of the woman (Julie) within the French marriage system, but it goes on to demonstrate the even greater miseries attached to the choices open to Julie's two sisters: either spinsterhood and drudgery or prostitution. The Brieux play (from 1897) obviously interested Shaw, who ponders these same three "choices" of the modern woman in his own "unpleasant" plays.
14 Shaw's comment on Wycherley is revealing in the context of this particular play: "I have nothing in common with Wycherley and Congreve except our art, and an indefensible love of acting for its own sake," *Shaw on Theatre*, pp. 174–75.
15 *The Quintessence of Ibsenism*, p. 26; also Bernard Shaw, *Major Critical Essays* (London, 1932), p. 15.

16 The second and third acts of the original are combined into one long second act in both the Standard Edition (1931) and the Penguin edition (Harmondsworth, 1946 *et seq.*) of *Plays Unpleasant.*
17 Henri Bergson, *Laughter: An Essay on the Meaning of the Comic,* trans. Cloudesley Brereton and Fred Rothwell (New York, 1937), p. 5.
18 Constable Standard Edition, p. 161.
19 Letter of November 4, 1895: Shaw, *Advice to a Young Critic,* p. 41.
20 See *The Theatre,* New Series 24 (December 1894), p. 332. Shaw himself denied using any such earlier title: *Advice to a Young Critic,* p. 9.
21 *Victorian Dramatic Criticism,* ed. George Rowell (London, 1971), p. 311.
22 William Winter, *The Wallet of Time* (New York, 1913), vol. II, pp. 509, 507–8.
23 "An Old New Play and a New Old One," *Saturday Review,* February 23, 1895: Shaw, *Our Theatres in the Nineties,* (London, 1932), vol. I, pp. 45, 47.
24 *Victorian Dramatic Criticism,* p. 312.
25 Letter of June 10, 1896: Shaw, *Advice to a Young Critic,* pp. 49–50.
26 *The Quintessence of Ibsenism,* p. 28; also *Major Critical Essays,* p. 17.

FURTHER READING

Meisel, Martin, *Shaw and the Nineteenth Century Theater,* Princeton, 1963.
Shaw, Bernard, *Advice to a Young Critic and Other Letters,* ed. E. J. West, New York, 1955.
Wisenthal, J. L. (ed.), *Shaw and Ibsen: Bernard Shaw's The Quintessence of Ibsenism and Related Writings,* Toronto, 1979.

6

DAVID J. GORDON

Shavian comedy and the shadow of Wilde

The careers of Bernard Shaw and Oscar Wilde followed very similar paths up until 1895. Both were born of Protestant stock in Dublin around the mid-fifties, and launched themselves as writers after settling in London during the seventies. For about five years both wrote apprentice work – trying out genres, seeking a style. At the same time, both were developing considerable skill as public speakers with a theatrical flair. From 1885 to 1888 they worked together, along with William Archer and George Moore, as anonymous book reviewers on the *Pall Mall Gazette*. Both were drawn to socialism, and probably it was an address of Shaw's at a Fabian meeting that inspired Wilde's "The Soul of Man Under Socialism."[1] At the turn of the decade each wrote and published an important, defining volume of criticism: *The Quintessence of Ibsenism* and *Intentions* (the latter including "The Decay of Lying," "The Critic as Artist," and the essay on socialism). And during the next few years, until that fateful February of 1895, each wrote five accomplished and still produced plays: by Wilde, *Salomé*, *Lady Windermere's Fan*, *A Woman of No Importance*, *An Ideal Husband*, and *The Importance of Being Earnest*; by Shaw, *Widowers' Houses*, *The Philanderer*, *Mrs. Warren's Profession*, *Arms and the Man*, and *Candida*.

At almost every step Wilde seems to have enjoyed an advantage, although there is only a little to suggest that Shaw, competitive but generous, envied or resented his compatriot. Wilde came to London trailing clouds of academic glory from Trinity College and Oxford; the self-educated Shaw arrived after four years of clerical work in a Dublin estate office. Their personal acquaintance (the families were acquainted in Dublin) probably began in 1880 at one of Lady Wilde's at-homes: Shaw later acknowledged that "Lady Wilde was nice to me in London" during that difficult period (*Pen Portraits*, p. 299). Although Shaw was getting known as a Fabian orator, Wilde was already famous enough by 1881 to have been invited by D'Oyly Carte to do a year's lecturing in America as an apostle of aestheticism, even if Shaw felt that Wilde's familiarity with any

124

art other than literature was secondhand compared to his own (*Pen Portraits*, pp. 301, 305). When it came to review assignments for the *Gazette*, Shaw, according to Michael Holroyd, was assigned trivial books whereas "other Irishmen on the paper were given major writers to review. George Moore wrote on Huysmans and Zola; Oscar Wilde on Dostoevsky, William Morris, Tolstoy, [and] Turgenev."[2] And as for the comedies of the nineties, Wilde's were all produced promptly in major theatres (*An Ideal Husband* and *The Importance of Being Earnest* were, in fact, running together and very successfully at the time of his disgrace) whereas *Widowers' Houses*, in the words of Stanley Weintraub, "had managed two unrewarding performances in December 1892, while *The Philanderer* had frightened away producers and *Mrs. Warren's Profession* had been proscribed by the Censor."[3] Despite all this, Shaw praised Wilde's work directly and indirectly. He (and Archer, and they alone among critics of reputation) defended *Salomé* against censorship.[4] He wrote to one correspondent in 1889: Wilde's "work [on the *Gazette*] was exceptionally finished in style and very amusing";[5] to another, in 1894: "Wilde's wit and his fine literary workmanship are points of great value."[6] He warmly praised *An Ideal Husband* in one of his first contributions to the *Saturday Review*,[7] and admired in incidental comments both *Lady Windermere's Fan* and *A Woman of No Importance*.[8] After the trials, Shaw drafted two petitions for a release from prison and a reduction of sentence. Again in 1897, just months after the release from prison, he nominated Wilde for membership to a British Academy of Letters. The one real blot on this good record was his impercipient review of *The Importance of Being Earnest*, which described the play as "inhuman," "mechanical," amusing but not touching, most likely a much earlier play refurbished (*Our Theatres*, vol. XXIII, pp. 43–46). And he compounded this insensitive judgment twenty years later, calling it Wilde's "first really heartless play," "essentially hateful" (*Pen Portraits*, p. 302). Stanley Weintraub comments with sympathetic insight (but ignoring the renewal of the attack): "Two plays [produced and acclaimed] in two months was too much even for Shaw. One had to have been manufactured earlier, and he took the second comedy's apparent lack of surface seriousness as its core" (*Shaw's People*, p. 45).[9]

Personal relations between the two writers were always courteous but the courtesy was strained. In a letter of February 23, 1893 Wilde acknowledges the receipt of *The Quintessence of Ibsenism* and sends *Salomé* in return: "You have written well and wisely and with sound wit . . . England is the land of intellectual fogs but you have done much to clear the air: we are both Celtic, and I like to think that we are friends: for these and many other reasons [mainly Shaw's effort to lift the censorship] Salomé presents herself to you in purple raiment."[10] Shaw has not yet received Wilde's play: "Salomé is still wandering in her purple raiment in search of me, and I expect her to arrive a perfect outcast, branded with inky stamps" (Shaw, *Collected Letters*, p. 384).[11] In return he will send *Widowers' Houses*, "which you will find tolerably amusing" (Shaw, *Collected Letters*, p. 384). And Wilde acknowledges this with a conceit that graciously arranges their current and forthcoming plays in an alternating pattern defining a new "Celtic School" (*Wilde Letters*, p. 339).

But it is apparent that, despite mutual respect, they did not really like each other, as Shaw indicated in the Harris letter when he remembers the "queer shyness" between them: "We put each other out frightfully; and this odd difficulty persisted between us to the very last" (*Pen Portraits*, pp. 300, 299). More important, they did not like each other's ideas. In particular Shaw disliked the doctrine of aestheticism that Wilde had taken over and developed from Walter Pater. Holroyd (*Bernard Shaw*, p. 75) finds this antagonism expressed as early as his first novel, *Immaturity*, in which an earnest and industrious young man named Smith is contrasted to a dilettante named Hawksmith who courts the favor of society. In its mature form, as in the Epistle Dedicatory to *Man and Superman*, it is expressed as a protest against style for its own sake (rather than as an aspect of effective assertion), a protest against "'art's sake alone' for which I would not face the toil of writing a single sentence." Richard Ellmann is at pains to show that "Art for Art's Sake" was a slogan Wilde repudiated because it implied a less energetic and morally complex view than he espoused (*Wilde*, pp. 310, 318). Shaw did, in fact, tend to degrade the aesthetic position associated with Wilde and, conversely, to exaggerate the contrasting quality of his own art, sometimes even calling it propaganda. Probably he sensed that his deep quarrel with the aesthetic position grew out of fundamental similarities with his own.

Both writers from the start attacked similar targets: duty, respectability, the sentimental view of poverty, the danger of self-denial and of ideal-driven goodness. Both shared a belief in the cardinal value of individuality – the major theme of "The Soul of Man Under Socialism" but also stressed in *The Quintessence* and in Shaw's work generally in the nineties. (After the turn of the century Shaw was more inclined to believe that "WE MUST REFORM SOCIETY BEFORE WE CAN REFORM OURSELVES," a heading in the preface to *Misalliance*.) As co-disciples of Ruskin, neither writer regarded Art and Life antithetically, believing instead that one enhanced the other. But Wilde obscures this because he uses the word "Life" in several senses (individuality, social custom, natural fact), just as Shaw obscures it by sometimes (and quite passionately) defending the words "art" and "artist" and sometimes belittling them: "Wilde wrote for the stage as an artist. I am simply a propagandist." This provocative self-libel ("Playwright," p. 127) is matched by his preface to *Mrs. Warren's Profession* in which Shaw claims that he wrote about prostitution "to draw attention to the truth" and "expose the fact" – although there are no such bald assertions in the play, only ideas carefully presented as characteristic of those who speak them.

The underlying similarities help to explain the fact that some words elevated in Wilde's vocabulary – beauty, passion, joy, romance, art – are by no means always degraded in Shaw's but are first purged of their degraded component and then embraced at a higher level. Words like "joy" in the mouth of *Man and Superman's* Devil ("I call on [the world] to sympathize with joy, with love, with happiness, with beauty") stigmatize him because they nauseate Don Juan, but the Epistle Dedicatory eloquently invokes "the *true* joy in life, the being used for a purpose recognized by yourself as a mighty one" (*my emphasis*). In connection with *Arms and the Man*, we will see again that the word "romance" is first purged of its degraded sense and that a higher sense, associated with power rather than passivity, then acquires a positive meaning.

But the differences growing out of these likenesses are what matter most, and they involve Shaw's and Wilde's opposite views of art – of their own art in practice and of the place of art itself in relation to life.

The artistic ideal which Shaw embraced from early on favored the robust and strenuous. Its models were found in the work of artists such as Bunyan, Handel, Blake, Shelley, Wagner, and Ibsen, antagonistic in spirit to Wilde's Romanticism, to the tradition of Keats, Swinburne, Pater, and the decadent movement deriving from Huysmans. If Wilde's creative imagination was stirred by the socially transgressive act or word made charming by high style, Shaw's was stirred by the idea of a Life Force, something between Schopenhauer's remorseless Will to Live and Blake's exuberant Will to Create. If Wilde's aestheticism morally polarized the beautiful and the ugly, Shaw's vitalism morally polarized energy and conventionality. A contrasting style of wit arose therefrom, best indicated by an example. With Proudhon's "Property Is Theft" in mind, Shaw's John Tanner ripostes (to Mendoza's "I am a brigand. I live by robbing the rich"): "I am a gentleman. I live by robbing the poor." This is a paradox with a strong ethical thrust, exploiting our perception of an absurdity inherent in the structure of capitalism. Wilde's Lady Bracknell also has something to say about property: "It gives one position and [because of encumbering 'duties'] prevents one from keeping it up. That's all that can be said about land." Her contradiction is less a paradox than an elegant irony, less a social protest than an enforcement of class superiority by the way the speaker rises above distress through a recourse to style alone.

Although Shaw was seldom a propagandist *in* his art (his art is didactic in tendency, but it does not preach socialism, and indeed only refers to it ironically), he certainly believed that art itself refined and improved us – a view shared by many educated people in his time even if it is now, after Auschwitz, a view put into serious question:

> Every step in morals is made by challenging the validity of existing concep-tions ... of conduct ... The claim of art to our respect must stand or fall with the validity of its pretension to cultivate and refine our senses and faculties. Further, art should refine our sense of character and conduct, of justice and sympathy, greatly heightening our self-knowledge, self-control, precision of action, and considerateness, and making us intolerant of baseness, cruelty, injustice, and intellectual superficiality or vulgarity
>
> ("The Sanity of Art," in *Works*, vol. XIX, pp. 314, 328–29).

For Wilde, in contrast, art leads, and should lead, nowhere. Speaking through Lord Henry Wotton of *Dorian Gray* he writes: "Art has no influence upon action. It annihilates the desire to act. It is superbly sterile."[12] Shaw, like Carlyle, would emphasize work or, more exactly, what the critic Alfred Turco, highlighting a phrase in *Cashel Byron's Profession*, calls "executive power."[13] Again like Carlyle, Shaw believed the road to freedom lay through self (and social) control: "anarchism" con-stituted a temptation for a socialist, but, as the title of one of his *Fabian Essays in Socialism* indicates, it is an "Impossibility." Wilde, on the other hand, was unworried about control, and admitted to being "something of an Anarchist" (Ellmann, *Wilde*, p. 328). Indeed, in "The Soul of Man Under Socialism," he writes emphatically: "All modes of government are failures"; "The mode of government that is most suitable to the artist is no government at all" (*Works*, pp. 1087, 1098–99). Wilde like Shaw was drawn to the idea of social evolution, but, rather than developing its implications, he was content to believe that the progress of which socialism speaks will heighten individualism.

When Shavian drama directly introduces opposing views of Art and Life, as it does most notably in the Hell scene of *Man and Superman*, the presence of Wilde's shadow is unmistakable. Harold Bloom with some reason finds an anxiety of influence evidenced in the tension between the hedonist Devil and the Shavian Don Juan who cannot rest as long as he can conceive something better than himself. Bloom puts it pithily:

> Shaw was genial only when he was not menaced, and he felt deeply menaced by the Aesthetic vision of which his Socialism never quite got free. Like Oscar

Wilde and Wilde's mentor Walter Pater, Shaw was a direct descendant of Ruskin, and his animus against Wilde and Pater reflects the anxiety of an ambitious son toward rival claimants to a heritage ... Shaw's lifelong animus against Pater and his repressed anxiety caused by Wilde's genius as an Anglo-Irish dramatist, emerge with authentic sharpness and turbulence as Don Juan and the Devil face off.[14]

A major reason that this act retains its vibrancy is that Shaw participates in his antagonist's argument; his Devil is never stronger than when he turns directly against man's vaunted brain and the capacity for self-improvement, the basis of Don Juan's (and Shaw's) faith. Bloom could have gone further in seeing *Man and Superman* as a quarrel with Wilde, for Octavius's worship of art vs. Tanner's friendly scorn is another version of it – a weaker version, to be sure, but significant in that it shows us that, even if the Shavian artist thinks of himself as a revolutionary rather than an artist, his verbal energy – not only in his dream but also in the comedy, the Handbook, and the Maxims – gives him away. And, although this has not been noticed, the Epistle Dedicatory is also a version of the same debate, with the critic A. B. Walkley (to whom it is addressed) standing in for Pater (whom Walkley admired) and Wilde. That, I think, is why Shaw flatters a critic who had written about his plays with distaste and why Walkley can serve as someone to react against in the fiercely eloquent peroration about the true joy of life, which seeks, in the spirit of Nietzsche, to raise selfhood from the merely human to the superhuman level.

It is surely not coincidental that this elaborate, threefold attack on Wilde occurs in a play written during the years immediately after Wilde's death, a play much wider in scope than anything Shaw had tried before. It is as if Wilde's death aroused in him a need to come to terms with the shadow of a persisting presence. Shaw's work thereafter is much less intense in this regard, consisting (apart from the role of Lady Britomart, genially indebted to that of Lady Bracknell) mainly of statements requested by Wilde's former friends (especially Frank Harris and Alfred Douglas) in which Shaw tries to judge the man more than his ideas.

During Wilde's lifetime, Shaw wrote nothing so suggestive of an anxiety of influence as his review of *The Importance of Being Earnest*. But his own comedies written about the same time develop contrasting comic strategies, and it is this contrast to which I now turn.

It is convenient to focus the contrast around a limited number of plays, and from Wilde this means the single play in which his comic genius is most completely represented. In the earlier comedies there was a certain disjuncture between the morality of melodrama and that of the dandy.[15] Edouard

Roditi observed of Wilde's first comedy that the "unrelieved earnestness of Lady Windermere contrasts too violently with the frivolity of most of the other characters."[16] Ian Gregor, writing on "Comedy in Oscar Wilde," added that the problem of the earlier comedies was "finding a world fit for the dandy to live in."[17] Peter Raby contrasted the world of *An Ideal Husband* with its one or two dandies to the world of *The Importance of Being Earnest* in which "every character participated in the role and stance of the dandy."[18] There seems to be a sense of guilt concerning the idea of a double life in the earlier comedies, but I would agree with Gregor that the world in *Earnest* is for once "a world of idyll, of pure play" (Bloom, "*The Importance*," p. 20); with Robert J. Jordan, in his "Satire and Fantasy in *The Importance of Being Earnest*," that it is a world of "innocence," "without evil" (Bloom, *The Importance*," p. 30); and with Harold Bloom who strongly denies in this play "any understructure of sin and guilt" (p. 9). It is as if the apparent source of unease in the earlier plays bubbles to the surface of *Earnest* and, sportively called "Bunburying," is bandied about. The plot taken literally suggests that Bunburying is having a last fling before marriage, but it is clear from the spirit of the whole play, capped by the final exchange between Jack and Gwendolyn ("Gwendolyn, it is a terrible thing for a man to find out suddenly that all his life he has been speaking nothing but the truth. Can you forgive me?" "I can, for I feel you are sure to change"), that the spirit of Bunburying is irrepressible. What Shaw himself wrote about *An Ideal Husband* fits *Earnest* better than anything he wrote about the latter play: "Wilde is to me our only thorough playwright. He plays with everything: with wit, with philosophy, with drama, with actors and audience, with the whole theatre" (*Our Theatres*, vol. XXIII, p. 10).

From Shaw's comedies of the nineties, I select three grouped around *Earnest*: *Arms and the Man* (1894), *You Never Can Tell* (1896), and *The Devil's Disciple* (1897). *Arms and the Man*, the first of the "pleasant" plays, is also the first to make apparent Shaw's own comic genius, and it was the first to enjoy some public success (a run of fifty performances at one of the smaller West End theatres). *You Never Can Tell* was composed just a few months after the production of *Earnest* that Shaw saw and reviewed, and is actually indebted to it in specific ways. And *The Devil's Disciple*, the first of the *Three Plays for Puritans*, discriminates further the moral positioning of characters in Shaw's comedies and thus sharpens our sense of the contrast between his and Wilde's technique.

About *The Importance of Being Earnest* two principal points will furnish the grounds for comparison with these plays of Shaw's. One concerns the basic lack of differentiation among characters; the other pertains to the genre of the play itself, its peculiar place in the comic tradition.

The characters of Wilde's masterpiece are, of course, played off against one another in different scenes but more for the sake of repartee and plot movement than to establish signficant differences in moral position. It is of little importance to contrast, in any systematic way, the dandyism of one character to the earnestness of another, though some critics have tried or partly tried to do so. All the characters speak what Ian Gregor calls the "language of the dandy ... at once critical and self-delighting" (Bloom, "*The Importance*," p. 21). "Almost everything [the characters] say is spoken for effect," observes Peter Raby (*A Reader's Companion*, p. 58). All seek to realize their own individualities in the "aesthetic Utopia" of *Earnest*, writes Susan Laity in an essay called "The Soul of Man Under Victoria: *Iolanthe, Earnest*, and Bourgeois Drama" (Bloom, "*The Importance*," pp. 139–40). Even the secondary characters "are erudite verbalists," comments Camille Paglia in "Oscar Wilde and the English Epicene," and she wittily describes Wilde's "original language" for his characters in this play as "*monologue extérieur*" (Bloom, "*The Importance*" pp. 91, 89). And Katharine Worth, in "The Triumph of the Pleasure Principle," catches the single quality of the speakers in Wilde's farce by noting that "no one is ever so agitated that he cannot take time to round a sentence" (Bloom, "*The Importance*" p. 59). In effect the play at every point turns substance into style and content into form. For me this is epitomized in Lady Bracknell's remark that the "two weak points in our age are its want of principle and its want of profile" – the neat alliteration quickly leveling morality and aesthetics.

The dandies of *Earnest* and the heroes of Shaw's plays are equally remarkable for their aplomb, and much comic effect is generated by both playwrights exploiting the incongruity between a bland, self-possessed manner of speech and startling, outrageous, or absurd matter. But Wilde's dandies are self-possessed because, paradoxically, there is no single self for them to defend, only a mask or persona to adopt opportunistically; it is in fact Wilde's main argument against "sincerity" that it must be false because there are many selves.[19] The Shavian hero, in contrast, is self-possessed – "keeps his head like a god" – because, like Karl Marx, "He has discovered the law of social development, and knows what must come."[20] If the Shavian hero implicitly promises to steer us toward an improved future, confident that destroying ideals will not result in chaotic drifting, the Wildean dandy, with no less aplomb (think of the Algernon/Jack muffin dialogue at the end of Act 2), finds a dizzying of one's sense of direction delightful, an end in itself.

The question of characterization involves the larger question of what kind of comedies we are comparing. Wildean and Shavian comedy both seem to be initiated by satire but before long they slide into something else.

Can we say that *Earnest* is a satire on upper-class manners? Certainly a number of snobbish, class-conscious attitudes are amusingly reflected, but satire soon turns fantastical. In the opening scene between Algernon and his servant Lane, for example, we seem to understand that the institution of marriage, as in a Restoration play, is providing the occasion for ridiculing remarks. But such remarks (numerous in the play) are mere pinpricks. The unique quality of the work lies elsewhere and starts to come into focus in this exchange:

ALGERNON: Good heavens! Is marriage so demoralizing as that?
LANE: I believe it *is* a very pleasant state, sir. I have had very little experience of it myself up to the present. I have only been married once. That was in consequence of a misunderstanding between myself and a young person.
ALGERNON: (*Languidly.*) I don't know that I am much interested in your family life, Lane.
LANE: No, sir; it is not a very interesting subject. I never think of it myself.

(Act 1, scene 1)

What is funny here is not exactly that marriage has taken a clever hit but that Lane refers to a serious subject in so droll and insouciant a way. His style, not his sincerity or insincerity, is what matters. Such dialogue trivializes a serious subject or, more exactly, displaces Wilde's own earnestness from subject matter to style.

Because the freedom from care that makes this sort of posturing possible is associated with the upper classes, we can say that the play not only displays the snobberies of this class (never mind that Lane is a servant) but also supports the privilege that makes them possible. As Raby puts it: "The intention is not primarily to satirize the ridiculous nature of some social rituals and taboos . . . but to infuse them with a new and independent life" (*A Reader's Companion*, p. 44). He shrewdly observes that Lady Bracknell's references to the horror of revolution are not *just* a joke because social order is what provides the basis for her life of privilege (p. 7). In Ellmann's words, in this style of wit, "We have the pleasure affirming the *ancien régime* and of rebelling against it at the same time" (*Wilde*, p. xvi). On the whole, class-related freedom from seriousness seems stronger than class-directed satire. That is to say, and in contrast to Shavian comedy, the subversive aspect of the play has little to do with any implied desire to undermine a social order but much to do with its undermining of sense, with its comic anarchy. Raby comments that the world of *Earnest* "is a mixture of the reassuringly stable and the chaotically surreal" (*A Reader's Companion*, p. 81). It is, one might say, a world where cigarette cases are lost and returned, where suitors propose, diaries are kept and muffins are eaten, but where the logic used to describe these worldly activities keeps sliding off the rails.

To what genre, then, does the play belong? If there is any consensus among critics, it is in locating it somewhere between the Anglo-Irish comic tradition established by Congreve, Goldsmith, and Sheridan on the one hand, and, on the other, the Victorian genre of "nonsense literature" as represented by Lewis Carroll and Edward Lear. To put it another way, it is satire turning repeatedly into farce but farce with a peculiar seriousness because it seeks not merely to resolve plot complications but, through its language, to define an aesthetic utopia, a guiltless "triumph of the pleasure principle." Its final recognition scene exploits the conventions of melodrama, the most moralistic of dramatic genres, but sends them up: the discovery of a long-lost mother is deflected onto an all-important handbag, of a long-lost father onto an all-important name in a reference book.

The Shavian comedies I will consider here for their contrasting strategies do not so much slide away from satire, as *Earnest* does; instead, they use satire to ridicule an entrenched but outworn moral position and then, reactively, spring forward to a new moral position more vigorous and heroic. The former position is called in *The Quintessence of Ibsenism* "idealist" because it idealizes in order to conceal its vulnerability, the latter "realist" because, as in Plato's antithesis of real and ideal, it has the power to dispel error and raise up truth. In *Arms and the Man* Bluntschli helps Raina to abandon her out-of-date idealizations of love and war whereupon the two will lead the way towards a new kind of realism; in *You Never Can Tell*, the parents whose grievances are nourished by Victorian ideals of duty and respect are forced to surrender them by the combined energy of the independent younger generation and the executive power of the mediating waiter and his formidable son; in *The Devil's Disciple* the position of the romantic, idealizing wife and that of the suave gentleman resist but are overcome by the love-and-life-defying heroism of a seemingly unlikely saint and a seemingly unlikely soldier. Shaw's heroes solve problems as agents of a progressive force, yet always some qualifying irony attends their head-of-the-pack achievements. In the traditional comedy of Shakespeare or Molière, a blocking figure stands apart from the social group and threatens its cohesion whereas in Shaw the hero himself stands against the social group. But Shavian comedy never forgets that there is something absurd as well as wonderful about an idiosyncratic stance.

The comic energy of *Arms and the Man* is generated at first by the clash between the romantic heroine (whose "Byronism" is seconded by her fiancé and by the Bulgarian unworldliness and aristocratic pretension of her family) and the practical and prosaic Swiss mercenary ("bourgeois to his

9   Incurable Romanticism: the opening scene in *Arms and the Man*: Andrew Gillies as Bluntschli and Donna Goodhand as Raina in the Shaw Festival's 1986 production of *Arms and the Man*

boots") who strips away her false idealism. To make that change in her credible, she must be shown as ripe for it, and, once the change is accomplished, she demonstrates an energetic realism in the most effectively set up farcical business of the play, when she and Bluntschli skillfully cooperate to extract a compromising photograph from the pocket of a coat under the noses of the confused family. But Bluntschli's heroism is not merely a matter of undermining error: in a fine surprise, we discover that he reinstates romance at a higher level. He claims to Sergius's amazement to have "an incurably romantic disposition," shown by the fact that he "climbed the balcony of this house when a man of sense would have dived into the nearest cellar...and came sneaking back here to have another look at the young lady when any other man of my age would have sent the coat back." More important, he then demonstrates a power to amaze in the marvelously efficient way he solves the practical problems – too difficult for Major Petkoff and Colonel Saranoff – involved in sending the Bulgarian troops back home. This prosaic or Shavian idea of romance is capped when

10   Pragmatism vs. Idealism: the opening scene in *Arms and the Man*: Simon Bradbury
as Bluntschli and Elizabeth Brown as Raina in the Shaw Festival's 1994 production of
Arms and the Man

he reads his hotelkeeper-father's will, which proves that he can offer a bride
the appurtenances of a good home – tablecloths, silverware, horses, etc. –
in quantities ridiculously beyond the means of any aspiring gentry. Such
achievements give new meaning to the word "bourgeois" – and to the word
"romance." The final line of the play – Sergius's "What a man! Is he a
man!" – captures the double view of him and clinches Shaw's comedy.[21] As
hero, Bluntschli is a bit lightweight, and his "chocolate cream soldier"
romance with Raina a bit sentimental, but *Arms and the Man* is still
effective comedy, and the ethical thrust of its action, the way it seeks to
alter rather than dissolve identity, marks a clear contrast to the Wildean
mode.

You Never Can Tell offers two comic situations. One is a duel of
experienced lovers each of whom takes pride in making conquests without
falling in love and each of whom, having unwillingly fallen in love, defeats
the resistance of the other by appealing from head to heart rather than
heart to head. (This situation is a more elegant version of what we find in
The Philanderer and anticipates the main plot of the comedy in *Man and
Superman* where matrimonial reluctance is extended to fantastic lengths
before a final capitulation.) The other situation involves a family of five in

which the estranged parents are stubbornly at odds: he calls himself Mr. Crampton and morosely nourishes a vague grievance against his wife; she calls herself Mrs. Clandon, has lived in Madeira before moving to a hotel on the Devon coast where Crampton lives, and has written a series of "Twentieth Century Treatises" whose ethical cast is unfortunately more Victorian than modern. The eldest child and mother's star pupil is Gloria, locked in amorous combat with a young dentist named simply Valentine. The other two children, Philip and Dolly, are youthful twins, and it is their witty and engaging insolence directed at the older generation (father, mother, and a lawyer known to both) that provides much of the play's charm.

Their spirit is iconoclastic, but in order for it to be effectual in bringing about a measure of reconciliation sufficient to prepare for the festive finale, it must be supplemented by the executive power of the ever tactful waiter, William, and his imperiously forceful son, an attorney named Bohun. Bohun's repeated wisdom is: "You think you won't but you will"; William's gentler version is "you never can tell." The force of the one and (especially) the easy suavity of the other win the day.

As a number of critics have noticed, the play is indebted to Wilde's *Earnest* in several ways. The most obvious is the search for the missing father and, in particular, the resemblance between Lady Bracknell's advice to Jack "to produce at any rate one parent, of either sex, before the season is quite over" and Valentine's advice to the twins: "in a seaside resort theres one thing you must have before anybody can afford to be seen going about with you; and thats a father, alive or dead." The similarity in the use of name-changes has also been noted, as has the wordplay on "earnestness," "too pervasive to be coincidence," according to Stanley Weintraub.[22] If Shaw's borrowings reflect rivalry, they are nonetheless used in a non-rivalrous spirit. Wilde wants to show that the name (the appearance) is more important than the thing (the reality). Shaw, in contrast and more conventionally, wants to show that name differences really point to more fundamental differences. *You Never Can Tell* actually produces the missing father so that a reconciliation and a marriage can go forward, and it does not so much pun on the word "earnest," like Wilde's play, as show how jesting and earnestness are closely related. Wilde's farce is in every sense gay throughout, its earnestness consisting of keeping out any judgment that forces a distinction between levels of seriousness, whereas Shaw's play, in his own opinion, "ought to be a very serious comedy, dancing gaily to a happy ending round the grim earnest of Mrs. Clandon's marriage and her XIXth century George Eliotism" (quoted by Raby, *A Reader's Companion*, p. 17).

The Devil's Disciple is subtitled a melodrama, and, accordingly, a morality of good and evil is well defined in it, but with a Shavian twist, as the play attempts to imitate the "diabolonian ethics" of Blake's "The Marriage of Heaven and Hell" in which good is aligned with a conventional Christianity and evil with a vitalistic one. The moral underpinning of the play is a kind of vitalism (a better term for it than Shaw's prefatory phrase "diabolonian ethics"), but it is no less a melodrama for that. Wilde's play has moments (like the final recognition scene) that imitate the *form* of melodrama, but, as Katharine Worth comments about Miss Prism's recognition of her long-lost handbag, "no melodramatic morality could survive the absurdity of this" (Bloom, *"The Importance"* p. 74). The structure of his play also allows Shaw to differentiate his characters' moral positions more finely than before, and thus sets off his art of characterization all the more clearly from Wilde's. The Dudgeon uncles who assemble for the reading of the will are satirized as hypocrites keeping up appearances, but Mrs. Dudgeon, though like them in this, verges on being a tragic figure as well since we are allowed to sense her bitter frustration, and it is pertinent to remember that Shaw modeled her on two of Dickens's tragicomic mothers, Mrs. Clenham and Mrs. Gargery. Richard's brother Christie is too doltish even to have an understanding of good and evil except as a mere form of words, while Richard himself is clever enough to understand these words in so original a sense that he confuses or frightens all the others – except of course, for different reasons, Parson Anderson and General Burgoyne. This is the first play Shaw wrote in which there are two heroes, the "saint" and the "soldier" (about which more in a moment), but he also provides two dramatically significant forms of resistance to their heroism. One comes from Anderson's wife Judith, described in stage directions merely as *"a sentimental character formed by dreams,"* but, though she remains confused and must be set down as one of Shaw's conventional idealists, she makes some telling protests against the inhuman aspect of the heroism of both her husband and the man whose self-sacrificing deed arouses her love. The other form of resistance to heroism comes from Burgoyne, whose role is not a large part in terms of lines but is likely to steal the show. Although lacking any itch for a higher vision (and wittily remarking on such desire in Richard), Burgoyne is free of the cant of his time and class, as shown in his scorn for Colonel Swindon, and he is, in contrast to Swindon, utterly self-possessed. According to the terms of *The Quintessence of Ibsenism*, he is less the idealist than the Philistine, but his candor gives him strength to match the strength of the Realist. (An earlier version of the role is Mrs. Warren, a later Ann Whitefield, both conscious hypocrites whom Shaw admires for using rather than being used by their society.)

The two heroes of *The Devil's Disciple* both have executive power; acting in a crisis with sudden courage, Richard saves Anderson and Anderson saves the town. The minister-turned-soldier is bolder in a physical sense, but the scapegrace-turned-minister is the hero whose motives the play is interested in. Why does Richard do it? He tells us that "a law of [his] own nature" prevented him from allowing another man to die in his place, and he implies that a particular other man, Anderson, inspired the elevation of his own character. Judith of course wants to believe he did it for love of her – wrong, to be sure, but Act 2 does suggest that it was in fact a reaction *against* the lower happiness of marriage and domestic tranquility that stimulated his access of moral strength. Perhaps the two motivational lines are congruent because Shaw at this time was working out (in what would become the argument of *The Perfect Wagnerite*, published in 1898) a dialectical or Hegelian conception of heroism that "attempts to formulate its own revolt against itself as it develops into something higher." I quote from the 1898 preface to *Candida*, a play whose Marchbanks, a poet tempted by domesticity but plunging at last out into the night (presumably toward a more heroic future), anticipates such a conception. The role of Dick Dudgeon develops this conception, and one might say that Shaw's Caesar – along with his critical interpretation of Wagner's Siegfried – provides its culmination.

The conception is evolutionary. Wilde himself as a man of his time was influenced by the idea of an evolutionary progress in social, not merely biological life, as he shows in "The Soul of Man Under Socialism." Evolution is the law of life, he says, and evolution will lead us to to further individualism, further self-realization, through the elimination of degrading poverty. But that is pretty much as far as his interest in the idea extends whereas Shaw was becoming deeply committed to an idea of "creative evolution." A two-pronged attack on both the rich and the poor remained an important part of his political philosophy, but what was required also was raising the moral level of the individual, and the principal agency of this improvement was the will, an unconscious force but one working inexorably and capable of enlisting something like conscious participation ("a will of which I am a part" is Andrew Undershaft's phrasing of the idea). Wilde does not attempt to represent any such idea dramatically but Shaw does, and this ideological difference can account for the difference in the tone of their satire. When it is a question of protesting some form of moral degradation, Wilde's touch is light, as when (in *A Woman of No Importance*) his dandy scores an Englishman galloping after a fox as "the unspeakable in full pursuit of the uneatable." A comparable protest in Shaw, the opening stage directions of *The Devil's Disciple*, aimed at the slaughter of the Revolutionary War, is Swiftian in style: "their *idealizations . . . convinced both Americans and English that the most highminded course for them to pursue is to kill as many of one another as possible.*"

During the half century between Wilde's death (1900) and Shaw's (1950), Shaw's reputation was high and Wilde's depressed. But this has been reversed during the second half of the twentieth century, and Shaw may be said once again, in a different way, to be shadowed by Wilde. Since Wilde is not self-evidently a stronger writer, and was certainly a less prolific one, the change is worth inquiring into by way of concluding this essay.

Wilde's increased appeal in our day has to do primarily, I think, with his tapping into our postmodern skepticism regarding objectivity, truth, and art. One is inclined to trace this skepticism back to Nietzsche, and, in so far as this is justified, it is significant that Nietzsche's influence in the first half of the century (on such writers as Yeats, Lawrence, Dreiser, London, and O'Neill) concerned mainly the question of power whereas in the second half it has concerned mainly the question of truth. Although Wilde remains a late Romantic and not a postmodern figure, he wrote with memorable flair about objectivity as an aspect of subjectivity, of truth as an aspect of fiction, and of art as an aspect of criticism.

Matthew Arnold famously told us, in "The Function of Criticism at the Present Time," that the critic's aim is "to see the object as in itself it really is." Walter Pater subtly altered this in his Preface to *The Renaissance*: "in aesthetic criticism the first step towards seeing one's object as it really is, is to know one's impression as it really is . . ." And Wilde, in "The Critic as Artist," sharpens Pater's idea to the point of wit and at the risk of absurdity: the true aim of the critic is "to see the object as in itself it really is not" (*Works*, p. 1030). Criticism had long wrestled with the problem that fiction can be seen as either a kind of truth or a kind of lying, but Wilde with engaging boldness puts this question to the side and, in "The Decay of Lying," locates as crucial the distinction between splendid lying and vulgar misrepresentation. As for Art, of course that word is often a shibboleth in Wilde's work, but in "The Critic as Artist" (a title phrase meant to startle but which would pass today as *un*remarkable), art is shown to be, paradoxically, an aspect of an activity traditionally considered subordinate to it: "There is no such thing as Shakespeare's Hamlet," his Gilbert declares, going on to develop the idea not only that critics see different things but that they ought to, because individuality is developed in the act of reading (*Works*, p. 1034). Shaw could never have written, as Wilde did, "It is the spectator and not life that art really mirrors" (*Collected Letters*, p. 268). And such a view is flattered by the critical biases of our own time.

On the other side of the equation, some Shavian values, especially those involved with socialism and communism, have suffered a clear loss of prestige in the latter half of the twentieth century. The fault of course is not Shaw's. A socialist ethos was in the intellectual air at the turn of the century whether one was strictly a socialist or not, but it is in the air no more. Our society, our technological civilization, faces problems that seem intractable to us and that Shaw was not in a position even to recognize. We hope now for survival or mitigation, hardly for the sort of moral progress that formed the basis of his vision. Self-improvement is not a dead idea, but the notion of collectively improving the quality of human beings by either political or biological means seems to most of us impracticable, perhaps even dangerous.

Harold Bloom sums up sharply the current reputation of the two writers: "the Aesthetic Vision of Pater and Wilde now appears to be Ruskin's abiding legacy, while Shaw's Fabian Evolution would seem to have been a Ruskinian dead end." (*George Bernard Shaw*, p. 2). Bloom, however, underrates Shaw both as stylist and as artist (vs. propagandist). Where the comedies of the nineties now appear weakest is not in being too doctrinaire but too timid. The Petkoff pretensions (library, bell, bathing more than once a week) and the seductions at century's end of "Byronism," the weak Victorianism of the parental generation in *You Never Can Tell*, the attempt to establish Richard as "the devil's disciple" because he is said to consort with smugglers and gypsies – such stuff is too easy, not vigorously enough imagined. But where the dramatic effect centers, in the tension between a heroic style of feeling and thinking and what resists or opposes it, the plays still come alive.

Finally the difference between the artistic goals of these two masters of dramatic comedy should not, I think, be expressed in terms of aesthetic evaluation but in psychological and historical terms. Shavian comedy seeks to resolve the will and firm up ego boundaries, Wildean comedy to dissolve the will and loosen ego boundaries – and both goals, although entailing different comic effects, can give audiences pleasure. Historically, Shaw derives from the Enlightenment; his test for art is whether it is true to "real life" and the "real world" – phrases used repeatedly in his 1894 essay, "A Dramatic Realist to His Critics." Wilde, in contrast, derives from the Romantic movement and tests art by its unreality, the vividness of its artifice: in his "Phrases and Philosophies for the Use of the Young," he tells us that "The first duty in life is to be as artificial as possible" (*Works*, p. 1205). I wish to avoid stating the comparison invidiously. One may have a preference here but it is not one that can be defended on strictly aesthetic grounds. As far as we can see, both playwrights will continue to hold their audiences for some time to come.

NOTES

1 The basis for this inference is a remark of Shaw's in his 1916 letter to Frank
Harris published as a preface to Harris's *Life of Wilde* and reprinted by Shaw
with minor changes in *Pen Portraits and Reviews*, vol. XXIX of *The Works of
Bernard Shaw* (London: Constable, 1930–38). I quote it from this source (cited
hereafter as *Pen Portraits*), p. 300: "Robert Ross surprised me greatly by telling
me, long after Oscar's death, that it was this address of mine that moved Oscar
to try his hand at a similar feat by writing 'The Soul of Man Under Socialism'."

2 *Bernard Shaw: The Search for Love* (New York: Random House, 1988), p. 210.

3 *Shaw's People: Victoria to Churchill* (University Park: Pennsylvania State
University Press, 1996), pp. 31–32. One might add that *Arms and the Man* was
first produced in 1894, *Candida* in 1897, *Mrs. Warren's Profession* in 1902,
and *The Philanderer* (professionally) in 1907.

4 Richard Ellmann, *Oscar Wilde* (New York: Knopf, 1987), p. 373.

5 Letter of May 9, 1889 to David J. O'Donoghue, in *Bernard Shaw: Collected
Letters*, ed. Dan H. Laurence (New York: Dodd, Mead, 1965), vol. I, p. 210.

6 Letter of November 19, 1894 to R. Golding Bright (*Collected Letters*, p. 460).
Shaw further defended Wilde in another letter to Bright (*Ibid.*, p. 480).

7 *Our Theatres in the Nineties: Criticism Contributed Week by Week to The
Saturday Review from January 1895 to May 1898 in Three Volumes*, in *The
Works of Bernard Shaw*, vol. XXIII, pp. 9–12. Hereafter cited as *Our Theatres*,
vol. XXIII (or vol. XXIV).

8 On *Lady Windermere's Fan*, see the comment tucked into Shaw's self-interview
concerning *Widowers' Houses*, "The Playwright on His First Play" (hereafter
cited as "Playwright'), reprinted in *The Bodley Head Bernard Shaw: Collected
Plays with their Prefaces*, ed. Dan H. Laurence (London: Max Reinhardt, The
Bodley Head, 1970), vol. I, p. 127. See also Ellmann, *Wilde*, p. 397. On *A
Woman of No Importance*, see Shaw, *Letters*, p. 491. Shaw also commended
Wilde generally as a playwright in *Our Theatres*, vol. XXIII (p. 115) and vol.
XXIV (p. 228).

9 In trying to understand Shaw's judgment of *Earnest*, one should consider also
that "heartless" is in this connection a peculiarly loaded word. Shaw had
applied it to himself in his letters to Ellen Terry and would again in those to
Mrs. Campbell. The Devil of *Man and Superman*, a Wildean figure, applies it to
the Shavian Don Juan. The critic A. B. Walkley, the addressee of the Epistle
Dedicatory, had implied it when he wrote of Shaw's plays generally (in 1902,
just before the Epistle was written): "No character exhibits real emotion"
(*Drama and Life* [Freeport, NY: Books Libraries Press, 1967], p. 45). Finally, it
is a word Wilde also used in his plays concerning characters like himself: Lord
Goring in *An Ideal Husband* is several times called "heartless" by his father, and
Algernon by Jack in *The Importance of Being Earnest* – and of course Shaw had
very recently seen these two plays.

10 *The Letters of Oscar Wilde*, ed. Rupert Hart-Davis (New York: Harcourt, Brace
& World, 1962), p. 332.

11 Sally Peters makes much of the words "branded" and "outcast," concluding that
Shaw himself inclined to homosexuality. (See her *Bernard Shaw: The Ascent of
the Superman* [New Haven: Yale University Press, 1996], p. 226 and

throughout). The record of his life and work does not support such an inference, nor do these words in context, which respond to Wilde's diction, require it. Shaw's sexual imagination was governed not by homoerotic but by mother-related incestuous wishes. Shaw's view of Wilde's homosexuality, moreover, was emotionally neutral, unlike his view of Wilde's drinking and other personal failings. His most direct comment on Wilde's homosexuality reflects the prejudices of its time, mitigated by a measure of enlightened doubt: "My charity to his perversion, and my recognition of the fact that it does not imply any general depravity or coarseness of character came to me through reading and observation, not through sympathy. I have all the normal, violent repugnance to homosexuality – if it be really normal, which nowadays one is sometimes provoked to doubt" (*Pen Portraits*, p. 303).

12 *Complete Works of Oscar Wilde*, introd. Vyvyan Holland (London: Collins, 1968), p. 163.

13 *Shaw's Moral Vision: The Self and Salvation* (Ithaca: Cornell University Press, 1976).

14 Harold Bloom, ed. and introd., *Modern Critical Views: George Bernard Shaw* (New York: Chelsea House, 1987), pp. 2, 10.

15 Ellen Moers, in *The Dandy: Brummell to Beerbohm* (New York: Viking, 1960), defines the dandy, which "haunted the Victorian imagination," as "a man dedicated solely to his own perfection through a ritual of taste. The epitome of selfish irresponsibility, he was ideally free of all human commitments that conflict with taste: passions, moralities, ambitions, politics, or occupations" (p. 13). Wilde, Beerbohm, and the new dandies of the 1890s, she implies, carried Brummell's sartorial "art of the pose" into literature, using wit, epigram, and paradox "to confound the bourgeois" (p. 288).

16 *Oscar Wilde* (New York: New Directions, 1947), p. 138.

17 In Harold Bloom, ed. and introd., *Modern Critical Interpretations: "The Importance of Being Earnest"* (New York: Chelsea House, 1988), p. 12. Hereafter cited as Bloom, *"The Importance."*

18 *"The Importance of Being Earnest': A Reader's Companion* (New York: Twayne, 1995), p. 34.

19 "Is insincerity such a terrible thing? I think not. It is merely a method by which we can multiply our personalities." This is from *The Picture of Dorian Gray* (*Works*, p. 112), and almost the same phrasing is used in "The Critic as Artist" (*Works*, p. 1048): "What people call insincerity is simply a method by which we can multiply our personalities."

20 R. W. Ellis (ed.), *Bernard Shaw and Karl Marx: A Symposium* (New York: Random House, 1930), p. 6.

21 Originally the final words were simply: "What a man! What a man!" (British Library Additional MS 50601). The change incorporates a suggestion of inhumanity in the superman. In Cecil Lewis's film version of the play, the phrasing was changed back to its original form, presumably to spare the audience a subtle effect.

22 *Shaw's People*, p. 51. See also Peters, *Ascent*, p. 227; and Raby, *A Reader's Companion*, pp. 93–96.

FURTHER READING

Beckson, Karl, *London in the 1890s: A Cultural History*, New York: Norton, 1992.

Beerbohm, Max, *Around Theatres*, New York: Taplinger, 1969, pp. 118–22, 188–91, 491–93.

Bloom, Harold, *The Anxiety of Influence: A Theory of Poetry*, London: Oxford University Press, 1973.

Brophy, Brigid, "The Great Celtic/Hibernian School," *Grand Street* 7:4 (1988), pp. 175–82.

Carpenter, Charles A., *Bernard Shaw and the Art of Destroying Ideals: The Early Plays*, Madison: University of Wisconsin Press, 1969.

Crompton, Louis, *Shaw the Dramatist*, Lincoln: University of Nebraska Press, 1969, chapters 2 to 6.

Dukore, Bernard, "Dolly Finds a Father: Shaw's Dramatic Development," *Papers on Language and Literature*, Winter 24:1 (1988), pp. 81–90.

Gagnier, Regenia, *Idylls of the Marketplace: Oscar Wilde and the Victorian Public*, Stanford: Stanford University Press, 1986.

Ganz, Arthur, *George Bernard Shaw*, London: Macmillan, 1983, chapter 4.

Gordon, David J., *Bernard Shaw and the Comic Sublime*, London: Macmillan, 1990.

Harris, Frank, *Oscar Wilde including "My Memories of Oscar Wilde" by George Bernard Shaw*, East Lansing: Michigan State University Press, 1959.

Hyde, Mary (ed. and introd.), *Bernard Shaw and Alfred Douglas: A Correspondence*, New Haven: Ticknor & Fields, 1982, pp. xi–xli.

Joseph, Gerhard, "Framing Wilde," in Regenia Gagnier (ed.), *Critical Essays on Oscar Wilde*, New York: G. K. Hall and Co., 1991, pp. 179–85.

Laurence, Dan (ed.), *The Bodley Head Bernard Shaw: Collected Plays with their Prefaces*, vol. I, London: Max Reinhardt, The Bodley Head, 1970.

McDowell, Frederick P. W., "Shaw's 'Higher Comedy' Par Excellence: *You Never Can Tell*," *The Annual of Bernard Shaw Studies* 7, ed. Alfred Turco, Jr., University Park: Pennsylvania State University Press, 1987, pp. 63–83.

Sedgwick, Eve Kosovsky, *Epistemology of the Closet*, Berkeley: University of California Press, 1990, chapter 3.

Valency, Maurice, *The Cart and the Trumpet: The Plays of Bernard Shaw*, New York: Oxford University Press, 1973, pp. 104–70.

Weiss, Samuel A., "Shaw, *Arms and the Man*, and the Bulgarians," *The Annual of Bernard Shaw Studies* 10, eds. Stanley Weintraub and Fred. D. Crawford, University Park: Pennsylvania State University Press, 1990, pp. 27–44.

Wisenthal, J. L., "Wilde, Shaw and the Play of Conversation," *Modern Drama*, 37:1 (1994), pp. 206–19.

7

FREDRIC BERG

Structure and philosophy in *Man and Superman* and *Major Barbara*

UNDERSHAFT: [startled] A Secularist! Not the least in the world: on the contrary, a confirmed mystic.

(*Major Barbara, Collected Plays*, vol. III, p. 110)[1]

Although very much a participant in the secular fervor of his times, Bernard Shaw, like his creation Andrew Undershaft, was also a confirmed mystic, and gradually this mysticism led him to a long-range solution to human problems, a solution he called the Life Force and a philosophy he called Creative Evolution. Over time, Shaw's plays became less social diatribes and more parables addressing what he saw as the basic human paradox: by the time the human mind begins to achieve its potential, the human body is ready for the dustbin. Creative Evolution, and its concurrent human development, were therefore based on a premise that that which furthered the evolution of the species toward the true development of the intellect was good, and that which hindered it was bad.

However, Shaw was aware of the need for clearly defined dramatic structures which would support his polemics without reducing the text to a lecture and the audience to lecturegoers. While he utilized many of the structures of the nineteenth-century theatre, the basic structure most often found in Shavian drama is the triangle, with its strong character conflicts allowing him to present his theories in a form that could both amuse and educate on stage.

This idea of a triangle, comprising three opposing points of view, as the basic structural element in Shaw is not new: he himself first called attention to it in the guise of his discussion of Ibsenism, where he labeled its three components the Realist, the Idealist and the Philistine.[2] Others have labeled the triangles by their plot components: the Father/Daughter/Suitor triangle, the Two-Suitor triangle, etc. I propose another nomenclature, using the characters Shaw himself placed in two corners of the triangle in *Man and Superman*, the Superman and the Devil, and naming the third corner by its function, the Object of their conflict. However, I am not using the term Superman in the Nietzschean, nor the term Devil in the Miltonic, senses. Rather, I mean them as the personification on stage of the basic conflict in all of Shaw's work: the battle between those who serve Creative Evolution, attacking "what is" and advocating the new, the different, the difficult, the unconventional; and those who unwittingly foil the progress of Creative Evolution by defending the old, the *status quo*, the easy, the conventional.

Although it was not until *Man and Superman* that Shaw assigned the attacker the title of Superman and the defender that of Devil, these terms can be carried backward and applied to characters and attitudes found from his first play onward. In these earlier plays, Shaw was defining and then refining this basic triangular dramatic structure and exploring how it could be best utilized to express his developing idea of the Superman, an idea he was attempting to present not abstractly, as a philosophical or literary conceit, but as an active dramatic character functioning within a framework of dramatic conflict. Whereas the contextual positions of the Superman and Devil are fixed, the Object is a variable whose movement propels much of the dramatic action of each play.

It is in *Man and Superman*, Shaw's first play of the twentieth century, that these character and philosophical concerns first clearly converged. This is the play in which Shaw first turned away from the nineteenth-century dramatic structures which had originally supported his work and began to develop the new forms which would sustain his later plays and influence the theatre of the twentieth century. Structurally, as Margery M. Morgan has noted: "The crux of *Man and Superman*, is the relation of the Hell scene in Act III to the rest of the play. Without it, as F. P. W. McDowell has observed, the title Shaw gave the whole is reduced to a mere quip: 'Superman' could only have reference to the woman who overrules the man."[3] Shaw, in his preface to the play, sanctioned the cutting of the entire third act including the dream sequence which has come to be known as *Don Juan in Hell*. However, to do so strips the play of its philosophical import, leaving only a basic Shavian comedy – granted, no small accomplishment – but not the first great play of the twentieth century.

What are the triangular structures of both the inner and outer plays; how are they constituted; how do they operate within both plays; how do they tie the two plays together? An examination of these questions will not only show the interdependence of the inner and outer plays, but also how they combine to express Shaw's philosophical purpose.

Does one triangle describe both the inner and outer plays? Shaw is very clear which characters in the outer play embody the characters in the inner one, and hence the triangle in the inner play is obvious. Shaw designates the

11 The "inner" triangle: the Hell scene, with Carole Shelley, Tony van Bridge,
Ian Richardson, Norman Welsh in the Shaw Festival's 1977 production of
Man and Superman

character in one corner of the triangle to be the Devil, the defender of Hell where the easy, conventional life holds sway; accords the position of Superman to his philosophical opponent Don Juan, the defender of Heaven where the few who see its import strive to bring about the higher life; and establishes that it is the newcomer to the afterlife, Doña Ana, who is the Object of their conflicting arguments. (The Statue is clearly shown to have already chosen Hell, although he can acknowledge the soundness of certain of Juan's arguments.) Although there are overtones of convention and unconvention in the two positions (always keeping in mind Shaw's unconventional idea of what is Heaven and what Hell), the philosophical differences between the two are far greater than these simple terms, extending beyond actions and behavior to purposes and reasons.

Given this triangle in the inner play, the triangle in the outer play obviously should be Tanner as Superman, Mendoza as Devil, and Ann as

Object. But how much philosophical difference is there between Tanner and Mendoza; in what context are we to see the former as unconventional when compared to the latter? Their politics are basically the same; each is a socialist, with a clear-eyed view of his economic situation:

MENDOZA: I am a brigand: I live by robbing the rich.
TANNER: I am a gentleman: I live by robbing the poor.

(*Collected Plays*, vol. II, p. 621)

Moreover, each is the most conventional of lovers. Tanner is the last to know that Ann has set her cap for him, and the least effective in dealing with her when he does know; Mendoza is a hopeless romantic, who has taken to a life of brigandage only in response to rejection of his love. It is true that Tanner runs while Mendoza swoons, but this difference is the result of the responses of their respective lovers, and again underscores their romantic conventionality. It is hard to view these two as Superman and Devil, notwithstanding the fact that Mendoza, outside of Act 3, hardly exists as a character in the outer play.

Beyond this, is Ann the Object; is she in any way converted by either of the men? On the contrary, it is she who is unchanging throughout the outer play, at all times certain of what she wants and how to go about getting it, and it is she who converts Tanner, while having little if anything to do with Mendoza. It is only as Doña Ana, in the inner play, that Ann is uncertain, and then only while the others are dealing in abstractions. When a concrete need is announced, that of a mother for the Superman, she immediately announces herself ready to fill the position. Moreover, the opposite is true of Tanner and Mendoza. They, as Superman and Devil, are quite at home amid the philosophical abstractions of the inner play, each certain of and unconvertible from his position; whereas in the outer play, their absolute certainty of the rightness of their positions leads to their constantly making fools of themselves.

With the inner triangle fixed, and the absence of one triangle tying together the inner and outer plays, we are forced to look elsewhere for the triangle in the outer play. What are the needs of this triangle; specifically, must it have Tanner as the Superman? Other than his dreaming himself so in Act 3, is there any justification for placing him in this position? As Eric Bentley has pointed out:

Tanner is a windbag. Indeed, the mere fact of the woman courting the man would probably not yield comedy at all were it not for a further and more dynamic reversal: the woman, who makes no great claim for herself, has all the shrewdness, the real *Lebensweisheit*, while the man, who knows everything and can discourse like Bernard Shaw, is – a fool. Tanner is, in fact, like

Molière's Alceste, the traditional fool of comedy in highly sophisticated intellectual disguise. Ann Whitefield, into whose trap Tanner falls, is the knave – in skirts.[4]

Not only is Ann more unconventional than Tanner, she is also more committed. She cannot (or will not) name it, but Ann Whitefield is in service to a cause: the Shavian Life Force. Instinctively, she understands the need to improve the species through generational reproduction, the constant striving upward toward "a mind's eye that shall see, not the physical world, but the purpose of Life, and thereby enable the individual to work for that purpose instead of thwarting and baffling it by setting up shortsighted personal aims as at present" (p. 663). It is this battle between the Life Force and "shortsighted personal aims" which is the Superman/Devil conflict in the outer play, and in this context it is easy to locate the Superman, Devil, and Object, and to see how the dramatic structure of the triangle sustains Shaw's agenda.

On one side is Ann, the instinctive Superman. Not only can she not articulate or defend her position, to be able to do so would betray her position. For articulating and defending a position is serving the shortsighted personal aims of the Devil. Man (used here as a non gender-specific term), as s/he exists in the real world of the outer play, does not have the Superman's capacity to deal with ideas or philosophies; our humanness keeps getting in our way. We are constantly sidetracked by egotism, the need for love, social proprieties, class differentials, political ideologies, and so forth. It is only in the incorporeal realms, where we will be free of our human failings, that we will have the ability and the time (eons and eons of it) to develop, shape, debate and reshape ideas worth having. In the brief life span that we know, the human brain has only time to begin to function, only time to begin to assimilate all of experience and digest it into a coherent philosophy. Before we can begin to do justice to our ideas, our bodies begin to fail us; our short-lived brains begin to deteriorate and all the great thinking we are poised to achieve is lost forever. The Shavian Life Force is the means of freeing the intellect from its corporeal bonds, of defeating this dichotomy of body and brain, the "*misalliance*" of a later play.

Shaw introduces this concept early in both the outer and inner plays. Ramsden's comment on Ann's father's death, "its the common lot, we must all face it some day" (p. 535), states the reason why all should be serving the Life Force. Later, Doña Ana tells Juan that she was "younger [at 70]: at 30 I was a fool" (p. 637). But of what use is it to feel younger (i.e. be smarter) at 70 when your body cannot sustain this and you will only be taking this greater wisdom to the grave? If we lived "*as far as thought can reach*" (the title Shaw gave to his only play portraying the results of Creative Evolution), we could keep applying this wisdom to gain ever newer and greater wisdom.

Arrayed against Ann are a variety of Devils, for every man in the outer play is in the service of shortsighted personal aims. The first, and easiest to see, is Roebuck Ramsden (whose name evokes his bull-in-a-china-shop approach). Ramsden is the Devil of temporal social/political/economical ideas, theories which, as Shaw makes clear, are transitory: in this "drama of ideas . . . everything depends on whether his adolescence belongs to the sixties or the eighties" (p. 534). Twenty years ago, Ramsden was in the forefront of social thought, on the so-called "cutting edge." But the slash of this cutting edge is quick; in twenty years Ramsden's ideas have become conservative and accepted. They have been replaced by those of the man one generation his junior, John Tanner.

Tanner certainly can be seen as unconventional when compared with Ramsden in the world of social ideas, but this is an ever changing condition: Ramsden was once the man of unconventional ideas, and Tanner's ideas will also become conventional with time. It is not radicals who become conservative with age; rather, radical ideas become accepted, and hence become conservative. For Shaw, truly unconventional people keep changing their ideas to stay on the cutting edge; staying true not to a set of ideas, but rather to the idea of new ideas.

Accordingly, in Act 1, Ramsden is the Devil, believing ideas are all-important (whether they be conventional or unconventional); and Tanner is the Object, who begins the play as the devil's disciple, in revolt about the specifics of ideas, but not their importance. Opposing them is Ann, the Superman, knowing (instinctively) that all ideas are transitory, and that the real importance is serving the Life Force by propagating the species. In the overall action of the outer play, she will convert Tanner to the service of the Life Force, away from political and social actions which are shortsighted personal aims, self-satisfying but unproductive. However, as her last line indicates, if he will serve the Life Force she will let him keep playing with his toys or ideas: "Never mind her, dear. Go on talking" (p. 733). (On the other hand, Ramsden, like Shaw, has never served the Life Force; he has no biological children, only godchildren and wards.)

But Ramsden is not the only Devil in the play; how could he be, for after Act 1 Ramsden himself is barely in the play? Instead, Shaw introduces a new Devil in each act: Straker in Act 2, Mendoza in Act 3 and Malone Sr. in Act 4. Not only do they serve to keep reenergizing the action, these three characters make up their own triangle of men who might appear to be Supermen in the real world: the mechanic (master of machines), the

12 An "outer" triangle: Act 1 of *Man and Superman* with Julie Stewart as Violet Robinson, Kate Trotter as Ann Whitefield, and Michael Ball as John Tanner in the Shaw Festival's 1989 production

romantic adventurer (master of his soul), and the new industrialist (who is buying mastery of England's social and historical institutions). But each of them is serving a shortsighted personal aim, and each of these characters can be said to be the Devil in his act, the representative of the temporally important.

Hence, in Act 2, Straker is the Devil. His machines, like Ramsden's ideas, will soon become outdated and be replaced by ever newer machines; it is he who tells Tanner of Ann's intentions, precipitating Tanner's flight and temporarily short-circuiting the workings of the Life Force; and both here and in Act 3, he is as full of middle-class morality as any Shavian Devil. Nevertheless, Shaw has a fondness for this Devil of machinery, because however temporary each specific machine, machinery itself can help to bring about the longer-lived bodies the Life Force is seeking. Accordingly, he gives Straker some "new" ideas about class and heritage (although these "new" ideas will also become outmoded and replaced), and he allows Straker to see through Tanner as Tanner saw through Ramsden: Straker's knowing description of his boss, "he likes to talk" (p. 589), is a preview of Ann's last line. As the Devil of the short Act 2, which bridges the real world of Act 1 and the eternity world of Act 3, Straker stands halfway between man and Superman and serves as a possible bridge between them.

Mendoza, the Devil in Act 3, sees himself as a romantic adventurer, but romance or love is not necessary to serve the Life Force and in fact emotions tend to get in its way. Moreover, Mendoza's adventures belong spiritually to Louisa and financially to Malone Sr. For all his bluster, he is passively fatalistic; sharing more than his occupation with William Boon, the waiter who believes *"you never can tell."* Ironically, although he is the Act 3 Devil, it is he who impedes Tanner's flight, thereby serving rather than hindering the Life Force.

While a representative character in his own right, Mendoza is also Octavius Robinson's surrogate in Act 3. Tavy is too young and poetic to be Shaw's idea of *the* Devil; for that Shaw needs an older, more experienced cynic like Mendoza, who provides a better opponent for Tanner than the easily vanquished Tavy. Shaw is continuing a dichotomy he has used in previous plays, the practical man versus the poet: Bluntschli and Sergius in *Arms and the Man*, Morell and Marchbanks in *Candida*, Anderson and Dudgeon in *The Devil's Disciple*; but here it is a dichotomy of romantic Devils, as if to reposition his previous "real world" Supermen.

Finally, Hector Malone Sr., the Devil in Act 4, has the pride and arrogance that comes with money. He believes he can buy anything – his son's obedience or an English abbey – by offering or withholding his wealth (which, like all things temporal has no value in the eternity world of the Superman). But the industrialist is at the mercy of the same parochial pride that drove him to seek wealth, and he would stand in the way of his son's happiness to assuage his Irish need to best the English. His son, meanwhile, is the mirror of his father and would condemn his wife to poverty to satisfy his pride. Fortunately, both are easily manipulated by Violet, who, being pregnant, is in even greater service to the Life Force than Ann, but has a Devil's commitment to the shortsighted personal aims of money.

Thus, Ramsden may be called the shortsighted Devil of ideas, Straker of machinery, Mendoza and Tavy of love, and the Malones (including Violet) of money, and the complete triangle for the outer play, with one Superman and seven Devils, expresses just how weighted down the real world is against the true Superman. However, Shaw does not rigidly stratify these Devils, and thus the Devil of ideas, Ramsden, does not understand Ann because of his romantic illusions about her; while the romantic Devil, Mendoza, leads a group of scruffy brigands who spend more time debating ideas than snatching purses.

In a world populated by so many shortsighted Devils, the Life Force demands a man worthy of serving it, and it is indicative of Ann's Superman qualities that she can recognize Tanner as such. Although in the throes of shortsighted personal aims – *The Revolutionist's Handbook* – Tanner has integrity and honor; he means to do the right thing, but as he never understands what is really happening, his good impulses lead him into foolishness. In Act 1, his decent motivations coupled with his misunderstanding of Violet lead him to make a fool of himself; and to show us that he has learned nothing during the course of the play, he does the same in Act 4 with Hector. In addition, he is impossibly dense in realizing that he, and not Tavy, is Ann's prey. But his basic goodness, coupled with Ann's basic shrewdness, will combine to produce children with qualities of each, and thus move the species slightly up the evolutionary ladder.

Therefore, the structural triangles of the inner and outer plays do not correspond, and the two parts of *Man and Superman* do not duplicate each other. Rather, they stand in contrast, each commenting upon the other and in combination expressing Shaw's developing philosophy of the true need and place for the Superman. Previously, the Superman had been the defender of a specific secular set of ideas, and Shaw had attempted to establish the character in a theatrical "real world," what Bentley calls "The World As It Is."[5] Here, Shaw is separating the Superman, establishing two different conflicts, two different goals, and two different worlds for her or him to operate in. Only when the Life Force provides the longevity which allows for full development of our mental capacities (now only possible in the death-induced immortality of the inner play) can ideas take primacy; and thus, in "the world as it is," the true Superman eschews the temporal, shortsighted personal aims of ideas (as well as machinery, love, and money) to serve the Life Force. When the needs of the Life Force have been accomplished, when our brains have been advanced to primacy over our bodies, then the Superman of ideas can step forward, and the Superman who serves the Life Force will be useless and out of place.

In the outer play, Ann is the Superman and Tanner the Object, while in the inner play these positions are reversed. In the outer play it is Ann who is effective: manipulating and dominating everyone with whom she comes into contact as she selfishly serves the greater need of the Life Force. Tanner, on the other hand, is, as Bentley says, a fool and a windbag; whose lengthy expressions of bombast Ann neatly deflates, Act by Act: "I am so glad you understand politics, Jack: it will be most useful to you if you go into parliament" (p. 575); "I suppose you will go in seriously for politics someday, Jack" (p. 599); and the aforementioned "Never mind her, dear. Go on talking" (p. 733).

When we move to the inner play, Ann is out of her element. Her concerns are temporal: her appearance, her honor, her reputation, her repentance. She is decidedly a spectator to the central debate, only able to enter fully near the end, when the subject shifts to worldly male–female relations. In the opening scene between Doña Ana and Don Juan, Shaw reverses the roles: he is constantly deflating her bombast. Her final line, "A father for the Superman" (p. 689), expresses her misunderstanding: the Superman already exists and fathers and mothers are useless here, but she is still thinking in those terms. The line is thus ironic, foolish, and transitional, back to the real world of the outer play, where a father for the Superman is a legitimate concern.

Similarly, Tanner goes from being the foolish pamphleteer of the outer play to the insightful exponent of the Shavian philosophy of Creative Evolution in the inner play. His speeches, while rambling at times, are a coherent statement of Shaw's ideas, and although the Devil is certainly given the opportunity to defend his position, often brilliantly, Juan/Tanner/Shaw is never at a loss for ideas or words to counteract the Devil.[6]

Underlying Shaw's theory of Creative Evolution is a belief that the ultimate goal of the Life Force is brain unencumbered by body, pure consciousness which will live eternally. The desire to apply one's will toward this end, is, to Shaw, the work of Heaven, while the passive acceptance of our current state is the sloth of Hell:

> . . . heaven, which is . . . the home of the masters of reality, and . . . earth, which is the home of the slaves of reality. The earth is a nursery in which men and women play at being heroes and heroines, saints and sinners; but they are dragged down from their fool's paradise by their bodies: hunger and cold and thirst, age and decay and disease, death above all, make them the slaves of reality: thrice a day meals must be eaten and digested: thrice a century a new generation must be engendered: ages of faith, of romance, and of science are all driven at last to have but one prayer "Make me a healthy animal." (p. 650)

This same contrast between inner and outer plays holds true in Shaw's use of the Devil. In the outer play there are a number of Devils; in the inner play there is only the Devil of love, Mendoza, for the romantic mind is the most antithetical to that of pure ideas. However, in this eternity of Heaven and Hell, where ideas take primacy, the question of the importance and viability of each specific idea is valid and worth discussing. Hence, the Devil of ideas, Ramsden, also exists in this world. But here he is not *the* Devil, merely a participant. The nature of his ideas precludes his being the Superman, and his rigidity (he is after all a statue) precludes his being the Object. By not being part of the Shavian triangle, he serves as a philosophical ground wire: the voice of middle-class reasoning keeping the philosophical debate anchored to the real world, but without Doña Ana's still existing ties to human concerns. Although he has already decided to throw in his lot with the Devil, he can appreciate the points of the Superman; even the Philistines are more advanced here.

In addition to these triangles, Shaw, in a brilliant twist of stagecraft, uses his own enemies, time (our mortality) and place ("the world as it is") to dramatically support his arguments; time and location underscore the contrast between the two parts of the play. The three acts of the outer play appear to follow the neo-classical unity of time, as all are set in daytime with each progressively a little later (this is indicated but not specified): Act 1 in the mid-morning, Act 2 at noon, Act 4 in the early afternoon. But actually, each is part of a different day and the unity of time is an illusion. Act 3, on the other hand, is set in the evening: out of sequence and thus separated from the others. The first two acts, where Tanner resists the Life Force, are set in England, where the Devil tells us he has "the largest following" (p. 648). The first act, the only interior, is set in an actual drawing room which reflects the act's roots in "drawing room" comedy; the second act is an exterior, but set close to the house: a driveway which serves to connect the (inner) house to the (outer) road, as the act connects the inner and outer plays. The last two acts are set in Spain, earthly home of the eternal Superman, Don Juan, and it is in these two acts that Tanner stops resisting the Life Force. Both are exteriors and both suggestive. Act 3, which contains both the inner and outer plays, is set along a road that is so remote that it could be anywhere at any time, even eternity; whereas Act 4 removes us from the road, suggesting we have reached our destination, and locates us in the garden of a Spanish villa. It is here that the service to Life Force is finally acknowledged, and the garden suggests the mythological starting point of man's evolutionary journey, the Garden of Eden.

Earlier, reference was made to F. W. P. McDowell's claim that without the inner and outer plays the title is "mere quip: 'Superman' could only have reference to the woman who overrules the man." But even a mere Shavian quip can have great depth and profundity, and in this case the title is a paradox which works on a number of levels. In the outer play, McDowell's quip is operative. The title differentiates Tanner and Ann – man and woman, man and Superman – the former the involuntary slave of shortsighted personal aims, the latter the voluntary servant of the long range needs of the Life Force. In the inner play, it both combines man (Tanner) and Superman (Don Juan) intellectually, as well as differentiating them physically: man (corporeal, mortal, inhabitant of the real world these characters have left behind) and Superman (incorporeal, immortal, inhabitant of the eternal world of ideas). Finally, this paradox connects the two plays. The outer play is set in the real world of man, while the inner play is set in the eternal world of the Superman, and the title expresses the basic conflict inherent both in the play and in Shaw's evolving philosophy of the purposes and goals of man and Superman.

Thus, as Michael Holroyd puts it, "the message of *Man and Superman* is that biological progress must precede intellectual development."[7] However, Shaw's next play, the mystical *John Bull's Other Island*, dealt despairingly with the relationships between his native Ireland and adopted England, and perhaps it was the intractability of this relationship (still apparent today) that led him to make another attempt to address man's abilities to influence this world. Three years after *Man and Superman*, Shaw wrote a more worldly and radical version of the demands of Creative Evolution in *Major Barbara*.

> UNDERSHAFT: My religion? Well, my dear, I am a Millionaire. That is my religion.
>
> (*Major Barbara, Collected Plays*, vol. III, p. 111)

If *Man and Superman* argues the limits of intellectual salvation until our bodies catch up with our brains, *Major Barbara* argues the possibility of religious and economic salvation; or more exactly the dependence of the former upon the latter. Shaw is still acknowledging the limitations of the body and man's temporal/corporeal inabilities to change the world; but, as with Straker in the earlier play, he is acknowledging the power of machinery (economics) to do the job, if we are willing to let it and suffer the dislocation of the consequences, including the need to disown our own middle-class morality: "That is what is wrong with the world at present. It scraps its obsolete steam engines and dynamos; but it wont scrap its old prejudices and its old moralities and its old religions . . . Dont persist in that folly. If your old religion broke down yesterday, get a newer and a better one for tomorrow" (p. 171).

Again, the basic structure of the play is triangular: Barbara Undershaft, the Salvation Army lass who is a true believer in her ability to do good in "the world as it is"; her fiancé, Adolphus Cusins, torn between love, religion, and classical thought as the means to serve mankind and hence not quite committing to any; and her father, Andrew Undershaft, who, whatever we may think of it, has a functional philosophy for dealing with the realities of this world, where poverty is "the worst of crimes" (p. 172). (As in *Don Juan in Hell*, this triangle is supplemented with a Philistine ground wire in the character of Lady Britomart.)

However, while the triangle in *Major Barbara* is not difficult to see, it has proven almost impossible for many to accept, for Shaw frames the argument paradoxically, making the merchant of death and destruction the

Superman voice of reason and progress, and the angel of religious mercy the Devilish voice of the easy and ineffective. Just as Tanner must learn the transitory nature of ideas, so Barbara finally realizes that to honestly bring salvation to others, she must first get "rid of the bribe of bread" (p. 184), and, by logical extension, the need for it. Finally, in this triangle it is Cusins who is the Object of this debate, synthesizing both sides by coming to understand Plato's paradox that "society can not be saved until either the Professors of Greek take to making gunpowder, or else the makers of gunpowder become Professors of Greek" (p. 178).

Undershaft, whose morality and religion "must have a place for cannons and torpedoes in it" (p. 90), is Shaw's greatest radical, and as such a true Shavian Superman. Possibly more than any other Shavian character, Undershaft engenders critical disagreement and discussion, even among the other characters in the play who call him "wicked" and "immoral" and refer to him in Devilish terms such as "Mephistopheles" and "The Prince of Darkness." A touchstone of Shavian Realism, he forces us to confront Shaw's premise that to truly serve the Life Force in "the world as it is," one must have Andrew's ruthless philosophy, faith in destruction, and understanding of the need for and sanctity of the dollar which destruction engenders. In three short years, Shaw has moved from an association with Tanner, the younger lover/husband/pamphleteer ineffectually and selfishly saving his bachelorhood, to an association with Undershaft, the mature mentor/father/doer saving souls by making guns.[8]

Barbara, on the other hand, is a Shavian Idealist who is also recognizable as the Devil in the play's triangle. While Shaw begins the play with Barbara as the focus, with her conflict between religion and action prefiguring *Saint Joan*, slowly Undershaft comes to dominate the play, until in the final act Barbara is almost lost in the battle between Andrew and Cusins, as Doña Ana is lost between Don Juan and the Devil. (It is interesting to note that although it is Barbara who is the title character, Shaw originally thought to call the play *Andrew Undershaft's Profession*.) In this regard, the two worlds of *Major Barbara* parallel the two worlds of *Man and Superman*. Like Ann, Barbara is the Superman of her earthly domain, but she has moved beyond Ann, whose domain was strictly private – the domesticity of the drawing room – to dominance in both her private and public worlds – the drawing room and the Salvation Army yard. However, both are temporal domains, and in Perivale St. Andrews, a world where true change can be effected, Barbara, like Ann in Hell, is helpless and overwhelmed. Although she declares herself ready to actively serve Andrew's philosophy, our last view of her is one of childishness: "Mamma! Mamma! I want Mamma" (p. 184).

13 From "Hell" to "Heaven": the triangle of Jim Mezon as Adolphus Cusins, Martha Burns as Barbara Undershaft, and Douglas Rain as Andrew Undershaft in the Shaw Festival's 1987 production of *Major Barbara*

As in *Man and Superman*, *Major Barbara* appears to follow the neo-classical unity of time, without the separate world of eternity: Act 1 takes place in the evening, Act 2 in the morning, Act 3 in the afternoon. But, as before and underscoring Andrew's call for scrapping the old, this is not the classical twenty-four hour day but rather three successive ones. The locations also serve Shaw, and Barbara and Andrew's domains may be seen literally as Hell and Heaven. Unlike the ironic Hell of eternity, the Salvation Army yard is a literal Hell – dirty and poverty-stricken – where the Salvation Army preaches acceptance of the earthly *status quo*, and, giving in to its corporeal needs, shortsightedly takes money for its immediate ends with no realization of long term ruin. Similarly, its clientele exist only in "the world as it is," and will do and say anything for immediate relief – both hypocritically, like Rummy Mitchums and Snobby Price, or sincerely but ineffectually, like Peter Shirley and Bill Walker. Paradoxically, Barbara, the only one to see beyond the immediate need for money, is "cast out" of this Hell as Satan was from Heaven, echoing Jesus' words: "My God: why hast thou forsaken me?" (p. 136).

Perivale St. Andrews, on the other hand, is a literal hilltop Heaven – clean, financially sound, and because of the nature of what is done there – destruction – ripe for salvation; Cusins tells us that "it needs only a Cathedral to be a heavenly city" (p. 158). It is only the Philistines, Lady Britomart and Charles Lomax, who dare express hypocrisy here, and Andrew's other two biological children, Sarah and Stephen, both show themselves ripe for their father's form of salvation.[9] It is here where the needs of serving the Life Force can be properly debated and a realistic plan of action – Cusins's inheritance – put forward. (The third location, Lady Britomart's drawing room, is simply a middle ground, where the domestic issues which drive the plot are discussed and resolved.)

However, while it is easy to see the literal uses of the settings, the Hell of the grimy and hypocritical Salvation Army yard and the Heaven of the hilltop overlooking the paradise of Perivale St. Andrews, it is also possible to look at these settings figuratively, and as such relate them closer to *Man and Superman*. In this view, the Salvation Army yard is the "world as it is," where our corporeal needs prevent us from dealing with the idea of our salvation in any but self-serving ways; and the hilltop overlooking Perivale St. Andrews is, ironically, Hell, the Hell of Don Juan and the Devil, which is a place to debate ideas but not institute them. Accordingly, the unseen town of Perivale St. Andrews is the same as the unseen Heaven of *Man and Superman* – the actual laboratory or crucible where the work of raising the species goes forth; and in the end Barbara and Cusins, like Juan, commit to it.[10]

From this perspective, these two plays form the literature of Shaw's religion of Creative Evolution: *Man and Superman* being the gospel of the Life Force and *Major Barbara* being the parable of the word made flesh. Just as Ann Whitefield must triumph in this world so Don Juan may triumph in the next, Andrew Undershaft must first triumph so Adolphus

Cusins (aided by his wife) can later triumph by bringing true religious and humanistic concerns to the power of Andrew's economic engine. But in *Major Barbara*, Shaw is shortening the time frame, and through his Superman of this world, Andrew, saying that the only way to shorten it to our lifetimes is to "make war on war" (p. 178), through radical and violent means:

> Poverty and slavery have stood up for centuries to your sermons . . . they will not stand up to my machine guns. Dont preach at them: dont reason with them. Kill them . . . When you shoot, you pull down governments, inaugurate new epochs, abolish old orders and set up new. (p. 174)

> Turn your oughts into shalls, man. Come and make explosives with me. Whatever can blow men up can blow society up. The history of the world is the history of those who had courage enough to embrace this truth. (p. 175)

Major Barbara can be seen as Shaw's most realistic and radical play, perhaps his most despairing. Blow it all up and start over, he seems to be saying; radical change is necessary and without it we can only wait and hope for the long haul of Creative Evolution. To accomplish any significant change now will require much more than bread and treacle, erudite knowledge of dead languages and ideas, or even conventional moral horror.

However, although he would later become fascinated by what he perceived as attempts to do so on both the political left (Stalin in Russia) and the political right (Mussolini in Italy), at heart Shaw knew that neither he nor we really want to take so radical a step, and thus we must continue to serve the Life Force and await the slow, continual progress of Creative Evolution.

NOTES

1 All quotations are from *The Bodley Head Bernard Shaw: Collected Plays with Their Prefaces*, vols. II (*Man and Superman*) and III (*Major Barbara*), ed. Dan H. Laurence (London: Max Reinhardt, The Bodley Head, 1971).

2 For a fuller discussion of these terms and their application to specific Shavian characters, see Arthur H. Nethercot, *Men and Supermen: The Shavian Portrait Gallery* (Cambridge, MA: Harvard University Press, 1954).

3 Margery M. Morgan, *The Shavian Playground: An Exploration of the Art of George Bernard Shaw* (London: Methuen, 1972), p. 100. The reference is to F. P. W. McDowell, "Heaven, Hell and Turn-of-the-Century London: Reflections upon Shaw's *Man and Superman*," *Drama Survey* 2, no. 3 (February 1963), pp. 245–68.

4 Eric Bentley, *Bernard Shaw* (reprint edn., New York: Proscenium Publishers, 1975), p. 170.

5 *Ibid.*, p. 170.

6 So long as Juan is expressing Shaw, his arguments are logical and cogent; when Shaw tries to express Juan, when he turns to earthly male–female relations, marriage and fidelity, the arguments become weak and at times foolish. Juan's speech beginning "'Perfectly' is a strong expression" (p. 671), is a perfect example of the holes in Shaw's thinking. He compares a married couple with galley prisoners, but despite Tanner's claims to being railroaded by the Life Force (which may very well be a reflection of Shaw's feelings about his own marriage), one hardly exercises as much choice in entering prison as one does in entering marriage, and married couples are not selected randomly, as Shaw acknowledges that prisoners are: "chain me to the felon whose number *happens* to be next before mine" (italics mine). Moreover, an incompatible marriage can be ended, but even Shaw can't believe jailers to be that accommodating to incompatible galley companions. Even if Shaw is merely arguing for the freedom to remain married but change one's sex partner, the prison analogy is pointless: the prisoners aren't free to briefly row with another partner; it's a monogamous relationship. Finally, the last line of the speech is the most ridiculous; no one pretends a prisoner is happy, that's why he's still in chains. As Shaw himself states, prisoners have only "accepted the inevitable," which is a far cry from being happy.

7 Michael Holroyd, *Bernard Shaw: The Pursuit of Power, 1889–1918* (New York: Random House, 1989), p. 78.

8 For a fuller discussion of this approach to Andrew, see Anthony S. Abbott, "Assault on Idealism: *Major Barbara*," in Rose Zimbardo (ed.), *Twentieth Century Interpretations of Major Barbara* (Englewood Cliffs, NJ: Prentice-Hall, 1970), pp. 42–57.

9 However, in order to become an active part of Perivale St. Andrews's salvation, one must embrace its violent methods. Barbara is described, in explosive imagery, as having gone "right up into the skies" (p. 185), and Sarah, a character who most commentators are at a loss to explain as anything more than decorative, becomes an Undershaft when she announces her willingness to let her body be blown up, at which moment Andrew, her father and "savior," appears to first see her as a person:

LOMAX: Your own daughter, you know!
UNDERSHAFT: So I see.   (p. 179)

10 For those who might wonder how this could be played on stage, I offer two examples from a recent production I directed. Near the end of the play, when Bilton refuses Andrew, who is carrying Lomax's matches, admission to the gunpowder shed, Andrew replies, "here you are" (p. 179), and, in Shaw's stage directions, gives the matches to the workman. Instead, Andrew crossed to Cusins and, saying the line, offered him the matches – obviously the symbolic keys to the kingdom – which Cusins, after hesitating, accepted. Similarly, at the end of the play, rather than all remaining on stage for Andrew's last line, Barbara shooed Cusins and the others off to house hunt with her, leaving Andrew alone on stage to knowingly say, "Six o'clock tomorrow morning, Euripides" (p. 185), leaving no doubt that the flustered Cusins would be there at Andrew's command.

FURTHER READING

Albert, Sydney P. "The Price of Salvation: Moral Economics in *Major Barbara*," *Modern Drama* 14 (1971), pp. 307–23.

Amalric, Jean-Claude, "Shaw's *Man and Superman* and the Myth of Don Juan: Intertextuality and Irony," *Cahiers Victoriens et Edouardiens: Revue du Centre d'Etudes et Recherches Victoriennes et Edouardiennes de l'Université Paul Vale* 33 (1991), pp. 103–14.

Baker, Stuart E., "Logic and Religion in *Major Barbara*: The Syllogism of St. Andrew Undershaft," *Modern Drama* 21 (1978), pp. 241–52.

Blanch, Robert J., "The Myth of Don Juan in *Man and Superman*," *Revue des Langues Vivantes* 33 (1967), pp. 158–63.

Bloom, Harold (ed.), *George Bernard Shaw's Man and Superman. Modern Critical Interpretations*, New York: Chelsea House, 1987.

  George Bernard Shaw's Major Barbara. Modern Critical Interpretations. New York: Chelsea House, 1988.

Dickenson, Ronald J., "The Diabolian Characters in Shaw's Plays," *University of Kansas City Review* 26 (1959), pp. 145–51.

Dukore, Bernard F., "The Undershaft Maxims," *Modern Drama* 9 (1966), pp. 90–100.

  "The Time of *Major Barbara*," *Theatre Survey: The Journal of the American Society for Theatre Research* 23, no. 1 (1982), pp. 110–11.

Frank, Joseph, "*Major Barbara*: Shaw's *Divine Comedy*," *PMLA* 72 (1956), pp. 61–74.

Leary, Daniel J., "Dialectical Action in *Major Barbara*," *Shaw Review* 12 (1969), pp. 46–58.

Matheson, T. J., "The Lure of Power and the Triumph of Capital: An Ironic Reading of *Major Barbara*," *English Studies in Canada* 12, no. 3 (1986), pp. 285–300.

McDonnell, Frederick P. W., "Heaven, Hell, and Turn-of-the-Century London: Reflections upon Shaw's *Man and Superman*," *Drama Survey* 2, no. 3 (1963), pp. 245–68.

Nickson, Richard, "The Art of Shavian Political Drama," *Modern Drama* 14 (1971), pp. 324–30.

Noel, Thomas, "Major Barbara and Her Male Generals," *Shaw Review* 22 (1979), pp. 135–41.

Rosador, Kurt T. von, "The Natural History of *Major Barbara*," *Shaw Review* 17 (1974), pp. 141–53.

Russell, Annie, "George Bernard Shaw at Rehearsals of *Major Barbara*," *Shaw Review* 19 (1976), pp. 73–82.

Weintraub, Stanley, "Exploiting Art: The Pictures in Bernard Shaw's Plays," *Modern Drama* 18 (1975), pp. 215–38.

  "Bernard Shaw in Darkest England: G.B.S. and the Salvation Army's General William Booth," *The Annual of Bernard Shaw Studies*, 10 (1990), pp. 45–59.

Weisenthal, J. T., "The Cosmology of *Man and Superman*," *Modern Drama* 14 (1971), pp. 298–306.

Zimbardo, Rose (ed.), *Twentieth Century Interpretations of Major Barbara: A Collection of Critical Essays*, Englewood Cliffs, NJ: Prentice Hall, 1970.

8

CHRISTOPHER INNES

"Nothing but talk, talk, talk – Shaw talk": Discussion Plays and the making of modern drama

In 1890, before he even began his career as a playwright, Shaw identified what he considered to be the defining quality for a new, non-traditional form of drama. From Aristotle on, action had been the core of drama; now Ibsen offered a radically different model. In *The Quintessence of Ibsenism* Shaw presented Ibsen as a socialist and a realist, whose naturalistic drama exposed all collective abstractions as damaging illusions, and promoted the "individual will" against "the tyranny of ideals." But beyond this, the key factor was that instead of the standard final-Act climax, Ibsen's characters sat down and talked. The clash of opinion replaced physical conflict, so that a play's resolution was the outcome of discussion.

As with so much of Shaw's writing, all this may seem an idiosyncratic distortion of its subject, but reveals a great deal about its author. The pamphlet was published in 1892, shortly before his first play *Widowers' Houses* appeared, and served as a manifesto for his theatrical aims. When Shaw delivered it as one of the lectures for a Fabian Society series on "Socialism in Contemporary Literature" two years earlier "The Quintessence of Ibsenism" had a more immediate target; and its politics were deliberately provocative in attacking the collectivist beliefs of other leading Fabians, such as Annie Besant (who had chaired Shaw's lecture) and Sidney Webb. However, the switch from action to discussion, that Shaw detected in Ibsen's work, corresponds with the fundamental Fabian approach to social change. Named after Fabius Cuncator, the Roman general who defeated Hannibal's superior forces by avoiding battle, the movement sought to reform society from within, by education, rejecting the violence of open revolution. And when carried over into drama, this commitment to the political effectiveness of intellectual persuasion is exactly analogous to resolving a play's action through dialogue. Ibsen thus becomes the prototype for a specifically Fabian form of theatre – and indeed Shaw makes the connection explicit by including the bust of Ibsen in the setting for one of his early plays, *The Philanderer*.

But these Ibsenite qualities also become the basis for Shaw's drama in a far more direct way. In fact *The Quintessence of Ibsenism* could be seen as a blueprint for the elements that are most quintessentially Shavian in Shaw's plays. The internal political argument over Fabian principles carried over into some of his major themes: the fallacies of idealism being ridiculed or demolished from *Arms and the Man* and *The Devil's Disciple* to *Saint Joan*, while the moral primacy of the individual will forms the basis for the concept of the Superman, which is expressed in the characterization of so many of his protagonists. The preference for dialogue over plot is even more central, since it leads to the one unique theatrical form that Shaw evolved: the Discussion Play.

Shaw was continually experimenting with theatrical form throughout his long career as a playwright: inverting melodrama, reshaping the historical chronicle-play, exploring musical structures, creating social and subliminal parallels in the outer and inner plays of *Man and Superman*, expanding the limits of performance in his eight-hour "metabiological pentateuch" *Back to Methuselah*. But all of these experiments either rely on pre-existing forms, or have analogues in other contemporary drama of the period. The only distinct theatrical form Shaw originated was what he labeled the "Disquisitory Play." The first to be given this subtitle was *Getting Married* in 1908; and this is closely linked to Shaw's next major play, *Misalliance*, completed in 1909 though not staged until 1910 and originally subtitled "A Debate in One Sitting."

It is striking that these have received less critical attention than any of Shaw's other major plays. This may be partly due to the fact that following their first performances they almost vanished from the stage until after Shaw's death. Even *Misalliance*, which has achieved a major place in the repertory over the last twenty years, only ran for eleven performances in 1910. Apart from an American production in 1917 it had just two brief revivals in England (1930 and 1939 – to respectful but puzzled reviews); and it was not until 1953, when a production was mounted on Broadway, that it first enjoyed public success. Yet these two plays have a central position in Shaw's work, and mark a culmination of Shaw's development over the first half of his career. Although several short plays – *The Shewing Up of Blanco Posnet, The Glimpse of Reality, Press Cuttings* and *The Fascinating Foundling* – intervene between Shaw's writing of *Getting Married* and *Misalliance*, these were clearly conceived as a pair; and they are the fullest expression both of subjects which had been preoccupying Shaw since his first novel, and of the style of drama which Shaw had been evolving over several of his preceding plays. At the same time, both were so far from the theatrical norms of the first half of the century as to be almost automatically disqualified from dramatic criticism. In fact these plays are among Shaw's most extreme stylistic experiments.

They represent such a different approach to dramatic construction that the reviewers of the time were unable to understand them. Indeed it has been argued that the vision of existence incorporated in *Misalliance* had to wait until the absurdist drama of Ionesco had been accepted, before it could be appreciated.[1] Yet the experimental nature of each play was effectually disguised by its apparently normative surface. This was clearly deliberate. Even more than with his earlier plays, Shaw controlled every detail of the first London productions, including recognizably naturalistic settings, which he designed himself: a twelfth-century Norman hall entirely appropriate to an episcopal palace; a very contemporary Edwardian conservatory attached to a *nouveau-riche* mansion in Surrey. In fact, (tongue-in-cheek) Shaw even summarized *Getting Married* as a stock farce, pointing out:

> It is the wedding day of the bishop's daughter. The situation is expounded in the old stage fashion by that old stage figure the comic greengrocer, hired for the occasion as a butler . . . The fun grows fast and furious as the guests arrive, invited and uninvited, with the most distracting malaprosity. [2]

With such a stylistic contradiction, it is perhaps hardly surprising that the initial critical reaction was (as Shaw accurately described it) "violent press hostility." By contrast Shaw always claimed that the public was appreciative. Thus at the opening of *Getting Married* "There was a splendid audience; and the excitement was immense" – while the critics "almost without exception, in articles of great length, assured the public that the play had been an unexampled failure; that it was intolerable and monstrously dull; that it was not a play at all; that it was . . . unintelligible" (accusations that Shaw later parodied in *Fanny's First Play*).[3] Typical comments were that Shaw had "degenerated into dullness for the very reason that he is so tremendrously in earnest" (*The World* on *Getting Married*), or reduced drama to the "debating society of a lunatic asylum – without a motion, and without a chairman. . . What [the characters] do is of little importance. . . they do not keep to the point because there is no point to keep to" (*The Times* on *Misalliance*). Later critics were equally negative, but from the opposite perspective, for instance dismissing *Misalliance* as "a tolerably dull entertainment based on an aimless narrative."[4] It is only very recently that their significance has been realized, but they still count as "Neglected Plays" (the title of the 1987 *Annual of Bernard Shaw Studies*).

Shaw's plays attack a remarkably wide range of issues, from specific abuses like rack-renting and medical malpractice, through socio-economic forces like industrial capitalism or imperialism, to philosophical generalities like eugenics and the conflict between intellectual and biological imperatives. However, the subject of *Getting Married* and *Misalliance* is a topic that he returns to more frequently than any other. Indeed, this subject underlies most of Shaw's other concerns because of his choice of comedy as a vehicle, with its traditional focus on love relationships leading to marriage; and in fact it could be argued that Shaw chose the standard comic form precisely *because* it dealt with this. The marriage laws – and contemporary Parliamentary debates on married women's property – had already fueled the action in Shaw's novel, *The Irrational Knot* (written in 1880), where various female characters advise the heroine. One makes the (deliberately shocking) equation between "respectable" marriage "to secure ourselves a home and an income" and "what we – bless our virtuous indignations! – stigmatize as prostitution. *I* don't mean ever to be married, I can tell you, Marian. I would rather die than sell myself forever to a man." Another – an actress, ironically dressed in harem costume – proposes the solution of monogamy without marriage, having "refused, as any decent woman in my circumstances would" to "make a regular legal bargain of going to live with a man. I don't care to make love a matter of money; it gives it a taste of the harem. . ." Ignoring their advice, Marian experiences the loss of economic and psychological independence in marriage, which forces her to seek a divorce and leads her to run away to America where "One can get free without sacrificing everything except bare existence. . . our marriage laws are shameful."[5]

Mrs Warren's Profession thirteen years later picks up directly on the marriage/prostitution comparison, while the immediately preceding play, *The Philanderer* (also written in 1893) is an illustration of "the grotesque sexual compacts made between men and women" which spring from the current "marriage laws."[6] Notoriously, its dramatic situation and main characters also mirror Shaw's personal life, with the New Woman being based on the jealously possessive Jenny Patterson – Shaw's first and possibly only sexual lover – and the fleeing "philanderer" as a very Shavian critic of idealism, described in the play as "the famous Ibsenist philosopher" (*Collected Plays*, vol. I, p. 156). The original Act 3 of *The Philanderer* – cut because Shaw came to realize that "I have started on quite a new trail and must reserve this act for the beginning of a new play" – has been called Shaw's first attempt at a discussion play. The whole of this deleted section focused on the issue of divorce. Again, as in *The Irrational Knot*, the characters decide to leave for America to avoid the intolerable legal requirements for divorcing in Britain; and the dialogue clearly forms the basis for one of the situations in *Getting Married*.

PARAMORE: . . . Julia doesn't care a button for me, and never did. We have no children: she has money enough of her own to be quite independent from me: there's no reason why we shouldn't remarry and make ourselves comfortable. Unfortunately our pig-headed law provides no decent way of doing this . . .

CHARTERIS: . . . Couldn't you give her a harmless smack in the presence of a witness and elope with some lady who has no character to lose and who would stay at a hotel under your name for a consideration . . .

PARAMORE: No. I'd rather defy the law openly than circumvent it by a squalid farce involving the degradation of a third party. [7]

The course of action indignantly rejected here has been carried out by one of the couples in *Getting Married*, fifteen years later. Nothing has changed; and the opprobrium is emphasized by the reaction of other characters, who fail to realize the wife's collusion, while the contrast between honorable motives and public shame reveals the legal requirements for divorce as ludicrously unreasonable:

REGINALD: (*out of patience*) Whats the good of beating your wife unless there's a witness to prove it afterwards? You dont suppose a man beats his wife for the fun of it, do you? How could she have got her divorce if I hadnt beaten her? Nice state of things that!
. . . I had to go to Brighton with a poor creature who took a fancy to me on the way down, and got conscientious scruples about committing perjury after dinner. I had to put her down in the hotel book as Mrs. Reginald Bridgenorth. . . Do you know what that feels like to a decent man? Do you know what a decent man feels about his wife's name? How would you like to go into a hotel before all the waiters and people with – with that on your arm? Not that it was the poor girl's fault, of course: only she started crying because I couldnt stand her touching me; and now she keeps writing to me. And then I'm held up in the public court for cruelty and turned away from Edith's wedding. (*Collected Plays*, vol. III, pp. 568–69)

While this might well sound simply comic – particularly today, when divorce is almost on demand and free from social stigma, even in England – the preface to the play emphasizes the reality and seriousness of the legal problems at the time, and a 1933 Postscript affirms its continuing relevance, since legislative reforms had still not addressed the underlying problem. In fact prefaces have a special role in the Discussion Play, with the ancillary material attached to *Getting Married* and *Misalliance* being among the most fully developed examples of Shaw's practice. In each case they were written three to four years after the play itself, and (like the rest of the prefaces) added for commercial reasons: to give each three-play collection a page-length comparable to a serious novel, thus not only allowing them to be published for a viable return but also encouraging readers to approach plays as significant literature, rather than ephemeral performance scripts. However, unlike Shaw's early prefaces, they are neither straightforward introductions to the material of the plays, nor part of his campaign to establish the public persona of "G.B.S." With *Man and Superman* the ironic "Dedication" and the appendix of "The Revolutionist's Handbook" become semi-fictional extensions of the drama on a different plane: the "Handbook" supposedly being the published political maxims of the intellectual genius in the play. But the prefaces written for both *Getting Married* and *Misalliance* are each considerably longer than the plays themselves.[8] While addressing the primary topic of conversation between the characters – indeed picking up on specific points in their arguments, and (particularly in *Getting Married*) even echoing specific phrases from the dialogue – they also cover a far wider spectrum of related issues.

Each preface has between fifty and seventy sections, with headings that range from defining the topic ("What does the Word Marriage Mean?"/ "What is a Child?") and outlining the problem ("The Economic Slavery of Women"/"The Manufacture of Monsters") to suggesting solutions ("Wanted: An Immoral Statesman"; "Divorce a Sacramental Duty"/"We must reform Society before we can reform Ourselves"; "Wanted: a Child's Magna Charta"). Notably these solutions contradict the dramatic resolutions arrived at by the characters in the plays. For instance, the various couples spend much of *Getting Married* attempting (with the best legal and religious advice) to draw up a "private contract" on the model of "ancient Rome" as a replacement for standard marriage – one of the key recommendations in the preface (*Collected Plays*, vol. III, p. 492) – only to find the task impossible:

> SOAMES: (*after a silence of utter deadlock*) I am still awaiting my
>   instructions . . .
>   (*rising with the paper in his hands*) Psha! (*He tears it in pieces*) So much for
>   your contract!   (*Collected Plays*, vol. III, p. 621)

These prefaces also move beyond the plays in other ways, comparing oriental and occidental variants of polygamy or discussing Darwinian theories of natural selection, and analyzing the social causes of the characters' problems that by definition lie outside their consciousness. Among these, the most striking to a modern eye are the connections Shaw draws between the family and imperialism, or between childhood education and economic exploitation.

The prefaces are clearly intended to counterbalance the comedy of the dramatic representation; and Shaw deliberately attempts to shock the readers with overstatements – for instance in asserting that "marriage enjoys the credit of a domestic peace which is hardly more intimate than the relations of prisoners in the same gaol" (*Collected Plays*, vol. III, p. 476) – or Swiftian "modest proposals" such as:

> I have more than once thought of trying to introduce the shooting of children as a sport, as the children would then be preserved very carefully [like pheasants] for ten months in the year, thereby reducing their death rate far more than the fusillades of the sportsmen during the other two would raise it.
> (*Collected Plays*, vol. IV, p. 101)

At the same time, set side by side with the prefaces, the plays are clearly ways of humanizing the issues, giving them an individual dimension – even though on that level the social problems are insoluble.

At first glance the two prefaces would seem to indicate that *Getting Married* and *Misalliance* deal with different subjects: the Marriage and Divorce Laws versus Children's Rights and Education. But closer reading shows that these are a continuum, complementary aspects of the same topic: family life as the immediate source of social exploitation and inequality. The first preface raises issues that are pursued at greater length in the second, as with a characteristically Shavian critique of all British personal relationships as slavery: "The theory that the wife is the property of the husband or the husband of the wife is not a whit less abhorrent and mischievous than the theory that the child is the property of the parent. Parental bondage will go the way of conjugal bondage" (*Collected Plays*, vol. III, p. 540). In the same way, the second preface refers back to arguments made in the first: for instance the destructive effect of idealized visions of marriage (*Collected Plays*, vol. IV, p. 138). And there is crossover too between the dialogue of one play and the preface of the other, as when the would-be philosopher tycoon of *Misalliance* denies that his philandering makes him "a bad husband. I'm not. But Ive a superabundance of vitality. Read Pepys' Diary" (*Collected Plays*, vol. IV, p. 197). This gnomic apostrophe to Pepys is only explainable by a comment in the preface to *Getting Married*: "If we take a document like Pepys' Diary, we learn that a woman may have an incorrigibly unfaithful husband, and yet be better off than if she had ill-tempered . . . one, or was chained for life to a criminal, a drunkard, or a lunatic" (*Collected Plays*, vol. III, p. 515). The plays are also explicitly linked as steps in a single line of stylistic development. In an "interview" (drafted by Shaw as self-promotion a week before the opening of *Getting Married*) Shaw pointed out that the play is closely related to the "Dream of Don Juan in Hell" from *Man and Superman*, which had been performed separately at the Court Theatre the previous year – an expansion of the same static disquisitory technique, but without the music which structures the argument between Don Juan and the Devil (*Collected Plays*, vol. III, p. 665). A similar "interview" which followed the production of *Misalliance* emphasized the parallels with *Getting Married*, presenting both plays as examples of "the higher drama" (*Collected Plays*, vol. IV, p. 257).

Indeed, the overall form of each is almost identical. Both are designed to be played without interval – although for *Misalliance* Shaw noted that "As the debate is a long one, the curtain will be lowered twice" for the "convenience" of the audience, who were asked "to excuse these interruptions" (*Collected Plays*, vol. IV, p. 11). In both almost all the physical activities which would be high points in conventional drama are deliberately kept offstage. Thus the wedding of the young engaged couple, which one would expect to be the climax of any play entitled *Getting Married*, not only takes place behind the scenes, but comes as a surprise when it is finally reported since the last time they were seen the would-be bride and groom had both been declaring marriage impossible (and indeed since none of the other characters are aware they have left, we are not even supposed to notice their absence). Even in *Misalliance* – which appears at first glance to have far more physical activity with an airplane crashing into the roof of the conservatory, a courtship carried out as a literal chase, and an acrobat as one of the leading characters, to say nothing of the standard melodramatic scene of a desperate revolutionary thrusting a pistol into the face of the capitalist tycoon with lurid oaths of vengeance (in advice to the actor Shaw stressed the rhetorical nature of these speeches) – what we see on stage is merely anticlimactic. The tycoon is completely unfazed by the pistol, and the confused revolutionary disarmed without effort. Acrobatics are limited to a discussion of juggling oranges while reading a Bible, while any more strenuous displays take place out of sight in a gymnasium; and all we are shown is the exhaustion of the men as each returns from their "exercise" with the fascinating female acrobat. The chase may start and finish in the conservatory, but its climax in which the pursuer becomes the pursued is reached way outside on a hilltop. As for the plane crash – notionally as spectacular as anything the modern megamusical could offer, combining as it does the helicopter of *Miss Saigon* with the falling chandelier in *Phantom of the Opera* – Shaw insisted that everything be left to the imagination by using a boxful of broken glass and having the actors look up and shout.[9]

Denying audiences' expectations of visual spectacle or physical excitement is of course one of Shaw's standard techniques: the most obvious example being the total omission of the Embassy Ball in *Pygmalion* which is not only explicitly built up to from the beginning of the play, but would (if played) provide the scene of Eliza's triumph over the false standards of society, and the vindication of Higgins's linguistic education as well as

Shaw's belief in social equality. However, the two Discussion Plays take this denial far further. Shaw claims to be matching the theatrical purity of ancient Greek drama in observing the unities of time and place; and in classical tragedy all physical actions are also reported instead of staged. It is specifically for these two works that Shaw coins the term "a play of ideas" – perhaps the most influential concept for later twentieth-century theatrical development – and in his view "the Greek form is inevitable when drama reaches a certain point in poetic and intellectual evolution" (*Collected Plays*, vol. III, p. 449). *Getting Married* and *Misalliance* are the only plays in which Shaw completely followed this formula, although *Heartbreak House* is sometimes grouped with them as a third Discussion Play.

Claiming antique models for a future-oriented modern form of drama seems contradictory; and indeed Shaw's classical references are merely attempts to win critical support for something entirely new by aligning it with an equally unconventional type of theatre (by turn-of-the-century standards), but one that evoked automatic respect. This becomes obvious in Shaw's provocative denial that *Getting Married* has any plot:

> If you look at any of the old editions of our classical plays, you will see that the description of the play is not called a plot or a story, but an argument. That exactly describes the material of my play. It is an argument – an argument lasting nearly three hours, and carried on with unflagging cerebration by twelve people and a beadle.   (*Collected Plays*, vol. III, p. 667–68)

However (as Shaw would have been well aware) when Claudius demands to know "the argument" of Hamlet's Mousetrap he is referring to the thesis of the play: by contrast Shaw's "argument" is not a description of the subject of *Getting Married*, but its theatrical form.

To illustrate the incongruity and unnaturalness of Christian marriage and its legal implications in England, Shaw's large cast of characters represents a range of conjugal relationships. These are designed to appear "normal" (despite press accusations of immorality[10]). None of the husbands are criminals, drunkards, or lunatics, or even ill-tempered; the wives show no evidence of being economically exploited. Quite apart from serious problems being inappropriate to comedy, Shaw's aim is to show that the law cannot accommodate the most "ordinary" couples, even when they try with the best will in the world. Only one of the three married pairs, however happy, corresponds to the legal fiction: Collins, the caterer-greengrocer and his wife, but she is so smotheringly maternal and single-mindedly uxorious that his "children all ran away from home" while he sees "family life" as being "in a cage." By contrast his brother's marriage is kept "fresh" because his wife (Mrs. George) is continually running off with other men and "the variety of experience made her wonderfully interesting" as well as providing conversational partners for her husband (*Collected Plays*, vol. III, p. 553). Even the most "respectable" marriage is a *ménage à trois*, the Bishop (whose daughter's wedding is the excuse for gathering all the characters together) carrying on an affair with a married woman – though, with typical Shavian irony, it turns out that this is purely spiritual since the relationship with his Incognita Appassionata will only be consummated "in heaven when she has risen above all the everyday vulgarities of earthly love" (*Collected Plays*, vol. III, p. 579).

These three variations on married bliss are set beside three other sets of people at different distances from the altar. One of the Bishop's brothers, a General, has proposed to Lesbia (the sister of the Bishop's wife) nine times over the past twenty years, and is refused a tenth time during the play because, even though she believes it her eugenic duty to have children, she refuses to sacrifice her independence by subordinating herself to a husband, as the law would require. The Bishop's other brother Reginald has arranged for his much younger wife, Leo, to divorce him because she has fallen in love with someone her own age, though in fact she wants to keep both men and would "like to marry a lot of men. . . to have Rejjy for everyday, and Sinjon for concerts and theatres and going out in the evenings, and some great austere saint for about once a year at the end of the season, and some perfectly blithering idiot of a boy to be quite wicked with" (*Collected Plays*, vol. III, p. 572). As for the Bishop's daughter, she and her fiancé have both been sent pamphlets on the law (with characteristically bold Shavian titles: DO YOU KNOW WHAT YOU ARE GOING TO DO? BY A WOMAN WHO HAS DONE IT, and MEN'S WRONGS) which have opened their respective eyes to the impossibility of getting a divorce even if a husband becomes a murderer, and to a husband's responsibility for his wife's debts. Since Edith is a social activist, whose public attacks on unscrupulous manufacturers for exploiting the female workforce will ruin Cecil by heavy damages for libel, both are calling the marriage off – even though the church is already packed with waiting wedding guests.

The whole play consists of a series of discussions to resolve these impasses, culminating in the unsuccessful attempt to draw up an alternative form of "private" marriage contract, and the summoning of Mrs. George (who being the Lady Mayoress is escorted by a Beadle *"in cocked hat and gold-braided overcoat, bearing the borough mace"*) as a clairvoyant with the power to speak through trances "as if it was the whole human race giving you a bit of its mind" (*Collected Plays*, vol. III, pp. 622 and 555). But the dramatic status of *Getting Married* as an "argument" goes beyond this. The Bishop, General, and Beadle – all in ostentatiously full uniform –

14 Discussion – with benefit of Clergy and Beadle, in the Shaw Festival's 1989 production
of *Getting Married*

represent symbolic positions, together with a curate in cassock and biretta standing for the law: the authorities of church, military and civil power, the all-male hegemony that upholds the social order. They form the official frame for argument, even if (in a typical Shavian reversal) as individuals they contradict the stereotypes, the Bishop becoming a devil's advocate and the General's medals being the result of trying to get himself killed for rejected love. And the structure of the play itself embodies a logical pattern of antithesis and accretion. The characters, each presenting one postulate, are introduced singly, one after the other – analogous to a discursive sequence. As alternative positions on marriage, they are juxtaposed, organized in different combinations, and conflated in a demonstration of rational process, while the numerical balance (three marriages, and three unwedded relationships) represents the formality of the reasoning.

At the same time, demonstrating the unreasonable nature of the legal and religious context for the argument, no logical process can offer a solution. Instead the conclusions are arbitrary, evade the problem, or revert to the original (unsatisfactory) premise. Thus although Mrs. George's oracular trance expresses a mystic sexuality that transcends marriage, it is her physical presence that by attracting Leo's lover reduces Leo to remarrying Reginald. Edith and Cecil finally get married (in an empty church, since all the wedding guests have given up waiting long before) after taking out insurance against libel suits – though Edith's reservations are simply ignored. And Lesbia, forced to refuse the General for the last time, will never bear the children society needs.

Perhaps in an attempt to get around the failure of traditional reasoning in the previous play, *Misalliance* incorporates a quite different logical structure. From William Archer on, critics have complained that this play lacks focus, is incoherent, or fails to define any central topic.[11] But rather than standard sequential reasoning, the pattern here embodies dialectical, lateral thinking; and Shaw gives a metaphoric image of the process through the acrobat's juggling display (which, promised but never performed, remains a purely intellectual construct):

> LINA: Put [the Bible] up before you on a stand; and open it at the Psalms. When you can read them and understand them, quite quietly and happily, and keep six balls in the air all the time, you are in perfect condition. . .
> (*Collected Plays*, vol. IV, p. 200)

The balls – or "silver bullets" that Lina would prefer as the hardest test of dexterity – are the multiple issues raised by the characters and kept in suspension during the play: parent–child relationships and the education of the public, class distinctions and political revolution, imperialism and democratic government, gender roles and eugenics, behavioral conventions and individual freedom, even acting versus talking. Although distinct, all can be brought into synthesis (the broader vision that Lina's Bible on one level represents) as a synoptic analysis of the whole social system.

The intellectual process operates through inversion, paradox, and divergence within repetition: all characteristic techniques of Shaw's drama, here subsumed into a mode of reasoning. Thus it is an aristocratic colonial governor who gives the most subversive social commentary (so much so that fifty years on Joe Orton picked a phrase from the speech as the epigraph for *Loot*):

> LORD SUMMERHAYES: Men are not governed by justice, but by law or persuasion. When they refuse to be governed by law or persuasion, they have to be governed by force or fraud, or both . . . anarchism is a game at which the police can beat you. (*Collected Plays*, vol. IV, p. 237)

By contrast the pistol-waving Marxist revolutionary turns out to have the most conventional bourgeois morality, and to be motivated by outdated and sentimental melodrama in seeking vengeance on Tarleton, the manufacturing magnate of underwear, not as a capitalist exploiter, but (being

Tarleton's illegitimate son) for the supposed "wrong" done to his mother. [12] Paradox is both physically embodied in Lina Szczepanowska, the Polish acrobat, a free spirit and gender-bending "man-woman or woman-man" who preserves her independence by risking her life daily, and in her profession. The description of her as an acrobat who walks "backwards along a taut wire without a balancing pole and turn[s] a somersault in the middle" (*Collected Plays*, vol. IV, p. 197) has been compared to one of Oscar Wilde's metaphors: "the way of paradoxes is the way of truth . . . To test reality we must see it on the tight-rope. When the verities become acrobats we can judge them."[13] And the action of the drama itself is shaped by reprises. Hypatia, Tarleton's bored daughter, asks her fiancé to invite his friend Percival to visit, and Bentley replies "Youd throw me over the moment you set eyes on him" – while her father describes her as wanting "things to happen. Wants adventures to drop out of the sky" and her brother smashes a china bowl to relieve his frustration (*Collected Plays*, vol. IV, pp. 168 and 185). This prefigures the much larger " *appalling crash of breaking glass*" when the airplane hits the conservatory; and the aviators, who literally drop from the sky, are indeed adventure (in the exotic form of Lina) and Percival, whom Hypatia is immediately attracted to and arranges to marry, leaving Bentley to be slung over Lina's shoulder and carried off by her in the airplane.

Although Shaw's voice is everywhere in *Getting Married*, with all the characters' points being echoed in the preface, his own marriage-model – sexless wedlock – is not included. However, *Misalliance* directly reflects Shaw's own family experience. The triangular relationship between Shaw's father, his Uncle Walter Gurly, and his mother's musical coach Vandaleur Lee is played on in the description of Percival's ideal family upbringing through having three fathers: a freethinking philosopher, an Italian priest (his mother's confessor) and his biological father who "kept an open mind and believed whatever paid him best" (*Collected Plays*, vol. IV, p. 166). Gunner, the illegitimate son who has just lost his mother and is shut into a dead-end job in a counting house, echoes Shaw's abandonment by his mother while working in a Dublin land agents.[14] And the play is also self-referential on other levels.

The characters are recognizable variations on figures from Shaw's earlier plays. Hypatia, with her animal energy and ruthless approach to husband-hunting – once she finds a suitable mate demanding that her father "buy the brute for me" – is a throwback to Blanche in *Widowers' Houses*. The highly intelligent but infantile Bentley is a clone of the poetic Marchbanks from *Candida*: as Shaw commented, "only the same hand could have produced both."[15] Tarleton, as a "captain of industry" who would prefer to

15   Adventure from the sky – enter the *Deus ex Machina*: Sharry Flett as
Lina Szczepanowska and Peter Krantz as Joseph Percival in the Shaw Festival's 1990
production of *Misalliance*

be a philosopher and is an enlightened philanthropist, echoes Undershaft's mix of financial power, realism, and progressive social engineering in *Major Barbara*. Even the eccentric and strikingly unique Lina is not only the most fully developed feminist, building on all his earlier versions of "the New Woman," who can legitimately declare herself "an Honest woman: I earn my living. I am a free woman: I live in my own house. I am a woman of the world. . . I am strong: I am skilful: I am brave: I am independent: I am unbought: I am all that a woman ought to be" (*Collected Plays*, vol. IV, p. 249). She is also the female equivalent of the Don Juan from *Man and Superman*, complete with notebook listing "proposals" from would-be lovers that duplicates Don Giovanni's famous record of female conquests in Mozart's opera.

The effect is to theatricalize the action, revealing the persona of "G.B.S." behind every aspect of *Misalliance*; and this is carried through into a highly contemporary type of deconstruction. The ostensible dramatic situation, which is specifically pointed by the play's title, is dismissed by the characters as a "question that occupies all the novel readers and all the playgoers. The question they never get tired of. . . The question which particular young man some young woman will mate with . . . As if it mattered!" Discussing literature, a young philistine demands "plot" and rejects drama "with nothing in it but some idea that the chap that writes it keeps worrying, like a cat chasing its own tail," demanding escapist theatre that makes him "forget the shop and forget myself from the moment I go in to the moment I come out" – while Tarleton refers specifically to Shaw's own work: "the superman may come. The superman's an idea. I believe in ideas. Read whatshisname" (*Collected Plays*, vol. IV, p. 238, 170, and 169).

This ironic deconstruction even extends to the Discussion Play form itself. Almost the first line of the play is "Lets argue about something intellectual" (*Collected Plays*, vol. IV, p. 145) – and the final lines are:

> TARLETON: Well I – er. . . I suppose – er – I suppose there's nothing more to be said.
> HYPATIA: (*fervently*) Thank goodness!   (*Collected Plays*, vol. IV, p. 253)

In announcing *Getting Married*, Shaw had defined his new drama as "Nothing but talk, talk, talk – Shaw talk" (*Collected Plays*, vol. III, p. 665) and now this is explicitly quoted by Hypatia:

> It never stops: talk, talk, talk, talk. That's all my life. All day I listen to mamma talking; at dinner I listen to papa talking; and when papa stops for breath I listen to Johnny talking.   (*Collected Plays*, vol. IV, p. 176)

Inevitably this expresses a deep ambivalence about reason, which is also reflected in the action of both plays. All the arguments are ultimately ineffective; and in each Shaw calls in a spiritual *Deus ex Machina* to resolve the problems: the clairvoyant Mrs. George in *Getting Married* and the "magical" Lina, literally a goddess descending from a machine in *Mis-*

alliance whose speeches all (as Shaw pointed out to Lena Ashwell, the first actress to play the role) carried "mystic meaning."[16]

By inventing the "play of ideas" Shaw created a prototype that set the conditions for a whole line in modern theatre, in England as well as abroad, from Bertolt Brecht and Edward Bond (both of whom labeled their work "rational drama") to Joe Orton. In extending the logic of argument to deconstructing and theatricalizing self-reference, he anticipated principles that have become associated with postmodernism. However, always a pragmatic playwright, Shaw seems to have concluded that these experiments were too far ahead of his time; and the critical reaction to them formed the frame for *Fanny's First Play*, staged just one year after *Misalliance*. Setting a "modern play" within a satire on (easily recognizable) Edwardian theatre critics, the whole piece becomes an ironic farewell to straight Discussion Drama. The pompous Trotter (aka A. B. Walkley, theatre critic for *The Times*, to whom Shaw had ironically dedicated *Man and Superman*) claims that

> these productions, whatever else they may be, are certainly not plays . . . one author, who is, I blush to say a personal friend of mine, resorts freely to the dastardly subterfuge of calling them conversations, discussions, and so forth, with the express object of evading criticism . . . I say they are not plays. Dialogues, if you will. Exhibitions of character, perhaps: especially the character of the author.   (*Collected Plays*, vol. IV, p. 365)

After Fanny has performed her (anonymous) play, the critics all argue about who might have written it – Pinero and Granville Barker are suggested, even Barrie – though Shaw is the last name to be mentioned. And in rejecting Shaw as a possibility they run through all the stock criticisms of his drama: intellect without emotion; characters as puppets, indistinguishable mouthpieces for their author; no plot; a down-market preference for "second-rate middle-class" instead of high society; "unpleasantness" instead of entertainment. Mirroring its dramatic situation, *Fanny's First Play* itself was produced anonymously (with Shaw mounting a tongue-in-cheek rumor campaign pointing to Barrie as the author) as a mocking challenge to the reviewers who had stereotyped his work and condemned his intellectualized, specifically modern theatrical form.

In many ways *Fanny's First Play* is a parody of Shaw's "play of ideas," with its heroine as a vociferously Fabian bluestocking suffragette from Cambridge – but paradoxically it was also a vindication of the Discussion Drama, transferring from the Court to the West End and running for over 600 performances. However, by that time Shaw had already discarded unadulterated arguments for more conventional compromises, with *Androcles and the Lion* (1912) playing off Wilson Barrett's immensely popular religious melodrama, *The Sign of the Cross*, and *Pygmalion* returning to the successful formula of *Plays Pleasant* in its inversion of conventional comedy.

NOTES

All quotations from Shaw's plays and prefaces are taken from *Bernard Shaw: Collected Plays with their Prefaces*, ed. Dan H. Laurence (New York, 1975).

1 For instance, R. J Kaufman, in *G. B. Shaw: A Collection of Critical Essays* (Engelwood Cliffs, NJ, 1965), p. 11.

2 Cited in Michael Holroyd, *Bernard Shaw: A Biography*, vol. II (New York, 1989), p. 199. Martin Meisel has even argued that *Getting Married* is an adaptation of Sardou: *Shaw and the Nineteenth Century Theater* (Princeton, 1963), pp. 265–66.

3 Shaw in *The Observer*, June 12, 1910, and *Bernard Shaw: Collected Letters: 1898–1910*, ed. Dan H. Laurence (New York, 1972), p. 781.

4 The reviews are cited by Holroyd, *Bernard Shaw*, pp. 204 and 244; Maurice Valency, *The Cart and the Trumpet* (Oxford, 1973), p. 292.

5 *The Irrational Knot* (New York, 1918), Book I, pp. 121–22; Book II, p. 220; Book IV, p. 357. For a discussion of British laws on women's rights and marriage in the nineteenth century, see Dolores Kester, in Rodelle Weintraub (ed.), *Fabian Feminist: Bernard Shaw and Woman* (University Park, PA, 1977), pp. 68ff.

6 *The Irrational Knot*, Book IV, p. 357.

7 Diary entry, June 17, 1893, and BM MS 50596 E pp. 31–33: cited in Brian Tyson, "Shaw's First Discussion Play: An Abandoned Act of *The Philanderer*," *Shaw Review* (September 1969), pp. 93 and 94.

8 In the case of *Misalliance*, for instance, quite apart from the difference between printed dialogue and consecutive prose, the preface runs 130 pages to the play's 111 pages of dialogue, and appended material adds a further 8 pages in the Laurence edition.

9 Undated letter to William Faversham, who mounted a US production of *Misalliance* in 1917: cited in Bernard Dukore, *Bernard Shaw, Director* (University of Washington Press, 1971), p. 117.

10 Lord Alfred Douglas, for instance, carried on a campaign in *The Academy* from May 13 to June 6, 1908 against *Getting Married* as "not only dull, but immoral" and corrupting "the British home." The "controversy" is reprinted in *The Annual of Bernard Shaw Studies* 9 (1966), pp. 66–74.

11 Cf. Valency, *The Cart and the Trumpet*, p. 293, William Archer, *The Old Drama and the New* (London, 1923), pp. 352ff., or John Dawick, "Stagecraft and Structure in Shaw's Disquisitory Drama," *Modern Drama* (December 1971), p. 280.

12 As an underwear manufacturer whose illegitimate son proves incapable of shooting him, Tarleton is a parodic amalgam of the haberdasher Gordon Selfridge and William Whitely, a contemporary businessman murdered by an unacknowledged illegitimate son in 1907 (cf. Holroyd, *Bernard Shaw*, p. 245).

His underwear business is also a deliberately bathetic parallel to the trade in womens' fashions that symbolizes Western decadence in Granville Barker's *The Madras House*.

13 *The Picture of Dorian Gray* in *The Portable Oscar Wilde*, ed. Richard Aldington and Stanley Weintraub (New York, 1981), p. 183. The comparison is made by J. L. Wisenthal, in "Wilde, Shaw, and the Play of Conversation," *Modern Drama* (Spring 1994), p. 216.

14 See Holroyd, *Bernard Shaw*, p. 246

15 Cited in *ibid.*, p. 245.

16 *Collected Letters*, p. 903.

FURTHER READING

Innes, Christopher, *Modern British Drama: 1890–1990*, Cambridge, 1992.

McDowell, Frederick P. W., "Shaw's Abrasive View of Edwardian Civilization in *Misalliance*," *Shaw Review* 23 (1988), pp. 63–76.

Sidnell, Michael J., "Misalliance: Sex, Socialism and the Collective Poet," *Modern Drama* 17 (1974), pp. 125–39.

Wisenthal, J. L., *The Marriage of Contraries: Shaw's Middle Plays*, Cambridge, MA, 1974.

9

RONALD BRYDEN

The roads to *Heartbreak House*

On June 8, 1917, Bernard Shaw invited a few friends to hear him read a new play, his first full-length piece since *Pygmalion*, written in 1913. Four of them were people with special knowledge of the materials that had gone into Shaw's cauldron: Henry Massingham, Gilbert Murray, Sydney Olivier, and Kathleen Scott, the widow of Scott of the Antarctic. They seemed likelier than most listeners to understand what he was up to in this, his most difficult work. Some perhaps were in a better position to understand it than he was – Kathleen Scott, undoubtedly, knew better than the playwright what motives had driven her husband to try and outface death in the hardest, most dangerous place on earth. Shaw may even have hoped they might help him to understand his play better himself.

For *Heartbreak House* had given more trouble coming to birth than any of his previous plays. He had started to write it on March 4, 1916, but three months later still had no clear idea where it was going. "I, who once wrote plays *d'un seul trait*," he wrote to Mrs. Patrick Campbell on May 14, "am creeping through a new one (to prevent myself crying) at odd moments, two or three speeches at a time. I don't know what it is about."[1] In November he read the first act to Lady Gregory, but told her he did not know how to go on, what he had written was so wild.[2] In December he confessed to William Archer that he still had only one act, and was stuck.[3]

Something broke the logjam for him early in 1917. It may have been his visit to the Western Front at the invitation of Douglas Haig, the British commander-in-chief. Shaw told the *Daily Chronicle* that he found the nightly bombardments finer than Tchaikovsky's 1812 overture.[4] Twenty-three years later, during another World War, he told Virginia Woolf in a letter that the conception of *Heartbreak House* came to him the weekend of June 17, 1916, when the Shaws, Webbs, and Woolfs found themselves in a houseparty at Wyndham Croft in Sussex.[5] Sitting on the terrace after dinner, they heard the distant thunder of artillery launching the offensive on the Somme. It sounds as if his tour of Flanders the following year linked with that experience, and with his memory of watching a German zeppelin sail over his house in Ayot St. Lawrence and fall "like a burning newspaper" near Potters Bar, brought down by fighter planes, on October 1, 1916.[6] They crystallized into Ellie Dunn's line in the last scene of *Heartbreak House*, as a zeppelin roars overhead: "By thunder, Hesione, it *is* Beethoven."

Stanley Weintraub's chronicle of Shaw's activities between 1914 and 1918, *Journey to Heartbreak* (1971), suggests how these wartime experiences combined in the play. The book does an admirable job of showing how Shaw's opposition to the war placed him for the first time on the sidelines of public events, in the limbo where *Heartbreak House* seems to take place, talking about history from somewhere outside of it. But by limiting itself to the years of the Great War, it fails to account fully for the play. In his preface to it, written in 1919, Shaw said that he began it before the first shots of 1914 were fired, at a time when "only the professional diplomatists and the very few amateurs whose hobby is foreign policy even knew that the guns were loaded."[7] This is confirmed by the letter he wrote to Lord Alfred Douglas telling how the figure of the play's protagonist, Captain Shotover, formed itself in his mind in 1913, when the actress Lena Ashwell told how her father, a retired sea captain, refused extreme unction unless he could have cheese with his communion bread.[8] (The old man's home in retirement, a sailing vessel moored in the Tyne, with living quarters for him in its stern and a drawing room and conservatory on its upper deck, inspired the play's setting.) But some of the concerns treated in the play reached even further back into Shaw's past. It seems clear that much of his difficulty in writing it came from trying to reconcile the wartime experiences which gave him its ending with the notions with which he had embarked on it six years or more earlier.

Working without a developed plot line in his head, he drew more than ever before on personal emotions and memories, conscious and semiconscious. Many of the feelings he needed to express were about things he needed to conceal from the public, and in some cases his wife. But more than that, he found himself needing to square an apocalyptic wartime ending with ideas he had had about plays he wanted to write before the war. Much of the power and richness of the play comes from the sense of emotions at work behind it too large to be expressed in its characters and situations. Much of its density and mystery comes from the shadowy movement below its surface of deeper, drowned patterns of meaning, the shapes of other plays it might have become lying like submerged mountain ranges beneath the play it is.

One of those plays was to be a variation on English themes in the manner of Chekhov. Shaw acknowledged this intention in his subtitle for the play, "A Fantasia in the Russian Manner on English Themes," but in the finished play his intention is clearer than Chekhov's direct influence. Shaw had first heard of Chekhov in 1905, possibly from his German translator Siegfried Trebitsch when the Moscow Art Theatre made its first foreign tour to Berlin. He wrote to ask Henry Irving's son Laurence, who read Russian, whether any of Chekhov's plays might suit the Stage Society, short of playwrights now that Shaw and Granville Barker were succeeding commercially at the Court Theatre. It was probably Shaw's advocacy that led the Society to stage *The Cherry Orchard* in May 1911, in an under-rehearsed and much derided production. Shaw attended it loyally, and also the first London staging of *The Seagull* by Maurice Elvey in March 1912. The Stage Society then mounted *Uncle Vanya* in May 1914. Coming out of its first performance, Shaw said to a friend: "When I hear a play of Chekhov's, I want to tear my own up."

The friend to whom he said this was Henry Massingham. He and Shaw had known each other since 1888, when Massingham, deputy editor of the *Star*, hired Shaw behind the editor's back to write music criticisms under the pseudonym Corneto di Bassetto. Shaw came to regard Massingham as "the perfect master journalist" and that rarest of rare birds, a first-rate editor. He was to value his qualities as an editor particularly during the war years. When Shaw's *Common Sense About the War*, published in the *New Statesman* in November 1914, led to his ostracism by every journal in London (including the *Statesman* itself, launched with £1,000 of his money), Massingham made space in his non-party weekly *The Nation* for the unhonored prophet's voice to be heard crying in the wilderness. They saw more or less eye to eye on the subject of the war. But their closest bond was probably the theatre. Massingham's daughter Dorothy had played the juvenile lead in Shaw's *Great Catherine* in 1913. Massingham had himself been a theatre critic, one of the few in Britain to recognize the nature and quality of Chekhov's plays when they first appeared in Britain. He had taken A. B. Walkley of the *Times* to task for complaining of implausibility in *The Cherry Orchard*, and of the play's mixture of tragedy, comedy, and farce. "Life is all these things, being made up of change and loss, and a certain sparkling recovery, and a grimly ludicrous, ironic play of unknown forces over it all," he wrote in the *Nation* on June 3, 1911. After seeing *Uncle Vanya* in 1914, he analyzed the ensemble nature of its writing and construction, "the way in which all these creatures are repelled from or attracted to each other, like the tremulous oscillations of electric needles."[9] If anyone could be relied on to understand what Shaw had taken from Chekhov in writing his play, it surely was Massingham.

The tentative title Shaw gave to his first draft of *Heartbreak House* was *The House in the Clouds*. (Later it became *The Studio in the Clouds*.) This indicates that his fantasia in the Russian manner was also the play he discussed before the war with his friend Gilbert Murray, which was to be a contemporary imitation of Aristophanes' *The Clouds*. Shaw had become intimate with Murray during the Vedrenne–Barker seasons at the Court Theatre, which grew out of Granville Barker's production of Murray's version of Euripides' *Hippolytus* in October 1904. Within the following year, Murray and Shaw became sufficiently close for Shaw to model his Greek scholar Adolphus Cusins in *Major Barbara* on the Oxford classicist, and to seek Murray's help when in difficulties writing an ending for the play. During the war, Murray embraced Shaw's suggestion that the postwar world should be policed by a supranational League of Nations, and he became one of the League's most faithful champions between the wars.

Aristophanes' *Clouds* is a satire on education in the Athens of the Sophists. Socrates, lumped inaccurately and unfairly among them, is caricatured in it as a subverter of traditional decency and decorum, teaching the young by twisted logic the right of sons to beat their fathers. The play's Chorus, dressed as clouds, present themselves as symbols and presiding deities of the new learning: volatile, shape-shifting, woolly, and chaotic. That Shaw should have visualized a contemporary comedy on such themes lending itself to treatment "in the Russian manner" suggests that he may have had Chekhov's *Seagull* in mind as a model rather than *Uncle Vanya* or *The Cherry Orchard*.

Because *The Cherry Orchard* is the Chekhov play invoked most specifically in Shaw's preface, and because of a few obvious parallels – bankrupt house, undisciplined servants, impending disaster – it is the work by Chekhov to which *Heartbreak House* has been most frequently compared. But in its concern for what one generation passes to the next, what values parents raise their children to honor and pursue, *Heartbreak House* is much closer to *The Seagull*, itself an oblique homage on Chekhov's part to the Russian novel he most admired, Turgenev's *Fathers and Sons*. The miasma of romantic bohemianism that hangs over the Shotovers' stranded ship of fools comes much closer to the atmosphere of the Sorins' love-infested house by its magic lake than to that of Madame Ranevsky's fading mansion among its cherry trees. Two-thirds of the way through the play, at the point where Aristophanic comedies usually bring forward the leader of the Chorus to speak the parabasis, the statement of the play's serious purpose, Shaw gives Captain Shotover his longest speech. It is about the generations rising to replace his own, and what they value.

I see my daughters and their men leading foolish lives of romance and sentiment and snobbery. I see you, the younger generation, turning from their romance and sentiment and snobbery to money and comfort and hard common sense. I was ten times happier on the bridge in the typhoon, or frozen into Arctic ice for months in darkness, than you or they have ever been. You are looking for a rich husband. At your age I looked for hardship, danger, horror, and death, that I might feel the life in me more intensely.[10]

What he says has more in common with Nina at the end of *The Seagull*, walking into the storm to pursue her vocation as an actress, than it does with the muted, relieved farewells Gayev, his sister and family say to their old lives in the last act of *The Cherry Orchard*.

Shaw had no children of his own, of course, to brood over as Captain Shotover broods over his progeny. But as he had turned in his twenties to his friends in the Fabian Society for a surrogate family to replace the broken one which starved him for love, so in his fifties he tended to look on the new generation of Fabians as substitutes for the children he and his wife Charlotte would never have. Both treated Harley Granville Barker, who joined the Society in 1901, as an adored adoptive son. A similar parental feeling seems to have led Shaw to push H. G. Wells into the Society two years later, and to invite Robert Loraine, who had played Jack Tanner in *Man and Superman* in New York, to join the first Fabian Summer School in North Wales as his guest and Charlotte's. (Shaw and Loraine nearly drowned together swimming in Tremadoc Bay.) But his highest hopes, and those of other old Fabians, centered on the Cambridge Fabian Club, a brilliant group of young people drawn toward socialism by the Liberal Party's landslide victory in 1906. Among its members were the poet Rupert Brooke, "the handsomest young man in England"; Hugh Dalton, the economist who became Chancellor of the Exchequer in the 1945 Labor government; James Strachey, younger brother of the biographer Lytton; and Arthur Waley, the future Chinese scholar. Women from Girton and Newnham Colleges, though still denied membership of the university, were admitted to the club. Several were daughters of old Fabians. Among them was Rosamund, daughter of the journalist Hubert Bland – though illegitimate, the product of one of Bland's extramarital affairs, she had been reared in the family by his wife, the children's writer Edith Nesbit. Amber Reeves was the daughter of the director of the London School of Economics, founded by Sydney Webb. Margery Olivier was the eldest of the four beautiful daughters of Shaw's old friend Sydney Olivier, one of the founding Fabians.

Shaw and Olivier had first met in 1884, brought together by Sydney Webb, with whom Olivier shared the duties of resident clerk at the Colonial

Office. Although it had been officially launched some months earlier, this was really the birth of the Fabian Society. Shaw, Webb, and Olivier became its three musketeers, with Olivier's Oxford friend Graham Wallas as their ingenuous d'Artagnan. It was they who wrote the key *Fabian Essays* in 1889 and dominated the society's activities well into the new century. Olivier had to withdraw somewhat in the 1890s, as colonial service overseas took him abroad for longer and longer periods, to British Honduras, the Leeward Islands, and other colonies in the Caribbean. In 1899, when appointed Colonial Secretary of Jamaica, he moved with his family to the island for five years. But the moment he returned in 1904, the Fabians seized on him to arbitrate the various disputes that had broken out in the society, mainly instigated by H. G. Wells.

Olivier was fitted for the task by an openness to new ideas (he instantly took to Wells) combined with an air of unquestionable authority. According to Shaw, who visited him there later, he ruled Jamaica as an enlightened despot, making no secret of the fact that his sympathies lay with the island's black peasantry rather than its white plantocracy. A tall, commanding figure with the pointed beard of a Spanish grandee (his nephew Laurence modeled his Shylock on him in 1969), he paid little attention to any judgments but his own – people usually came around to agreeing with him in a year or two, he told Shaw.[11] He followed his own judgment in the education of his daughters. In Jamaica, they learned to play polo in the grounds of King's House, and were taught at home by tutors, until the new Sussex coeducational school Bedale's became available for his youngest daughter, Noel. Rupert Brooke's attempt to persuade his mother, the domineering "Ranee," to invite two of the Olivier daughters to visit their home in Rugby was scotched by a woman she met who had recently returned from Jamaica. "The Oliviers!" she exclaimed to the alarmed Ranee. "They'd do *anything*, those girls!"[12]

What the Olivier girls did most, apparently, with the help of the Cambridge Fabian Club and its summer schools, ski trips, and other activities, was fall in love with Rupert Brooke. H. G. Wells's chief interest in the Fabian Society, apart from taking it over and displacing its old rulers, was to make it the instrument of his desire for a new, freer sexual morality. He found eager disciples in the Cambridge Fabian Club. It was said that Hubert Bland arrived in the nick of time to stop Wells and his daughter Rosamund from boarding a train together at Paddington station for some clandestine destination in the west. In 1909 Wells embarked on an affair with Amber Reeves, then the club's treasurer, and fathered a child with her. The scandal might have been hushed up – Amber accepted an offer of marriage from a chivalrous young Fabian barrister named Blanco White –

had Wells not made it the subject of his next novel, *Ann Veronica*. The old Fabians just succeeded in holding the society together by forcing Wells to resign and say it was because of political differences.

By then Olivier and his wife were back in Jamaica. He had been recalled by public demand to be governor of the island when an earthquake destroyed Kingston, the capital, in 1907. Their daughters stayed in England to pursue their educations, chaperoned by Margery. Rupert Brooke used his Fabian friendship with Margery as a means to pursue them. The first object of his admiration was Brynhild, the beauty of the family, named after the heroine of William Morris's *Sigurd the Volsung*. Then in June 1908 the whole family visited Cambridge to see the Marlowe Society perform Milton's *Comus*, with Brooke, its founder, as the Attendant Spirit. Brooke met for the first time and was instantly fascinated by the youngest of the sisters, Noel, then fifteen. For the next two years they wrote each other jokily flirtatious letters, met occasionally, and Brooke wrote Noel poems, the best of them his 1909 sonnet "Oh! Death will find me long before I tire / Of watching you." Then in September 1910, when Noel was seventeen and Brooke twenty-three, they entered into a secret engagement, which Brooke proceeded to break two years later by having an affair with another Cambridge Fabian, Katherine Cox.

How much of this the Olivier parents knew when Shaw and his wife visited them in Jamaica in January 1911 is impossible to tell. It seems likely that Margery, fulfilling her responsibility for her younger sisters, prevented Noel's relationship with Brooke from developing into an affair. It seems more than likely that, recognizing Brooke's attentions to herself as a way of gaining access to her sisters, she felt used. She may have told her mother that much. But it seems unlikely that the friends spent a week together in the new, earthquake-proof King's House without discussing the convulsive history of the Cambridge Fabian Club under Wells's tutelage, and the acid comments passed by Beatrice Webb on the Fabian summer schools, to the effect that their participants seemed more interested in each other than in social reform. Shaw's surrogate children included Olivier's daughters. Years later, in the 1930s, he gave Brynhild money to rescue a farm which her feckless husband was in danger of losing. One of the many reasons why he may have invited Olivier to hear his play was perhaps to make sure he had not too obviously let the figures of his old friend and his children show behind those of the ancient Ulysses with a Jamaican wife and siren daughters.

There was another way that Shaw might have heard of Rupert Brooke's courtship of the Olivier girls. During the 1905–06 season at the Court Theatre, he received an anonymous fan letter from "Miss Charming,"

Poste Restante, Godalming, which he could not resist answering. Miss Charming turned out to be Erica Cotterill, a first cousin of the Brookes, a daughter of a Fabian schoolmaster. For the next seven years, she kept bursting in on his life, until Charlotte Shaw insisted he forbid her their house. When he advised Erica to join a socialist society, she joined the Fabians and followed him home from lectures. When he invited her to lunch in the country, she camped in the woods near Ayot St. Lawrence and roared up to their house next day on a motor bicycle. Having learned in the theatre what a Shavian superwoman should be like, she tried to make herself one in real life. She was a nuisance, possibly slightly unhinged, but Shaw saw something touching in her. Nobody, not even he, seemed to be able to tell her what to do with her life, except to get married and raise children. Understandably, she refused all advice. As imperious in her way as her aunt, Rupert Brooke's mother the Ranee, she followed her own impossible course, demanding that Shaw love her, insisting on arranging her life to suit her own ideas rather than other people's. Many Shaw biographers have observed that something of Erica turns up in the character of Ellie Dunn in *Heartbreak House*, but few point out the extent to which Ellie shares Erica's unshakeable feminist obduracy about leading her own life as she thinks best.

Erica Cotterill's cousinship to him is the only reason for Rupert Brooke's name to appear in any biography of Shaw, but he is an important if invisible presence at the center of *Heartbreak House*. The play is Shaw's meditation on why so great a majority disagreed with him and welcomed the Great War with inflammatory excitement. Brooke, the brightest and best of the Cambridge Fabians, who might have been expected to join Bertrand Russell and Lytton Strachey in socialist pacifist resistance to the war, instead had made himself the voice of his generation with the sonnet "Now God be thanked Who has matched us with His hour." After his death from blood poisoning in the Aegean in April 1915, Winston Churchill described him in the *Times* as "all that one would wish England's noblest sons to be in days when no sacrifice but the most precious is acceptable." A few weeks earlier, the Dean of St. Paul's read his sonnet "The Soldier" – "If I should die, think only this of me" – at a Sunday service. From then on, Brooke was the hero of every war-lover in Britain, the strongest of the voices that drowned out Shaw's *Common Sense About the War*. *Heartbreak House* was Shaw's attempt to understand the feelings Brooke had summed up. It asks like *Fathers and Sons* and *The Seagull* "Where did we go wrong?"

Brooke's answers in his sonnet are imprecise. He talks of how the God of the war has "wakened us from sleeping" and caused the young

> To turn, as swimmers into cleanness leaping,
> Glad from a world grown old and cold and weary,
> Leave the sick hearts that honour could not move,
> And half-men, and their dirty songs and dreary,
> And all the little emptiness of love.

It is possible to detect a certain amount of posturing in the poem, the relief of a young man with doubts about his sexuality welcoming the opportunity to prove himself manly to the core. But Shaw could recognize the disgust with Britain's prewar society as something Brooke held in common with others, including himself. Was what he had to say so different from the statement made implicitly by Robert Scott in his ill-fated Antarctic expedition of 1912? Shaw had imbibed enough Marx at an early age to be accustomed to dialectical thinking. Captain Shotover expresses in the play the need for human beings to feel the fear of death sharply in order to feel the life in themselves more intensely. Presumably Shaw had invited Kathleen Scott to hear his play's final speeches to this effect and respond to them from the point of view of Scott's widow. Unfortunately, worn out by her war work at the Ministry of Pensions, Kathleen Scott dozed off and had to be excused before the end of Shaw's reading. He forgave her, insisting on reading the end of the play to her the following day.

In the event, there was no way of representing the voice of Brooke's and Scott's generation in *Heartbreak House*. Shaw's stage direction describing the first entrance of Randall Utterword, the youngest male in the play, is a reminder that there were no actors to be found in wartime of conscriptable age: "He has an engaging air of being young and unmarried, but on close inspection is found to be at least over forty." Hector Hushabye, a handsome fifty-year-old, can represent H. G. Wells, winning the love of Ellie Dunn as Othello won that of Desdemona by telling far-fetched stories about anthropophagi and men whose heads grow beneath their shoulders. Ellie can speak for Erica Cotterill and the bright young women of the suffragette movement such as Rebecca West, with whom Wells had had an affair similar to the one with Amber Reeves, and fathered another child, in 1914. The Shotover sisters can be prevented from bringing the Olivier girls to mind by incorporating elements of Leslie Stephen's daughters, Virginia Woolf and Vanessa Bell, as well as characteristics, in the case of Hesione Hushabye, of Shaw's own Circe Mrs. Patrick Campbell, and of Ottoline Morell, the fantastically dressed queen of a court of Bloomsbury and Cambridge conscientious objectors on her estate at Garsington. Captain Shotover can combine the voices of Shaw himself and Sydney Olivier. But there can be no young men of fighting age in the play. The small change of young people's flirtations and infatuations which provide the action of earlier country house comedies such as *Misalliance* are not possible in *Heartbreak House*.

This makes it hard to describe precisely what the action of the play consists of. Shaw obviously used the label "in the Russian manner" as a license for writing a play in which nothing seems to happen, but he was perfectly aware that beneath the apparent boredom of Chekhov's inconsequent conversations, hearts are broken, lives blighted, and hopes destroyed just as dramatically as in any Pinero melodrama. But the speech-to-speech action of *Heartbreak House* is elusive for other reasons. It is hard to say what outcomes result from the various encounters between characters, scene by scene, unless one follows up a clue Shaw dropped, apparently artlessly, when writing to Lawrence Langner of the New York Theatre Guild before the play's world premiere in 1920. He told Langner of his habit of working out the moves in his plays with chess pieces on a chessboard – "if the actors follow the stage directions exactly as they are written in the play, they cannot possibly go wrong." There is plenty of evidence that this had long been Shaw's custom. But *Heartbreak House* is the only play of Shaw's in which the characters could actually be said to correspond to the pieces on a chessboard, and the action of the play to consist of a series of confrontations in which one character either "takes" another or fails to do so, as chess pieces do.

The analogy breaks down only at the absence of the chessboard's castles – instead of actual castles on the board, Shaw has his two imaginary entities, Heartbreak House and Horseback Hall, the palaces of the liberal-intellectual bohemia he described in his preface, and of the English Junker-class he identified in *Common Sense About the War*. The two houses have their white queen and black queen, Ariadne Utterword and Hesione Hushabye, and there are a white king and black king, Captain Shotover and Boss Mangan, who look imposing but turn out to be circumscribed in their movement, as the kings of the chessboard are. (Mangan makes a less regal figure than Shotover, but it should be noticed that when the black king is removed from the board by a German bomb, the game is over.) Each queen also has a knight caracoling in broken-backed motions about her – Hector Hushabye about his wife, Randall Utterword about his sister-in-law – and I would argue that the play's two male Dunns can be seen as black and white bishops: Billy Dunn a former pirate who has reduced burglary to a pious form of moral blackmail; Mazzini Dunn, a martyr of old-fashioned liberalism who has become a well-meaning tyrant to his child. Ellie Dunn, of course, begins the play as everybody's pawn, but as she makes her way across the board, immobilizing first one king and then the other, she triumphantly turns herself into yet another queen, the spiritual bride of Captain Shotover, as ordinary pieces do in chess's younger cousin, draughts.

It would probably be a mistake to dress a production of the play in a manner that recalled *Alice Through the Looking Glass*, but it could be helpful to actors to think of what their characters are up to as "taking" one another, in the chess sense of the word. Hector has "taken" Ellie before the play begins. Ariadne proceeds to "take" Hector, and Ellie to "take" Mangan, while Hesione Hushabye, to her surprise, fails to "take" Mazzini Dunn, the only man she ever met "who could resist me when I made myself really agreeable." Mazzini literally takes Billy Dunn prisoner when he finds him burgling the house, and Ellie, discarding Mangan in the last act, takes Captain Shotover as her "spiritual husband and second father," a mystic marriage of the kind Shaw claimed later to have felt between himself and William Morris's daughter May, and perhaps the relationship Shaw would have wished for himself when young with Morris in his messianic old age. The action of the scenes in which these takings happen is not really action in the normal sense of the word. Characters measure themselves against each other in a Darwinian fashion, and decide either to embrace or discard each other. They are like the subtexts to the debates in *Getting Married*, with most of their texts abandoned – in effect, each character executes the kind of judgement on each other that is executed on the characters of *The Simpleton of the Unexpected Isles*, a play with many affinities to *Heartbreak House*, when Judgment Day comes. In *The Simpleton*, heaven's judgment consists of sweeping off the board those characters who serve no useful purpose. Those whose lives can be said to be useful are spared to continue them. Hector Hushabye cries out for such a judgment in the last act of *Heartbreak House*, declaring that its denizens are useless, dangerous, and ought to be abolished. In their small way, the two-character scenes of *Heartbreak House* are microcosms of the universal judgment it moves toward.

They are only indirectly, however, part of that movement. As the equivalencies I have suggested indicate, there is no coherent opposition of black and white in Shaw's chess game, only a set of individual contests, some between black and black (Hesione Hushabye, the black queen, for example, "takes" Mangan, the black king) or white and white (for example, Ariadne Utterword chastising her knight Randall at the end of the second act). Shaw never found the consistent plot that would join the Graeco-Russian comedy he mused on before the war to the apocalyptic ending that his wartime experiences brought him. The apocalypse, as is presumably the supernatural nature of such events, arrives out of nowhere, heralded by some foreboding prophecies by Shotover and Hector Husha-

16 The palace of sleep – Ellie Dunn dreaming of Othello: Marti Maraden as Ellie Dunn, with Jim Jones and Ric Sarabia as the Gardener's Boys, in the Shaw Festival's 1985 production of *Heartbreak House*

bye, but having no direct causal connection with the previous events of the play. The bridge that connects the beginning of *Heartbreak House* to its ending is of a non-narrative kind, constructed by means that belong more to music than to drama. The real action of the play is its movement away from narrative sequence toward its final fire from heaven. Shaw described it as well as anyone has in an interview with the *Sunday Herald* before the play's London opening in 1921: "The heartbreak begins, and gets worse until the house breaks out through the windows, and becomes all England with all England's heart broken."[13]

In the end, the unique brilliance of *Heartbreak House*, which makes it unlike any play written before it, was the result of Shaw's recognition that there was no narrative connection to be made between the play's beginning and ending. Its action consists of the unmooring of the play from the reality in which it begins, floating it above and beyond that reality like an airship, and bringing it home on target to the reality of air war in 1917. Had the play been staged in 1917, as Shaw presumably intended when he gave it a cast of over-forty male actors, the audience would have watched the curtain go up on a country house weekend of the kind that provided the matter of innumerable Edwardian comedies. Since Ellie is penniless, Hesione wears Pre-Raphelite draperies, and Ariadne has just returned from the colonies, none of the play's women enter in clothes that betray any particular year. One would be free to suppose that the reality in which the play is set is the unreality of any upper-class Edwardian play of wit, flirtation, and snobbish class warfare. But gradually that unreal reality becomes more and more unreal, its characters protesting that normal people do not behave as they do, as they behave less and less theatrically. And suddenly an aimless, typically Edwardian discussion about the frequency of local night trains ushers in the thunder of zeppelins overhead, and the time is clearly 1917, the reality in which the play ends the same chilly wartime reality that waits for the audience in the streets outside the theatre.

The real action of the play is the artifice with which Shaw brings about this passage from an illusion of unreality to an illusion of reality. He uses two main devices. The first is presenting the Shotovers' ship-shaped house on the Downs as a palace of sleep, where everything may have been asleep for a hundred years or alternatively may just have dropped off, to dream uneasily of a nightmare future. The play begins with Ellie nodding off to sleep over her copy of *Othello*, while her hostess has drowsed off upstairs arranging flowers (poppies and mandragora, no doubt) in a guest room. In the second act, Ellie puts Boss Mangan to sleep in a hypnotic trance, and Ariadne tongue-lashes Randall to tears, like a fractious child, to make him drowsy for bed. In the third act, Mazzini Dunn comes down to join the dreamers on the terrace in pyjamas and a flamboyant dressing-gown, declaring that he feels perfectly at home so dressed at Heartbreak House, and is reminded by Ariadne that this would not be the case in any normal, well-run English country house of the kind she would prefer. Meanwhile Captain Shotover, deprived of the rum that keeps him awake, has drifted off to sleep in Ellie's arms. After the initial sound of a clock striking six at the opening of the play, the audience never knows the time. The night takes on the endlessness and formlessness of the small hours, while the watchers in the house sit entranced by moonlight that reminds Hesione of the night in *Tristan and Isolde*. Part of the sense that the house has drifted away from its moorings in reality comes from this carefully created illusion that time has stopped, and the mundane reality of daytime receded.

Shaw's other device is an equivalent unmooring of the Shotovers' house from its geographical position in the here and now. Mostly this is achieved by letting Captain Shotover expand the world of the play into the world of his memory and ancient perspective on life. The means by which he does this vary from details as small as his asking Ellie to "favour me with your name," a usage with the period courtliness of his Regency youth, and his talk of the wooden figurehead of his ship the Dauntless, which his son-in-law Hastings Utterword so resembled, back in the age before iron and steam conquered the seas, to his refusal at his age "to make distinctions between one fellow creature and another." There are also of course the hundred small ways in which he treats the house as if it were a ship, blowing his captain's whistle and shouting "All hands aloft!" when a burglar is discovered upstairs and telling Nurse Guinness to "take him to the forecastle." Above all, he makes the house feel as if it were a flimsy, impermanent structure. "I came here on your daughter's invitation," protests Mangan, when the captain upbraids him for wanting to marry a young girl. "Am I in her house or yours?" "You are beneath the dome of heaven, in the house of God," Shotover replies. "What is true within these walls is true outside them. Go out on the seas; climb the mountains, wander through the valleys. She is still too young."[14] Whenever Shotover comes on stage, he makes the floor seem to heave like a deck, the timbers of the house seem to creak like a ship's at sea. A director might do worse than to make these effects happen in a production, if his stage were capable of them.

Much of the difficulty *Heartbreak House* encountered from critics in its early productions was surely the result of the fact that it was never played as it was designed to be played, in wartime. Its world premiere was staged by the Theatre Guild in New York in 1920, its first London production by J. B. Fagan the following year. Shaw says in his preface that he withheld the play from production in 1917 because he recognized that national morale must come first in time of war, and *Heartbreak House* might have lowered morale. He may also have recognized that no management was likely to take a chance on it while theatres were filled by such things as *Chu Chin Chow* and *The Maid of the Mountains*, unless it could boast a star as great as Mrs. Patrick Campbell. He read her the play in July 1917. She admired it with reservations; but the only parts she would be interested in playing, she told Shaw, would be either Ellie Dunn or Shotover himself. Not until twelve years later did Shaw admit to her that he had modeled Hesione Hushabye on her.

As a result, *Heartbreak House* had to wait for real success in the theatre until the Second World War, when Robert Donat staged it at the Cambridge Theatre in London in March 1943, playing Captain Shotover himself. Deborah Kerr, then twenty-two, played Ellie Dunn. By then, the worst German air raids on London were over and the V-1 rocket raids had not yet begun. But audiences seeing the play could receive directly the unique effect Shaw had designed it to produce. What began as an Edwardian comedy lifted out of its period, to float in a timeless twentieth-century mixture of disillusion and presentiments of disaster, and ended in the present, with bombs raining down on England. There has scarcely been a year since in which Shaw's extraordinary theatre poem, as authentic a myth for imperial Britain as Blake's prophetic books, has not seemed uncannily relevant to the civilization whose end it foresaw.

NOTES

1 *Bernard Shaw and Mrs. Patrick Campbell: Their Correspondence*, ed. Alan Dent (New York: Knopf, 1952), May 14, 1916.
2 Lady Gregory, *Journals* (London: Putnam, 1946), November 19, 1916.
3 *Bernard Shaw: Collected Letters*, ed. Dan H. Laurence (New York: Viking, 1985), vol. III, December 12, 1916.
4 Shaw's three articles for the *Chronicle*, published March 5, 7, and 8, 1917, are reproduced in *What I Really Wrote About the War* (London: Constable, 1931).
5 *Bernard Shaw: Collected Letters*, ed. Dan H. Laurence (New York: Viking, 1988), vol. IV, May 10, 1940.
6 Letter to Beatrice Webb in *Collected Letters*, vol. III, October 5, 1916.
7 *The Bodley Head Bernard Shaw: Collected Plays with their Prefaces*, ed. Dan H. Laurence, 7 vols. (London: Max Reinhardt, The Bodley Head, 1970–74), vol. V, p. 12.
8 Michael Holroyd, *Bernard Shaw: A Biography*, 5 vols. (London: Chatto and Windus, 1988–92), vol. III, p. 9.
9 Victor Emeljanow, *Chekhov: the Critical Heritage* (London: Routledge, Kegan Paul, 1981), p. 129.
10 *Collected Plays*, vol. V, p. 146.
11 Shaw's description of Olivier is drawn from his preface to Olivier's *Letters and Selected Writings*, ed. Margaret Olivier (London: Allen and Unwin, 1948).
12 *Song of Love: the Letters of Rupert Brooke and Noel Olivier*, ed. Pippa Harris, 1991 (London, Bloomsbury, 1991), p. xxvi.
13 *Collected Plays*, vol. V, pp. 183–85.
14 *Ibid.*, p. 88.

FURTHER READING

Delany, Paul, *The Neo-Pagans: Rupert Brooke and the Ordeal of Youth*, New York: Free Press, 1989.
Weintraub, Stanley, *Journey to Heartbreak: the Crucible Years of Bernard Shaw*, New York: Weybright and Talley, 1971.
Woodfield, James, "Ellie in Wonderland: Dream and Madness in *Heartbreak House*," *English Studies in Canada* (1985).
Wright, Anne, *Literature in Crisis*, London: Macmillan, 1984.

10

MATTHEW H. WIKANDER

Reinventing the history play: *Caesar and Cleopatra, Saint Joan,* *"In Good King Charles's Golden Days"*

Defining the history play

When the Players arrive at Elsinore, Polonius details the genres and sub-genres of the Elizabethan theatre in which they excel: "tragedy, comedy, history, pastoral, pastoral-comical, historical-pastoral, tragical-historical, tragical-comical-historical-pastoral, scene individable, or poem unlimited" (*Hamlet*, II.ii). The joke makes clear that even at the time when histories were enjoying their greatest popularity, as Herbert Lindenberger puts it, "the boundaries between historical drama and recognizable genres such as tragedy and romance are often quite fluid."[1] Defining historical drama in the age of Shakespeare, Irving Ribner draws a distinction between plays in which the playwright "assumes the function of the historian," and "romantic drama using historical figures" with "no attempt to accomplish the serious purpose of the historian."[2] What Ribner sees as the distinguishing feature of the Elizabethan history play Shaw singles out as his own special claim: Shaw, too, insists that he is a serious historian and that such dramas as *Caesar and Cleopatra, Saint Joan,* and *"In Good King Charles's Golden Days"* must be evaluated as contributions to historical knowledge. At the same time, Shaw, with characteristic playfulness, suggests that attention to detail, one "serious purpose of the historian," is of little interest to him: "I never worry myself about historical details until the play is done; human nature is very much the same always and everywhere," he told Clarence Rook. "Given Caesar, and a certain set of circumstances, I know what would happen, and when I have finished the play you will find I have written history."[3] Shaw's claim to find a higher historical truth than that found by pedants worrying the details draws its force from a long tradition of rivalry between historians and playwrights that characterizes discussion of historical drama ever since Shakespeare.

Shaw shows his awareness of this rivalry by identifying *Saint Joan* with the Elizabethan chronicle history play form (its subtitle is "A Chronicle

Play in Six Scenes"). *Caesar and Cleopatra* he calls more bluntly "A History"; and *"In Good King Charles's Golden Days,"* "A True History That Never Happened." In this last instance, he explicitly raises questions about the relationship between historical fact and historical truth that also have a long tradition. Aristotle, in the *Poetics*, first raises the distinction between plays about events that have happened and plays about events that may happen, and declares that poetry "is more philosophical and a higher thing than history: for poetry tends to express the universal, history the particular."[4] Renaissance critics like Sir Philip Sidney agreed, finding history deficient in its bondage to particulars. Thomas Rymer, in *A Short View of Tragedy* (1692) pugnaciously paraphrased Aristotle's famous dictum: "Poetry is led more by Philosophy, the reason and nature of things, than History; which only records things higlety, piglety, right or wrong, as they happen."[5] Shaw recasts the ancient dialectic of poetry and history in the *Preface* to *Saint Joan*. Only by means of an "inevitable sacrifice of verisimilitude" can he secure "sufficient veracity" in his representation of figures from the past.[6]

While Shaw makes his most pointed claim to the status of historian in these three plays, singling them out from Shaw's output as specifically belonging to the genre of history play is to set aside a profusion of other plays that touch on history in a number of ways. Martin Meisel adds to these three *The Man of Destiny*, "A Fictitious Paragraph of History"; of Shaw's dramas, Meisel argues, this short play most closely resembles "the Scribe–Sardou strain of historical romance, with its diplomatic intrigues, contested papers, and amorous concerns."[7] *The Devil's Disciple*, labeled by Shaw "A Melodrama," also belongs to that nineteenth-century popular form of melodrama in which a historical figure enters into a fully fictional plot, as General Burgoyne does here. *The Dark Lady of the Sonnets* could well be classified with plays about the lives of famous poets: a brief vogue for such *"Dichterdramen"* existed during the 1840s in Germany. *Arms and the Man* is set against the backdrop of the Serbo-Bulgarian war of 1885, though Shaw admitted to requesting the facts from an authority and adding them to a play that was substantially finished; and of *Great Catherine* he confesses that the play offers a bravura turn for an actress but will "leave the reader as ignorant of Russian history now as he may be before he has turned the page" (*Collected Plays*, vol. IV, p. 899). J. L. Wisenthal argues that "many of Shaw's plays can profitably be seen in the light of his thinking about history," not only those set in a historical present, like *Heartbreak House*, *Major Barbara*, and *John Bull's Other Island*, but also those, like *Back to Methuselah*, that project present history into the future.[8]

Such uncertainty about naming and definition dominates discussion of historical drama. Its status as a genre separate from comedy and tragedy dates from the First Folio's division of Shakespeare's works into Polonius's first three categories. But Elizabethan practice was more vague: *The Merchant of Venice*, for example, first appeared in Quarto as "The Most Excellent Historie of the Merchant of Venice," and *Richard III*, which we now classify with the history plays, was first published as *The Tragedy of Richard the Third*. *King Lear* enjoyed publication first as a "True Chronicle Historie" and then was classified among the tragedies in the Folio. Shaw's assertion that in *Saint Joan* he runs the gamut of the genres – "the romance of her rise, the tragedy of her execution, and the comedy of the attempts of posterity to make amends for that execution" (*Collected Plays*, vol. VI, p. 66) – refers back to the infinite variety of the Elizabethan history plays.

Reinventing the history play (1): English historical drama after Shakespeare

Shaw's reinvention of the history play takes place most importantly in a context of English theatrical practice. The Victorian theatre prized above all the historical. Nineteenth-century production of Shakespeare's plays in England was dominated by the desire for historicity in settings. Lavish and accurate costuming, expensive reconstruction of palaces and castles, detailed reenactments of coronations and royal weddings, were all features of productions that severely cut Shakespeare's texts as they ravished the eyes of the spectators. Antiquarians offered their expertise to ensure, for example, that the courtiers in James Robinson Planché's *King John* (1823) would be "sheathed in mail, with cylindrical helmets and correct armorial shields."[9] When playing W. G. Wills's *Charles I* (1872), Henry Irving carefully imitated the famous Van Dyke portraits in his stage makeup: "It was as though one of Van Dyke's portraits had stepped out of its frame and been endowed with life," one critic enthused.[10]

This kind of pictorial accuracy was challenged in the 1890s by William Poel and the Elizabethan Stage Society, who staged amateur performances of the plays of Shakespeare and his contemporaries on stages designed to emulate the Elizabethan platform stage, and also in authentically Elizabethan sites, such as the halls of the Inns of Court. As theatre reviewer for the *Saturday Review*, Shaw agreed with Poel's principal goal: "It is only by such performances that people can be convinced that Shakespear's plays lose more than they gain by modern staging." Poel's productions did away with the pictorial set and stressed instead the costumes and music of the Elizabethan period. "[N]othing like the dressing of his productions has been seen by the present generation," Shaw wrote in 1898: "our ordinary managers have simply been patronizing the conventional costumier's business in a very expensive way, whilst Mr. Poel has achieved artistic originality, beauty, and novelty of effect, as well as the fullest attainable measure of historical conviction . . . The result, on the whole, is that those who have attended the performances have learnt to know the Elizabethan drama in a way that no extremity of reading the plays – or rather reading *about* the plays and pretending to have read them – could have led them to, and this, I take it, is what Mr. Poel promised our literary amateurs."[11] Shaw's enthusiasm for Poel's experiment was of course tempered by his critique of particular performers, and indeed Poel's liberation of Shakespeare from the tyranny of the Victorian set designer often led to a quirky, equally pedantic Elizabethanism. Poel's claim to a higher degree of authenticity in staging could be countered by the scenic designer's claim to a higher degree of authenticity to history.[12] Planché's barons in Shakespeare's *King John* looked like real medieval barons; Poel's Elizabethans always looked like Elizabethans. In both instances the claim of historicity evokes a counterclaim of anachronism: a charge which, as we shall see, Shaw came to delight in inviting for his historical plays.

The kind of authenticity represented by Henry Irving in the guise of Van Dyke's portraits of Charles I was prized not only in staging, but also in a play's portrayal of historical figures. Just as Irving was supposed to look like Charles, his actions and conduct in the play were expected to cohere with a reputation fixed in narrative and pictorial sources, a whole tradition of "Victorian historical iconography," as Stephen Watt puts it. Historical figures were in a sense stock characters: the sentimentalization of Charles I's domestic life led in Wills's play to a focus on the king as husband and father. Wills caused a small outburst of outrage by characterizing Cromwell as greedy and ambitious, a "slanderous invention" according to critics, which Wills defended as attested in "numerous contemporary pamphlets."[13]

In concentrating on Charles's devotion to his family and wringing pathos from Henrietta Maria's desperate interventions, *Charles I* is typical of English historical drama ever since the Restoration. Daunted by vigilant censorship, English dramatists from about 1680 shied away from the political implications of their stories. Censorship was fully institutionalized in the Licensing Act of 1737. The first play suppresed by the act, Henry Brooke's *Gustavus Vasa* (1739) was a historical play, thought to offer in its portrayal of a Swedish patriot ("The Father of His Country" is the subtitle) an invidious parallel with the government. But Brooke's play actually relocated the cause of Gustavus's rebellion against the Danes in a private amorous intrigue. English dramatists generally focused on the domestic lives of historical figures, staging their private passions and sorrows and leaving the business of history – the story-lines of their plays – in the hands of villainous statesmen. Secret loves, private jealousies, misdirected letters, trivial causes of great public events: these all add up to a dramatic historiography that dominated the nineteenth-century stage as thoroughly as did the elaborate, authenticated pageantry of set decor.

English historical drama before Shaw also featured what Nicholas Rowe called, introducing his *Tragedy of Jane Shore* (1714), "Imitation of Shakespeare's Style." Rowe's claim called down immediate ridicule from such contemporaries as Swift and Pope. Oaths, archaisms, clumsy locutions – "Avaunt, base groom!" – became, despite the scorn of some, the language of history on the English stage. Such overcharged language also ruined experiments in verse tragedy like Shelley's *Cenci*, as Shaw argued: working within the form originated by Otway and Rowe, Shelley "certainly got hold of the wrong vehicle." Shaw continues: "The obligations imposed on him by this form and its traditions were that he should imitate Shakspere in an un-Shaksperean fashion by attempting to write constantly as Shakspere only wrote at the extreme emotional crises in his plays . . ."[14] Finding the *right* vehicle for dramatizing past history becomes for Shaw a quest to find a language for the past that is not an inadvertently parodic emulation of Shakespearean style. "Hence the shock of Londoners," effuses Niloufer Harben, "when Shaw's Julius Caesar came on the stage speaking plain English!"[15]

Reinventing the history play (2): Shakespeare and European Romanticism

The identification of Shakespeare with historical drama was absolute, not only on the English stage in the eighteenth and nineteenth centuries, but on the French and German stages as well. Neither country had a Renaissance tradition of historical drama. French drama in the seventeenth century was resolutely uninterested in the French past, recent or otherwise. Instead, the classical dramatists concentrated on ancient Greece and Rome for their stories; Voltaire, who set out to flout the restraints and decorums of the classical stage in his dramatic work, was the first to introduce medieval French settings into his plays. Voltaire professed admiration of Shakespeare, whom he saw as a cudgel with which to bludgeon the eighteenth-century French literary and theatrical establishment. After Voltaire, the French Romantic playwrights, such as Victor Hugo in his preface to *Cromwell* (1827), and critics such as Stendhal in his highly influential *Racine and Shakespeare* (1823) actively championed Shakespeare's irregularities of structure and inconsistencies of style as a way to rejuvenate French drama. Likewise, German playwrights of the late eighteenth-century *Sturm und Drang* school saw in the Shakespearean history play a way to shrug off the dominance of French classical forms and to create a uniquely German dramatic tradition.

Shaw's insistence that the English theatre recognize its own European context – most conspicuous in his championship of Ibsen – carries through into his approach to the problem of historical drama. While Shakespeare, as understood and staged by the professional London theatre, was a stultifying influence, to Schiller and Goethe his raw Gothic power was an inspiration. German dramatists, as Benjamin Bennett has put it, had the advantage over English dramatists, who "obviously could not dream of becoming the English Shakespeare."[16] The dream of becoming the German, or, for Victor Hugo, the French, Shakespeare, on the other hand, led Shakespearean imitation in a different direction for those not disadvantaged by being forced to compete in the same language.

"Shakespearo-Manie," the passion to imitate Shakespeare and create a national historical dramatic tradition, was a widespread phenomenon. "At the end of the eighteenth century," Philip Edwards argues, "Shakespeare's English history plays, which had contributed powerfully to England's national awareness at the end of the sixteenth century, began a new life, profoundly important and long-lasting, in developing a sense of national awareness in other countries."[17] In Germany, Friedrich and August Wilhelm Schlegel, Shakespeare's translators, called for a national poet to give to Germans a past, as Shakespeare had given a past to the English. Schiller, in particular, seemed to fill this bill.

No playwright before Shaw dramatizes so powerfully the rivalry between historian and dramatist as does Schiller. Schiller served as Professor of History at the University of Jena, and wrote a narrative history of the Thirty Years' War. Schiller found the partisanship of the sources he consulted in his research for this work distasteful. At one point, describing the death of Gustavus Adolphus, Schiller contrasts contemplation of the higher truth of Providence to the mudane duty of the historian: "By whatever hand he fell, his extraordinary destiny must appear a great interposition of Providence. History, too often confined to the ungrateful task of analyzing the uniform play of human passions, is occasionally rewarded by the appearance of events, which strike like a hand from heaven into the nicely adjusted machinery of human plans and carry the mind to a higher order of things."[18] Schiller carried this desire to think of a "higher order of things" rather than confine himself to the "ungrateful task" of history into his tragic trilogy, *Wallenstein*. Here Schiller adds to history a fictitious couple, Max and Thekla, who not only function as a love-interest but also rebel against the limitations of the moral, political, historical world in which they find themselves cast adrift. Wallenstein, Schiller's character, only reluctantly performs the actions history records him as performing, wondering aloud at his own motivations. The challenge to historical fact in Schiller's historical drama, though, reaches its peak in *The Maid of Orleans*, where, according to Shaw, we find Joan "drowned in a witch's caldron of raging romance." Schiller provided Joan with a love-interest, of course; but he went further and deprived her of her trial and her death at the stake. Instead, she falls gloriously on the field of battle. "Schiller's Joan has not a single point of contact with the real Joan, nor indeed with any mortal woman that ever walked this earth," Shaw complained. While Shaw deplored "Schiller's romantic nonsense" (*Collected Plays*, vol. VI, pp. 40, 41–42), Schiller in his historical plays sought, as Shaw would do, to offset the deficiencies of history by drama-tizing higher, essential truths.

Also insistent on the primacy of the artist over the mere historian was Shaw's near-contemporary August Strindberg. Strindberg's astonishing output includes twelve plays on Swedish history and four "world-historical plays," devoted to Luther, Socrates, Moses, and Christ. Most of these were written between 1898 and 1902; Strindberg planned cycles of both Swedish and world-historical plays, but never completed either. In 1903, Strindberg published an essay entitled "The Mysticism of World History" in which he projected a vision of history as "a colossal chess game with a solitary player moving both black and white."[19] Characters in Strindberg's historical plays find themselves in the grip of forces they do not understand, rewarded and punished by an inscrutable Providence.

Hegel, Buckle, and Marx

Shaw seems to be unaware of Strindberg's historical plays, but, as Strind-berg's use of the phrase "world-historical" makes clear, Strindberg was, like Shaw, attracted to Hegel's view of history. According to Hegel, history is a dialectical process, a constant opposition and negotiation between the poles of Freedom and Necessity. The human spirit pushes toward freedom and self-knowledge, but as it moves from one phase to the next it generates contradiction and opposition. Only the world-historical individual can intuit the next phase, and act "instinctively to bring to pass that which the time required." Such individuals derive their "purpose and vocation not from the calm, regular course of things, sanctioned by the existing order, but from a secret source whose content is still hidden and has not yet broken through into existence."[20] Hegel is here speaking of Julius Caesar, but his language can apply accurately not only to Saint Joan, but also to the Isaac Newton of *"In Good King Charles's Golden Days"*; Napoleon and even General Burgoyne, in Shaw's historical melodramas, likewise seem prescient, in touch with the "secret source" from which the future will spring.

"Did you ever read Buckle's History of Civilization?" Shaw asked a friend; "If not, *do*." Strindberg, too, professed himself fascinated by the work of Henry Thomas Buckle, whose *History of Civilization in England* (1857–61) applied scientific principles to the writing of history and pointed out the operation in history of evolutionary laws. "One error conflicts with another; each destroys its opponent, and truth is evolved," Buckle declared. Strindberg, like Shaw, admired Buckle's celebration of iconoclasm and skepticism, and in his first history play, *Master Olof* (1872), he offered a hero who challenged received ideas. Subtitled "What is Truth?," Strindberg's play endorsed Buckle's contention that "the authors of new ideas, the proposers of new contrivances, and the originators of new heresies, are benefactors of their species."[21] From Buckle both Strindberg and Shaw derived a view of history as an evolutionary struggle of ideas in conflict. Strindberg, converted to an idiosyncratic Christian mysticism after his mental breakdown in the late 1890s, came to repudiate Buckle's positivist methodology. While Shaw, too, was skeptical of Buckle's full-throated endorsement of material, technological, and industrial progress, his historical dramas show heroes in conflict with their societies, "authors of new ideas, proposers of new contrivances, and originators of new heresies," and indeed propose them to be "benefactors of their species." "Shaw as historian belonged very much to the idealist schools of the nineteenth century; for he presented ideas, embodied in men, as the realities of history, and will, not accident, as its driving energy," declares Martin Meisel.[22]

Shaw recommended in *The Intelligent Woman's Guide to Socialism and Capitalism* further reading not only in Buckle but, of course, in Marx. "I was completely Marxed," Shaw said (in 1934) of his early reading of *Das Kapital*; "When I read *Das Kapital* by Marx," Bertolt Brecht declared in 1926, "I understood my plays." For Brecht, Marx was "the only spectator" for whom he would write. "Karl Marx changed the mind of the world by simply telling the pursepproud nineteenth century its own villainous history," the Son declares in *Buoyant Billions* (*Collected Plays*, vol. VII, p. 318), and Shaw in numerous locations endorses this view. The celebration of material progress by Victorian historians, especially Thomas Babington Macaulay, invited "Marxian debunking."[23] As a Fabian socialist, Shaw adopted much of Marx's theory of the economic forces that shaped history and applied Marxian critique to Macaulay's view of Victorian capitalism as the highest expression of personal liberty.

In Macaulay, the idea of progress animates the history of England, and the goal to which progress leads is Macaulay's own time. This "Whig interpretation of history," as Herbert Butterfield called it, uses the present as a historical endpoint, a vantage point from which the past becomes intelligible. In a sense, it is winner's history: every earlier event can be seen as contributing to current conditions which are wholly satisfactory. For Shaw, as for Brecht, current conditions, based upon savage inequities in the distribution of property and exploitation of labor, are deplorable. More Hegelian than Marxist in his dramaturgy of ideas and in his celebration of world-historical individuals, Shaw saw Marx as a strong counter to the late-Victorian complacency enshrined in Macaulay's Whig interpretation of English history.

Anachronism

According to Butterfield, viewing the past from the perspective of the present leads inevitably to anachronism: "The study of the past with one eye, so to speak, upon the present is the source of all sins and sophistries in history, starting with the simplest of them, the anachronism."[24] Anachronism is also the means by which Shaw most plainly shocks the audiences of his historical plays and challenges their preconceptions about the past. Just as Poel's Elizabethan experiments challenged Victorian ideas about representational authenticity in staging, Shaw uses anachronism to offer a serious critique of the positivist Whig historiography of popular historians such as Macaulay. Similarly, Brecht – who offered up "Three Cheers for Shaw" early in his career (1926) – insisted later on the importance of "historicizing": "By means of historicizing, an entire social system can be observed from the viewpoint of another social system."[25] What Brecht would develop into a full-fledged theory of theatre based upon making the strange familiar and the familiar strange – a strategy of "alienation" or *Verfremdung* – Shaw anticipates in his persistent and playful use of anachronism in his history plays.

Caesar and Cleopatra (1899)

A glaring example of this strategy is Shaw's portrayal in *Caesar and Cleopatra* of Britannus, Caesar's secretary. A Romanized Briton, dressed in blue, his *"serious air and sense of the importance of the business at hand is in marked contrast to the kindly interest of Caesar, who looks at the scene,*

17 Anachronistic details – Ancient Briton with Eyeglass: Caesar (Douglas Rain) discussing
civilization with Britannus (Herb Foster) in the Shaw Festival's 1983 production of
Caesar and Cleopatra

which is new to him, with the frank curiosity of a child" (*Collected Plays*, vol. II, p. 198). Britannus, pompous and humorless, defends his bureaucratic blue suit. "Is it true that when Caesar caught you on that island," Cleopatra asks, "you were painted all over blue?" "Blue is the color worn by all Britons of good standing," Britannus stiffly responds. "In war, we stain our bodies blue; so that though our enemies may strip us of our clothes and our lives, they cannot strip us of our respectability" (*Collected Plays*, vol. II, p. 222). Here Shaw conflates the blue body-painting of the primitive Briton with the imperial civil servant's cult of "respectability." Likewise, Britannus invokes the regular churchgoing of the responsible Victorian in confronting Caesar: "What Briton speaks as you do in your moments of levity? What Briton neglects to attend the services at the sacred grove? What Briton wears clothes of many colors as you do, instead of plain blue, as all solid, well esteemed men should? These are moral questions with us" (*Collected Plays*, vol. II, p. 241). Here the juxtaposition of British domestic sobriety with the paganism of the "sacred grove" takes on a further dimension of anachronism in the biblical echo of Joseph's coat of many colors.

Shaw carries the joke further in his endnote to the play: "I find among those who have read this play in manuscript a strong conviction that an ancient Briton could not possibly have been like a modern one." Shaw parodies the theories of Hippolyte Taine, whose history of Britain insisted on the centrality of race and climate in determining national character. "We have men of exactly the same stock, and speaking the same language, growing in Great Britain, in Ireland, and in America," he argues. "The result is three of the most distinctly marked nationalities under the sun." The characteristics of the British type, he continues, would have been more pronounced in ancient Britain: indeed "exaggerated, since modern Britain, disforested, drained, urbanified, and consequently cosmopolized, is presumably less characteristically British than Caesar's Britain" (*Collected Plays*, vol. II, p. 300). The intellectual footwork here is dazzling. The putative critic, discomfited by the appearance of a modern bureaucratic character-type in what calls itself, after all, "A History," is disarmed by the invocation of climatological theory. The accusation that Britannus is a modern type is turned on its head; an ancient Briton would have to be even more quintessentially "British" than a modern, Shaw counters. By pretending to universalize the type of the Macaulayan complacent imperialist, Shaw in effect points to its narrow identification with its own class and place in time.

Shaw insisted in a 1902 letter proposing a production in Vienna upon changing Britannus so that the Austrian audience could make the proper identification: he requested "Britannus changed into an echt Wiener bourgeois, and a splendid *mise en scène*." This remark of course makes nonsense out of the whole climatological argument that Shaw would later offer in the published version of the play. He wants his audience, British or Viennese, to see in Britannus a representative of a particular class, not a particular "nationality." For a Polish production of the play, Shaw suggested replacing Ra's references to England in the Prologue with references to Poland, and he helpfully explained to the play's French translators that "Egypt for the Egyptians" was a "phrase of the Liberal politician Sir William Harcourt." Britannus is even described in a stage direction as "*unconsciously anticipating a later statesman*" when he echoes Disraeli's formulation, "Peace with honor."[26]

The play satirizes the decorums of British imperial culture while at the same time celebrating the imperial vision of Caesar. For in Julius Caesar both Hegel and Shaw saw a world-historical figure, and Shaw's source, Theodor Mommsen's *History of Rome*, similarly saw Caesar as a magnetic hero – "the entire and perfect man," in Mommsen's words.[27] But Shaw's presentation of his hero is complex, part debunking, part glorification. In

Caesar's address to the Sphinx, at the beginning of the play, both elements mingle: Caesar's portentous declaration that he has found "no air native to me, no man kindred to me, none who can do my day's deed, and think my night's thought" is undercut by Cleopatra's greeting – "Old gentleman" (*Collected Plays*, vol. II, p. 182). Nonetheless, the action of the play shows Caesar to be in tune with the Life Force and out of sympathy with Britannus's advocacy of business as usual in the empire.

In writing about Caesar as a world-historical figure, Shaw was also throwing down the gauntlet to Shakespeare. "The truce with Shakespear is over," he trumpeted in a review of a production of *Julius Caesar*. Shakespeare stands exposed in *Julius Caesar* as "a man, not for all time, but for an age only, and that age, too, in all solidly wise and heroic aspects, the most despicable of all the ages in our history." Shaw lambasts Shakespeare for his inability to dramatize Caesar as a "great man": instead we are given a "silly braggart": "There is not a single sentence uttered by Shakespeare's Julius Caesar that is, I will not say worthy of him, but even worthy of an average Tammany boss."[28] Ra, in the 1912 prologue to the play, chides the audience for expecting *Antony and Cleopatra*: "Do ye crave for a story of an unchaste woman? Hath the name of Cleopatra tempted ye hither?" (*Collected Plays*, vol. II, p. 166). As Wisenthal wittily observes, Shaw makes it clear how little Cleopatra has learned from Caesar, when, at the end of the play, she dreams of Mark Antony: "The full measure of Cleopatra's inferiority is her preference to be in Shakespeare's play rather than Shaw's."[29]

In his attack upon Shakespeare, Shaw sets himself up as a historian who can see through Shakespeare's prejudices and limitations. Shakespeare, Shaw argued in "Bernard Shaw and the Heroic Actor," created in Julius Caesar "nothing but the conventional tyrant of the Elizabethan stage adapted to Plutarch's Roundheaded account of him." There is a staggering anachronism in the identification of Plutarch as a "Roundhead": for what Shaw is actually taking on is the Whig historiography of Macaulay that saw in the Civil War a step in the direction of liberty. "Shakespear's sympathies were with Plutarch and the Nonconformist Conscience, which he personified as Brutus," Shaw continues. "From the date of Shakespear's play onward England believed in Brutus with growing hope and earnestness until the assassination in the Capitol was repeated in Whitehall, and Brutus got his chance from Cromwell, who found him hopelessly incapable, and ruled in Caesar's fashion until he died, when the nation sent for Charles II because it was determined to have anybody rather than Brutus" (*Collected Plays*, vol. II, pp. 309–10). This rant utterly misreads Shakespeare's play, transforms Shakespeare into a kind of Macaulay, and wildly stretches the

18 Debunking mythologies – heroes as ordinary people: Douglas Rain as Caesar and
Marti Maraden as Cleopatra in the Shaw Festival's 1983 production of
Caesar and Cleopatra

parallel to the breaking point. Yet in it Shaw represents himself as defending historical accuracy against Shakespeare's, Plutarch's, and Macaulay's depredations.

Shaw acts out his rivalry with Shakespeare by reinventing *Julius Caesar* as a simplistic Whig allegory of the English Civil War and then chiding Shakespeare for perpetrating such a slander. In a similar strategy of appropriation, he claimed that *Caesar and Cleopatra* was "a chapter of Mommsen and a page of Plutarch furnished with scenery and dialogue, and that a boy brought to see the play could pass an examination next day on the Alexandrian expedition without losing a mark" (*Collected Plays*, vol. II, p. 312). That is, Shaw acts out his rivalry with professional historians by suggesting that he has had expert advice (consulting with Gilbert Murray) and that his critics cannot distinguish between pure fancy and transcribed Plutarch. Shakespeare becomes an ally in the campaign to establish the play's historical authenticity: like a Shakespearean chronicle play, Shaw's is "the real thing, the play in which the playwright simply takes what the chronicler brings him and puts it on the stage as it is said to have happened" (*Collected Plays*, vol. II, p. 311). Tellingly, Shaw here recasts Ranke's famous dictum that history reports the past *"wie es eigentlich gewesen"* –

as it really happened – with the suggestion that historical narratives themselves may not be trustworthy. Between what *really* happened and what "is said to have happened" opens up the gulf of historical narrative.

In an interview about *Arms and the Man*, Shaw argued that historical narratives necessarily followed the rules of literary composition. "Why, you cannot even write a history without adapting the facts to the conditions of literary narrative, which are in some respects much more distorting than the dramatic conditions of representation on stage," Shaw pointed out. Like Schiller, he finds that source material is already contaminated by the interests of the creators of original documents themselves: "[A]ll reports, even by eyewitnesses, all histories, all stories, all dramatic representations are only attempts to arrange the facts in a thinkable, intelligible, interesting form – that is, when they are not more or less intentional efforts to hide the truth, as they often are." Here Shaw gives voice to ideas that are currently associated with the work of Hayden White. In an extensive study of nineteenth-century historians, White argued that historical narratives follow rules of literary genre even as they claim a higher responsibility to fact than literature. "The contributions of Marx and Nietzsche to the 'crisis of historicism' of the late nineteenth century," White argues, "consisted in their historicization of the very concept of objectivity itself."[30] For Shaw, too, the category of historical "fact" itself is suspect, dependent upon narrative for its intelligibility. History *never* represents "what really happened."

Saint Joan (1923)

Shaw thus straddles a fence by on the one hand adopting a posture of skepticism toward historical source material and on the other hand insisting that his historical plays are more faithful to the sources, more seriously researched, than those of his predecessors. In *Saint Joan*, Shaw takes care to place his play among other plays about Joan, among them Shakespeare's hostile representation of "Joan the Pucell" in *Henry VI, Part One*. Shaw speculates that Shakespeare began by making Joan a "beautiful and romantic figure," but was persuaded by his "scandalized company" that such a representation would never do. Or, possibly, Shakespeare was called in as a play doctor, to tinker with a "wholly scurrilous" earlier version, "shedding a momentary glamor on the figure of The Maid." Voltaire's mock-epic, *La Pucelle*, comes in for critique, and of Schiller's play Shaw concludes "that it is not about Joan at all, and can hardly be said to pretend to be" (*Collected Plays*, vol. VI, pp. 39–40). Shaw sets out to stage Joan, as both a real person and a world-historical figure, in touch with the Hegelian "secret source" of the future.

Because telling the truth about the real Joan involves assessing her historical importance in the long term, Shaw insists upon dramatizing not only her life but its subsequent re-evaluations in her rehabilitation and canonization in the Epilogue. Unlike the run-of-the-mill Jeanne d'Arc melodramas, Shaw's play takes into account the Maid's continued presence in history. In so doing, it pushes the limits of the form of historical drama. *Caesar and Cleopatra*, Meisel argues, "though aggressively heterodox toward certain conventions of contemporary historical drama" remains bound to Victorian conventions of "spectacle and costume." However, Shaw also teases the Victorian reliance on spectacle by listing scenes such as the Burning of the Library and the Capture of the Pharos in the program for the 1899 copyright performance: scenes which then remain firmly offstage. In *Saint Joan*, Shaw promised to "ignore the limitations of the nineteenth century scenic stage as completely as Shakespear did," and the play moves toward the Shavian genres of Discussion, in its presentation of the debates among Cauchon, Lemaître, and Warwick, and Extravaganza, in the Epilogue.[31]

Again the effect is of startling and audacious anachronism. Taking a leaf from Thucydides' pages – in which the Greek historian admits to inventing appropriate speeches for his figures to deliver – Shaw insists that Cauchon, Lemaître, and Warwick are represented as "saying the things they actually would have said if they had known what they were really doing. And beyond this neither drama nor history can go in my hands." Thus Shaw's trifling with "verisimilitude" in matters of fact serves the higher goal of "veracity." The anachronistic ability of Warwick and Cauchon to anticipate Joan's later significance allows an audience to appreciate implications of which the historical originals of these characters must have been unaware. As Shaw puts it, "they were part of the Middle Ages themselves, and therefore as unconscious of its peculiarities as of the atomic formula of the air they breathed" (*Collected Plays*, vol. VI, pp. 73–74). Pondering Joan's insistence upon following her voices, Warwick comments: "It is the protest of the individual soul against the interference of priest or peer between the private man and his God. I should call it Protestantism if I had to find a name for it." "Scratch an Englishman, and find a Protestant," observes Cauchon, dourly. "Well, if you will burn the Protestant, I will burn the Nationalist," Warwick concludes, for his primary anxiety is about Joan's threat to the feudal system.

Shaw even includes a Britannus-type in this debate about Joan. "Certainly England for the English goes without saying," concurs the Chaplain: "it is the simple law of nature. But this woman denies to England her legitimate conquests, given her by God because of her peculiar fitness to rule over less

19 Shifting the time scale – bringing history into the present: George Dawson as Warwick and Michael Ball as Cauchon in the "tent scene," in the Shaw Festival's 1993 production of *Saint Joan*

civilized races for their own good." It is a measure of the Chaplain's benighted *simplicitas* that he echoes the Macaulayan imperial theme at the same moment in which he fails to notice what Shaw sees as the truth about Joan. "I do not understand what your lordships mean by Protestant and Nationalist," he says, "you are too learned and subtle for a poor clerk like myself. But I know as a matter of plain commonsense that the woman is a rebel; and that is enough for me" (*Collected Plays*, vol. VI, p. 139–40). For two authors whom Shaw admires, Buckle and Ibsen, the figure of the rebel embodies the challenge of the future to the past. "In short," Shaw declares in the preface, "though all society is founded on intolerance, all improvement is founded on tolerance, or the recognition of the fact that the law of evolution is Ibsen's law of change" (*Collected Plays*, vol. VI, p. 57).

"And now tell me," Joan asks after she learns that she has been made a saint in 1920, "shall I rise from the dead and come back to you a living woman?" Nobody wants that: even the Gentleman who brings her the news must "return to Rome for fresh instructions." Joan is as much ahead of her time in 1920 as she was four hundred years before. Her plea at the end of the play – "O God that madest this beautiful earth, when will it be ready to receive thy saints? How long, O Lord, how long?" – looks back over the span of time between her trial, her rehabilitation, and her canonization. It also looks forward to a future which only rebels and visionaries can imagine (*Collected Plays*, vol. VI, p. 206–08).

The Epilogue to *Saint Joan* epitomizes a paradoxical historiography.[32] Generally speaking, historians tend to think teleologically – seeing history as moving towards a goal, like Macaulay's free British Empire – or cyclically – seeing history as a consisting of repetition and return. Shaw portrays Joan in the Epilogue as the rebel, unwelcome to the intolerant in any age, and as an embodiment of the possibility, over the very long term, of change. Shaw's historiography is in the short term pessimistic and cyclical – the hidebound attitudes of Britannus and the Chaplain are always with us – and in the long run evolutionary. The contrast with W. B. Yeats, whose theory of history is precisely the reverse – in the long run cyclical but in the short run evolutionary – is illuminating. The idea of geological time, which fascinated the Victorians, suddenly allowing the possibility of eons of evolution rather than the orthodox 6,000 or so years of history since creation calculated by Archbishop Ussher, liberated Shaw to see history as both constantly repetitive and always subject to the law of change.

"*In Good King Charles's Golden Days*" (1939)

"Did not the late Archbishop Ussher fix the dates of everything that ever happened?" Charles II asks Isaac Newton on the day in 1680 when Shaw brings these figures (who never met) together in his "True History That Never Happened." "Unfortunately he did not allow for the precession of the equinoxes," Newton counters (*Collected Plays*, vol. VII, p. 223). By the end of the first scene, Newton has experienced what Shaw calls in the preface "a flash of prevision," and he "foresees Einstein's curvilinear universe" (*Collected Plays*, vol. VII, p. 206). The irruption into Newton's quiet house in Cambridge of King Charles, the Quaker George Fox, and the painter Godfrey Kneller (along with Charles's brother James and three of Charles's mistresses) has not only ruined Newton's day, but changed the universe. His "life's work turned to waste, vanity, folly" Newton must repudiate the book correcting Ussher's chronology that he has been working on:

> And what have you and Mr. Fox done to that book? Reduced it to a monument of the folly of Archibishop Ussher, who dated the creation of the world at four thousand and four, BC, and of my stupidity in assuming that he had proved his case. My book is nonsense from beginning to end. How could I, who have calculated that God deals in millions of miles of infinite space, be such an utter fool as to limit eternity, which has neither beginning nor end, to a few thousand years? But this man Fox, without education, without calculation, without even a schoolboy's algebra, knew this when I, who was born one of the greatest mathematicians in the world, drudged over my silly book for months, and could not see what was staring me in the face.
>
> (*Collected Plays*, vol. VII, p. 274)

Newton's epiphany comes as the result of an anachronism that Shaw singles out for his reader's attention in the preface. Alluding to the "eternal clash between the artist and the physicist," Shaw "invented a collision between Newton and a personage whom I should like to have called Hogarth; for it was Hogarth who said 'the line of beauty is a curve,' and Newton whose first dogma it was that the universe is in principle rectilinear." Instead, Shaw gives the quote and the role of artist to Godfrey Kneller, endowing him also with "Hogarth's brains." Why? "In point of date Kneller just fitted in." Apparently it is not historically irresponsible to invent a collision between physicist and artist, and not intolerably anachronistic to put in the artist's mouth words not spoken until much later by another artist: but it would be unacceptable to transpose Hogarth, "by any magic," to 1680.

Later on, Shaw confesses, "I have made Newton aware of something wrong with the perihelion of Mercury. Not since Shakespear made Hector of Troy quote Aristotle has the stage perpetrated a more staggering anachronism. But I find the perihelion of Mercury so staggering a laugh catcher (like Weston-super-Mare) that I cannot bring myself to sacrifice it." Here the rules of history and the rules of comedy come into conflict, and Shaw cheerfully resolves the conflict in favor of comedy, though, of course, he is "actually prepared to defend it as a possibility" (*Collected Plays*, vol. VII, p. 205).

Shaw may rule here in favor of the "laugh catcher," but the play also insists on offering a version of Charles II that is corrective of the image portrayed by Macaulay. Macaulay's Charles is indolent and affable, easily run by his mistresses, secretly a pawn of Louis XIV. Shaw's Charles is witty, percipient, and quite aware that he is taking Louis XIV's money and returning nothing of value. He foresees with (anachronistic) clarity the troubles his brother James will run into and the eventual invitation to "Orange Billy" and Macaulay's Glorious Revolution. Charles enjoys playing his mistresses off against each other, and in the play's second scene he discloses the full measure of his loyalty and affection for his wife. Catherine of Braganza sets the record straight: "You have never been really unfaithful to me," she declares; "You are not lazy: I wish you were: I should see more of you." At the end of the play she reminds him to put on his wig: "Nobody would take you for King Charles the Second without that wig" (*Collected Plays*, vol. VII, p. 292; 295; 301). With this tribute to the tradition of Victorian pictorialism the play comes to a close.

Shaw, history, and drama

Shaw "gives the theatre as much fun as it can stand," Brecht wrote in "Three Cheers for Shaw," and in his engagement with history we see his playfulness in full force.[33] His delight in the staggering anachronism, his assault as a kind of intellectual "terrorist" (the word is Brecht's) upon preconceived, heroic, pictorial notions of appropriate representation of the past, his bumptious arrogation to himself of total authority over history – all these constitute a serious challenge to the high prestige enjoyed by narrative history in the late nineteenth century. By recognizing that history follows rules of narrative construction, Shaw is able to exploit what is fictive in his sources and contrast it to the more immediate truth of dramatic representation. Shaw's history plays are modern, Stephen Watt argues, in that they "heighten the audience's consciousness of its own participation in a theatrical event" by breaking illusion.[34] The technique of anachronism, blurring categories and forcing the question of what, exactly, changes over time and what remains the same, is crucial to this enterprise. Shaw demands that his audiences, like the readers of the extra-theatrical discussions which accompany his plays, actively think about the historical vision he expresses. As he forces his audiences to engage in debate, Shaw anticipates Brecht's vision of a new theatre for the scientific age.

Historical drama, as Lindenberger insists, enacts the tension between literature and reality, between the present and the past, between theatrical immediacy and historical distance. Shaw insists on making his audiences think historically, and he does so by emphasizing the artificiality and arbitrariness of the kinds of historical narratives they tend uncritically to accept. Proclaiming his drama's higher truth, critiquing the bias of historians and the fragmentary nature of historical documentation, Shaw anticipates Hayden White's critique as he at the same time returns to a Shakespearean claim of equal authority with the historian. "History, Sir, will tell lies, as usual," Shaw's General Burgoyne says in response to the question, "What will History say?" (*Collected Plays*, vol. II, p. 131). Strindberg entitled one of his Blue Book essays "Lie-History," and enjoyed pointing out that Herodotus, the Father of History, was also the Father of Lies. This skepticism is modern, to be sure, but it also has a long tradition, in which historical drama necessarily participates. Shaw's reinvention of the history play restores to lying its full fictive dignity and gives to anachronism and factual error the status of alternative truth. In their glorification of paradox, the history plays figure importantly in Shaw's larger project of the constant reinvention of himself.

NOTES

1 Herbert Lindenberger, *Historical Drama: The Relation of Reality and Literature* (Chicago: University of Chicago Press, 1975), p. x.
2 Irving Ribner, *The English History Play in the Age of Shakespeare* (New York: Barnes and Noble, 1965), p. 3; p. 267.
3 Quoted by J. L. Wisenthal, *Shaw's Sense of History* (Oxford: Clarendon Press, 1988), p. 61.
4 *Aristotle's "Poetics,"* trans. S. H. Butcher, introduction by Francis Fergusson (New York: Hill and Wang, 1961), p. 68.
5 *The Critical Works of Thomas Rymer*, ed. Curt A. Zimansky (New Haven: Yale University Press, 1956), p. 163.
6 Bernard Shaw, *The Bodley Head Bernard Shaw: Collected Plays with their Prefaces*, ed. Dan H. Laurence, 7 vols. (London: Max Reinhardt, The Bodley Head, 1970–74), vol. VI, p. 74. Paul Hernadi, in *Interpreting Events: Tragicomedies of History on the Modern Stage* (Ithaca: Cornell University Press, 1985), discusses the dialectic of "veracity" and "verisimilitude" in *Saint Joan*, pp. 17–21.
7 Martin Meisel, *Shaw and the Nineteenth Century Theater* (Princeton: Princeton University Press, 1963), p. 355.
8 Wisenthal, *Shaw's Sense of History*, p. vii.
9 J. R. Planché, *Recollections and Reflections* (London: Tinsley Brothers, 1872), vol. I, p. 56.
10 Review in the *Post* quoted by Stephen Watt, "Historical Drama and the 'Legitimate' Theatre: Tom Taylor and W. G. Wills in the 1870s," in Judith L. Fisher and Stephen Watt (eds.), *When They Weren't Doing Shakespeare: Essays on Nineteenth-Century British and American Theatre* (Athens: University of Georgia Press, 1989), p. 201.
11 *Our Theatres in the Nineties: Criticisms Contributed Week by Week to the Saturday Review from January 1895 to May 1898*, in vols. XXIII–XXV of *The*

Works of Bernard Shaw (New York: W. H. Wise and Co., 1931), vol. XXII, p. 198; vol. XXV, p. 381.

12 For fuller discussion of Poel's work, see J. L. Styan, *The Shakespeare Revolution: Criticism and Performance in the Twentieth Century* (Cambridge: Cambridge University Press, 1977); see also Jonas Barish, "Is There 'Authenticity' in Theatrical Performance?" *Modern Language Review* 89 (1994), pp. 817–31.

13 Watt, "Historical Drama," p. 201; Wills quoted, p. 205.

14 Quoted by Meisel, *Shaw and the Nineteenth Century Theater*, p. 3.

15 Niloufer Harben, *Twentieth Century English History Plays: From Shaw to Bond* (Totowa, NJ: Barnes and Noble Books, 1988), p. 6.

16 Benjamin Bennett, *Modern Drama and German Classicism* (Ithaca: Cornell University Press, 1979), p. 63.

17 Christian Dietrich Grabbe coined the word in his essay, "Über die Shakespearo-Manie" (1827); Philip Edwards, *The Threshold of a Nation: A Study in English and Irish Drama* (Cambridge: Cambridge University Press, 1979), pp. 191–92.

18 Friedrich Schiller, *History of the Thirty Years' War*, trans. A. J. W. Morrison (New York: Harper Brothers, 1846), p. 264.

19 August Strindberg, "Världshistoriens Mystik," in John Landquist (ed.), *Samlade Skrifter*, vol. LIV (Stockholm: Bonnier, 1920), p. 353. My translation.

20 G. W. F. Hegel, *Reason in History*, trans. Robert S. Hartman (Indianapolis: Bobbs-Merrill, 1953), pp. 39–40.

21 Shaw quoted by Wisenthal, *Shaw's Sense of History*, p. 21; Buckle quoted by Wisenthal, *Shaw's Sense of History*, p. 127n.

22 Meisel, *Shaw and the Nineteenth Century Theater*, p. 375.

23 Shaw quoted from a letter to St. John Ervine (1936) in Wisenthal, *Shaw's Sense of History*, p. 19; Bertolt Brecht, *Schriften zum Theater*, ed. Werner Hecht, in *Gesammelte Werke* (Frankfurt: Suhrkamp, 1967), vol. XV, p. 129; my translation.

24 Herbert Butterfield, *The Whig Interpretation of History* (1931; rpt. New York: Norton, 1965), pp. 31–32.

25 "Three Cheers for Shaw" is John Willett's translation of "Ovation für Shaw," in *Brecht on Theatre*, ed. and trans. John Willett (New York: Hill and Wang, 1964), p. 10–13; *Der Messingkauf* quoted from Brecht, *Schriften zum Theater*, vol. XVI, p. 653; my translation.

26 Letter to Siegfried Trebitsch, quoted by Meisel, *Shaw and the Nineteenth Century Theater*, p. 361; other remarks quoted by Wisenthal, *Shaw's Sense of History*, p. 102.

27 Mommsen quoted by Harben, *Twentieth Century English History Plays*, p. 28.

28 Shaw, *Our Theatre in the Nineties*, vol. XXV, pp. 313–14.

29 Wisenthal, *Shaw's Sense of History*, p. 61

30 Shaw quoted by *ibid.*, p. 49. Hayden White, *Metahistory: The Historical Imagination in Nineteenth-Century Europe* (Baltimore: Johns Hopkins University Press, 1973), p. 280; see also White's *The Content of the Form* (Baltimore: Johns Hopkins University Press, 1988).

31 Meisel, *Shaw and the Nineteenth Century Theater*, p. 361; p. 365.

32 Stephen Watt, in "Shaw's *Saint Joan* and the Modern History Play," *Compara-*

tive Drama 19 (1985), discusses "Shaw's almost paradoxical philosophy of history" with reference to Hayden White, pp. 82–83.
33 *Brecht on Theatre*, p. 11.
34 Stephen Watt, "*Saint Joan* and the Modern History Play," p. 76.

FURTHER READING

General

Ludeke, H., "Some Remarks on Shaw's History Plays," *English Studies* 36 (1955), pp. 239–46.
Roy, R. N., *George Bernard Shaw's Historical Plays*, Delhi: Macmillan Co. of India, 1976.
Whitman, Robert F., *Shaw and The Play of Ideas*, Ithaca: Cornell University Press, 1977.

Caesar and Cleopatra

Couchman, Gordon W., *This Our Caesar: A Study of Bernard Shaw's Caesar and Cleopatra*, The Hague: Mouton, 1973.
Harrison, G. B., *Julius Caesar in Shakespeare, Shaw, and the Ancients*, New York: Harcourt, Brace, 1960.
Larson, Gale K., "*Caesar and Cleopatra*: The Making of a History Play," *The Shaw Review* 14 (1971), pp. 73–89.
Weintraub, Stanley, "Shaw's Mommsenite Caesar," in Philip Allison Shelley and Arthur O. Lewis, Jr. (eds.), *Anglo-German and American-German Crosscurrents: 2*, Chapel Hill: University of North Carolina Press, 1962.
Wisenthal, J. L., "Shaw and Ra: Religion and Some History Plays," *Shaw: The Annual of Bernard Shaw Studies 1: Shaw and Religion*, ed. Charles A. Berst, University Park: Pennsylvania State University Press, 1981, pp. 45–56.

Saint Joan

Fielden, John, "Shaw's *Saint Joan* as Tragedy," *Twentieth-Century Literature* 3 (1957), pp. 59–67.
Hill, Holly, *Playing Joan: Actresses on the Challenge of Shaw's Saint Joan: Twenty-Six Interviews*, New York: Theatre Communications Group, 1987.
Hollis, Christopher, "Mr. Shaw's *St. Joan*," *Shaw: The Annual of Bernard Shaw Studies 2*, ed. Stanley Weintraub, University Park: Pennsylvania State University Press, 1982, pp. 155–170.
Huizinga, Johan, "Bernard Shaw's Saint," in *Men and Ideas: History, the Middle Ages, the Renaissance: Essays*, trans. James S. Holmes and Hans van Marle, New York: Meridian, 1959.
Silver, Arnold Jacques, *Saint Joan: Playing with Fire*, New York: Twayne, 1993.
Stowell, Sheila, "'Dame Joan, Saint Christabell,'" *Modern Drama* 37 (1994), pp. 421–36.
Tyson, Brian, *The Story of Shaw's Saint Joan*, Kingston: McGill-Queen's University Press, 1982.

Weintraub, Stanley (ed.), *Saint Joan: Fifty Years After, 1923/4–1973/4,* Baton
  Rouge: Louisiana State University Press, 1973.

"In Good King Charles's Golden Days"

Evans, T. F., " '*In Good King Charles's Golden Days*': The Dramatist as Historian,"
  Shaw: The Annual of Bernard Shaw Studies 7: The Neglected Plays, ed. Alfred
  Turco, Jr., University Park: Pennsylvania State University Press, 1987,
  pp. 259–79.
Keynes, John Maynard, Lord, "G. B. S. and Isaac Newton," in Max Beerbohm,
  et al., *G. B. S. 90: Aspects of Bernard Shaw's Life and Work*, ed. Stephen
  Winsten, New York: Hutchinson, 1946.

11

TRACY C. DAVIS

Shaw's interstices of empire: decolonizing at home and abroad

Playing around the edges of monolithic binaries is one of Shaw's trade-marked strategies. Some might call it his perversity, others the common stock of comedic reversal. A more precise technical term might be parataxis: the setting side by side of statements or concepts without explicitly indicating their relationship. As an ironicist, Shaw consistently draws out our assumptions about the relationship, teases out unexpected complications from the logical follow-through of those assumptions, then displays the fallacy of the universe being as simple and stable as we might ever assume. The paratactic concepts frequently resemble the most familiar tropes of dramatic literature: the struggle between the sexes, monogamy versus infidelity or polygamy, class conflict, and the native versus the foreign. But just as Britain was a hybrid of many nations, the Empire was a hybrid of many peoples, and iconoclasts were made by many forces, Shaw's plays are complicated by more than merely the rivalry of women and men, the contest between poet and philistine, the incompatibility of hero and coward, or the mutual exclusivity of respectability and unfettered naturism. Rather, his plays frequently are exercises in the theatricalization of per-formances around and between such concepts. Altogether, they suggest prolonged meditation on the dilemma of colonization: never achieving postcolonialism because institutions of power are not dismantled, but exploring the varieties of subjection resulting from policies of hegemony metonymically embodied.

In several of the plays most blatant in their critiques of colonialism, *Caesar and Cleopatra* (1898), *John Bull's Other Island* (1904), and *St. Joan* (1923), Shaw engages the colonial metaphor in cultures resistant of a colonizing nation's charms, as the call of "Egypt for the Egyptians" is echoed by "Ireland for the Irish" and "France for the French," utilizing anachronism to draw parallels to contemporary British politics of the most high-blown sort and foregrounding his own identification as an Irishman within debates about Home Rule. In another set of plays forming the focus of this essay, Shaw alternates between setting his polemics in the heart of Britain and the imaginary outposts of empire. In mundane details of plotting, Shaw consistently likens the micropolitics of households and inter-gender relations to questions of statecraft, inviting comparisons between the state of marital bonding and the utterly unnatural coupling of ruler and colony. *Candida* (1895) provides the paradigmatic example of Shaw's ability to relate the microeconomy and power of a household to the macroeconomic concerns of global capitalism, its product (colonialism), and the complicity of colonialism in gender ideology and racism. Here, as elsewhere, the *ménage à trois* inspired Shaw. Perhaps because in his own life he kept finding himself on different points of the romantic triangle, he experienced the interstitial poignancy of "betweenness" to great paratactic effect.

In the parsonage of St. Dominic's (East London), the Reverend James Morell believes he is a responsible socialist, operating on the principle that "We have no more right to consume happiness without producing it than to consume wealth without producing it."[1] Morell is kind and equitable to his employees, asking them to share no hardships greater than his own. His father-in-law Burgess used to offer less than subsistence wages to sweated female garment workers, but Morell now accepts him as a self-styled "moddle hemployer" because he fired all the women, replaced them with machines, and pays excellent wages to the men who remain to oversee the equipment. This is the chink in Morell's thinking: he does not look at the root cause of capitalist profit that motivates Burgess, and thereby misses the fundamental relationship between the exploitation of women and their dispensability from the economic equation. What he thinks is merely "Prossy's Complaint" – his stenographers' propensity to stay with him for low wages and participate in household labor simply because they are enamored with him – is merely a trumped-up sentimentalized version of Burgess's methods, displacing the dependency of economic necessity for romantic attraction. This is not simply a matter of class exploitation – the transliteration of Burgess's Cockney accent precludes that conclusion – but a matter of one gender's willingness to extend unlimited credit (in the form of fidelity and nurturing) and the other gender's willingness to exploit this credit fulsomely for its own glory or profit. There is no denying, in this formulation, that domestic work has everything to do with the relationship of wage labor to capital which, for a socialist such as Shaw, is the relation-ship at the heart of all that ails society.[2]

The young idealist poet Eugene Marchbanks questions the equilibrium in the parsonage. His involvement in the Morell household is seemingly his first experience with a stable nuclear family. He establishes himself, at least in Morell's mind, as a rival for Candida's affections. Discovering that Candida takes part in household labor by filling the lamps, blackleading, and slicing common onions, he is struck with "poetic horror," preferring to hold to Patmorean values of the household angel with unsullied hands, equating the "idle, selfish, and useless" with the "beautiful and free and happy."[3] Morell believes that the context in which he earned Candida's love (in the scullery or the pulpit) does not matter as long as it was done honorably: "*I did not take the moment on credit; nor did I use it to steal another man's happiness,*" as Marchbanks clearly aims to do.[4] Morell believes himself to be an honest trader. He believes himself on solid ground as long as this model of transaction is stable. He wants to be the husband-as-honest-broker, with his wife as recipient of the fair deal, returning affection for social good. But Morell's tussle with Marchbanks in Act 3 is motivated by his sudden uncertainty about Candida's affections. He suffers a crisis of categories and wants Candida to resolve it by choosing between them. Shaw composes a delightful moment of dramatic irony:

> MORELL: We have agreed – he and I – that you shall choose between us now. I await your decision.
> CANDIDA: (*slowly recoiling a step, her heart hardened by his rhetoric in spite of the sincere feeling behind it*) Oh! I am to choose, am I? It is quite settled that I must belong to one or the other.

In this moment, the *Doll's House* resonance is clearest. The Candida who, earlier that day, pulled her husband to the easy chair and sat on the carpet beside his knee in order to sue for more time together, *might* in this later moment turn thoroughly conventional or utterly defiant. Without missing a beat, Morell responds firmly, "Quite. You must choose definitely." Candida says nothing – but it is an interstitial nothing that Marchbanks comprehends, at least in part.

> MARCHBANKS: (*anxiously*) Morell: you dont understand. She means that she belongs to herself.
> CANDIDA: (*turning on him*) I mean that, and a good deal more, Master Eugene, as you will both find out presently. And pray, my lords and masters, what have you to offer for my choice? I am up for auction, it seems. What do you bid, James?[5]

She takes the high ground, morally and literally. Seating Morell in the children's chair, Marchbanks in the visitor's chair, and herself in the easy chair, she reveals that she has no crisis of categories. She theatricalizes the two men's status and, claiming the power to choose rather than merely being allowed it, takes the weaker of the two. Explaining Morell's life to him (how his coddled childhood and idolized manhood have caused no end

20   The triumph of the female over the poet: Duncan Ollerenshaw as Marchbanks
appealing to Seana McKenna as Candida in the Shaw Festival's 1993 production
of *Candida*

of trouble to the women who cared for him) and revealing herself to be all
the female categories wrapped up into one (wife, mother, sister, and mother
to his children), it is a scenario that Marchbanks promptly abandons.
Whether repelled, matured, enlightened, or hardened it is not clear but he
departs, claiming to know a secret.

This primal scene of middle-class, Christian, socialist, monogamous,
heterosexual, procreatively successful family life demonstrates perfectly
how if we understand a household we have understood the world, and if
we understand housework we have understood the world's economy.
Through Marchbanks, Shaw forces attention away from the pumped-up

socialist orator onto the domestic front. Through the sharing of household duties in the parsonage there is a claim to dispersing the economic servitude that normally goes to married women (and the Third and Fourth Worlds), yet by holding rigidly to categories Morell clings to the most fundamental dyads of nineteenth-century British life: the husband and wife, and master and servant. Candida proclaims in the last moments, "I make him master here, though he does not know it, and could not tell you a moment ago how it came to be so."[6] By *making* him master, over and over on a daily basis, he never really *is* master. Instead, Morell exists on the feminine side of the binary, not a husband but a dependent, not a provider of economic opportunity but one who is protected and enabled by the silent complicity of another in his fictions about his strength, industry, and dignity. But while he exists on the feminine side, he is still the man. And while the feminine side is typically aligned with the colonized in terms of global politics, the lie that colonizers tell themselves about the colonized nation's dependency on them is more than evident in Candida's superior strength, yet she is still the woman.

Homi Bhabha refers to Nadine Gordimer's *My Son's Story* but could well be describing *Candida* when he insists "It . . . requires a shift of attention from the political as a pedagogical, ideological practice to politics as the stressed necessity of everyday life – politics as a performativity."[7] In *Candida*, this comes out clearly during Morell's moment of public triumph (a rousing speech to the Guild of St. Matthew), when Shaw focuses attention onto the private realm of the parsonage by dramatizing a scene between Candida and Marchbanks rather than dramatizing Morell's concurrent declamation. It would seem to be a clear contrast of the Habermasian binary of public and private, yet by the end of the Act this comfortable split is questioned by the multiple demonstration of the inappropriateness of simple categories. To give a single example, Proserpine Garnett discovers she likes champagne, breaks her pledge of abstention, yet claims she is only a "beer tee-totaller." Thus, categories can be disposed of without important consequences, but what actually remains is probably what operated all along: an existence interstitial to the binaries, that flexes ideology in the everyday vicissitudes of responding to desires. The play ends as Morell and Candida embrace – a tacit acceptance that they will continue to perform "marriage" much as before – but a more complex picture underpins it as an institution.

Getting Married (1908), written a decade after Shaw wed Charlotte Payne-Townshend, concerns another frocked household, this time the bishopric of Chelsea in the west of London. Categories are rather elastic in this topsy-turvy household where the Bishop's study is in the scullery, the family councils are in a medieval kitchen out of all human and budgetary proportion, the greengrocer is the family's confidant, and polyandrously inclined women are welcome as long as they are charming. For a bishop's household, the sacraments are remarkably out of vogue. The Bishop's brother Reginald is in the divorce court, his sister Lesbia criticizes the law for not allowing her to have children without the appendage of a husband, and the Bishop himself has recommended to four prime ministers that the divorce law must be amended or the propertied classes may finally strike against the institution of marriage.

Lesbia presages the crisis when she remarks that "an English lady is not the slave of her appetites. That is what an English gentleman seems incapable of understanding."[8] On the morning of her wedding, the Bishop's daughter Edith has received the pamphlet "Do You Know what You are Going to Do? By a Woman Who has Done It." Meanwhile, her fiancé Cecil has received Ernest Belfort Bax's essays on men's wrongs.[9] These writings enlighten them about the laws prohibiting women from suing for divorce except on grounds of adultery, no matter how heinous the husband's behavior, and the laws that will obligate Cecil to take financial responsibility if his wife is sued for libel. Edith rejects whatever appetites she might have for Cecil, and the afternoon's wedding is called off. Cecil, who is responsible for his mother's and sister's upkeep, is justifiably concerned about his liability, for if after marriage Edith proclaims publicly that the factory owner Slattox has "two hundred girls in his power as absolute slaves" he could lose all his net worth and his mother could go starving. Edith's political conviction takes precedence over the "private" arrangement of marriage, and she refuses to censor her speech.

It is noteworthy that fear of naming an industrial slavery in their midst is what motivates the play's crisis and most of its serious consideration of the marriage sacrament. The alternative of a legal contract is proposed, and the Bishop's solicitor-turned-cleric attempts to draw it up to suit everyone. The debates reveal the underlying ideologies that gruesomely prop up marriage. When Lesbia proposes that children should belong to the mother, Reginald swears "I'll fight for the ownership of my own children tooth and nail," showing that the relationship is one of property, not affection.[10] But countering the idea that children are the result of non-productive labor – and thus "free" like the earth, water, native peoples, or other forms of "Nature" available for capital exploitation – Edith insists that procreation is work that should be rewarded with a stake in the offspring as realizable property.

EDITH: It seems to me that they should be divided between the parents. If Cecil wishes any of the children to be his exclusively, he should pay me a certain sum for the risk and trouble of bringing them into the world: say a thousand pounds apiece. The interest on this could go towards the support of the child as long as we live together. But the principle would be my property. In that way, if Cecil took the child away from me, I should at least be paid for what it had cost me.[11]

Believing in the same ethic but taking it to a sexist extreme, Reginald sees the whole venture of marriage as if it should be a guaranteed investment against risk: "I think it jolly hard that a man should support his wife for years, and lose the chance of getting a really good wife, and then have her refuse to be a wife to him."[12] A slave could not so refuse.

The late entrance of the fabled Mrs. George, wife to a coal merchant who happens to be the Mayor, sharpens the terms of the debate while supposedly brokering a solution to the stalemate. In love, she says while possessed by a trance, women give the ultimate gift: "eternity in a single moment, strength of the mountains in one clasp of your arms, and the volume of all the seas in one impulse of your souls."[13] This is sheer essentialism, but the fact that women bear the price of sexual union – the torture of childbirth – whereupon men only heap more burdens upon them is biologically axiomatic. Shaw takes the analogy further, into the realm of marital politics:

MRS. GEORGE: I carried the child in my arms: must I carry the father too? . . . Was it not enough? We spent eternity together; and you ask me for a little lifetime more. We possessed all the universe together; and you ask me to give you my scanty wages as well. I have given you the greatest of all things; and you ask me to give you little things. I gave you your own soul: you ask me for my body as a plaything. Was it not enough? Was it not enough?[14]

It is economic coercion. It is exploitation. It is the enslavement of all married women, not a mere two hundred in a factory, for like slavery there is no way for a women to say no other than to run to another master; no way to end his unrestricted appropriation of her body; no way to refuse the tyranny of a husband's demands except by colluding to break the law and deceive society. It is strong stuff for 1908, and little wonder Shaw could only portray it as spoken in a mesmeric fit. It goes way beyond the practical reform of suffrage to the very heart of the domestic and political economy of the British, at home and abroad.

Misalliance (1910) resumes the idea, meditating on childrearing to make a broader context for family life. Lord Summerhays, formerly governor of "a place twice as big as England" where the interracial mixing "civilizes them" while it "uncivilizes us" to the detriment of the British, is completely incapable of managing his son, Bentley. Having lived "so long in a country where a man may have fifty sons, who are no more to him than a regiment of soldiers . . . I'm afraid Ive lost the English feeling about it."[15] Tarleton, the underwear entrepreneur, is made to ironically proclaim imperialism a fine thing that broadens the minds of the English, whether they are subjected to it by the Romans or propagate it themselves as at the present moment.[16] Summerhays unhesitatingly proclaims government by tyranny and fraud acceptable if it maintains order; a parallel between the governor abroad and the industrialist in his factory or the patriarch at home is tempting, stemming from his daughter Hypatia's hint that to keep her from earning a living she was kept a prisoner.[17] Bonds of love, it seems, stand in the way of female independence, which is why Lina the Polish acrobat (who literally drops in from the sky) proclaims her refusal to be supported by any man "and make him the master of my body and soul."[18] This, evidently, is what separates Poles from Britons. Members of her family regularly risk life and limb, but marriage just goes too far.

In *Pygmalion* (1913), Shaw again depicts female dependence as the central theme, tying it metaphorically to the classic dyads of male and female, master and slave, colonizer and colonized. Henry Higgins, the Pygmalion who understands all about *how* people talk but grasps nothing of what they *mean*, thinks he can dispose of the new improved Eliza into the marriage market, but explicitly disavows this as an economic relationship:

> LIZA: I sold flowers. Now youve made a lady of me I'm not fit to sell anything else. I wish youd left me where you found me.
> HIGGINS: Tosh, Eliza. Dont you insult human relations by dragging all this cant about buying and selling into it.[19]

He cannot see the brutality of his own behavior in using Eliza as an amusing experiment, objectifying her as a product of his own skill, then taking her presence as perpetual slipper-fetcher for granted. The colonizing metaphor is solidified by the marital theme of the last act: not only in Doolittle the dustman's sadly reversed circumstances which no longer enable him to cohabit with Eliza's stepmother (the "natural way"), but also in the question of Eliza's disposal. By taking away Eliza's independence as a kerbstone flower seller, Higgins in effect enslaved her, and she complied. Higgins deludes himself into thinking that she can return to his household after her triumph at the ball, and in the name of good fellowship assume a new position neither as experiment nor slave but as someone he really cares for but with whom he has no romantic entanglement.[20] The self-satisfied manner in which Higgins is left on stage, abandoned by women (just like

Torvald in *A Doll's House*, who faces a new life but barely knows it), rattling the change in his pocket and chuckling to himself, is completely ironic. For all his knowledge, he is master of nothing and no one. He knows much about how people talk, but nothing of who they are. Eliza likened herself to a child in a foreign country, having forgotten her own language, yet she learned enough of the master's knowledge to abandon him yet coexist.[21]

Writing *Heartbreak House* (1919) in the midst of global war, Shaw's parataxis of empires and households implies an outcome with higher stakes than before. Men's world is, supposedly, that of business while women's is marriage.[22] But this is sustained mostly by shams. The imposing industrialist Mangan is just the front man for syndicates and has no great wealth of his own; the dashing Hector is no adventurer at all but merely his wife's pet; the burglar is no burglar at all but just an extortioner; and even the Captain who seeks "the seventh degree of concentration" is an old duffer of an inventor addicted to rum, whose greatest pride is his Caribbean African wife. Amidst the standard romantic permutations of the country house weekend plot, Shaw counterpoints the Captain – who "sold himself to the devil in Zanzibar" – against his son-in-law, Lord Hastings Utterword, governor of every British colony in succession. These are the two men of the world, and perhaps Hastings's non-appearance in the play (like the Captain's alleged wife) underlines the metaphoric import of his value. The Captain perpetuated exotic rumors about himself in order to maintain discipline in unruly and unjust circumstances, but argues that nothing like this applies to the *ingénue* Ellie Dunn, and hence she should not sell herself into marriage.

> CAPTAIN SHOTOVER: I had to deal with men so degraded that they wouldnt obey me unless I swore at them and kicked them and beat them with my fists. Foolish people took young thieves off the streets; flung them into a training ship where they were taught to fear the cane instead of fearing God; and thought theyd made men and sailors of them by private subscription. I tricked these thieves into believing I'd sold myself to the devil. It saved my soul from the kicking and swearing that was damning me by inches.[23]

He might be referring to distant ports, but on the other hand he is also accurately describing the British system of naval impressment in place for hundreds of years and only recently (the play premiered in 1919) abandoned in favor of a less predatory form of conscription. His daughter Ariadne's philosophy is similar, regulated in proportion to whomever she is disciplining. Children she "smacked . . . enough to give them a good cry and a healthy nervous shock," whereupon they "were quite good afterwards."[24] A thief, at least abroad, could be beaten and sent away: she recommends the application of "a good supply of bamboo to bring the British native to his senses" too, as remedy for what ails the nation.[25] England, it is asserted through the analogy of house as ship and domesticity as the ship of state, must learn to navigate or it will founder and be lost. Perhaps another way of stating Ariadne's position is that England must revert to its indigenous brutality, indigenously applied.

However exotic the Captain's love life has been, apparently his English daughters are not the strengthened products of miscegenation. Hesione's black hair, at any rate, is only a wig. If, in the typical formulation of colonialism, white males are free at the expense of women's domestication and the racial other's colonization, *Heartbreak House* depicts the emotional dependence of men upon women, the capitalist's complete lack of autonomy, the corruption of English country life with soft Bohemianism, and the asserted but never staged discipline of colonial rule. In the *mise-en-scène*, there are no children, foreigners, or even horses present to subjugate, and women very consistently rule over men. Thus, this play is as much about England foundering blindly on the brink of destruction by a German dirigible as the lies embedded in an entire belief system based on empire, entrepreneurial savvy, rule by consent, and the superiority of leisured British gentility. In the final moments, as the Zeppelin drifts overhead, destruction booming like Beethoven, the public world comes spectacularly crashing into the private, disrupting the garden idyll. Nothing could be a more apt theatricalization of the end of British insularity, the delusion of glory, or the question of which home fires are to be kept burning: hearths or houses in the cataclysmic deaths of the two practical men of business (Mangan and the burglar) and the demolition of manse and clergyman. If free enterprise and religion are so vulnerable, it bodes very badly for empire. Still, Shaw stopped short of dismantling empire. Perhaps he felt optimistic (though mistakenly), on the eve of the League of Nations' inauguration, that history was doing the work for him.

Twenty years earlier, Shaw wrote another meditation on the concept of justice in the scramble for empire. In *Captain Brassbound's Conversion* (1899) an English judge, Sir Howard Hallam, is held to ransom in a Moroccan castle by the pirate Captain Brassbound, whose West Indian mother was maltreated by Sir Howard. It just so happens that Brassbound is Sir Howard's nephew, which renders this something of a family feud even though Hallam readily grants Brassbound his rightful plantation lands, glad to be rid of the money pit overseas. On the face of things, Hallam seems doomed – England will certainly not treat this incident like a replay of General Gordon's siege at Khartoum and send whale boats and camel corps to his rescue – but the Sheikh Sidi el Assif readily trades Sir Howard

21   Woman and Empire: captivating the Sheikh in Shaw Festival's 1979 production of
Captain Brassbound's Conversion

for his sister-in-law, Lady Cicely Waynflete, the iconoclastic lady traveler modeled after Mary Kingsley.[26] Her habit is to greet all men civilly by looking them in the face and saying "howdyedo." Thus, the Sheikh is captivated by his own prisoner. She has a talent for taking charge, reorganizing every masculine institution into a better regulated and harmonious entity in such a way that "half a dozen such women would make an end of law in England in six months."[27] Gunboat diplomacy, however, courtesy of the Americans, breaks the impasse much faster.

Brassbound is tried by the American gunboat captain, but excused when he learns of the insults showered on Brassbound's mother by the complainant. Lady Cicely – the only woman in the cast – is the key to all of this, for she not only tames the "ferocious" infidels and improvises rules of evidence in the makeshift courtroom, but completely subjugates Brassbound with all his piratical ways, in the course of exercising her great leadership potential. Brassbound offers to serve under her – in matrimony – as he did under Gordon at Khartoum. With all his bullying ways and command by force, until he met her he had missed the real secret of command: look people in the face and say "howdyedo." But the play averts a matrimonial ending by Lady Cicely's timely break from Brassbound's mesmerism, and in so doing theatricalizes the parataxis. By breaking the mesmeric gaze she rescues him while he, in Lady Cicely's words, makes a glorious escape. A white woman, daughter of a peer, will not rule over a miscegenated, non-English, colonial, pirate captain. By maintaining the one hierarchy of man over women, the hierarchies of empires, nations, and peoples remain intact. Justice, governance, and biological sex roles are all depicted as unstable, but ultimately the forces of history and incident do not succeed in changing anything.

Despite the steady state ending, *Captain Brassbound's Conversion* might be said to speak ambiguously and reverberate with crisis as Lady Cicely is left alone on stage "in a strange ecstasy" and proclaiming glory. As David Spurr asks of all colonial travel writing:

> Is it the voice of an individual writer, the voice of institutional authority, of cultural ideology? . . . In the colonial situation as well as in its aftermath, this ambiguity in writing itself joins with the logical incoherence of colonial discourse to produce a rhetoric characterized by constant crisis, just as colonial rule itself continually creates its own crisis of authority. The anxiety of colonial discourse comes from the fact that the colonizer's power depends on the presence, not to say consent, of the colonized.[28]

In some ways, the text speaks paradigmatically of colonial relations and their continuance, for the primitive and the civilized are juxtaposed and the existence of one justifies the supremacy of the other. But Shaw ironizes the formula by juggling the elements between Cicely and Brassbound. Just as Cicely rejects the weaker side of assigned femininity, Brassbound compounds the authority accorded masculinity with the abjection of not being fully white or fully British. For the duration of Cicely's trance, chaos is explored; but since this chaos is paratactic to marriage, what is Shaw suggesting about traditions of how the comic genre restores order by concluding with a wedding? And what categories are left for this non-couple who are respectively rescuer and escapee? Shaw takes us to the brink of a border region but, as usual, can only theatricalize what exists in tension with it.

Another play, set largely on a mountainous coastline and, like *Heartbreak House*, also meditating on the war of 1914–18, uses Shaw's system of antitheses to suggest that though something has irrevocably changed since World War I, its aftermath is not yet known. *Too True To Be Good* (1931) depicts a supposedly invalided daughter who decides to run away with her felon nurse/chambermaid and the nurse's burglar/clergy accomplice. All three abscond with the Patient's pearls and diamonds to a climatically auspicious British outpost, where they live off the proceeds of the jewelry and scheme to add to the coffers by collecting a ransom for the Patient. (The case is patterned after Redivious Oliver, who as a teenager traveled in Italy and sent word to his step-father that he had been captured. The ransom was paid and Redivious lived handsomely off it.)[29] The Patient, now sunburned, muscular, and agile, masquerades as the native servant of the nurse, who poses as a Countess. The pretences of nativism and rank are both extreme, for Shaw describes the Patient as "*en belle sauvage* by headdress, wig, ornaments, and girdle proper to no locality on earth except perhaps the Russian ballet," and the Countess – lacking a Higgins to tutor her up from the rank of chambermaid – assumes a dialect that is "a spirited amalgamation of the foreign accents of all the waiters she has known."[30] Thus, they have transparently assumed their cultural "other": for the wealthy invalid it is ruddy native servitude, while for the chambermaid thief it is the titled pan-European. But the Patient is the only character who, in Shaw's convoluted manner of assigning names, is never given a forename and is addressed only by a nickname (Mops, after her surname Mopply) or her original function as the "Patient." She is never personalized, and thus remains emblematic, as in a morality play.

The military men assigned to recover the Patient from her supposed brigand captors are also topsy-turvy: the Colonel holds fast to principles of discipline and rank, advocating that enlisted men not even be treated as human, but really prefers to keep himself idle by painting in watercolours; Private Meek (modeled after Lawrence of Arabia) is the thoroughly capable fellow who appears to the Colonel to be a halfwit but has in fact resigned several commissions in favor of his present rank; and the brawny Sergeant who captivates the Countess's attention is a theologian and feminist. It is this Sergeant who supplies one of the unifying themes of the play through his pondering of Bunyan's meaning of the Pilgrim's wandering in the wilderness of the world, without trails, and in horror of the destruction that will come to those waiting like sheep in the Cities of Destruction.[31] This metaphor is especially applicable to the Patient, who tires of being free and happy, away from her mother's overindulgence, and grows to see nature as both dull and full of wanton evil (her Eden turned to the earthly). It also applies to the governments responsible for the war that has disillusioned so many, and which now do not know where to flee from their accumulations of corpses and debts. An Elder evangelist (actually father to

Reverend Aubrey, the Countess's accomplice) proclaims the end of New-
tonian rational determinism. Science has replaced it with an atomic algebra
that mocks both Free Will Catholicism and the Protestant's belief in private
judgment. No purpose or design is apparent in the electron's path: the
world is neither created *à la* Creationism nor engineered *à la* Darwinism,
but random. One by one, the characters recognize themselves in an abyss,
seeking the means to be saved. Like postmodernists, the characters are
stuck in a world whose meanings are as immaterial as discourse, while
Shaw, the stalwart modernist, seeks to understand causes and to vainly
prescribe and not just criticize.

Too True To Be Good sets up several important questions for the world's
decolonization and prospective transition into postcolonialism. The mal-
ingering feminine apparent in the Patient of Act 1 is easily expunged by
contact with a mountainous outpost of British colonialism, but her recovery
began with the opening of a window and contact with fresh air and the
pragmatism of the thieving class which suggested a way out of her sickly
confinement. Thus, her cure was not really abroad but always near at hand.
The surreal giant measles microbe at her bedside, made ill by the Patient's
feminized invalidism – a topsy-turvy joke whereby the patient makes the
disease sick – is instantly cured. The microbe, which Shaw refers to as The
Monster, is likened to the colonized native: a sort of invalided Caliban. It
was going about its business doing its own thing when this particularly
noxious woman sickened it beyond measure. While one usually thinks of a
disease invading a host, in Shaw's paradoxical world the Patient colonized
the Monster by feigning weakness when she was really strong. With the
microbe cured, the Patient is freed of one colonial burden and embarks on a
tourist's quest for escape, using her wealth to plunge into the world beyond
her country's shores. A metaphoric colonizing of disease is replaced with an
economic version. In the process, she is besieged by parasitic "tourist
agencies, steamboat companies, railways, motor car people, hotel keepers,
dressmakers, servants, all trying to get my money by selling me things I
don't really want" all over the world, as if it was not the same sun
everywhere.[32] Thus, just as she directed her "tourist's gaze" on the "un-
civilized world," her own people attempted to exploit her. She really wanted
to settle down, nest, and raise children, but instead she was preyed upon by
these capitalists selling soporifics. In other words, in order to develop a
conscience and a critique of the global economy, the Patient in turn becomes
the exploited, just as the invading disease was sickened by its victim.

The military has no authority over the indigenous peoples of Act 2 and 3,
yet Private Meek's ingenuity in setting off harmless maroons (explosives
such as those used in World War I to warn of air raids) deceives the tribes

22   Inverting hierarchies: Simon Bradbury as Private Meek issuing commands to
William Webster as Colonel Tallboys in the Shaw Festival's 1994 production of
Too True to be Good

into thinking that there is a sizeable British garrison rather than a mere handful of soldiers. It is the empire in its final phase, literally, as a crumbling presence on far-flung shores, all boom and little bite, proclaiming sovereignty over Crown Colonies but not even able to muster a representative government. Nevertheless, in a nostalgic refrain of greater empire, another Gordonesque mission to save a Briton (this time a supposedly delicate female) wins the Colonel more kudos than would the rescuing of the titled judge in *Captain Brassbound*. Both the maroon ploy and the recovery of the Patient are due to Meek, yet the Colonel is knighted. The British officer increases his authority at home (as Sir Tallboys, with his wife Lady Tallboys at his side) in a cynical allusion to a government improving its chances of reelection by populist association, and Meek not inheriting the world (though the Colonel has no authority whatever in the foreign land). The Colonel not only gives Meek the control of the outfit, but also is without authority in respect to his relationship with the natives: he has no contact with genuine indigenes and hence can have no mastery over them. But how much longer will the native peoples be as easily fooled by a few detonated maroons as are the Britons at home by a titled indolent watercolorist?

The metaphor of the colonizing man and the colonized woman is overthrown by the Countess, long known for her fickleness in discarding men after ten days, but this time restrained by the Sergeant who forces her to engage her "top storey" (intellect) as well as her "ground floor" or "lower centres" (sexual drives).[33] It is only high-class status, such as the Patient's, that enables a woman to be broken sufficiently to be dull *and* remain constant. Since the war, the Countess has been knocking down domestic institutions like an earthquake, but it is she who at the end of the play goes off to be married, and the Patient who will found an unorthodox sisterhood. As a rich woman, the Patient's soul had starved on a diet of religious selfishness and her class's snobbery; thus, the sisterhood will be neither religious nor elitist. But the flaw in her thinking is that she idealizes it as an army, and the recent war has put an end to any peace of mind that comes from military organizations. The military existed to kill the wrong people – innocents slaughtering innocents – and doing so at great remove since new technology enabled bombs to be detonated from forty miles away. Playing with the binary of male and female, and reversing the usual assignments of civilized and savage, Shaw suggests that the Patient will not succeed in forging a new female civilization even though she will come closest, amongst all the characters, to progress.

So, in this Patient/Pilgrim's "dream" of journeying to a mountainous place, suffering perils, shedding lies, and spouting the refrain to the childish pastoral "Mary had a Little Lamb" (back to front), where will she find salvation? Not at home, for Shaw despairs of making England sensible. Not abroad, for she must be in a compromised position *vis-à-vis* the peoples with whom she cohabits. If she is to clean up the world, and keep it clean, where will she reside and how shall she proceed? In the aftermath of such horrific war, young people eschew disguising themselves from each other with idealism; their faith was destroyed, along with buildings and scenery. The young see through the holes in their elders' rags and wonder what to do. But ultimately, Shaw offers little guidance in this regard. As he says in his concluding stage directions, "fine words butter no parsnips": evangelists are the hot air that fan the flame of true Pentecostalism, and though women of action may be his idea of the way forward, their actions are as yet unimaginable (and unstageable?) in any detail. Also, a feminist would likely add, as long as Shaw remains the spouting evangelist there is unlikely ever to be a clearer picture. The Patient is actually thwarted in her desire to breed, so Shaw's optimism in the strengthening of successive generations, shown in much earlier plays such as *Man and Superman* (1903) and *Major Barbara* (1905), has no place here.

If there is any ambiguity about the ascription of these paratactic readings of any of the earlier plays, about *The Simpleton of the Unexpected Isles* (1934) there can be no doubt whatsoever. Michael Holroyd reads the play as steeped in Shaw's infatuation with the Soviet Union, and reflecting his belief in it as a socialist heaven, but it has many other contemporaneous resonances with the decay of Britain in the latter phase of Empire.[34] World War I not only challenged British ideas about the glory of war, but brought the Dominion nations into battle on a large scale in defense of the United Kingdom. While experiencing greater independence – going, in Shaw's terms, from the world's childhood into a period of its "responsible maturity" – the colonies peopled principally by whites may have reluctantly sent their soldiers yet they upheld British ideas about racial superiority and preferred British affiliation to cultural or political domination by any other power.[35] After all, it was Australia that led the movement to exclude a covenant recognizing racial equality from the League of Nations' charter in 1918. In colonies where whites governed a large indigenous population, the path to commonwealth was more ideologically fraught. India's Congress was declared illegal in 1932, and its leader Mahatma Ghandi was arrested. A campaign of civil disobedience against British rule absorbed India during the period when Shaw was traveling in Asia and the Pacific, and as he wrote *The Simpleton*. The independence of colonies was widely sought but the course by which they would achieve it was yet to be determined.

Shaw seems to say in *The Simpleton* that for Europeans life in the colonies was intolerable so long as they insisted on retaining European ways and values exclusively. The clerk in the Isles' emigration office (note: not an immigration office) regards himself as an indispensable functionary, building Empire in the style of Cecil Rhodes. But his problem is that he always "throws back" what is given him, and abruptly ends his life with a bullet through the head. His supervisor, the Emigration Officer (later to emerge as Hugo Hyering, political secretary to the Isles) weeps "A man's a slave here worse than a nigger," yet discovers that when he takes life as it comes on the behest of a female visitor from abroad and assimilates to indigenous ways, life becomes more than tolerable (he later marries her).[36] In the Prologue, the climate is blamed, yet later on the Unexpected Isles newly emerged from the sea are depicted as an Edenic garden. It literally took Hyering a kick in the butt and a flying leap from a cliff to realize the intrinsic value of the place.

This play is chiefly concerned with moral worth rather than any form of monetary economics. Nevertheless, the arrangements of domesticity and the heterosexual marriage compact move the plot. Hyering formerly complained that he could not afford to marry a white woman and that native women were too well educated and refined to be interested in white men, who are ignorant and foul-smelling. But financial problems are not at the root of the European's doomed sterility: it is that Englishmen are taught useless things such as classical languages and sports rather than vital things such as how to feed and clothe themselves and reproduce. It is the typical Shavian formula of characters seeing in the world what they themselves are, while being unable to know themselves. The indigenous island Priestess, Prola, appropriately wonders whether it is "really kind to treat them according to their folly instead of to our wisdom?"[37] Sir Charles and Lady Farwaters succumb to fascination about the culture, but other visitors must be strongarmed into paying due attention.

In the twenty-four years that intervene between the Prologue and first act (i.e. a similar interval as between the commencement of World War I and the premiere of the play), the Priest and Priestess Pra and Prola unite with the Farwaters and Hyerings in a domestic experiment of six parents raising four progeny melding Eastern and Western cultures and bloodlines. The parents are never specified, and so these progeny are perhaps the most blatantly theatrical of all Shaw's parataxes: six made four, but which six, or rather which pairings amongst the six? Now in early adulthood, the children named Maya, Vashti, Janga, and Kanchin – which Shaw glosses as Love, Pride, Heroism, and Empire – regard themselves collectively as a single entity.[38] But another entity must be provided in order to let the females breed, for this is no Ptolemeic dynasty.[39] Enter the Simpleton, Iddy (for "Idiot"), a Church of England clergyman marooned on the Unexpected Isles after being kidnapped by pirates from his Somerset parish. The *ménage à six* want Iddy to lend respectability to their enterprise and a moral conscience to the children, while the offspring are driven by lower desires. Iddy is reluctant to join the Superfamily on the grounds that Church of England clergymen generally have only one wife at a time. But when he finally interlinks his arms with Maya and Vashti, and they "vanish in black darkness," all scruples are set aside.[40] He prefers the fairer of the two, but the morality of Clapham Common does not extend much beyond British shores: in the majority of the Empire, polygamy and miscegenation are the order of the day. Thus, for a potential second generation, racial purity is challenged, while for a third generation the basic domestic unit of the nuclear heterosexual family is scorned.

The momentousness of this for empire is spectacularly dramatized. The Empire's fleets assemble in the harbor on behalf of this "impotent simpleton."[41] Sir Charles, the governor, is besieged with as many demands to end the relationship as he receives congratulations. Every faction in the Empire, and many outside it, seek to impose their ideas on everyone else. But diplomats' ultimata are ignored, and the old order collapses. England dissolves its Empire, "Downing Street declares for a right tight little island," and a new scramble for domination is unleashed.[42] Ireland is enraged by this treason, Canada proclaims its status as premiere Dominion, Australia pronounces itself the metropolitan Dominion, New Zealand challenges this and instigates a butter blockade, South Africa announces the expulsion of all Britons from the continent, and the Pope celebrates the "passing away of the last vain dream of earthly empire."[43] If this is a Soviet parable, then the hasty announcement of Prola's promotion to Empress seems out of keeping with any socialist utopia that even Shaw could muster. Instead, this could be seen as the newly independent state replicating all the folly of foreign systems, and significantly it is the children who are most keen on this plan. The children advocate killing the world's human lemmings, and living for their flag and Empress, anything to defend the Isles' eternal queendom.

A peel of gunfire and volley of trumpets heralds the advent of an angel announcing Judgment Day while shaking bullets and lead shot from its robes. The English-speaking peoples will be judged first, followed by the USA, Australasia, Scotland, and Ireland (whose languages, as far as heaven is concerned, are not English). Those who cannot justify themselves are stricken, and disappear. It is a wonderful application of the Good versus Bad dyad, but of course it is by Shaw's rules. Thus, judgment is particularly devastating to politicians, peers, the stock exchange, Anglicans, physicians, and celebrities. The Eastern parts of the Empire, however, are almost untouched apart from the four hedonistic children of the Superfamily. And in what may be regarded as Shaw's most progressive statement on the ideal marriage, Prola explains to Pra:

> Ive never allowed you or any other man to cut me off my own stem and make me a parasite on his. That sort of love and sacrifice is not the consummation of a capable woman's existence: it is the temptation she must resist at all costs.[44]

They made a good pair, sustaining each other's intellect, supporting each other's dreams, and keeping each other from social ruin. The Unexpected Isles, they conclude, and the world – as a synecdochal contiguity – make the same errors and suffer from the same responses to insecurity and calamity. Creative life (preferably the unpredictable) needs this combination of male and female, taking life as it comes, living with imagination and brains, and looking eastward.

So, what might Shaw be suggesting as possible routes to a true postcolonialism? New hybridities, certainly. A generous helping of social reductionism. A culture that redistributes the idea of gender assignments, respecting biology but regarding the origins and keepers of wealth as broadmindedly as the definition of wealth itself. A society that knows the relatedness of behavior at home to behavior abroad, and the attitudes of the private citizen to the conduct of governments. An enlightened politics that is performed, not just espoused, and which reaches into the most fundamental aspects of private life.

Perhaps what goes along with this is a closer examination of what constitutes Shaw's parataxes, and why they are acceptable in a comedic frame. Shaw rarely, if ever, recalibrates the binaries, but the paratactic pairs can provide more surprises for the productive politics of home and world, work and economics, liberation and power, or discipleship and wisdom by siting the interstices. Sometimes, the antitheses collapse, and therein lies the drama. But being a product of his times, and hence a modernist, Shaw never abnegates his characters of responsibility: the means to full decolonization, and the goal of some day achieving the true *post*colonial rests heavily upon them.

NOTES

1 George Bernard Shaw, *Complete Plays with Prefaces*, 6 vols. (New York: Dodd, Mead, 1963), vol. III, p. 204.
2 See Claudia von Werlhof, "Women's Work: the Blind Spot in the Critique of Political Economy," in Maria Mies, Veronika Bennholdt-Thomsen, and Claudia von Werlhof (eds.), *Women: The Last Colony* (London and New Jersey: Zed Books, 1988), pp. 13–26.
3 *Complete Plays*, vol. III, p. 236.
4 *Ibid.*, p. 254.
5 *Ibid.*, p. 264.
6 *Ibid.*, p. 267.
7 Homi Bhabha, *Location of Culture* (London: Routledge, 1994), p. 15. Performativity refers to the discursively determined practices of individuals belying their relationship to normative categories such as gender, class, or race. See Judith Butler, *Bodies That Matter: on the Discursive Limits of "Sex"* (New York and London: Routledge, 1993).
8 *Complete Plays*, vol. IV, p. 405.
9 Most likely, Shaw refers to *The Legal Subjection of Men* (London: New Age Press, 1908).
10 *Complete Plays*, vol. IV, p. 453.
11 *Ibid.*
12 *Ibid.*, p. 455.
13 *Ibid.*, p. 477.
14 *Ibid.*
15 *Ibid.*, pp. 113, 147.
16 *Ibid.*, p. 148.
17 *Ibid.*, pp. 191, 198.
18 *Ibid.*, p. 202.

19 *Complete Plays*, vol. I, p. 257.
20 *Ibid.*, pp. 276–77.
21 *Ibid.*, p. 271.
22 *Ibid.*, p. 535.
23 *Ibid.*, p. 565.
24 *Ibid.*, p. 575.
25 *Ibid.*, pp. 555–56, 583.
26 Author of *Travels in West Africa* (1897), *West African Studies* (1899), and *The Story of West Africa* (1899), based on her travels in 1893 and 1894–95. About her, MacDonald wrote "Mary Kingsley, alone with Fang cannibals in the equatorial jungle of Gabon, is to her companions – as near as they can judge – a white man: she has the authority and knowledge of the imperial power." Robert H. MacDonald, *The Language of Empire: Myths and Metaphors of Popular Imperialism, 1880–1918* (Manchester: Manchester University Press, 1994), p. 39.
27 *Complete Plays*, vol. I, p. 668.
28 David Spurr, *The Rhetoric of Empire* (Durham, NC: Duke University Press, 1993), p. 11.
29 John M. East, *'Neath the Mask: The Story of the East Family* (London: George Allen and Unwin, 1967), p. 90.
30 *Complete Plays*, vol. IV, p. 663.
31 See John Bunyan, *The Pilgrims's Progress* (1678).
32 *Complete Plays*, vol. IV, p. 704.
33 *Ibid.*, p. 690.
34 Michael Holroyd, *Bernard Shaw. Volume III: 1918–1950, the Lure of Fantasy* (New York: Random House, 1991), pp. 290–91.
35 *Complete Plays*, vol. VI, p. 598.
36 *Ibid.*, pp. 545, 555.
37 *Complete Plays*, vol. IV, p. 554.
38 These Sanskrit terms may be more accurately translated as Illusion, i.e. a worldly or earthly physicality, for Maya; war for Janga; and gold for Kanchin. Precisely what Shaw means by choosing Vashti is ambiguous: she has a part in the book of Esther, as the Persian queen repudiated by Ahasuerus (Xerxes I, ruled 486–65 BCE). Perhaps it is this element that is recalled in the plot.
39 Compare *Caesar and Cleopatra* in *Complete Plays*, vol. III, pp. 392–93.
40 *Complete Plays*, vol. VI, p. 578.
41 *Ibid.*, p. 581.
42 *Ibid.*, p. 588.
43 *Ibid.*
44 *Ibid.*, p. 609.

FURTHER READING

Alexander, Jacqui M. and Chandra Talpade Mohanty, *Feminist Genealogies, Colonial Legacies, Democratic Futures*, London: Routledge, 1996.
Ashcroft, Bill, Gareth Griffiths, and Helen Tiffin, *The Empire Writes Back: Theory and Practice in Post-Colonial Literatures*, London: Routledge, 1989.

Ashcroft, Bill, Gareth Griffiths, and Helen Tiffin (eds.), *The Post-Colonial Studies Reader*, London: Routledge, 1995.

Davis, Tracy C., *George Bernard Shaw and the Socialist Theatre*, Westport: Greenwood and Praeger, 1994.

Donaldson, Laura E., *Decolonizing Feminisms: Race, Gender, and Empire-Building*, Chapel Hill and London: University of North Carolina Press, 1992.

Gainor, J. Ellen, *Shaw's Daughters: Dramatic and Narrative Construction of Gender*, Ann Arbor: University of Michigan Press, 1991.

Hutcheon, Linda, *The Politics of Postmodernism*, London: Routledge, 1989.

Waugh, Patricia, *Practising Postmodernism/Reading Postmodernism*, London: Edward Arnold, 1992.

12

T. F. EVANS

The later Shaw

In 1923, Shaw wrote *Saint Joan*, which he called "A Chronicle," a description that he had never previously given to a play. The play was performed with great success, first in New York in December 1923 and in London in the following year. Shaw was awarded the Nobel Prize for literature for 1925 (despite his well-known aversion to such awards), and, although the prize was given for the entire corpus of a writer's contribution to literature, there can be little doubt that the judges were greatly influenced by the success of *Saint Joan*. After *Saint Joan* Shaw did not write another play for five years. In 1924, however, his sister-in-law Mrs. Mary Cholmondeley, asked him to send her "a few of your ideas of Socialism." She wanted the notes for a study circle in her home county of Shropshire. This was when the Soviet Union had come into being and Britain had had her first Labor government. Shaw threw himself into the task with energy and enthusiasm. He said that he enjoyed the exercise because it was "real brain work, not romancing and inventing but reasoning hard" and "a real hard literary job, all brains instead of writing plays."[1] Exasperatingly, the work proved more demanding than he had expected. Originally planned as a booklet of about 50,000 words, it ended as a large volume of well over 200,000 words. The book was finally published in 1928 with the title *The Intelligent Woman's Guide to Socialism and Capitalism*.

The title of the book has given some readers (and perhaps more of those who have not read it) the impression that it was specifically planned as a primarily feminist work. This was not so. Shaw chose the title, partly because the work was, in fact, written in response to a request from intelligent women and partly because he was determined to write something as far removed as possible from conventional works on economics and politics and allied subjects because the great majority of such works were written in dry and unreadable academic jargon. In addition all the books were addressed to men. Shaw declared that, "You might read a score of them without ever discovering that such a creature as a woman had ever existed. In fairness let me add that you might read a good many of them without discovering that such a thing as a man ever existed."[2] He was determined, therefore, to write in an understandable language, although, as several critics have been only too ready to point out, he was not writing for the "ordinary" woman or man so much as for the more middle-class type of reader who had certainly had more than a rudimentary or elementary education. The book is written in an almost lighthearted or jaunty style even when it is dealing with questions of finance or politics that are not readily understood by those who have only a superficial knowledge of those subjects. It is open to speculation to what extent Shaw's experience in writing stage dialogue contributed to his ability to express himself so fluently and easily on matters of abstruse content, but he had spent many hours in earlier years in committee work and speaking on platforms to audiences who might not be expected to respond easily to the language of the university senior common room or the leading articles of *The Times*. Whatever the background of his approach, the work is an astonishing production and it has been seriously neglected by students and scholars of Shaw.[3]

He threw himself into his subject in his opening paragraph, advising his reader, "dear madam," not to read anything else that had been written on socialism before she and her friends had settled the question of how wealth should be distributed in a respectable civilized country. His solution was equality. Everybody should have the same income. It is impossible to summarize such a work but it can be said that few readers who last until the end will fail to see a little more clearly than before many features of the economic and political system. Ramsay MacDonald, the Labor Prime Minister of the 1920s who became the leader of a later, Conservative-dominated coalition, no doubt went far beyond rational bounds when he said, in a conversation reported by Shaw's German translator, Siegfried Trebitsch, that the work was "after the Bible . . . the most important book that humanity possesses,"[4] but there is an inherent nobility in it that outweighs the sense of exasperation felt by those who cannot accept all, or even any of the conclusions. Shaw's peroration, in which he declares that his socialist remedy for the ills of society will result in a view of life where "the base woman will be she who takes more from her country than she gives to it . . . and the lady will be she who, generously overearning her income, leaves the nation in her debt and the world a better world than she found it," will not impress all readers but even some who are not converted to socialism may nevertheless find it moving. Shaw's final word is "By such ladies and their sons can the human race be saved, and not otherwise."[5]

The publication of *The Intelligent Women's Guide* left Shaw free to return to writing plays. The work involved in writing the *Guide*, intense and demanding as it had been, had affected neither his determination nor his ability to continue to write for the theatre. In the years that followed the appearance of the *Guide*, from the end of 1928 to the outbreak of war in 1939, he wrote ten plays, seven of which were full-length. In view of the time and effort that he had spent on non-dramatic work, it was hardly surprising that, when he returned to the theatre, political themes became prominent in his plays. Thus, of the ten plays, four, all of them full-length, had the word "political" in their descriptive subtitles, a term that he had never previously applied to any of his plays. The effect of the concentration on political themes that had produced the *Guide* may be discerned clearly in several of the other plays as well. It seemed that his dramatic creation was given a new incentive in the political direction as a result of his labors on what he had called the "confounded book." It is beyond doubt that the failure of Labor governments to bring about in practice any of Shaw's socialist ideals and what he came to consider the failure of British parliamentary government in general during the years before the 1939 war, and the serious deterioration in the international situation, had an important effect on the plays that Shaw wrote during the decade. In November 1928, he began *The Apple Cart*, his first play since *Saint Joan* and he finished it on December 29. It was first presented in Warsaw in June 1929 and the first English production was at Malvern on August 19, 1929. The Malvern Festival had been conceived by Shaw's friend, Barry Jackson, in part as a tribute to Shaw, and Shaw had agreed to write a new play for the festival. For the next decade, Shaw felt under an obligation to provide plays for the annual festival and four of the full-length plays in the thirties were given their first English performances at Malvern. It may be that Shaw felt a greater freedom in writing plays for first production in a small provincial festival than in the West End of London. An additional cause of the remarkable burst of regular productivity during the decade could well have been the sense that time was passing – he was eighty in 1936 – and while he still felt capable of writing, he realized that this could not go on forever. As he wrote to Nora Ervine, the wife of his friend and fellow dramatist, St. John Ervine on May 12, 1934: "Old age is telling on me. My bolt is shot as far as any definite target is concerned and now, as my playwright faculty still goes on with the impetus of 30 years vital activity, I shoot into the air more and more extravagantly without any premeditation whatever."[6] There may be a connection here between the use of the word "extravagantly" and his description of several of the plays of this later period as "extravaganzas."

Shaw's entire background as a political campaigner, a Fabian socialist, a vestryman and borough councillor, and his general political disposition, meant that he was always opposed to the established Conservative or Liberal parties and, when it became a political force, he always supported the Labor party in national and local government elections. Nevertheless, he was never a slavish follower of any party line and he always set himself against the crudity of using his plays as propaganda. In fact, it was frequently observed that he tended to give those of his characters who might be putting forward a point of view which was not his own, a far more sympathetic presentation than might have been expected. When he considered this question late in his career, he summed up what had always been his attitude by saying in a letter to Erich Strauss, dated August 4, 1942, "you cannot make out why I, being a Republican and a Communist, do not write plays in which all the kings are villains and all the Socialists angels. That is the very crudest dramatic practice, and is never convincing."[7] The words are particularly appropriate to the first play of the series, *The Apple Cart*, which is set in a future some years ahead and presents a conflict between the British King, Magnus, and a government, led by a Prime Minister, Proteus, clearly based on Shaw's one-time admirer Ramsay MacDonald, who, however, is said not to have recognized himself when he saw the play.

The play concerns a serious crisis, when the government ministers contend that Magnus, the King, has gone beyond his constitutional powers by flagrantly interfering with the functions of government. The strength of the play lies in the conflict between the King and his ministers, with the dramatically effective picture of one man against the majority. The conflict has been found by some critics to be unfairly unbalanced because the King is seen as a man of charm and integrity as opposed to a collection of either rogues or simpletons who are merely playing the usual political game. Shaw himself dealt with the criticism in the preface to the published play (written as were all the prefaces, after the play, not before). He said that he did not accept that the conflict had been unfairly presented. He wanted the King and the ministers to meet on a basis of equality in personal ability and good sense. He assumed the equality but went on to say that it was "masked by a strong contrast of character and methods which has led my less considerate critics to complain that I have packed the cards by making the King a wise man and the minister a fool." (It is possible here that D. H. Lawrence's advice should be followed that, in interpreting literary works, the reader should trust the tale and not the artist.) What Shaw maintained that he intended to emphasize in the play, and he does give this idea important prominence, was that the real conflict was not between the King and the ministers but "between both and plutocracy, which, having destroyed the royal power by frank force under democratic pretexts, has bought and swallowed democracy" (*Collected Plays*, vol. VI, p. 252). There is much that is prophetic in the play, ranging from the attack on uncontrolled plutocracy to views on the changing position of the Royal Family. (The King, a man of great charm and ability, bears no resemblance to any real occupant of the British throne.)

Continuing topicality has helped *The Apple Cart* to be very popular in regular revivals. Among the actors who have played Magnus was Noel Coward, who as a fellow playwright was a great admirer of Shaw's dramatic technique. Criticism through the years has varied from declarations that the play is "verbose" and a minor work, to a claim by Irving Wardle in *The Times*, writing on a production in central London in 1986, that there is a major revival of the play every ten years and "each time it is rediscovered as a play for today."[8] Certainly it always speaks to the public mind when there is a mood of disillusion with politicians and when Shaw's view of the decay of parliamentary democracy appears to be gathering public acceptance. Sometimes, the criticism of the play is swayed by specifically political considerations as, for example in the response of another critic who, when he saw a revival in 1977, said that though he generally admired Shaw, he found the play marked and marred by "contempt for the masses" and Shaw's attitude of "blinkered elitism."[9]

The next play, while called, as was *The Apple Cart*, "A Political Extravaganza," differs greatly from its predecessor in both tone and temper. The play was called *Too True to be Good* and, in a letter to his French translator, when he had just finished writing the play, Shaw said that it contained "burglars, brigands, a stolen necklace, a military expedition and a battle actually fought on the stage." He added that "these stirring incidents are only pretexts for speeches of unprecedented length and solemnity."[10] The play is an odd mixture of realism and fantasy with settings in a luxurious English bedroom and a sea beach near the edge of a desert in a mountainous foreign country. It concerns the adventures of three young people, a man and two women, of the post-1918 generation. Shaw purports to show them setting out "to have a thoroughly good time with all the modern machinery of pleasure to aid them. The result is that they get nothing for their money but a multitude of worries and a maddening dissatisfaction" (*Collected Plays*, vol. VI, p. 400). While these elements are present in the play, it would be a remarkably perceptive member of the audience who would describe the play in these terms after seeing it without the benefit of Shaw's preface from which these words are taken. Kidnapped by a clergyman-burglar and his accomplice who is her nurse, a young woman escapes from an overpowering mother. At the end of the first act, the audience is addressed directly by a microbe, who has been infected by the disease from which the young woman patient has been said to be suffering. He declares that "The play is now virtually over; but the characters will discuss it at great length for two acts more" (*Collected Plays*, vol. VI, p. 455).

The final act of the play includes long expositions of different views, touching principally on religion and politics, by the various characters. Shaw wrote in the *Malvern Theatre Book* for 1932 in connection with the first production in England, at Malvern, after the play had been presented in New York, that he knew his business as a playwright

> too well to fall into the common mistake of believing that because it is pleasant to be kept laughing for an hour, it must be trebly pleasant to be kept laughing for three hours. When people have laughed for an hour, they want to be serio-comically entertained for the next hour; and when that is over they are so tired of not being wholly serious that they can bear nothing but a torrent of sermons.[11]

This reasoning, which is sophistry to some extent, gives Shaw the opportunity to end the play with a long sermon from the clergyman-burglar. Shaw wrote in his final stage direction that "fine words butter no parsnips" and added that "the author, though himself a professional talk maker, does not believe that the world can be saved by talk alone." In spite of this assertion, it is hard not to assume that Aubrey is speaking Shaw's own thoughts, but the author appears to have it both ways by declaring that "his own favourite is the woman of action", that is, the patient herself (*Collected Plays*, vol. VI, p. 528).

The next full-length play was *On the Rocks*, written a year after *Too True to be Good* and first presented not at Malvern but in London in November 1933. The play is termed "political" but it is not labeled as an extravaganza. It may be weaker than the first plays of the group, perhaps because it is not relieved by farce or knockabout comedy but consists solely of talk. The talk is excellent, and carries on Shaw's analysis of the political situation, showing an even more marked concern with what he considered the failure of British parliamentary democracy. The leading figure is another British Prime Minister, Sir Arthur Chavender, under whom Britain has gone "on the rocks." A Liberal confronted by the serious problem of rapidly growing unemployment, he turns to Marx for a solution. The situation proves too much for him and he admits it, deciding to retire, but telling his wife that he will hate the man who carries through the necessary reforms "for his cruelty and the desolation he will bring on us and our like" (*Collected Plays*, vol. VI, p. 734). The play ends inconclusively with the mob marching on Downing Street and being dispersed by mounted police.

In the distance, as the curtain falls, can be heard the voices of the unemployed continuing to sing Edward Carpenter's socialist hymn, "England Arise," to the accompaniment of the baton-thwacks of the police.

On the Rocks is not of the quality of either *The Apple Cart* or *Too True to be Good*. The political analysis is not as convincing as in *The Apple Cart* and it lacks both the depth and the entertaining variety of *Too True to be Good*. It has not been revived in central London, but a performance at the Chichester Festival Theatre in 1984 did bring out some of the quality of the play. It was enhanced by being played at a time when there was serious discontent in connection with the strike of the coalminers, and the appearance on the stage at the end of the play of armed police in full riot equipment gave the play a touch of urgent topicality in which much of the rhetoric and discussion could be seen to be more relevant than might otherwise have been thought.

If it was surprising that *On the Rocks* has been neglected by central London for so long, it is even more astonishing that the next play, *The Simpleton of the Unexpected Isles*, written in 1934, has been performed in central London in a club theatre only, and has thus still to be seen in either one of the big subsidized theatres or the commercial West End. The play, which perhaps deserves most of all Shaw's later plays the term "extravaganza," is not so described but is called "A Vision of Judgment." It was written a year after *On the Rocks* and was first performed by the Guild Theatre of New York early in 1935 and at Malvern later in that year. *The Simpleton* is certainly an odd play and unlike anything that Shaw had previously written, except, perhaps, parts of *Back to Methuselah*. It defies adequate summary but it concerns among other subjects a group marriage, which is racially mixed, of three couples who produce four children, delightful in their own way but not endowed with conscience; the intervention of an English clergyman who is engaged to supply that deficiency; the future of the British Empire; the superiority of eastern religions to western, and the imminence of the Day of Judgment. This last event is announced by a very unorthodox angel who alights to declare that a judgment is being executed whereby "the lives which have no use, no meaning, no purpose, will fade out . . . Only the elect shall survive." He goes on to explain that "the Day of Judgment is not the end of the world, but the end of its childhood and the beginning of its responsible maturity" (*Collected Plays*, vol. VI, p. 825). Shaw noted with sardonic humour that, in the view of a New York critic who saw the first performance of the play, he had shown himself as a dignified monkey pelting the public "with edifying coconuts." He took the criticism lightheartedly, saying that his latest play was always considered a disaster and that when he wrote

23   The Angel of Judgment as minor bureaucrat: Roger Honeywell as the Angel explains the End of the World to disbelieving denizens of the Unexpected Isles in the Shaw Festival's 1996 production

another, the critics would point to the great qualities of *The Simpleton*. This has not happened, and, as indicated above, the play has been seriously neglected. The unfavorable view taken by the critics in New York and by many readers of the printed text elsewhere is to be accounted for, partly at least, by the views expressed by Shaw in the preface. There, he argues, as he had done in the preface to *On the Rocks*, for the extermination, as a political necessity, of "untameable persons who are constitutionally unable to restrain their violent or acquisitive impulses" (*Collected Plays*, vol. VI, p. 576).

Shaw completed *The Simpleton* on April 26, 1934. He began writing *The Millionairess* the following day. This has had a stage history almost as bizarre as that of its predecessor. *The Millionairess* was first presented in Vienna in January 1936 and the first production in English was in Melbourne in March of the same year, followed by the first production in England, which was by a small repertory company in Bexhill-on-Sea, Sussex, in November. It was performed at the Malvern Festival in 1937 and in Westport, Connecticut in 1938. A production planned for central London, with Edith Evans in the leading role, fell through with the outbreak of the war, although it was staged at one of the little theatres in

24 Taking the pulse of power: Nicola Cavendish as Epifania Fitzfassenden and George Dawson as The Egyptian Doctor in the Shaw Festival's 1991 production of *The Millionairess*

1944. It was only finally presented in the West End of London in June 1952 and the production went to New York in October. The leading part in both cities was taken by the film actress, Katherine Hepburn. She had been thought by Shaw to be ideally suited to the role in the 1930s but the part did not then attract her. At the time of Stalin, Mussolini, and Hitler, and his own ever growing disillusion with British democracy, Shaw was becoming more and more attracted by the idea of the old trade unionist Hipney in *On the Rocks* who had said that he was "for any Napoleon or Mussolini or Lenin or Chavender that has the stuff in him to take both the people and the spoilers and oppressors by the scruffs of their silly necks and just sling them into the way in which they should go with as many kicks as may be needful to make a thorough job of it" (*Collected Plays*, vol. VI, p. 719). The eponymous heroine of *The Millionairess*, who bears the striking name of Epifania Ognisanti di Parerga Fitzfassenden, is a non-political female incarnation of all the kind of modern dictators called to mind by Hipney, although the play is not overtly political in a narrow sense. (The play, when printed was given a "Preface on Bosses.") The other side of her character is shown when she meets an Egyptian doctor who is totally overwhelmed by her powerful personality, and, after a career in which she has imposed her will brutally on everyone with whom she comes into contact, she ends the play with a striking and moving declaration in favor of what she calls "this infinitely dangerous heart tearing everchanging life of adventure that we call marriage" (*Collected Plays*, vol. VI, p. 966).

Shaw's powers as a playwright were now clearly on the wane but there were still works to come in which some of his old gifts revealed themselves. His concern with the rapidly deteriorating international situation and the inexorable drift toward another great war, led him to his next play. This was *Geneva*, "another political extravaganza," written in three months at the beginning of 1936 and first played on the stage at Malvern in August 1938 and transferred to central London in November 1938. It thus straddled the crisis that was temporarily resolved by the agreement at Munich in September and Shaw, for all his eighty years, could certainly not be blamed for being behind the times. When the play was first presented and published in book form, it was given the descriptive subtitle, subsequently dropped, of "a fancied page of history." In a note printed in the program to the first London production, Shaw wrote that the critics were sure to complain that he had "not solved all the burning political problems of the present and future in it, and restored peace to Europe and Asia. They always do."[12] He professed himself flattered but exasperated by being considered both ominiscient and omnipotent but he was also infurated by the demands made upon him. All he could do, he said, was "to extract comedy and tragedy from the existing situation and wait to see what will become of it." *Geneva* was very well received as an up-to-date comment on the international scene at the time but with the passage of the years, such figures as Hitler, Mussolini, and Franco lost their topical appeal and revivals have tended to show that the play was perhaps not well enough written or constructed to survive without it.

Fortunately, the next full-length play, the last to be written before the war and the one which almost brought to an end Shaw's career as a playwright, restored the balance to a great extent and may well be the best play ever written by an octogenarian, certainly in English. This was "*In Good King Charles's Golden Days*," a title which is a quotation from the anonymous eighteenth-century song, "The Vicar of Bray." Shaw returned to a favorite method of his, in taking a fresh look at historical characters. The result was a stylish and witty series of conversations between King Charles II and a number of his subjects. These include the astronomer Isaac Newton, the Quaker George Fox, the painter Godfrey Kneller, as well as the King's brother, James, Duke of York (later to become King James II), a selection of the King's mistresses, and, in the final short scene, his Queen, Catherine of

Braganza. Shaw's friend, St. John Ervine ranked the greater part of the play among Shaw's best work, commenting that "the characters are mature and brilliantly drawn, each full of his own idiosyncracy, each stamped with the ineradicable lines of life." It was only late in the play, in Ervine's opinion, that Shaw fell away and allowed Charles II "to spout like a lecturer at a Fabian Summer School."[13] The first production of the play was at Malvern in August 1939 and it was transferred to central London in May of the following year. The Dunkirk evacuation took place during the short London run and in view of what was happening in the present, it was not easy to think of past history nor to focus on the future changes called for in the preface – which, in a special return to the theme of the intelligent woman, expounded the idea of the "coupled vote" in elections with each vote being cast for a pair of candidates, one man and one woman. (The play proved its continuing popular appeal in a brilliant 1997 Shaw Festival production, and a revival in England by the National Theatre is long overdue.)

It has been suggested earlier that the plays of the 1930s were marked by a greater and certainly more obvious concern with politics than any series of plays at earlier periods in Shaw's career as a playwright. There was always a tension in Shaw between the politician and the dramatist. At times, his own comments caused confusion. Thus, when his first play, *Widowers' Houses*, was published in book form in 1893, he declared, at the end of the preface (which he did not have reprinted in the Standard Edition in 1928), that the value of the play of which he had no doubts was "enhanced by the fact that it deals with a burning social question, and is deliberately intended to induce people to vote on the Progressive side at the next County Council election in London" (*Collected Plays*, vol. VI, p. 46). The fact that Shaw later omitted this preface may indicate that he thought that to say that the play was written with a definite vote-winning purpose might be going too far. In fact, it is very much to be doubted whether any of Shaw's plays taken by itself could induce anyone to change voting intentions. It would be a very shrewd reader or spectator who could decide how to vote as a result of studying any of the specifically political plays from, for example, *John Bull's Other Island* to the series that began with *The Apple Cart*. Late in his life, Shaw dealt specifically with his approach in his reply to Erich Strauss in the letter of August 4, 1944, already mentioned above. Strauss had appeared to suggest that, because Shaw had apparently given the better of the argument in *The Apple Cart* to the King and not to the democratically elected politicians, he had rejected democracy in favor of a dictatorship, royal or otherwise. His reply was:

> As a Socialist it is my business to state social problems and to solve them. I have done this in tracts, treatises, essays and prefaces. You keep asking why I

do not keep repeating these propositions Euclidically in my plays. You might as well ask me why I dont wear my gloves on my feet or eat jam with a spade.[14]

This does not altogether dispose of the criticism, or solve the dilemma. To lighten the tone of *The Apple Cart* in some places, he had, in fact, presented some of the members of the cabinet as boobies or scoundrels. In a letter to J. E. Vedrenne in 1907, he wrote of his work as "a series of music-hall entertainments thinly disguised as plays"[15] but, theatrically attractive though this practice usually was, it was not free from danger when the dramatist was trying to say something really serious beneath the surface of the fun. He appeared to think, at times at least, that, as he wrote in a letter to Graham Wallas in 1927, anyone who had to get a grip in Parliament had to be either an actor or an ambitious scoundrel.[16] In any event, Shaw wrote to Harold Laski on July 27, 1945 that William Morris "saw clearly that the sophisticated politicians were even more hopeless than the romantic tinkers and costers, and that the House of Commons was impossible as an organ for Socialism."[17]

If Shaw was often thought to be primarily a "political" dramatist and if this view, although too simple to be strictly accurate, was partly his own fault, it sprang from his continuing interest in politics throughout the whole of his life, an interest that could not fail to be represented in his work for the stage. Only second, however, to his interest in politics, was his interest in religion and he remarked often that these two subjects were the only ones of real value to thinking men and women. Some of his plays were directly and deeply concerned with different aspects of religious belief. For example, as suggested above, *Too True to be Good* contains important elements of Shaw's thinking on religious themes. Religion is both prominent and important in *The Simpleton*. The priest and priestess, Pra and Prola, adopt a specifically quietist oriental attitude with their insistence that the future will not belong to those who follow the old rules but, in the words of Prola "to those who prefer surprise and wonder to security" (*Collected Plays*, vol. vi, p. 840). This almost mystical approach sounds the note on which the play ends as they hail the life to come.

There is one final comment on the plays of this last decade of the playwright's career and this concerns technique. When Shaw began as a critic of the London theatre, he took up two positions. The first was opposition to the concentration of a leading theatre, the Lyceum, on the works of Shakespeare, in whose social views he asserted that no educated and capable person of the day had the faintest interest and whose work he considered, in part at least, artificial and foolish. The second and complementary position was a determined advocacy of the work of Ibsen. This championing of Ibsen was concerned not simply with the subject matter of the plays but with the technique. In *The Quintessence of Ibsenism*, first written in 1891, Shaw maintained that when the play was simply a question of a love affair or of a crime, there was nothing for the characters to discuss.[18] When, however, people went to the theatre for something other than the repetition of stereotyped plots of this kind, what were needed were "interesting" plays. By this term Shaw meant plays in which problems of conduct and character of personal importance to the audience were raised and discussed. Shaw gradually developed the type of what he called "a disquisitory play" (*Getting Married*) and "a debate in one sitting," the description he gave to the full-length *Misalliance*. In 1912, his friend William Archer said that he suspected Shaw "of sometimes working without any definite scenario, and inventing as he goes along."[19] Shaw declared in a newspaper article "My Way with a Play" in *The Observer* as late in his life as September 29, 1946:

> Instead of planning my plays I let them grow as they came, and hardly ever wrote a page foreknowing what the next page would be. When I tried a plot, I found that it substituted the absorbing interest of putting it together like a jigsaw puzzle (the dullest of all operations for the lookers-on) for communicable dramatic interest, loading the story with deadwood and spoiling it.[20]

Shaw did not have a closed mind to theatrical experiment. This was shown very clearly in his reactions to Sean O'Casey's experimental work, *The Silver Tassie*, which was rejected by W. B. Yeats, when it was submitted to the Abbey Theatre in 1928. Shaw was deeply impressed and wrote to O'Casey praising the variety in the work, with, especially, "the climax of war imagery in the second act."[21] He was in a small minority in his appreciation of O'Casey's expressionism in this work but it has to be admitted that Shaw does not seem to have taken a great interest in expressionist developments in the theatre elsewhere, in Germany for example.

By the time he reached *Too True to be Good*, he had adopted the idea of the extravaganza, which gave him the liberty to abandon the conventional style of plot altogether. It was not surprising, therefore, that when this play was revived in London in the years after the war, comparisons were made with what seemed to be the plotless plays of such *avant-garde* dramatists as Beckett, Ionesco, and Pinter. This play and *The Simpleton* had as little in keeping with the conventional West End plays of the 1960s as Shaw's earliest plays had had with the orthodox constructions of the stage of the 1890s.

It was not only in the contents and construction of his plays that Shaw revealed his ability to move with the times. He found himself looking for a changing style of the actual presentation of the plays in the theatre and also changes in the physical construction of the playhouse itself. Thus, as in the 1890s, he had mocked and derided the Irving style of presenting Shakespeare and had championed the reforms of such as Poel and Barker who almost went back to Shakespeare's own playhouse and style of presentation, so Shaw rejected the conventional West End type of theatre auditorium and called for something more appropriate to the style of play to which he was turning himself. Thus, as long before the final plays as 1923, he had written a paper for his friend, the New York producer, Lawrence Langner, who was to be responsible for pioneer productions of several of the later Shaw plays. His article was entitled "Wanted: a New Sort of Theatre for an Old Sort of Play."[22] Delighting, as always, in paradox, Shaw, who sometimes called himself a new and revolutionary dramatist but at other times declared that he was a most old-fashioned playwright, advocated a return to the theatre on more or less Shakespearean lines. He was greatly impressed by the possibilities of the then growing cinema, in which he saw that photography could do, in rapid changing of scenes, what all the designers and carpenters employed by Irving at the Lyceum had failed to do, despite the time and money lavished on them. Shaw maintained that "no theatre is likely to be generally useful in the future unless its stage is so constructed that it can present a play in fifty scenes without a break." He went on to mock the methods of presentation in the nineteenth-century theatre with "the stage being a mere hole in the wall at the narrow end, through which you peeped at a remote *tableau vivant* resembling a pictorial advertisement of the best rooms in the latest hotel." He stopped short of advocating a "theatre in the round" but his views do not seem very different from those of the directors and producers who have gone in that direction. *The Simpleton* was played in the round in the Orange Tree production in 1995 and succeeded admirably.

Shaw wrote one final full-length play after the remarkable decade of playwriting that ended with *"In Good King Charles's Golden Days"* in 1939. This was *Buoyant Billions*, which he had actually begun in 1936, abandoned in 1937, taken up again in August 1945, and completed in July 1947. He described the play in the preface as "a trivial comedy which is the best I can do in my dotage." He asked for forgiveness for the piece, and added that it would not rub in the miseries and sins of recent wars, which he urged his readers to forget. He made no greater claim for this late work than that it was an example of "smiling comedy with some hope in it" (*Collected Plays*, vol. VII, p. 311).

This was in 1947. Before that, however, his thoughts had taken a more constructive direction. When, in 1912, he had written to his friend, Mrs.

Alfred Lyttelton, that he had "a book on Socialism to write – *the* book on Socialism," this idea became, after long delay, *The Intelligent Woman's Guide*. He had told Mrs. Lyttelton that this meant that he would be "replunged into Socialism . . . even into journalism, perhaps: a horror at my age."[23] At a very much later age, he threw himself into socialism and even "journalism" once again. At the beginning of the 1939 war, he took on the task of writing another book on economics and politics. He told his friend Gilbert Murray that this was to be "a Penguin sixpenny stating the facts that persons ought to know before they are allowed to vote or present themselves for election." The book was published in 1944 as *Everybody's Political What's What?* (not a Penguin and costing very much more than sixpence). As with *The Intelligent Woman's Guide*, he found that the writing went rather more slowly than he would have liked. In a letter to Lord Alfred Douglas, he wrote on December 27, 1941: "My book, which I thought would be finished this year, is a mass of senile ramblings and repetitions. I shall never get it into any very orderly sequence. But perhaps my second childhood may go down with the mob better than my maturity did."[24] He may have done himself an injustice. Certainly, the book does not stand comparison with *The Intelligent Woman's Guide*. After nearly twenty years and when the author, practised though he was in clear exposition both on the stage and off, had lost something of his energy and skill, the later book lacks the clarity and coherence of the earlier and, at times, seems both jokey and jerky. Nevertheless, the American critic, Edmund Wilson, who, while admiring most of Shaw's plays of the 1930s, had written scathingly of his politics at that time, now felt that "even at the points where Shaw's thinking conspicuously fails in coherence, there is still a kind of general wisdom that soaks through the cracks of his argument."[25]

The final period of Shaw's dramatic production, from *Saint Joan* to his plays of the 1930s may be seen as, in themselves, a paradoxical representation of the whole of his writing life. For one who employed paradox to such a great extent in his own style of writing and thought, this in itself is an exquisite example of paradox. Thus, while it may be an exaggeration to suggest that Shaw proved to be most facetious when trying to be serious but showed himself as most serious when, in fact, intending to be facetious, it has certainly something of the truth in it. This may be illustrated by the summing-up of the critic Martin Meisel after he had examined Shaw's plays of the later period:

> As a group, Shaw's Extravaganzas are unquestionably the most under-appreciated of his plays. Just as the best of the Discussions are thought to be, from a theatrical point of view, static, argumentative, and dialectically over-

25   Intellectual Extravaganzas: Shaw (Al Kozlik) and fantasy (Lisa Waines as Maya) in the
Shaw Festival's 1996 production of *The Simpleton of the Unexpected Isles*

refined, while in fact they are full of farcical activity, vigorous character, and broad theatricalism, so the Extravaganzas are thought to be theatrically crude, allegorically dull, and relatively empty, while in fact they are inventive, exciting, and as full of meat as an egg.[26]

Meisel went on to suggest that the disregard of realistic canons in the later plays could be "deplored as evidence of Shaw's declining abilities only from the standpoint of doctrinaire dramatic naturalism." He concluded by remarking on the paradox that Shaw "capped his heterodox career, having always made the greatest intellectual claims for the drama, by making nineteenth-century Extravaganza the vehicle for his drama of ideas." From a different angle, G. K. Chesterton, a regular sparring partner of Shaw, always took the view that his old friend and adversary was more likely to be right when he was being flippant than when he was trying to be serious.

Despite the efforts that he made sometimes to speak in one capacity rather than the other, it was almost impossible for Shaw the "clown" to be absent from Shaw the "serious thinker" and vice versa. Thus, while in *The Intelligent Woman's Guide*, he made a deliberate attempt to write a work of exposition rather than entertainment, it was impossible for him to write in a style that was essentially different from that in which he wrote his plays and prefaces. Admittedly, the deliberately facetious or flippant is rarely to be seen in *The Intelligent Woman's Guide* but, in both this work and the later *Everybody's Political What's What?* his ability to use the homely or everyday illustration in his arguments makes his style of writing far nearer to that employed in his plays and as remote as possible from that of all but a small number of the usual writers of books on political or economic subjects which he found "written in an academic jargon" that was "unbearably dry, meaning unreadable" to the reader who was not specialized. It was not only in style that the works of exposition resembled the plays. The symmetry of the appearance of the two works, almost as bookends as it were, at either side of the corpus of plays written in the decade may tend to suggest the idea of essential difference. This is not so. Ideas worked out in *The Intelligent Woman's Guide* are clearly to be discerned in the plays. Examples are, of course, the discussions of the working or failures of parliamentary democracy in various plays and the disquisition on economic matters in *The Millionairess*. In the reverse direction, as it were, Shaw considers his profession as a dramatist in the chapter on "The Aesthetic Man" in *Everybody's Political What's What?* and says that "the artist's workshop is the whole universe as far as he can comprehend it; and he can neither contrive nor dictate what happens there: he can only observe and interpret events that are beyond his control."

In the last year of his life, an opportunity arose for Shaw to make a final public pronouncement on the function of the dramatist. Terence Rattigan, himself a popular and successful dramatist, wrote an article in the *New Statesman and Nation* with the title "The Play of Ideas." He contended that the theatre was dominated by "the play of ideas" under the continuing influence of Ibsen and Shaw, but he thought that plays should be primarily "about people and not about things." The editor invited Shaw to reply. He agreed, but suggested that other dramatists should first be invited to put their views and he would come in at the end and "wipe the floor with the lot."

In his reply, Shaw admitted that there were ideas at the back of his plays but this did not make them mere speeches or leading articles. The criticism was "an old story" and he contended firmly that "without a stock of ideas, mind cannot operate and plays cannot exist. The quality of a play is the quality of its ideas."[27] He then abandoned Rattigan and launched into a long exposition of his own development as a dramatist, influenced by the Greeks, Shakespeare, and opera. Perhaps his shrewdest thrust in his own defense was the observation that there were differences in mental capacity between playwrights. "One playwright is capable of nothing deeper than short-lived fictitious police and divorce court cases of murder and adultery. Another can rise to the masterpieces of Aeschylus, Euripides, and Aristophanes, to *Hamlet, Faust, Peer Gynt*, and – well, no matter." Six months after these characteristically self-confident assertions, Shaw's long career as public entertainer and "the greatest world teacher ever to have arisen from these islands"[28] came to an end.

NOTES

Quotations from Shaw's plays and prefaces are taken from the *Bodley Head Bernard Shaw: Collected Plays with their Prefaces*, ed. Dan H. Laurence, 7 vols. (London, 1970–74). Quotations from *Bernard Shaw: Collected Letters*, also ed. Dan H. Laurence, 4 vols. (London, 1965–88) are given in the following notes.

1 *To a Young Actress: The Letters of Bernard Shaw to Molly Tompkins* (London, 1960), pp. 89 and 90.
2 Bernard Shaw, *The Intelligent Woman's Guide to Socialism and Capitalism* (London, 1928), p. 465.
3 An exception is Gareth Griffith, *Socialism and Superior Brains* (London, 1993).
4 Siegfried Trebitsch, *Chronicle of a Life* (London, 1953), p. 277.
5 *The Intelligent Woman's Guide*, p. 463.
6 Letter to Nora Ervine, in St. John Ervine, *Bernard Shaw* (London, 1956), p. 555.
7 Letter to Erich Strauss, *Collected Letters*, vol. IV, p. 632.
8 Irving Wardle, *The Times*, February 22, 1987, and see also Adam Nicolson, *Sunday Telegraph*, September 18, 1996.
9 Michael Billington, *Guardian*, July 27, 1977.
10 Letter to Augustin Hamon, July 4, 1931, *Collected Letters*, vol. IV, p. 241.
11 Reprinted in *Shaw on Theatre*, ed. E. J. West (London, 1959), p. 217.
12 Raymond Mander and Joe Mitchenson (eds.), *Theatrical Companion to Shaw* (London, 1954), p. 261.
13 Ervine, *Bernard Shaw*, p. 569.
14 Letter to Erich Strauss, *Collected Letters*, vol. IV, p. 633.
15 *Bernard Shaw's Letters to Granville Barker*, ed. C. B. Purdom (New York, 1957), p. 77.
16 Letter to Graham Wallas, *Collected Letters*, vol. IV, p. 80.
17 Letter to Harold Laski, *Collected Letters*, vol. IV, p. 749.
18 *The Quintessence of Ibsenism*, in Bernard Shaw, *Major Critical Essays*, Standard Edition (London, 1932), p. 137.
19 William Archer, *Playmaking* (London, 1912), p. 43.
20 Reprinted in *Shaw on Theatre*, p. 267.
21 Eileen O'Casey, *Cheerio, Titan* (London, 1991), p. 45.
22 Lawrence Langer, *GBS and the Lunatic* (New York, 1963), p. 287.
23 Letter to the Hon. Mrs. Alfred Lyttelton, *Collected Letters*, vol. III, p. 142.
24 Letter to Alfred Douglas, *Collected Letters*, vol. IV, p. 622.

25 Edmund Wilson, *Classics and Commercials* (London, 1951), p. 243.
26 Martin Meisel, *Shaw and the Nineteenth Century Theatre* (Princeton, 1963), p. 427.
27 Reprinted in *Shaw on Theatre*, p. 289.
28 Irving Wardle, "The Plays," in Michael Holroyd (ed.), *The Genius of Shaw* (New York, 1979), p. 149.

3
THEATRE WORK AND INFLUENCE

13

JAN McDONALD

Shaw and the Court Theatre

Introduction

In his introductory remarks to Lillah McCarthy's autobiography, *Myself and My Friends* (1933), Shaw wrote of the Court Theatre experience: "It did not seem an important chapter when we were making it: but now, twenty years after its close, it falls into perspective as a very notable one."[1]

When the Court Theatre venture was properly launched in the autumn of 1904 by Harley Granville Barker and J. E. Vedrenne, G. B. Shaw was known as a minor novelist, a highly rated music and drama critic, and a failed playwright. A leading article in *The Era* (May 14, 1904) attributed his incontestable lack of success to his didacticism, his dehumanizing of characters, and his idiosyncratic egotism that revealed itself even more distastefully when his plays were performed rather than read. In March 1905, the leader in the same paper referred to "'The Bernard Shaw Boom" at the Court Theatre. By 1907 when the Barker–Vedrenne partnership was planning a move to the larger Savoy Theatre after an artistic triumph and at least a respectable financial outcome at the Court, no less a theatrical knight than Sir Herbert Beerbohm Tree was extolling Shaw's virtues as a dramatist who had by this time been happily acknowledged by the presence of the King, the Prince and Princess of Wales, the Prime Minister, and numerous notable politicians at his Court productions.

The Court between 1904 and 1907 was, in fact, the "Shaw Theatre," since 701 out of 988 productions were of Shaw's plays. These financed the experimental matinées of the work of Barker, Galsworthy, Hankin, and Masefield and kept the enterprise viable. In return, the Barker–Vedrenne management provided Shaw with the ideal theatrical conditions in which his plays could succeed. He was able to direct his own work with a group of actors sympathetic to his political stance and to his dramaturgical and theatrical technique of harnessing tradition in the pursuit of the innovative. The commercial set-up of the West End was anathema to him, as were the star-system, the hierarchy of the actor-managers, and the fashion for lavish settings and exquisite costumes. The Court management believed that "the play was the thing" and, in an ideal context for innovation, built up an audience prepared to be shocked, amused, or jolted from complacency by Shaw, the arch-iconoclast.

In three years, a new dramatic genius had been created in an unfashionable little theatre outside the West End orbit, with the help of a group of actors whose names were unknown beyond the Sunday evening performance circuit.

The legacy of the 1890s

Much of the groundwork for the success of the Court experiment had been done by the small "alternative" stage companies that sprang up in the 1890s, notably the Independent Theatre Society (ITS) founded by J. T. Grein, "the prince of theatre enthusiasts," in 1891, William Archer's New Century Theatre, and above all, the Stage Society, which rose from the ashes of the defunct ITS in 1899. The endeavors of the pioneers who worked in difficult circumstances with no regular company, no permanent theatre or rehearsal space, and extremely limited funds, nevertheless resulted in the establishment of a group of young actors interested in the challenge of "difficult" roles presented by the best of continental drama, in a growing body of native playwrights who sought to create an intellectual literary alternative to the postprandial escapism of society drama, and in a small but increasing audience for a theatre of social commitment and moral debate. Most specifically, the Societies provided the Court with its principal dramatist, G. B. Shaw, its director, Harley Granville Barker and a nucleus of actors on which the management could draw with confidence.

While Shaw was inevitably critical of the short rehearsal periods, the difficulties of recruiting actors and the lack of technical facilities, he was quick to acknowledge the importance to the dramatist of the right to fail. "The main point is that the Stage Society game is by no means to be despised, and that if the people who scorned the old Independent Theatre had written for it all they could, several of them would have been expert dramatists now."[2]

Shaw's first play, *Widowers' Houses*, was produced by the ITS in 1892. "It was the existence of the Independent Theatre that made me finish that play, and by giving me the experience of its rehearsal and performance, revealed the fact (to myself among others) that I possessed the gift of "fingering" the stage. Everything followed from that."[3]

The Stage Society's inaugural production was *You Never Can Tell* in

1899 and between that date and the establishment of the Barker–Vedrenne management at the Court in 1904, the Society produced *Candida* (1900), *Captain Brassbound's Conversion* (1900), *Mrs. Warren's Profession* (1902), and *The Admirable Bashville* (1903).

On the incorporation of the Stage Society in 1904, Shaw and his wife were the first (and only) life members. He was a member of the council of management and served on both the casting and the production committees. In acknowledging that "I owe the Society as much as it owes me,"[4] Shaw was not referring only to the provision of a stage for his dramatic experiments. It was through the Stage Society that he came into contact with Harley Granville Barker, "altogether the most distinguished and incomparably the most cultivated person whom circumstances had driven into the theatre at that time."[5]

The story of Shaw's initial dismissal of Charles Charrington's choice of the young Barker to play Marchbanks in the Stage Society's production of *Candida* and his subsequent conversion to wholehearted admiration of the latter's talent has been well rehearsed. Barker's success in the role led to his being cast as Captain Kearney in *Captain Brassbound's Conversion* and Frank in *Mrs. Warren's Profession*. Soon Shaw was convinced not only of his histrionic ability, despite reservations that Barker was too "fastidious and low-toned" for the full-blooded Shavian drama, but also of his originality as a dramatist and a director. Barker's directorial debut was for the Stage Society in April 1900, a triple bill of two Maeterlinck plays, *Interior* and *Death of Tintagiles*, and *The House of Usna* by "Fiona McLeod." It was also for the Stage Society that he directed his own play *The Marrying of Ann Leete* in 1902, and co-directed with the author, Shaw's *Cashel Byron's Profession* in the following year. "Shaw found in Barker first the juvenile actor he wanted, then the manager and co-director he needed; for sixteen years Barker was his chief stage resource."[6]

Barker, like Shaw, was always to acknowledge the opportunities and the encouragement proffered by the Stage Society and its predecessors but also like Shaw, he became increasingly frustrated by its limitations. "I think that the Independent Theatre – The New Century – the Stage Society have prepared the ground and the time is ripe for starting a theatre upon their lines upon a regular however unpretending basis."[7]

The principles of the Court experiment

In his much quoted letter to William Archer of April 21, 1903, "a seminal document in the Edwardian reform of the stage,"[8] according to Dennis Kennedy, Barker suggested that this theatre might be the Court in Sloane

Square where he proposed to "run a stock season of the Uncommercial Drama: Hauptmann – Sudermann – Ibsen – Maeterlinck – Schnitzler – Shaw – Brieux, etc." *Pace* the "etc." Shaw is the only English-speaking dramatist included. Despite Archer's reservations about the youth – Barker was only twenty-three – and inexperience of his correspondent, he had none about his vision, a vision that would culminate in a National Theatre for which Archer himself had tirelessly worked throughout the 1890s. Thus when almost a year later J. H. Leigh of the Court Theatre asked Archer's advice on a director for *Two Gentlemen of Verona* to feature his wife, Thyrza Norman, he suggested Harley Granville Barker, who agreed, provided that he could also produce six matinées of *Candida*, which had not yet had a public performance. Shaw reputedly took very little interest in the event, but Charlotte Shaw secretly promised £160 as a guarantee against loss, fortunately never claimed, as the play was popular and brought the sceptical Shaw royalties of £31 3s. Nonetheless, the totally uninterested Shaw had a few words to say on the advertisements: "Unless every advertisement is headed TUESDAYS, THURSDAYS and FRIDAYS in colossal print the scheme will fail because people will get confused about the dates which are perfectly idiotic."[9]

The success of *Candida* was consolidated by Barker's production of *Hippolytus*, Gilbert Murray's translation of Euripides' drama, for the New Century Theatre. J. E. Vedrenne, the Court's business manager saw that the *avant garde* could be profitable and entered into a partnership with Barker that was to last four years.

The Court repertoire fell into four categories: first, examples of the best of European contemporary drama, plays by Ibsen, Hauptmann, Schnitzler, and Maeterlinck; secondly, Gilbert Murray's lyrical (and totally anglified) translations of Euripides' tragedies, *Hippolytus*, *Electra*, and *The Trojan Women*; the largely naturalistic work of the "new" dramatists, such as Barker, Hankin, and Masefield; and, finally, and most importantly, the dramas of G. B. Shaw. During the three seasons from 1904 to 1907, there were premières of six plays by Shaw. *John Bull's Other Island* launched the project in November 1904, *Man and Superman*, a co-production with the Stage Society, was produced in May 1905, followed by *Major Barbara* in November. *The Doctor's Dilemma* (November 1906), *The Philanderer* (February 1907), and *Don Juan in Hell*, the hitherto unperformed third act of *Man and Superman* (June 1907), were all mounted in the last season at the Court. There were in addition regular revivals of *Candida* and *You Never Can Tell* and *Captain Brassbound's Conversion*.[10]

In some quarters there was disquiet about the domination of the Court repertoire by Shavian drama, notably from William Archer, a staunch supporter of the venture and a good friend to Barker and to Shaw. But with the possible exception of Barker himself, and he was certainly less prolific, there were few playwrights of calibre with work ready for production. Shaw's attempts to encourage his literary friends, for example, H. G. Wells, to write for the stage were unsuccessful, and John Galsworthy, a recent convert to the theatre, was only beginning his career with *The Silver Box*, produced at the Court in 1906.

Significantly, the actors, and particularly actresses, were highly supportive of the variety of roles offered. Lillah McCarthy, who created the part of Ann Whitefield in *Man and Superman*, wrote: "[Ann Whitefield] was a new woman and she made a new woman of me"[11] and Edith Wynne Mattison's reply to the toast to the Court actors at the end of the management concluded: "Our authors have fitted us out with an entirely new gallery of theatrical portraitures, freeing us from the conventional classifications which have done injustice for humanity too much on the English stage."[12]

Yet although Shaw was the dramatist whose work was most frequently performed at the Court, his contribution went beyond that of providing as he put it "a series of first-rate music hall entertainments, thinly disguised as plays."[13] He directed his own work, advised on the direction of others, on the choice of repertoire and other artistic matters, and from time to time took a practical interest in the theatre's finance and administration. Above all, despite his own success and the opportunities it brought for personal remuneration through long runs on the commercial stage, he remained unfalteringly true to the principles of the company and to its pioneering mission.

The radical ethos of the company suited Shaw's own political outlook. The most successful Court plays (those by Barker, Galsworthy, and Hankin, as well as Shaw's) put forward what the critic, Desmond MacCarthy, called "a critical dissenting attitude towards conventional codes of morality."[14] Lillah McCarthy, who played many Shavian heroines, referred to the Court Theatre as a "mission hall" and to Shaw as "the General Booth of this Salvation Army."[15] The atmosphere of commitment to social reform, using the stage as a platform, suited very well the Fabian Society stalwart who wrote, "Although my trade is that of a playwright, my vocation is that of a prophet."[16] The Court audience of serious-minded intellectuals, writers, artists, and socialists, who found little to amuse them in the self-reflecting upper-middle-class dramas of the West End commercial stage, was hungry for these prophecies. Shaw insisted that it was less of an audience than a congregation. *Punch* (December 13, 1905) detected "not a theatre-going but rather a lecture-going, sermon-loving appearance" in the spectators of *Major Barbara*.

Backstage, no less than in the auditorium, such egalitarian and radical principles prevailed. The hierarchy of the actor-manager's company was toppled in the Court's commitment to what the actress, Edith Wynne Matthison, described as "a sense of brotherhood and sympathy, firmly based on economic equity and artistic opportunity." The Court could never afford high salaries, nor did the management want to pay them, for the actor who demanded a star salary was probably not a Court actor anyway, and Barker firmly believed that economy in management often helped rather than hindered artistic achievement. Lewis Casson writes that £1 1s od per matinée was paid to first-rate actors at the Court, although a few actors, of which he was one, were on low-salaried seasonal contracts. Many actors, including Lillah McCarthy, who turned down a £30 a week contract from Charles Frohman to keep her Court "twelve-pound look," willingly accepted a drop in salary in return for interesting work with serious-minded and talented fellow actors.

Although Court salaries were low by West End standards, the actors were in no sense exploited, as Edith Wynne Matthison makes clear: "There were no groans of the ill-paid and sweated in our midst."[17] Indeed, it would have been surprising if there had been, for Court actors were prominent in the reform of the Actors' Association in 1907. The aim of the Reform Party, which included Barker, Henry Ainley, Lewis Casson, Edith Wynne Matthison, and Clare Greet from the Court, was to prevent the Association turning into a mere social club and to force it to consider seriously the financial difficulties of the profession. Largely thanks to their activities, the minimum weekly wage for a speaking part was established at £2 per week.

Many of the Court performers were deeply involved with the Actresses' Franchise League, the theatrical wing of the women's suffrage movement and the Court staged what is probably the best propagandist play on the subject, Elizabeth Robins's *Votes for Women!* in 1907, both Shaw and Barker having a hand in the final version.

The spirit of this company of pioneers that sought to reform the theatrical profession and, indeed, society itself was expressed artistically in the commitment to the idea of ensemble playing and the eradication of the "star system." Barker, in thanking his actors for their work over three seasons at the Court, said, "I would rather think of them as a company than as individuals, brilliant individually as they may be, for I feel very strongly that it is the playing together of a good company which makes good performances."[18] Lillah McCarthy maintained "at the Court, the whole was greater than the part . . . there were no stars. We were members of a theatrical House of Lords: all equal and all Lords."[19] As early as 1894,

Shaw had criticized the actor-manager/star system in that it limited the production of new plays to those with parts suited to the actor-manager, thereby excluding works, for example Ibsen's social prose dramas, which have female protagonists. It also prohibited experimentation as commercial considerations of necessity took precedence over the impulse to encourage any play or production that might be a financial risk. He advocated "the break-up of the actor-manager system by the competition of new forms of theatrical enterprise"[20] – exactly what the Court seasons were to prove to be.

The cult of the "star" personality, Shaw believed, led to plays being performed simply as a vehicle for his/her self-expression rather than as a cohesive work of art. When the "star" is given something worthwhile to say or do, s/he is at a loss. "To your star actor the play does not exist except as a mounting block. That is why comparatively humble actors, who do not dare to think they can succeed apart from the play, often give better representations than star casts."[21]

Apart from any artistic reservation Shaw had about star performers, he quickly realized that in the Court context, they were a financial burden. In a letter to Vedrenne (May 16, 1906) he wrote, "All our real successes John Bull and Superman have been with modest youthful casts . . . Will a fashionable leading lady in The D's D. [The Doctor's Dilemma] draw the difference between her salary and Miss Lamborn's?"[22]

A second principle of the Court philosophy was to avoid at all costs the pernicious long-run system, whereby largely for commercial reasons in a bid to recoup the vast investment in scenery and costumes, managements sought to keep a production on stage for as long as possible in London and then tour it in the provinces. This blatant commercialism did little for the acting profession: first, the actors were bored and unstimulated, playing the same roles over an extended period, and secondly, with all the main theatres being committed to long-running shows, there were fewer opportunities for experienced actors to gain employment or for young actors to learn. Barker had decried the long-run, maintaining that "it reduced to automatism the art of acting." Shaw, in an essay entitled "Qualifications of the Complete Actor" in the *Drama Review* (September 19, 1885), wrote, "The number of parts played by a metropolitan actor must be astonishingly small in proportion to the number of nights they have played." He is particularly concerned about the effect this paucity of experience would have on their future careers.

The Court Theatre operated a system whereby new work was introduced as a series of six matinées and if the play were successful it would be revived later in an evening bill. This gave the author and the actors time to rework the production with the experience of having played it before an audience. But no production, however successful, ran for more than six weeks.

The actors were appreciative of a system that allowed them a range of playing opportunities and were happy to be cast in small parts as well as in major roles. But for the system to work, actors of both versatility and stamina were required. In May 1905, Granville Barker played John Tanner in matinées of *Man and Superman* and Eugene Marchbanks in the evening performances of *Candida*; Louis Calvert, in the same season, played The Waiter in *You Never Can Tell* in the afternoon and Broadbent in *John Bull's Other Island* in the evening; Lewis Casson in October 1905 played "another gentleman" in *The Wild Duck* matinées and Octavius Robinson in *Man and Superman* in the evening bill; and Edith Wynne Matthison in January 1906 went from Electra to Mrs. Baines in *Major Barbara*. A regular feature of the Court actor's work was the movement from one large part to another, from a walk-on to a major role and from a Greek play to a play by Shaw. No actor or actress could coast through a Court season with a good profile and a pretty dress. The short-run system stretched actors, who had the ability to develop in different styles and to meet the challenges of the system.

Shaw recognized that he had little in common with the dominant mode of theatre at the turn of the century and that his plays would never enjoy success in that context. The ideals and ethos of the Court under Barker's direction provided him with a perfect opportunity, which he seized, bringing distinction both to himself and to the management.

G. B. Shaw as a director

"The art of producing [i.e. directing] plays . . . is as much in my profession as writing them,"[23] proclaimed Bernard Shaw. Indeed he believed that the best director was the play's author if at all possible but if s/he were not directing s/he should keep well away from the production. With typical flamboyance he announced himself to be the only good director for his plays, indeed a *sine qua non* to their successful staging: "Amateurs cannot perform my plays. Professionals cannot unless I am there to help them" (*The Era*, December 29, 1906).

He was indeed largely responsible for the direction of all his own plays at the Court, and even when his absence necessitated Barker's initiating the rehearsals, he invariably came in at the end of the process, dismissed Barker's delicate effects, replaced the younger man's "Debussy" with his own "Verdi," let the actors rip, and raised the production into the realms of grand opera. Yet when he undertook his first major Court production, *John Bull's Other Island* in 1904, he was comparatively inexperienced. He certainly learned "on the job" as it were, and does admit, in a more modest mode, that he was taught by excellent actors.

Shaw wrote two major essays on his principles and practice of directing, namely "The Art of Rehearsal" (1922) and "Rules for Directors" (1949). These together with the literally thousands of notes he took during rehearsals form the basis of Bernard Dukore's *Bernard Shaw: Director* (1971), which remains the principal work in this area.

Shaw believed that the first and most important step in the directing process was the choice of a good and appropriate cast. "Get your cast right, and get them interested in themselves and in the occasion, and stage management [i.e. directing] can be done without, though it does no harm when it does not get in the way of the acting."[24] His letters and notebooks in colour-coded inks display the various combinations and permutations he explored before reaching a conclusion. Often actors whom he admired were the basis of his characters, although the initial model was not always in the event able to play. But, in the main, he chose a team that would complement one another's skills, actors of suitable ages and personalities who would, above all, provide the correct orchestration and vocal contrasts for the play. Ann Casson, daughter of Lewis Casson, a regular Court player commented:

> Shaw worked orchestrally. When he cast his plays, he always cast them [thus] . . . you need a tenor voice for that, you need a bass voice for that, a soprano, an alto. You're casting them as instruments, and if you want to know how to play a part, you've got to know what quality of voice is needed for it.[25]

Shaw expected actors with skill and training, technical expertise in movement and diction, who could rehearse the phonetic alphabet as singers rehearse scales. "As a producer I went back to the forgotten heroic stage business and the exciting or impressive declamation I had learnt from old-timers like Ristori, Salvini and Barry Sullivan."[26] He was indeed fortunate as many of the Court company, including Granville Barker, himself "crazy mad about elocution," had worked with the pioneer Shakespearian producer, William Poel, who had insisted on "learning the tunes" of a play before any moves were made and whose dedication to the art of stage speech was handed on to the company in Sloane Square. As Lewis Casson confirmed, "Barker and Shaw would not have been able to achieve what they did had they not had at their disposal actors of a distinct type, trained speakers brought up in a tradition where there was an art of stage speech."[27]

26   The rhetoric of melodramatic acting: Deborah Lambie as The Lady and Stuart Hughes
as Napoleon in the Shaw Festival's 1993 production of *The Man of Destiny*

Shaw was correct in seeking out actors with highly developed skills in
diction as his plays presented three difficulties for the actors: first, the length
of the speeches, from the point of view of memory as well as of delivery, and
secondly, they often contained difficult and highly intellectual arguments.
The third difficulty was that Shaw was an Irishman. "Shaw wrote and spoke
in an Irish idiom and the English actor couldn't reproduce it," wrote Lewis
Casson. All his pleas for rhetoric may have been an attempt to transfer the
subtlety of his own Irishness to the English actor. Certainly all his rehearsal
notes and letters show a desire for a bigger style than the actors were used to
employing in modern plays. Shaw wanted more actors with Lillah
McCarthy's training in melodrama – "saturated with declamatory poetry
and rhetoric from her cradle, she learned her business out of London by
doing work in which one was either heroic or nothing."[28]

Shaw was somewhat contradictory in his statements regarding the degree
of intellectual or interpretative skills that he required from his cast – "In
selecting the cast no regard should be given to whether the actors understand the play or not (players are not walking encyclopedias)"[29] – and he
satirizes amusingly that species of director who enters into long discussions
about Nietzsche or the Oedipus complex rather than focus on the practi-
calities of getting a performance together. Yet in seeking to cast *Major*

Barbara, he proclaimed that "Nothing but a cast of geniuses will be of the slightest use."[30] Barker maintained Shaw wanted "a Barry Sullivan with your brains"[31] if such a thing were possible. J. T. Grein's review of the revival of *You Never Can Tell* at the Court in May 1905 attested to the fact: "Shaw's plays require 'brainy' actors all round: there are no minor parts, and no room for the animated automata who crowd our stage today. Vedrenne and Barker have gathered together a little company of players who in intelligence and keenness could hardly be bettered" (*Sunday Times*, May 7, 1905).

Shaw, himself, in an open letter to Alexander Bakshy in *The New York Times* (June 12, 1927) clearly states the ideal balance of imagination, intelligence, and technical skill in a Shavian performer.

> . . . my plays require a special technique of acting, and in particular, great virtuosity in sudden transitions of mood that seem to the ordinary actor to be transitions from one "line" of character to another. But, after all, this is only fully accomplished acting; for there is no other sort of acting, except bad acting, acting that is the indulgence of imagination instead of the exercise of skill.

Yet there was a further dimension that Shaw and Shaw's dramas demanded of actors. Dennis Kennedy asserts that Shaw needed "actors capable of projecting a socially critical attitude inside comic characters."[32] The critic of *The Spectator* (February 26, 1910) in a review of *Misalliance* had reached a similar conclusion, commenting on the fact that Shaw appeared to have established "a new convention of acting, rather formal, and tending a little towards caricature – the very opposite of the acting in *Justice*" (that is of psychological naturalism).

Shaw has been accurately described as being "of" the New Drama movement rather than "in" it. He was not a disciple of naturalism, although he admired Barker's dramaturgical and directorial skills in this vein. While he maintained that his aim was to "make the audience believe that real things are happening to real people," he was in fact introducing a further, nonnaturalistic, level into his work, by promoting a style of writing and of performance that encouraged distanciation rather than identification, seeking a comic objective response rather than an empathetic subjective one. A twentieth-century critic, Daniel Leary, expressed it as follows: "He was attempting to confront his spectators with glimpses of reality, have them shift their habitual stance, question their professions of belief. He did it by making the audience feel uneasy, by reversing reversals, by disturbing patterns of coherence."[33]

Sybil Thorndike, an actress who worked frequently with Shaw and whose husband, Lewis Casson, was a regular player at the Court, said the same thing from the point of view of a performer: "A landscape is much more vivid if one looks at it head downwards – one sees colour in greater contrast, everything is heightened in tone, and Shaw stood on his head, and made us stand on our heads also to shock us into awareness."[34]

This "alienation effect" is evident in his stage directions, lengthy admittedly because so many of his early plays had been published before they were performed, but also of great value to a director and to actors as they indicate what is to be thought of a character, outlining the actor's attitude toward a role, rather than seeking the performer's empathy with a character. Like Barker and Galsworthy, Shaw establishes a credible milieu and social environment but he goes further in providing, and simultaneously demanding from the actor, an objective assessment that must become part of the "showing" of the part to the audience.

In this he is nonnaturalistic, pursuing more than a representation of "real life," rather a blatant theatricality: "my dramatis personae are, as they should be, of the stage, stagey, challenging the actor to act up to them or beyond them, if he can"[35] – that is, actors with the skill not only to retain "inner truth" but to broaden the interpretation sufficiently to convert it into a representative of a social type, a prefiguring of later Brechtian theory.

Shaw prepared meticulously before the rehearsal period.

Every move, every piece of business, indeed the placing of every piece of furniture and prop on stage was worked out beforehand with the aid of a chessboard and its moving pieces. With the promptbook already prepared, there was no room for improvisation. This blueprint, one might almost say "modellbuch", was made ready out of courtesy to the actors, who, Shaw believed, did not want to waste their time in doing the director's job for him. In any event, the actors, each involved in his/her own part or piece of action, cannot manipulate the audience's focus of attention. That was the task of the director or "conductor":

> . . . if you take care that they never distract attention from one another . . . that when the audience is looking at one side of the stage and somebody cuts in on the other, some trick (which you must contrive) calls the attention of the audience to the new point of view or hearing . . . then you will at the first rehearsal get a command of the production that nothing will shake afterwards.[36]

Shaw was, without a doubt, the author of the performance as well as of the script. His first meeting with the company generally took the form of his reading of the text to the performers, a fairly commonplace procedure at the time, but Shaw's execution of it, together with his capacity in rehearsals to demonstrate the way he wanted something done, has been commented upon frequently by his actors. There was no question of imitation: Shaw conveyed an idea, a tone on which the performers could build. John Pollock, his secretary while directing at the Court, commented: "His system was based on the tone in which each line of the dialogue was delivered . . . famous artists like Kate Rorke, Louis Calvert and Sydney Fairbrother took from him precisely the tone he wanted . . . McCarthy, Gwenn, Page and Casson learned or perfected their art from G.B.S."[37]

Lillah McCarthy, one of those "learning her art" according to Pollock, was most appreciative of the teacher: "With complete unselfconsciousness he would show us how to draw the full value out of a line. He could assume any role, any physical attitude, and make any inflection of his voice, whether the part was that of an old man, a budding girl or an ancient lady."[38]

Yet these brilliant demonstrations were signposts of a way to follow, not molds to be filled. One of Shaw's "Rules for Directors" was: "show how the passage should be done as a suggestion, not an order; and exaggerate your demonstration sufficiently to prevent the player giving a mere indication of it. A performance in which the players are all mimicking the director, instead of following his suggestions in their own different ways, is a bad performance."[39]

Lewis Casson, through his daughter, Ann, herself an actress, cast an interesting gloss on Shaw's demonstration sketches of a speech or a character:

> I believe he was a marvellous actor [when reading his plays]. So person to person he could do it absolutely superbly, but Father didn't think he would be able to sustain an entire performance . . . He was very good at getting [the actors] to understand the character, and . . . line readings . . . but not any good at translating that into technical terms so that they would be able to play it in a large auditorium.[40]

Hence his reliance on the actors' own technical skills.

Shaw would have liked to follow Poel's example in spending several weeks with his actors round a table discussing not the meaning but the "tunes" of the play, but, unlike Poel and the Elizabethan Stage Society, Shaw was part of a commercial enterprise at the Court, however enlightened that commercialism might be. He was constrained by the normal four-week rehearsal period and he realized fully that one has to write for the theatre one is in. Nevertheless he wanted a six-week long preparation time and felt that only after about the tenth performance was the production really taking shape. The Court system of "tryout" matinees followed by an evening run if the production were proved successful was an ideal model for writing and directing of an experimental kind. Unlike Barker, who was famous for working himself and his actors late into the night, Shaw only rehearsed for three hours at a stretch, from 9am to 12 noon.

The first week was spent largely in blocking the play, answering questions on meaning and running each act through with actors still very much "on the book." In weeks two and three when the performers were learning and absorbing their lines, he withdrew from the stage, never interrupting but writing his famous little notes on details of performance, staging, and setting that were either conveyed verbally to actors after rehearsal or delivered by letter. He held it to be quite unreasonable to interrupt an actor searching for a line or coming to terms with a role. The final week, Shaw was back on stage, interrupting, pulling the whole together, primarily dealing with matters of pace, pitch, orchestration (again), and focus. He looked for contrast in mood, tone, and tempo between the units of the play, and between the voices of the actors who should beware of taking pitch or speed from each other.

Shaw's treatment of his actors, at any rate face to face, was almost invariably courteous. While as Lillah McCarthy put it, he was "serious, painstaking, concentrated and relentless in pursuit of perfection," he had perfect manners, a real respect for the individual's personality, and never, according to Sybil Thorndike "gave a performance of being of producer." Although, significantly, he viewed rehearsals as "art," the creative act was executed in private with no outsiders allowed. Even William Archer, a good friend to Shaw, Barker, and the whole Court enterprise, and Lillah McCarthy's mother were excluded from rehearsals of *The Doctor's Dilemma*. The actors should not be asked to "perform" publicly too soon, and the director should not perform *qua* director at all. Actors were called only when they were needed so that their time was respected. He believed that one should not comment on a fault unless one knew exactly how to correct it. Lillah McCarthy verified that this principle was upheld in the Court rehearsals: "Even when something was wrong he would say nothing until he had found out how to get it right. He never criticised unless a scene was hopeless; and then he made fun of it and of everybody, including himself."[41]

He was opposed to endless repetition of the same scene – another difference from Barker who is reputed to have gone through the Messenger's speech in *Hippolytus* some fifteen times. Shaw wrote to Barker in April 1906 giving advice on *Captain Brassbound's Conversion* in the early stages of which the latter was involved: "Go straight through and dont let them stop for anything. In any case, the policy of sticking at it until we get it is a vulgar folly. Let them take their failure and the shame of it home and they will think about it and pull it off next time."[42]

Shaw was clearly of the opinion that in "the art of rehearsal" the number of contact hours between director and actor were of no more importance than the work which the actor did on his/her own, aided, of course, by Shaw's paperchase of "notes."

In Shaw's opinion, "The perfect producer lets his actors act; and is their helper at need not their dictator."[43] He saw himself not as a schoolmaster but as a collaborator with fellow artists. Indeed, much of the "hard work" of directing lay in "the social effort of keeping up everyone's spirits in view of a great event." Bad temper, in the guise of "temperament," ruined the social interaction, and just as in any social situation, different people had to be treated differently according to their personalities and their artistic competence. He distinguished between "born actors" whom one just left alone and "spook actors" who needed a great deal of help. There was a wide spectrum in between, with Lillah McCarthy very much at the top end:

> The reward for being perfect was to be absolutely ignored, and perhaps corrected for a misplaced comma. When he came along with his notebook, an actor who had done very well would say "Have you nothing for me, Mr. Shaw?": and the reply would be, "Nothing. You're all right. I don't take the least interest in you," a maddening sort of compliment.[44]

While Shaw's conduct of rehearsals can be gleaned only from the comments of his actors and his own *post hoc* writings on the role of the director in the theatre, many of his notes and letters to his casts still exist.[45] These comment regularly on movement, the interpretation, delivery, and intonation of individual lines, on timing, and on the overall rhythm of the scene. The most common instruction is "Play to–," meaning either "play to" a particular line, thus indicating a "phrase" in the overall rhythm of the scene or, more commonly, "play to" another actor, clearly indicating both the need for interaction and for focus of attention. An example of the first comes in the notes for *Man and Superman* in the scene between Hector, Violet, Octarius, and Ann in Act 4.

> Hector It *is* a blow. Oct play to this
> Violet – Play to "I want to be a man."
> Oct – "She'll accept you" play to this.
> Ann – Play to "not so sure of that".

The creation of an ensemble proved a problem to Shaw in *Major Barbara* as Louis Calvert as Undershaft had great difficulty with the part. A sympathetic note to Granville Barker read, "You – poor devil – have to play with Calvert all the way through, play to him, play at him, play on him, play around him"[46] and an impassioned tirade to the offending actor showed Shaw at his most barbed: "you are ruining the end of the second act by your enormous, desolating, oblivious to everybody absent-mindedness: you must try to help the others . . . a good actor must work!"[47]

As far as movement is concerned, there are sometimes sketches to indicate groupings and changes in stage position: sometimes the instructions are given verbally. An example from the 1905 revival of *You Never Can Tell* reads:

> Dolly cross more expressively before the explanation
> Gloria sit at upper end of sofa
> Barker keep R of C when talking to servant – don't mask Phil

Movement and rhythm are the subject of an instruction to Lillah McCarthy as Ann Whitefield:

> In the third act, when Malone, Ramsden and Tanner go off making a great cackle and fuss, do not begin the scene with Tavy until the noise is over and the audience's attention has quite come back to you. Just wait, looking provokingly at Tavy, until there is a dead silence and expectation and then say, without the least hurry, "Won't you go with them Tavy?" Otherwise you will not get the new key and the slow movement.[48]

Notes on intonation and stress abound. From *Man and Superman*, "Ramsden – the most infamous under *my* roof – violent enough to fill the pause" and from *Don Juan in Hell*, "Juan's sighs are not loud enough with his back to the audience, gesture needed: The Life Force is *stupid*: *This* is not fair: Phili*stine*: Hell is the *home* of unreality." A letter to Ellen Terry in March 1906, prior to her appearance as Lady Cecily Waynflete, gives her both the stress and the subtext of her lines.

> (a) Have you thought of the GRANDEUR of wickedness? Grand! That's the word. Something grandly wicked.

> (b) If you take a man and pay him £500 a year, and HAVE – Ah, that's it! Beautiful phrase! Happy expression!
> Just think of it HAVE policemen and courts and laws
> and juries to DRIVE him into it. HAVE! Ah *Have*![49]

Lewis Casson maintained that Shaw's interest was solely in the interpretation of the words of the play, and that he was totally uninterested in the visual aspects of the production. "In his whole history as a producer of his own or anyone else's plays, I never knew Shaw take any serious practical interest in anything beyond the casting and the acting. All the rest, including scenery, costumes, lighting and grouping was of minor importance."[50] With respect to Casson, Shaw's rehearsal notebooks prove that this was not the case, and, although in accordance with Court policy costly settings were avoided, his notes demonstrate that he had a firm grasp of practical points about setting that could make the actor's task easier, for example in the notes for *Candida*, "See that there is a hook for Pross in the bookcase," "Reading lamp must be polished." His instructions regarding the production of *John Bull* include the following comments on the set, which should not be "typically Irish,"

> The same mountain backcloth will do for the three scenes in Act II but in the second scene, the stone must be removed, the round tower pushed as a wing and the scene disguised by the change in the lighting. Sc. I Act IV must be shallow as the hill must be ready set behind it: for the change must not occupy more than one minute at the very outside.

These are hardly the instructions of a man totally uninterested in scenery.

The notebooks show too that he had a keen eye for mistakes in costume and makeup, for example, in *Candida*, "Pross, must have a plainer blouse" and "Lexy too white behind the cheek"; in *You Never Can Tell*, "Gloria – dress wrong" and "Waiter – make-up too pale and drawn – not sunny enough"; and *Major Barbara*, "Barbara's make-up is too red, Undershaft too young, Cremlin's make-up absurd." A letter to Lillah McCarthy about her dress for Ann Whitefield reveals in Shaw an instinct for getting a nuance of character into even such a small piece of costume as a ribbon, "Don't have light blue ribbon with the white muslin: use violet or purple – not artless simplicity – pomegranate splendour." Lillah McCarthy also recounts in her autobiography how during rehearsals of *The Doctor's Dilemma*, Shaw sent her to see Judith Lytton's hair decoration as a model for Jennifer Dudebat's jewelled headdress in the scene immediately following her husband's death. "I went to her in London and, for my instruction and delight, she piled her hair high upon her head and strung it with bands of sapphires, rubies and pearls . . . I went back to the theatre and with my suggestions and Shaw's invention, Neville Lytton made the head-dress which so shocked the first night audience."[51]

There is in Shaw's notebooks and letters sufficient evidence to disprove Casson's statement on the one-sidedness of Shaw's direction and to demonstrate that, although scenically spectacular productions were certainly not within the financial means or part of the artistic philosophy of the Court, attention to the positioning of actors on stage and to their appearance within the set were matters to be taken seriously indeed.

The only designer whose name appeared on a programme during the Vedrenne–Barker seasons was Charles Ricketts, who provided scenery and costumes for *Don Juan in Hell*. Shaw was very keen to work with him although the collaboration between the artist and the wordsmith was not without difficulties. Ricketts wrote in his *Journal*, "Like all men of letters, speaking of beauty [Shaw] viewed it as a sort of agreeable compromise, and the essence of moderation, instead of its being a supreme form of controlled exaggeration."[52] Ricketts's plans for Doña Ana "in an Infanta hoop and a perfect collection of virgins, Holy Hearts and Memento Moris in nests of lace," Don Juan "a creature of silver and purple," and the Commendatore "in Roman armour, buskins, ruff and sash," "frightened Shaw who wanted nothing that would take away from the dignity of the figure, the comedy should be in the words . . ." Nonetheless, Shaw, admittedly with hindsight, gave full approval to Ricketts's final design in an open letter to *The Mask* in 1926. "Twenty years ago Charles Ricketts made a stage picture of the third act of Man and Superman which neither he nor any other in Europe has surpassed, or can surpass."

Shaw received innumerable tributes from his actors. J. L. Shine, who played in *John Bull's Other Island*, wrote, "You are a man worth working for, and if your brilliant play is not efficiently rendered, we alleged actors and actresses deserve extermination, for your god-like patience and courteous consideration, combined with your skilful and workmanlike handling of detail has been a revelation to me."[53]

Annie Russell, in a talk entitled *GBS at Rehearsals of Major Barbara* in April 1908, said "I have never seen actors so cleverly handled. No-one taught, but we were always encouraged, always told 'why'. Our talents were never belittled and we were made to feel proud of our powers. This is one reason why the Court Theatre of London . . . has the reputation of 'discovering' so many good actors."[54]

The critics' recognition of Shaw's power as a director, is shown in the *Daily Chronicle's* review of *Major Barbara* on November 28, 1905: "That he does make people act as they never act elsewhere is at any rate one quite indisputable proof of Mr. Shaw's genius."

The influence of the Court experiment

Inspired by the success of their venture at the Court Theatre, in 1907 Granville Barker and Vedrenne moved to the larger Savoy Theatre in the West End. The same formula of experimental matinées and short evening runs was continued, many of the same actors were involved, and the program of plays was chosen on the same principles. Shaw made a substantial financial investment in the new venture and, although he had personal reservations about the change in ethos that the move inevitably implied – the playing of the National Anthem at the first performance, for example, he regarded as "a hideous solecism, a symptom of moral decay" – he remained supportive.[55] His letters show that he was continually trying to whip up enthusiasm in the rather jaded management, but, no doubt from the best of intentions, he decided he should have a less high profile, leaving the way clear for younger, less well-known dramatists. Yet it was the success of the Shaw plays that had made the Court financially viable as well as bringing it artistic distinction. Further, Shaw, contrary to his practice at the Court, did not direct the three revivals of his plays staged at the Savoy, *You Never Can Tell*, *Arms and the Man*, and *The Devil's Disciple*, leaving the task to Barker, who was not an ideal director of Shavian drama. The Forbes Robertson production of *Caesar and Cleopatra* "imported" for a five week run was well below standard.

Shaw's professional and psychological withdrawal from the Savoy season was by no means the only reason for its failure, and he did after all bear the brunt of the financial losses when it ended in March 1908. But the unfortunate turn of events does underline the enormous contribution that his plays and his directing of them had made to the success of the Court.

The real legacy of the Court experiment lay in the establishment of repertory theatres out of London, in Manchester (1908), in Glasgow (1909), and in Liverpool (1911). Residents of these cities had shown a keen interest in the "new drama" movement by establishing *avant-garde* societies as offshoots of the ITS and the Stage Society. The people who belonged to such societies wanted serious plays of literary merit, well acted and well directed. The Vedrenne–Barker management of the Court became their inspiration and their model and they presented many plays by the dramatists which it had nurtured. Glasgow produced nine of Shaw's dramas, including *Man and Superman*, with Barker and Lillah McCarthy "guesting" in their original parts. *You Never Can Tell* was revived many times by popular plebiscite, and there was a private performance of the banned *Mrs. Warren's Profession*. All three companies staged *Candida*, and Manchester revived Shaw's first play *Widowers' Houses*. Whereas Glasgow almost adopted Shaw as its "house dramatist," Manchester favored Galsworthy, who wrote new pieces for the company, and, in addition, it took up the classical aspect of the Court's repertoire with productions of Murray's translations of *Hippolytus* and *The Trojan Women*. The Court tradition of presenting the best of European drama, most notably plays by Ibsen, was likewise continued. The first production in Britain of a play by Chekhov was Glasgow Repertory Theatre's presentation of *The Seagull* in 1909.

The group of actors who worked in the provincial companies included a great many veterans of the Court. The acting style was praised for its intelligence in representing the author's meaning, its integration of all parts into a coherent whole, the excellence of the diction, and the balance between stylized and naturalistic playing. The Court actors also provided directors for the companies, most notably Lewis Casson and Madge McIntosh. Younger performers trained in the highest standard of histrionic art were fed into the London theatre, and the provinces once again provided the practical experience that theatrical novices had lacked since the demise of the stock companies. Regrettably, only the Liverpool Repertory Theatre survived the First World War, yet the seeds sown in Manchester and Glasgow bore fruit later, so that both cities are now centers of theatrical activity, professionally and academically. The flourishing of the repertory theatres throughout Scotland and England which are as much Britain's National Theatre as the edifice on the South Bank, owes its origins to the initiatives of the early pioneers, most notably Barker and Shaw at the Court.

NOTES

1 Lillah McCarthy, *Myself and My Friends* (London: Butterworth, 1933), p. 1.
2 Letter from G. B. Shaw to H. G. Wells, September 20, 1904, in *Bernard Shaw: Collected Letters, 1898–1910*, ed. Dan H. Laurence (London, Sydney, Toronto: Max Reinhardt, 1972), p. 456.
3 G. B. Shaw, Introduction to J. T. Grein, *The World of Theatre: Impressions and Memories* (1921), in *Shaw on Theatre*, ed. E. J. West (New York: Hill and Wang, 1959), p. 137.
4 Quoted in Allan Wade, "Shaw and the Stage Society," in R. Mander and J. Mitchenson (eds.), *Theatrical Companion to Shaw* (London: Rockcliff, 1954), p. 287.
5 G. B. Shaw, "Granville Barker: Some Particulars," *Drama*, NS (Winter, 1946), reprinted in *Shaw on Theatre*, p. 260.
6 Dennis Kennedy, *Granville Barker and the Dream of Theatre* (Cambridge: Cambridge University Press, 1985), p. 62.
7 Letter from Harley Granville Barker to William Archer, April 21, 1903. C. Archer, *William Archer: Life, Work and Friendships* (London: Allen and Unwin, 1931), pp. 272–73.
8 *Granville Barker and the Dream of Theatre*, p. 18.
9 Letter from G. B. Shaw to Harley Granville Barker, September 27, 1903, in *Bernard Shaw's Letters to Granville Barker*, ed. C. B. Purdom (London: Phoenix House, 1956), p. 20.
10 *Man and Superman* was the most popular play by Shaw at the Court with 176 performances, followed by *You Never Can Tell* (149), *John Bull's Other Island* (121), *Captain Brassbound's Conversion* (89), *Major Barbara* (52), *The Doctor's Dilemma* (50), *Candida* (54), and *Don Juan in Hell* (8).
11 *Myself and My Friends*, p. 63.

12 Dinner in honour of H. Granville Barker and J. E. Vedrenne, July 7, 1907, Criterion Restaurant, London (British Library, 010325/ff/503).

13 Letter from G. B. Shaw to Harley Granville Barker, March 4, 1907, *Bernard Shaw's Letters to Granville Barker*, p. 77.

14 Desmond MacCarthy, *The Court Theatre* (London: A. H. Bullen, 1907), p. 15.

15 *Myself and My Friends*, p. 62.

16 G. B. Shaw, "About Actors and Acting," in *Shaw on Theatre*, p. 215.

17 Barker–Vedrenne Dinner, July 7, 1907.

18 *Ibid.*

19 *Myself and My Friends*, p. 90.

20 G. B. Shaw, "The Theatrical 'World' of 1894," in *Shaw on Theatre*, p. 52.

21 G. B. Shaw, "The Art of Rehearsal," in *Shaw on Theatre*, p. 153.

22 Letter from G. B. Shaw to J. E. Vedrenne, May 16, 1906, *Bernard Shaw's Letters to Granville Barker*, p. 61.

23 Bernard F. Dukore, *Bernard Shaw, Director* (London: George Allen and Unwin, 1971), p. 20.

24 Letter from G. B. Shaw to Granville Barker and J. E. Vedrenne, April 21, 1907, *Bernard Shaw's Letters to Granville Barker*, p. 81.

25 Barbara J. Small, "Interview with Ann Casson," in Daniel Leary (ed.), *Shaw's Plays in Performance* (University Park and London: Pennsylvania State University Press, 1983), p. 175.

26 Sydney Fairbrother, *Through an Old Stage Door* (London: Frederick Muller, 1939), p. 233; G. B. Shaw, "An Aside," in *Shaw on Theatre*, p. 220.

27 Lewis Casson, "G.B.S. and the Court Theatre," *The Listener*, July 12, 1907.

28 Stanley Weintraub, *Shaw – an Autobiography, The Playwright Years* (New York: Weybright and Talley, 1971), p. 32.

29 G. B. Shaw, "Rules for Directors," in *Shaw on Theatre*, p. 280.

30 Letter from G. B. Shaw to Granville Barker, August 3, 1905, *Bernard Shaw's Letters to Granville Barker*, p. 52.

31 Kennedy, *Granville Barker and the Dream of Theatre*, p. 64.

32 *Ibid.*

33 G. B. Shaw, "The Art of Rehearsal," *Shaw on Theatre*, p. 153; Daniel Leary, "From Page to Stage to Audience," in *Shaw's Plays in Performance*, p. 3.

34 Sybil Thorndike, "Thanks to Bernard Shaw," in *Theatrical Companion to Shaw*, p. 15.

35 G. B. Shaw, "How to Write a Play," in *Theatrical Companion to Shaw*, p. 149.

36 G. B. Shaw, "The Art of Rehearsal," in *Shaw on Theatre*, p. 155.

37 John Pollock, *Time's Chariot* (London: John Murray, 1950), p. 202.

38 Lillah McCarthy, "How Bernard Shaw Produces Plays," in *Shaw's Plays in Performance*, p. 176.

39 G. B. Shaw, "Rules for Directors," in *Shaw on Theatre*, p. 283.

40 Barbara J. Small, "Interview with Ann Casson," in *Shaw's Plays in Performance*, p. 176.

41 Sybil Thorndike, "Thanks to Bernard Shaw," *Theatrical Companion to Shaw*, p. 14. Lillah McCarthy, "How Bernard Shaw Produces Plays," in *Shaw's Plays in Performance*, p. 176.

42 Letter from G. B. Shaw to Granville Barker, April 14, 1906, *Bernard Shaw's Letters to Granville Barker*, p. 58.
43 G. B. Shaw, "Granville Barker: Some Particulars," *Drama*, NS (Winter 1946), reprinted in *Shaw on Theatre*, p. 267.
44 G. B. Shaw, "The Art of Rehearsal," *Shaw on Theatre*, p. 158; *Shaw's Plays in Performance*, p. 167.
45 Many of Shaw's notes for various productions are in the British Library: *You Never Can Tell* and *Candida* – Add. 50731; *Man and Superman, You Never Can Tell, John Bull's Other Island*, and *The Philanderer* – Add. 50732; *Major Barbara* – Add. 50733; *The Doctor's Dilemma* and *You Never Can Tell* – Add. 50734; and *Man and Superman* – Add. 50735. Shaw's "Instruction to the producer of John Bull's Other Island" is Add. 50515.
46 Letter from G. B. Shaw to Granville Barker, August 3, 1905, *Bernard Shaw's Letters to Granville Barker*, p. 52.
47 Letter from G. B. Shaw to Louis Calvert, November 18, 1905. Quoted in Sidney P. Albert, "Shaw's Advice to the Players of Major Barbara," *Theatre Survey*, 10, 1 (May 1969).
48 Letter from G. B. Shaw to Lillah McCarthy, June 7, 1905, *Collected Letters*, p. 528.
49 Letter to Ellen Terry, March 14, 1906, *Collected Letters*, p. 609.
50 Lewis Casson, "G.B.S. and the Court Theatre," *The Listener*, July 12, 1907.
51 *Myself and My Friends*, p. 85.
52 Charles Ricketts, *Self Portrait* (London: P. Davis, 1939), p. 127.
53 Letter from J. L. Shine to G. B. Shaw, October 30, 1904, *Collected Letters*, p. 462.
54 Annie Russell, *Theatre Survey*, 10, 1 (May, 1969).
55 *Shaw/Barker Letters*, p. 104.

FURTHER READING

Dukore, Bernard F., *Bernard Shaw, Director*, London: George Allen and Unwin, 1971.
Evans, T. F., (ed.), *Shaw: The Critical Heritage*, London: Routledge and Kegan Paul, 1976.
Holroyd, Michael, *Bernard Shaw, Volume II, 1898–1918: The Pursuit of Power*, London: Chatto and Windus, 1989.
Kennedy, Dennis, *Granville Barker and the Dream of Theatre*, Cambridge: Cambridge University Press, 1985.
MacCarthy, Desmond, *The Court Theatre*, London: A. H. Bullen, 1907.
Mander, R. and J. Mitchenson (eds.), *Theatrical Companion to Shaw*, London: Rockcliff, 1954.
Purdom, C. B. (ed.), *Bernard Shaw's Letters to Granville Barker*, London: Phoenix House, 1956.
West, E. J. (ed.), *Shaw on Theatre*, New York: Hill and Wang, 1959.
Woodfield, James, *English Theatre in Transition, 1881–1914*, London and Sydney: Croom Helm, 1984.

14

J. L. WISENTHAL

"Please remember, this is Italian opera": Shaw's plays as music-drama

Stick to my plays long enough, and you will get used to their changes of key & mode. I learnt my flexibility & catholicity from Beethoven; but it is to be learnt from Shakespear to a certain extent. My education has really been more a musical than a literary one as far as dramatic art is concerned. Nobody nursed on letters alone will ever get the true Mozartian joyousness into comedy.

(Shaw to Max Beerbohm, 1900)

[L]et the people in your next play have a little will and a little victory, and then you will begin to enjoy yourself and write your plays in the Shavian Key – D flat major, vivacissimo.

(Shaw to Siegfried Trebitsch, 1906)

"It is not enough to see Richard III: you should be able to *whistle* it." Such is Shaw's advice in his weekly music column in *The Star* in 1889, which he devoted to a current production of Shakespeare's history play. There was orchestral music that had been composed for the production, but Shaw's comment is directed at *Richard III* itself as a piece of music, and he reviews the acting as a musical performance, talking about a "magnificent duet," for example, and a "striking solo." Richard Mansfield's "execution of his opening *scena* was . . . deeply disappointing," and in a staccato passage "he actually missed half a bar" by dropping a syllable from a word. Mansfield occasionally "made fine music for a moment," but his performance as a whole was a musical failure. "It is a positive sin for a man with such a voice to give the words without the setting, like a Covent Garden libretto" (*Shaw's Music*, vol. i, pp. 586–91).

This is from one of the hundreds of music reviews that Shaw wrote during his six years as a regular music critic (between 1888 and 1894). And all these weekly columns represent only part of Shaw's career as a writer about music, a career that extended over a period of seventy-four years, and that included his still influential book on Wagner's *Der Ring des*

Nibelungen – The Perfect Wagnerite in 1898. Dan H. Laurence's edition of *Shaw's Music* collects the lifetime's work into three volumes that run to a total of 2,688 wonderfully readable pages. Shaw's music is a crucially significant element in his non-dramatic writing, in his plays, and in his life.

Shaw's mother was a singer (a mezzo-soprano) and a professional music teacher; and he was brought up in an environment of music-making in Victorian Dublin. In 1894 he recollected part of his musical background in an essay on "The Religion of the Pianoforte," in which he emphasized – as he did elsewhere as well – the extent to which his artistic education was musical rather than literary. An important event in his life, he said, was learning to play the piano "at the age of sixteen or thereabouts." "I learnt the alphabet of musical notation from a primer, and the keyboard from a diagram. Then . . . I opened Don Giovanni and began. It took ten minutes to get my fingers arranged on the chord of D minor with which the overture commences; but when it sounded right at last, it was worth all the trouble it cost." He then worked out his own fingering for scales, and

> soon acquired a terrible power of stumbling through pianoforte arrangements and vocal scores; and my reward was that I gained penetrating experiences of Victor Hugo and Schiller from Donizetti, Verdi, and Beethoven; of the Bible from Handel; of Goethe from Schumann; of Beaumarchais and Molière from Mozart; and of Mérimée from Bizet, besides finding in Berlioz an unconscious interpreter of Edgar Allan Poe. When I was in the schoolboy-adventure vein, I could range from Vincent Wallace to Meyerbeer; and if I felt piously and genteelly sentimental, I, who could not stand the pictures of Ary Scheffer or the genteel suburban sentiment of Tennyson and Longfellow, could become quite maudlin over Mendelssohn and Gounod.
>
> (*Shaw's Music*, vol. III, pp. 111–12)

It is, I think, relevant to Shaw's own dramatic works that his main exposure to much nineteenth-century European drama would have been through operas that used plays by Scribe, Schiller, and Dumas *fils*, for example, as sources for libretti. This is one of the reasons why he thinks of drama in musical terms.

It is significant that Shaw, according to this autobiographical reminiscence in his Pianoforte essay, began his piano-playing career with Mozart's *Don Giovanni*, for this opera, which he knew from singing it in the years before his piano-playing began, always remained for him one of the summits of human accomplishment, and a work of art that profoundly affected his own career as an artist. During the Mozart centenary in 1891, Shaw wrote that "in my small-boyhood I by good luck had an opportunity of learning the Don thoroughly, and if it were only for the sense of the value of fine workmanship which I gained from it, I should still esteem that lesson the most important part of my education. Indeed, it educated me artistically in all sorts of ways" (*Shaw's Music*, vol. II, p. 482). And it is significant too that Shaw in "The Religion of the Pianoforte" also recalled the pleasure that he gained from the operas of a composer like Gounod, for in his plays he derived a great deal from works that he regarded as by no means first rate.

One of the friends whom Shaw most liked and respected was Sir Edward Elgar. It was Shaw who persuaded the BBC, late in Elgar's life, to commission his Third Symphony (left uncompleted), and it was Elgar who dedicated his "Severn Suite" to Shaw. It was Elgar, too, according to Michael Holroyd, who while opening a Bernard Shaw exhibition at Malvern, "told his audience that G.B.S. really knew more about music than he did."[1] Shaw also had some personal acquaintance with Richard Strauss, whose operas he championed,[2] most notably *Elektra* when it was attacked by Wagner's biographer Ernest Newman in 1910 (*Shaw's Music*, vol. III, pp. 594–623). Shaw had met Strauss in 1914, and then again at a luncheon given by Elgar in London in 1922,[3] and years before there had been talk about Shaw writing a libretto for him. In 1907 Shaw responded to the London opera impresario Henry Mapleson who had offered him a commission to provide an opera libretto for Saint-Saëns: "Unfortunately I have a prior engagement with Richard Strauss, which is at present rather hung up by the fact that I want to write the music and he wants to write the libretto, and we both get along very slowly for want of practice."[4] During the same year Shaw instructed his German translator not to approach Strauss to compose incidental music for *The Admirable Bashville*, which was so trivial that the composer would be offended by the suggestion. But Shaw had other collaborative possibilities in mind: "I wish he would compose the incidental music for the Hell Scene in Superman – a Mozartian fantasia by Richard would be magnificent. But I should like enormously to do a new libretto for him."[5] Shaw also thought about the possibility of doing a libretto for Elgar. "I wonder whether Elgar would turn his hand to opera," he wrote to Mapleson. "I have always played a little with the idea of writing a libretto; but though I have had several offers, nothing has come of it" (*Theatrics*, p. 86). Dan H. Laurence introduces this letter with the information that "Shaw was frequently solicited for opera or operetta librettos," for composers including Richard Strauss, Sir Arthur Sullivan, André Messager, and Oscar Straus (*Theatrics*, pp. 85–86). Another composer who apparently – and intriguingly – was interested in an operatic collaboration with Shaw was Puccini, who, according to Puccini's biographer, "sounded out" the playwright for a possible libretto in around 1913.[6] Nothing came of any of these inquiries, but they do reveal something of

Shaw's involvement in the musical life of his day, which included friendships with other composers as well.

Shaw not only spoke of the importance of music in his education, but he also frequently emphasized the specific importance of music in his career as a dramatist. Here is one of his characteristic statements on this subject:

> My method, my system, my tradition, is founded upon music. It is not founded upon literature at all. I was brought up on music. I did not read plays very much because I could not get hold of them, except, of course, Shakespear, who was mother's milk to me. What I was really interested in was musical development. If you study operas and symphonies, you will find a useful clue to my particular type of writing.[7]

And here is another, in a 1916 letter to his would-be biographer Demetrius O'Bolger:

> [I]t is a pity you are not steeped in XVIII and XIX century music as deeply as in literature; for my plays bear very plain marks of my musical education. My deliberate rhetoric, and my reversion to the Shakespearean feature of long set solos for my characters, are pure Italian opera. My rejection of plot and *dénouement*, and my adoption of a free development of themes, are German symphony . . . I daresay I learned something from Gounod as well as from Fra Angelico as to the ease with which religious emotion and refined sexual emotion can be combined. (*Collected Letters*, vol. III, p.374)

This comment to O'Bolger, and others like it, have not gone unnoticed in scholars' discussions of Shaw as a dramatist, but in my view such assertions have not generally been taken with the full seriousness that they call for – or rather that the plays themselves call for. No element in Shaw's dramaturgy has been so underestimated and under-explored as music. When Shaw declares that he learned his trade from Mozart (*Collected Letters*, vol. IV, p. 432); or when he tells Molly Tompkins that "if you dont know Mozart you will never understand my technique" (*Collected Letters*, vol. III, p. 754); or when in the year in which his first play appeared he argues that the "quartets, &c., so often found in Donizetti and Verdi, to my mind shew how much superior opera is to the spoken drama" (*Shaw's Music*, vol. II, p. 535); or when he makes the remarkable assertion in a 1936 lecture that "I write exactly like Shakespear and I find if only people will get the rhythm and melody of my speeches, I do not trouble myself as to whether they understand them, so to speak; once they get the rise and fall of them they are all right" (*The Drama Observed*, vol. IV, p. 1473) – when Shaw says this sort of thing, he is providing an invaluable guide to the reading, watching, and producing of his plays.

It is highly instructive, too, to notice Shaw's way of talking about the theatre in musical terms (as in the *Richard III* review), and about musical works in theatrical terms. "The truth is," he proclaims in an 1890 music column, "that no man can conduct a Beethoven symphony unless his instincts are not only musical, but poetic and dramatic as well" (*Shaw's Music*, vol. I, p. 924). The three composers who are for him supremely dramatic are Beethoven, Mozart, and Wagner. Mozart he sees as "a prodigiously gifted and arduously trained musician who is also, by happy accident, a dramatist comparable to Molière" (*Shaw's Music*, vol. III, p. 526), and *Don Giovanni* in particular as nothing less than "the world's masterpiece in stage art" (*The Drama Observed*, vol. II, p. 577). The heir of Mozart and Beethoven in the realm of music-drama is Richard Wagner. In *The Perfect Wagnerite* there is a section entitled "The Nineteenth Century," in which Shaw (drawing no doubt upon Wagner's own 1851 book *Opera and Drama*) argues that Mozart and Beethoven laid the foundations of music that dramatically expresses human emotion – as opposed to absolute, decorative music that merely constructs a pleasing sound-pattern. "After the *finales* in Figaro and Don Giovanni, the possibility of the modern music-drama lay bare." Wagner went beyond Mozart in that as his own librettist he had dramatic poetry rather than inferior libretti to work with; and he went beyond Beethoven in that a "Beethoven symphony (except the articulate part of the ninth) expresses noble feeling, but not thought: it has moods, but no ideas. Wagner added thought and produced the music-drama" (*Shaw's Music*, vol. III, pp. 528–33). This is what Shaw saw himself as doing fifty years later to the theatre of the late nineteenth century: adding thought and producing music-drama. In *Opera and Drama*, Wagner argues for the need to make opera dramatic, and he violently rejects Meyerbeer as an operatic trivializer. Shaw's desire is to make drama operatic, and with a similar (though better-humored) vehemence he rejects Sardou as a theatrical trivializer. Shaw, working from the side of theatre rather than music, continues Wagner's campaign to create a genuine music-drama, and both composers[8] defend this art-form against the degradation that emanates from Paris.

In this realm of music-drama, then, the heir of Mozart, Beethoven, and Wagner is Bernard Shaw. We could look at just about any of his more than fifty plays in this context, but I have selected two of the best examples to examine in some detail. One is Shaw's musical re-working of Mozart: *Man and Superman*; and the other is Shaw's musical re-working of Wagner: *Major Barbara*.[9]

The production of *Richard III* that Shaw reviewed in 1889 had a small orchestra, consisting of two flutes, two oboes, two clarinets, two bassoons, two horns, drums, and strings (*Shaw's Music*, vol. I, p. 590). The presence of an orchestra as part of a dramatic production was a common feature of theatres in the late nineteenth century; see, for example, Shaw's 1892 review of Beerbohm Tree's *Hamlet* with music by the composer George Henschel, which is actually an article about "the position of the composer in the theatre" (*Shaw's Music*, vol. II, pp. 521–27). A production today of such plays as *Man and Superman* and *Major Barbara* could benefit significantly, I think, from a revival of this practice of orchestral accompaniment. Each of these plays could be staged with a small orchestra – or even better, if financial and spatial resources permitted, a large one.

One part of *Man and Superman* where this orchestra would be particularly valuable is the Hell scene, which is not only a kind of vocal string quartet but is also thoroughly operatic. The Hell scene is at the thematic and musical center of Shaw's version of *Don Giovanni*, which is what the whole of *Man and Superman* is, and it draws on other musical sources too. "What has become of the music in the hell scene of Man & Superman?" Shaw protested to the producer of a BBC radio production in 1946. "It is needed as a blessed relief to the cackle as well as for its proper effect." Shaw insisted that the music be included, and he told the BBC what to play.

> If you cannot add it to the record you must get the theatre orchestra to stand by. At the entrance of the statue the two first chords of the overture to Don Giovanni must crash out fortissimo in the broadest measure. When the devil appears the opening staves of Le Veau d'Or, the song of Mephistopheles from Gounod's Faust, rattles out. At the end, when Ana cries "A father for the Superman" the band bursts out with "unto us a child is born" from Handel's Messiah, and makes a resounding and triumphant finish.
>
> (*Collected Letters*, vol. IV, p. 779)

In Shaw's printed text of the Hell scene, music is included for the entrance of each of the four characters. The scene begins with a section of the overture to *Don Giovanni* (bars 193–204). Tanner, Mendoza, and Straker have fallen asleep, and the audience sees "*utter void.*"

> *Then somewhere the beginning of a pallor, and with it a faint throbbing buzz as of a ghostly violoncello palpitating on the same note endlessly. A couple of ghostly violins presently take advantage of this bass*

Then Don Juan appears.

For a moment he raises his head as the music passes him by. Then, with a heavy sigh, he droops in utter dejection; and the violins, discouraged, retrace their melody in despair and at last give it up, extinguished by wailings from uncanny wind instruments, thus: –

It is all very odd. One recognizes the Mozartian strain . . .

(*Collected Plays*, vol. ii, pp. 631–22)

As Ana enters, we hear "*Donna An[n]a's song to Ottavio*"

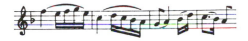

"*the whisper of a ghostly clarinet turning this tune into infinite sadness*" (*Collected Plays*, vol. ii, p. 632); this is the beginning of the Mozartian Anna's plaintive, superbly beautiful Act 2 aria "Non mi dir, bell'idol mio."

Similarly, the entrance of the Statue is signaled by the appropriate bars from *Don Giovanni*, the beginning of the overture – the chords that Mozart's score repeats (with the addition of trombones) when the Statue enters during the dinner scene in Act 2. In *Man and Superman* the dialogue ensures an audience will not miss the musical point:

> DON JUAN. Hush! Listen! (*Two great chords rolling on syncopated waves of sound break forth: D minor and its dominant: a sound of dreadful joy to all musicians.*) Ha! Mozart's statue music. It is your father.

Juan's first words to the Statue are "Ah, here you are, my friend. Why dont you learn to sing the splendid music Mozart has written for you?" – to which the Statue replies that "Unluckily he has written it for a bass voice. Mine is a counter tenor" (*Collected Plays*, vol. ii, pp. 640–41). The Statue music is heard again at the moment of Juan's departure for Heaven: the Statue "*wafts a final blast of his great rolling chords after him as a parting salute. A faint echo of the first ghostly melody comes back in acknowledgment*" (*Collected Plays*, vol. ii, p. 687).

The entrance of the Devil is signaled in a way that musically expresses the clash of values in the Hell scene. Into the sublime realm of Mozart there obtrudes a different kind of music altogether, the second-rate, debased sound (as Shaw heard it) of Gounod's *Faust*. "*At the wave of the statue's hand the great chords roll out again: but this time Mozart's music gets grotesquely adulterated with Gounod's*" (*Collected Plays*, vol. II, p. 643) – that is, with the passage from *Faust* that Shaw identified in the letter to the BBC producer: "Le veau d'or," the brazen celebration of the golden calf by which Méphistophélès vigorously introduces himself in the Kermesse scene in Act 2. The contrast between this and the ominous solemnity of the *Don Giovanni* passage is extreme; just the type of dramatic clash that Shaw's plays characteristically seek. The passage from Gounod has its own kind of force, and an audience will be attracted rather than repelled by it, so that the musical encounter between Mozart and Gounod places before us two kinds of attraction: a Blakean marriage of Heaven and Hell. Gounod's *Faust*, which represents the values of Hell, is no doubt the sort of thing that is much enjoyed at the "grand musical service" at the Devil's palace that is to follow the defection of Juan to Heaven (*Collected Plays*, vol. II, p. 688). "Hell," says Don Juan, "is full of musical amateurs: music is the brandy of the damned" (*Collected Plays*, vol. II, p. 646), and a decade before *Man and Superman* Shaw remarked in a music column that he would decline to attend all the productions of *Faust* during the coming summer, in order to prevent Gounod's opera "growing on me like brandy" (*Shaw's Music*, vol. II, p. 464). So there is a rich subtext to the musical introduction of the Devil in the Hell scene, and this moment is an important part of the whole dramatic structure of *Man and Superman*. An operatic production of the play would make the most of it, with the audience's attention being drawn to such matters in the theatre program.[10]

The musical contrast between Mozart and Gounod is a struggle, too, between German and French operatic composers,[11] which is a prominent subject in Wagner's *Opera and Drama* (where French degradation is represented by Meyerbeer). This national dialectic appears in another form later in the Hell scene, in a musical quotation from Act 2 of *Don Giovanni*. Toward the end of Mozart's opera, just before the Statue's arrival during the dinner scene, Donna Elvira reviles Don Giovanni, provoking his defiant response in "Vivan le femmine," exultantly singing the praises of women and wine. In the Hell scene of *Man and Superman*, the Devil and the Statue are recalling Juan's former days as a well-regarded denizen of Hell.

> THE DEVIL: You remember how he sang? (*He begins to sing in a nasal operatic baritone, tremulous from an eternity of misuse in the French manner*)
> Vivan le femmine!
> Viva il buon vino!
> THE STATUE: (*taking up the tune an octave higher in his counter tenor*)
> Sostegno e gloria
> D'umanità.   (*Collected Plays*, vol. II, p. 645)

Here again there is a mingling of musical styles; and once again Mozartian sublimities are adulterated with elements of French opera. And once again an audience is musically reminded of the intimate connection between *Man and Superman* and *Don Giovanni*.

There are other quotations from *Don Giovanni* that are crucial to Shaw's profoundly intertextual music-drama. One of them is optional, and is not in the text of the play but only mentioned by Shaw in the Epistle Dedicatory in what might seem to be just a playful suggestion. "Octavius I take over unaltered from Mozart," he says, "and I hereby authorize any actor who impersonates him, to sing 'Dalla sua pace' (if he can) at any convenient moment during the representation" (*Collected Plays*, vol. II, p. 519). I do not know how many actors or directors have taken Shaw at his word, but in my ideal production of *Man and Superman* Don Ottavio's tender, graceful aria from the first act of *Don Giovanni* would indeed be sung by Octavius (who, incidentally, will "go a good deal to the opera" in his permanent bachelorhood, according to Ann [*Collected Plays*, vol. II, p. 715]). One good spot for his aria would be after his duet with Ann in Act 4 (*Collected Plays*, vol. II, p. 718) which is soon followed by Tanner's scene with Mrs. Whitefield.[12] In *Don Giovanni*, Ottavio's aria is followed immediately by the entrance of the Don and Leporello, the scene that includes Don Giovanni's "Finch'han dal vino," the amazingly energetic, spirited aria that contrasts so strongly with the languid decorousness of Ottavio's. There should be precisely the same contrast between *Man and Superman*'s attractively energetic, intellectually licentious rebel and his conventional, lyric-tenor "rival." The singing of "Dalla sua pace" would bring out this contrast musically, and at the same time the audience, luxuriating in the aria, would feel that Octavius is not just a comic butt; he has his music too.

Two other important musical quotations from *Don Giovanni* are actually in the text of *Man and Superman*. One of these transposes a memorable passage of the Commendatore's to Don Juan: "Di rider finirai pria dell'aurora," the Commendatore threatens in his chilling opening utterance in the cemetery scene in Act 2, calling Don Giovanni "Ribaldo, audace!" ("By dawn your laughter will be ended . . . Audacious ribald!").[13] In *Man and Superman* this passage is transposed into a comic key:

> DON JUAN: Audacious ribald: your laughter will finish in hideous boredom before morning.
>
> THE STATUE: Ha ha! Do you remember how I frightened you when I said something like that to you from my pedestal in Seville? It sounds rather flat without my trombones.
>
> DON JUAN: They tell me it generally sounds flat with them, Commander.
>
> (*Collected Plays*, vol. II, p. 652)

It would be desirable for an audience to hear the relevant music in this piece of dialogue, and in my final example of musical quotation from *Don Giovanni* it would be, I believe, an even more valuable part of the audience's dramatic experience. This is the scene near the end of *Man and Superman* in which Tanner finally succumbs to Ann's desire to marry him.

> TANNER: I will not marry you. I will not marry you.
> ANN: Oh, you will, you will.
> TANNER: I tell you, no, no, no.
> ANN: I tell you yes, yes, yes.
> TANNER: No.
> ANN: (*coaxing – imploring – almost exhausted*) Yes. Before it is too late for repentance. Yes.
> TANNER: (*struck by the echo from the past*) When did all this happen to me before? Are we two dreaming?   (*Collected Plays*, vol. II, p. 728)

In this passage we have a close reenactment of the famous confrontation in *Don Giovanni* between the Don and the Commendatore late in Act 2. "Pentiti, cangia vita. / È l'ultimo momento," the Statue threatens – "Repent! Change your way of life! It's your last chance!"

> IL COMMENDATORE: Pentiti!
> DON GIOVANNI: No!
> IL COMMENDATORE: Sì.
> DON GIOVANNI: No! No!
> IL COMMENDATORE: Ah tempo più non v'è! [Now there is no more time!]
> (*Mozart Libretti*, pp. 214–15)[14]

The scenes occur in the same part of the dramatic and musical patterning of each work: the climactic moment just before the end. In *Man and Superman*, just as in *Don Giovanni*, the other characters pour back onto the stage right after the vanquishing of the protesting hero, and conventionally celebrate his defeat in a celebratory ensemble finale (with a closing chorus of "*Universal laughter*" [*Collected Plays*, vol. II, p. 733]). In each case the Don Juan figure is vanquished, but in *Man and Superman* Tanner has come to the realization that to marry Ann means a eugenic evolutionist's Heaven rather than (as be believed before the dream sequence in Act 3) a sentimental voluptuary's Hell. Thus Mozart's tragedy is turned into Shavian comedy – a transformation that is highly characteristic of Shaw's dramaturgy. Now, all of this would become much more part of the play in a production that does the Tanner–Ann scene in a manner that brings its original inescapably to mind – and ear. The music can profitably be heard in a literal, orchestral way, as well as in the delivery of the dialogue, which should come close to singing.

In fact, the whole of *Man and Superman*, and all of Shaw's plays, should be spoken in a way that approaches singing. "Opera taught me," Shaw wrote at the end of his life, "to shape my plays into recitatives, arias, duets, trios, ensemble finales, and bravura pieces to display the technical accomplishments of the executants" (*The Drama Observed*, vol. IV, p. 1527).[15] Here is one good example of a Shavian aria:

DON JUAN: Pooh! why should I be civil to them or to you? In this Palace of Lies a truth or two will not hurt you. Your friends are all the dullest dogs I know.
They are not beautiful: they are only decorated.
They are not clean: they are only shaved and starched.
They are not dignified: they are only fashionably dressed.
They are not educated: they are only college passmen.
They are not religious: they are only pew-renters.
They are not moral: they are only conventional.
They are not virtuous: they are only cowardly.
They are not even vicious: they are only "frail."
They are not artistic: they are only lascivious.
They are not prosperous: they are only rich.
They are not loyal, they are only servile;
not dutiful, only sheepish;
not public spirited, only patriotic;
not courageous, only quarrelsome;
not determined, only obstinate;
not masterful, only domineering;
not self-controlled, only obtuse;
not self-respecting, only vain;
not kind, only sentimental;
not social, only gregarious;
not considerate, only polite;
not intelligent, only opinionated;
not progressive, only factious;
not imaginative, only superstitious;
not just, only vindictive;
not generous, only propitiatory;
not disciplined, only cowed;
and not truthful at all: liars every one of them, to the very backbone of their souls. (*Collected Plays*, vol. II, p. 681)

I have divided the text into aria-like lines here (with a bit of introductory recitative), but however one prints this speech it calls out for musical treatment. On the stage it should be almost sung, and it could (for example) be made to sound recognizably like Figaro's "Largo al factotum" in the first act of Rossini's *Il Barbiere di Siviglia*,[16] with Rossini's orchestral accompaniment between phrases just as in the original aria. Juan's "Your friends are all the dullest dogs I know" aria is only one instance of the musical nature of Shaw's dramatic language; almost every speech in the Hell scene would do very well too, and of course my point is that all of Shaw's dramatic works are, as he himself said, shaped operatically into arias, duets, trios, and so on. To find more examples, one just needs to open a collection of Shaw's plays and whistle along to pieces of dialogue. Then one can see what Shaw meant in telling a correspondent in 1908 that one difficulty in having Richard Strauss use one of his plays for a libretto is that "my plays are already in a sense set to music: that is to say, to their own music" (*Theatrics*, p. 91).[17] And one can see, too, what Shaw meant when he said that getting the rhythm and melody, the rise and fall, of his speeches, is more important than understanding them.

   Another of Shaw's dramaturgical principles that derives from opera is the importance of contrast among the voices that we hear. In a revealing statement very late in his life (1949) Shaw advised that directors, in selecting a cast, should ensure that actors' "voices should not be alike. The four principals should be soprano, alto, tenor, and bass. Vocal contrast is of the greatest importance" (*The Drama Observed*, vol. IV, pp. 1516–17).[18] This is certainly a principle for a director to keep very much in mind in casting *Man and Superman*, and I will offer one possible way of achieving vocal contrast:

> Tanner/Juan: tenor (cf. Faust in both Gounod's *Faust* and Boïto's *Mefistofele*)
>
> Mendoza/Devil: baritone (specified in the text – "*a nasal operatic baritone*")
>
> Ramsden/Statue: bass (cf. the Commendatore in *Don Giovanni*; the counter-tenor business is a joke)
>
> Ann/Ana: soprano (cf. Donna Anna in *Don Giovanni*, Marguerite in *Faust*, Margherita in *Mefistofele*)
>
> Octavius: tenor (cf. Don Ottavio in *Don Giovanni*)
>
> Straker: bass-baritone (cf. Leporello in *Don Giovanni*)
>
> Violet: mezzo-soprano (in *Don Giovanni* her original, Donna Elvira, who rails against the Don as Violet rails against Tanner, is a soprano, but I have lowered the pitch in the interest of contrast with Ann).

This is not the only way to do it, and one might, for example, want to preserve the parallel with *Don Giovanni* by casting the Don Juan figure as a baritone or bass-baritone, but the important point is to have as wide a range of vocal pitches as one can, so that one part of a duet (let us say) is noticeably distinct from the other. This, as we have seen, is the method advocated by Shaw, who said in a discussion of radio drama in 1947 that "A cast in which all the voices have the same pitch and pace is as disastrous as it would be in an opera" (*Shaw's Music*, vol. III, p. 762).

It is not irrelevant or accidental to *Major Barbara* that two of the characters' names come from the late-Victorian musical world: Cusins from Sir William Cusins, who succeeded Wagner as conductor of the London Philharmonic in 1867 and continued until 1883; and Undershaft's partner Lazarus from Henry Lazarus, a leading clarinetist of the period. One of the very few things that we learn about this offstage silent partner in *Major Barbara* is that he likes chamber music; Undershaft describes Lazarus as "a gentle romantic Jew who cares for nothing but string quartets and stalls at fashionable theatres" (*Collected Plays*, vol. III, p. 167).

Undershaft's own musical tastes are very different. His particular instrument is the trombone – that quintessentially Shavian instrument that in *Don Giovanni* is associated with Undershaft's fellow bass, the Commendatore. In the first act of *Major Barbara*, Undershaft is invited by Barbara to come to her Salvation Army shelter. "Can you play anything?" she inquires. Her father replies that in his youth he earned money from stepdancing, and "Later on, I became a member of the Undershaft orchestral society, and performed passably on the tenor trombone" (*Collected Plays*, vol. III, p. 88). Toward the end of the act he offers to play his instrument during the alternative version of family prayers that he proposes: "If Barbara will conduct a little service in the drawing room, with Mr. Lomax as organist, I will attend it willingly. I will even take part, if a trombone can be procured" (*Collected Plays*, vol. III, p. 92). The next act, in which a trombone is procured, culminates with Undershaft playing it exultantly (*Collected Plays*, vol. III, p. 136).

Other characters also have their instruments. Cusins's is another of Shaw's favorites, the drum ("I would give anything to play the drum," Shaw confided to his readers in a music column [*Shaw's Music*, vol. I, p. 858]). Cusins' drum is a conspicuous part of the set for much of Act 2: "*A drum is heard in the shelter . . . Adolphus [Cusins] enters from the shelter with a big drum*" (*Collected Plays*, vol. III, p. 113). Shortly thereafter he kisses Barbara "*over the drum, evidently not for the first time, as people cannot kiss over a big drum without practice*" (*Collected Plays*, vol. III, p. 115), and near the end of the act he joins Undershaft in their irresistibly high-spirited orchestral exit (to which I will return in a moment). Also a member of this impromptu Salvation Army band is Barbara's colleague Jenny Hill, whose instrument is the tambourine.

In Act 1, Charles Lomax's instrument is the concertina.

> BARBARA: Cholly: fetch your concertina and play something for us.
> LOMAX: (*jumps up eagerly, but checks himself to remark doubtfully to Undershaft*) Perhaps that sort of thing isnt in your line, eh?
> UNDERSHAFT: I am particularly fond of music.
> LOMAX: (*delighted*) Are you? Then I'll get it. (*He goes upstairs for the instrument.*)
> UNDERSHAFT: Do you play, Barbara?
> BARBARA: Only the tambourine. But Cholly's teaching me the concertina.
>
> (*Plays*, vol. III, p. 87)[19]

Lomax is soon "*heard at the door trying the concertina*" (*Collected Plays*, vol. III, p. 88), and when it is time for him to play there is a characteristic moment in which a musical choice expresses a clash of competing values in the play.

> LOMAX: Hadnt I better play something?
> BARBARA: Yes. Give us Onward, Christian Soldiers.
> LOMAX: Well, thats rather a strong order to begin with, dont you know. Suppose I sing Thourt passing hence, my brother. It's much the same tune.
> BARBARA: It's too melancholy. (*Collected Plays*, vol. III, p. 91)

Of these two pieces by Sir Arthur Sullivan, Lomax's choice, the more sombre "Thou Art Passing Hence," represents traditional, controlled, conventional religious feeling; it was part of the music done with Wilson Barrett's religiously conventional play *The Sign of the Cross* in 1896, and its inclusion was noted by Shaw at the time (*The Drama Observed*, vol. II, p. 496). "Onward, Christian Soldiers," on the other hand, represents the joyous, assertive religious life that is the really positive element in the Salvation Army. The musical values of the Salvation Army are victorious by the end of Act 1, when all the characters except Stephen have moved to the drawing room for Undershaft's prayer service, with Lomax as "organist" on his concertina and Barbara on her tambourine: "*Onward, Christian Soldiers, on the concertina, with tambourine accompaniment, is heard when the door opens*" (*Collected Plays*, vol. III, p. 94).

In Act 2, the victory of Undershaft's values over those of the Salvation Army is also expressed musically, in the Dionysian orchestral scene that we have already glanced at. But in this scene it is the context that signifies Undershaft's triumph; the music itself is fitting for both him and for the Salvation Army, and it expresses the joyous energy that they share. For Shaw, it is this energy of its music that defines the nature of the Salvation

Army. The year after he wrote *Major Barbara*, he reviewed a concert of Salvation Army bands, and he commented that one of the bands

> had the peculiar combination of brilliancy and emotional quality which is and ought to be the distinctive Salvationist musical characteristic. The other bands had it occasionally when playing favorite hymn tunes; but the Clapton band never lost it, and combined it with a joyous vivacity of style and clear jubilant tone which stamped it as *the* Salvationist band *par excellence*.
>
> (*Shaw's Music*, vol. III, pp. 590–91)

This would be a good way of characterizing the nature of *Major Barbara* itself, and all the qualities cited here are very much in aural evidence when the band strikes up in Act 2. In a music review in 1889 Shaw mentioned in passing that Donizetti's choruses "have been discovered by the Salvation Army: I heard one of their bands playing *Per te d'immenso giubilo* capitally one Sunday morning last year" (*Shaw's Music*, vol. I, p. 634). This is the chorus sung by the guests at the beginning of the heroine's wedding in Act 1, Scene 2 of *Lucia di Lammermoor*; while the heartbroken (offstage) Lucia is forced to reject her apparently unfaithful beloved and marry another man, everyone else on the stage is celebrating the joyful occasion. In *Major Barbara*, the heartbroken heroine must watch and listen while all the others celebrate the defection of her beloved Salvation Army (the similarities of plot in this scene extend further, but let us stick to the music). Undershaft has just handed over the cheque with which he buys the Salvation Army:

> CUSINS: (*in a convulsion of irony*) Let us seize this unspeakable moment. Let us march to the great meeting at once. Excuse me just an instant. (*He rushes into the shelter. Jenny takes her tambourine from the drum head.*)
>
> MRS. BAINES: Mr Undershaft: have you ever seen a thousand people fall on their knees with one impulse and pray? Come with us to the meeting. Barbara shall tell them that the Army is saved, and saved through you.
>
> CUSINS: (*returning impetuously from the shelter with a flag and a trombone, and coming between Mrs. Baines and Undershaft*) You shall carry the flag down the first street, Mrs. Baines (*he gives her the flag*). Mr. Undershaft is a gifted trombonist: he shall intone an Olympian diapason to the West Ham Salvation March. (*Aside to Undershaft, as he forces the trombone on him*) Blow, Machiavelli, blow.
>
> UNDERSHAFT: (*aside to him, as he takes the trombone*) The trumpet in Zion! (*Cusins rushes to the drum, which he takes up and puts on. Undershaft continues, aloud*) I will do my best. I could vamp a bass if I knew the tune.
>
> CUSINS: It is a wedding chorus from one of Donizetti's operas; but we have converted it. We convert everything to good here, including Bodger. You remember the chorus. "For thee immense rejoicing – immenso giubilo –

immenso giubilo." (*With drum obbligato*) Rum tum ti tum tum, tum tum ti
ta –

BARBARA: Dolly: you are breaking my heart.

(*Collected Plays*, vol. III, pp. 134–35)

Then after Barbara refuses the tambourine that Cusins offers to her, and
removes her Salvation army badge, the others march off.

> CUSINS: (*calling to the procession in the street outside*) Off we go. Play up,
> there! *Immenso giubilo.* (*He gives the time with his drum; and the band
> strikes up the march, which rapidly becomes more distant as the procession
> moves briskly away*).
>
> MRS. BAINES: I must go, dear. Youre overworked: you will be all right
> tomorrow. We'll never lose you. Now Jenny: step out with the old flag. Blood
> and Fire! (*She marches out through the gate with her flag.*)
>
> JENNY: Glory Hallelujah! (*flourishing her tambourine and marching.*)
>
> UNDERSHAFT: (*to Cusins, as he marches out past him easing the slide of his
> trombone*) "My ducats and my daughter"!
>
> CUSINS: (*following him out*) Money and gunpowder!

(*Collected Plays*, vol. III, p. 136)

The musical quotation from Donizetti in this scene expresses heightened
emotion in a way that goes beyond language, and the dramatic impact of
the scene is decidedly intensified by the music the audience hears.

Lucia di Lammermoor brings actual operatic music onto Shaw's stage,
but it is not the only operatic moment in *Major Barbara*. The play is full of
effects that derive from opera – such as Cusins's recitative and the other
characters' chorus in Act 3:

> CUSINS: Well, I have something to say which is in the nature of a confession.
> SARAH:
> LADY BRITOMART: } Confession!
> BARBARA:
> STEPHEN:
> LOMAX: Oh I say! (*Collected Plays*, vol. III, p. 163)

Or take all the aria-like speeches in this third act, including the tenor–
soprano scene near the end with its big arias. Or there is the irruption of
the Mephistophelian Undershaft into the respectable abode of Lady
Britomart in Act 1, which musical accompaniment (along with a suitable
note in a theatre program) could connect with one of the nineteenth-
century Faust operas that Shaw was very much familiar with: Boïto's
Mefistofele. Reviewing a production of this opera in 1889, Shaw described
the strong effect of its Prologue in Heaven, drawing attention to "the
tremendous sonority of the instrumentation at the end, with the defiant

devil's whistle recklessly mocking each climax of its grandeur, [which] literally makes us all sit up" (*Shaw's Music*, vol. I, p. 645). The defiant devil's whistle which Shaw thought he detected at the end of Boïto's orchestral Prelude is explicitly heard in Act I of the opera, and then at the end of its Epilogue: "Trionfa il Signor," sings the defeated Mefistofele, "ma il reprobo fischia!" ("The Lord has prevailed, / but the reprobate whistles!").[20] Versions of this whistle could be heard in a number of places in *Major Barbara*, as Shaw's Mephistophelian ironist Undershaft disturbs the complacencies of other characters – see, for example, his final line of the play ("Six o'clock tomorrow morning, Euripides" [*Collected Plays*, vol. III, p. 185]), which is very much a devil's whistle recklessly mocking the climax of Barbara's and Cusins's grandeur.[21]

Major Barbara is (among other things) a Faust story, about the temptation of the scholar by the Mephistophelian man of the world – and Cusins does in fact call Undershaft Mephistopheles (*Collected Plays*, vol. III, p. 124). When Shaw thought about the Faust legend, he had in mind not so much Goethe's verse-drama as the two operatic versions that were much more widely known in the second half of the nineteenth century than they are now: Gounod's *Faust* and Boïto's *Mefistofele*. Each of these, at the end of its first act, has a memorable temptation scene between the scholar-tenor and the Mephistophelian bass. Anyone who listens to these two scenes and then reads *Major Barbara*'s temptation scene in Act 2 will, I think, be struck by the possibilities of bringing elements of Gounod's and Boïto's versions into a production. At the heart of the encounter between Cusins and Undershaft is the contrast that we must hear between the sonorous, authoritative, sometimes mocking bass and the much lighter tenor; and this is precisely the nature of both of the operatic scenes. Listen to the recitative that opens the scene in *Major Barbara*, and notice that it begins with Cusins flourishing "*his drumsticks as if in the act of beating a lively rataplan*" and that it ends with Undershaft's sonorous, authoritative bass "Yes," at which point "*The cadence of this reply makes a full close in the conversation.*" What follows is Cusins's tenor aria, with his own accompaniment on the drum at the end of it (I will not divide the lines this time, but the reader will see how easily this can be done):

CUSINS: Father Undershaft: you are mistaken: I am a sincere Salvationist. You do not understand the Salvation Army. It is the army of joy, of love, of courage: it has banished the fear and remorse and despair of the old hell-ridden evangelical sects: it marches to fight the devil with trumpet and drum, with music and dancing, with banner and palm, as becomes a sally from heaven by its happy garrison. It picks the waster out of the public house and makes a man of him: it finds a worm wriggling in a back kitchen, and lo! a woman! Men and women of rank too, sons and daughters of the Highest. It takes the poor professor of Greek, the most artificial and self-suppressed of human creatures, from his meal of roots, and lets loose the rhapsodist in him; reveals the true worship of Dionysos to him; sends him down the public street drumming dithyrambs (*he plays a thundering flourish on the drum*).

(*Collected Plays*, vol. III, p. 115–17)

One of Undershaft's big arias, the *"cold and sardonic"* "Have you ever been in love with Poverty," follows a few minutes later (*Collected Plays*, vol. III, p. 121), and it might be listened to after one has just heard his counterpart's aggressive, defiant "Sono lo spirito" in Boïto's opera – the aria that features the devil's whistle (and Boïto's scene, by the way, includes a handshake between the two characters, just as in *Major Barbara*).

Another operatic source of *Major Barbara* that certainly should not be left out of account in a reading or a production of the play is Wagner's *Der Ring des Nibelungen*, which Shaw regarded as "the central masterpiece of religious music in our times" (*Shaw's Music*, vol. III, p. 393). There has been some critical attention to relationships between *Major Barbara* and *Der Ring*, but it has mostly confined itself to themes in the literary rather than the musical sense, and thus to Wagner's libretto as opposed to his score.[22] If musical allusions to *Der Ring* are included in a production of *Major Barbara* as music-drama, they could bring out some of the striking correspondences between Shaw's characters and Wagner's. Undershaft (bass) is Shaw's Wotan and Alberich (the latter of whom is bass in *Der Ring*); Cusins (tenor) is his Siegfried; Barbara (soprano) is his Brunnhilde; and Lady Britomart (mezzo-soprano or contralto) his Fricka (who is soprano in *Der Ring*, but I have again altered the pitch for Shavian vocal contrast). These correspondences work out with remarkable closeness, especially when one sees *Der Ring* in the light of Shaw's *Perfect Wagnerite*, and the connections between Shaw's characters and Wagner's could be actually heard as well as thought about. One excellent source of music for *Major Barbara* in *Der Ring* would be the second act of *Die Walküre*, in which Wotan/Undershaft, Fricka/Lady Britomart, and Brunnhilde/Barbara sing in ways that relate to their dramatic positions in Shaw's play. The correspondences between some of Wotan's music here and Undershaft's major arias, it seems to me, are especially compelling.

When Shaw came to revise *Major Barbara* for Gabriel Pascal's 1941 film (for which Sir William Walton wrote the score),[23] one of the scenes he added brings – in a way – another opera into the play. In Shaw's screenplay, soon after everyone has arrived at the munitions foundry at

Perivale St. Andrews they visit the Labor Church there for a concert of televised, recorded music on a large screen. Undershaft explains that he has had his favorite record put in ready for them; then Lady Britomart pushes a switch and the screen is filled with "*an orchestra of a hundred performers in evening dress tuning their instruments,*" along with a chorus and four principal singers. A filmed announcer says that "What you are about to hear is a fragment from a dead opera by the Italian composer Giacomo [*sic*] Rossini, who in Europe a hundred years ago ranked as high as Handel in our own country. The subject is the miraculous passage through the Red Sea by the Israelites in their flight from Egypt." Because this subject is no longer of any importance to us, he explains, the libretto has been brought up to date by making the Red Sea a symbol of the socialist revolution.

> ANNOUNCER: We have not altered a note of the music: we have only given it such a wealth of orchestration as Rossini would himself have given it had the great resources of Undershaft and Lazarus been within his reach. The words alone are brought up to date. For Rossini at his greatest today there is only one conductor: Arturo Toscanini.[24]
>
> (*Toscanini enters, baton in hand, and takes his place at the conductor's desk.*)
>
> ANNOUNCER: Ladies and gentlemen: Arturo Toscanini. (*He leaves the platform.*)
>
> (*Toscanini raises his baton; and the quartet and chorus from Rossini's Moses in Egypt follows, accompanied by the Wagnerian orchestra. At the famous modulation into G major the organ is added.*)

What follows – or at least what would have followed, if the whole sequence had not been omitted from the film – is the inspiring Preghiera ("Dal tuo stellato soglio") from the third act of Rossini's *Mosè in Egitto*, with a new libretto that Shaw wrote with considerable difficulty (see *Collected Letters*, vol. IV, pp. 542–43); the revised words have to do with the task of moving from destruction to creation. This whole sequence (which is to be found in Dukore's edition of *Collected Screenplays*, pp. 335–37) may be seen as a late tribute to Rossini from the playwright who during the composer's centenary half a century earlier had called him "one of the greatest masters of claptrap that ever lived," and had exclaimed: "I cannot say 'Rest his soul,' for he had none; but I may at least be allowed the fervent aspiration that we may never look upon his like again" (*Shaw's Music*, vol. II, pp. 562, 570). In the film version of *Major Barbara*, we have a further example of Shaw's plays drawing on composers whom he did not place anywhere near the front rank – as Martin Meisel has shown he did with nineteenth-century playwrights as well. And we have a good reason to

27   The music of Shaw's words: Louise Marleau as Julia Craven with Paxton Whitehead as
Leonard Charteris in the Shaw Festival's 1971 production of *The Philanderer*

make use of the powerful, faith-affirming Preghiera music from *Mosè* in productions of Shaw's play.

In *Man and Superman* and *Major Barbara*, much of the music is operatic, but music of all sorts pervades Shaw's plays. To note just a few conspicuous examples, we hear two pianos in *The Music Cure*; a saxophone in *Buoyant Billions*; a bucina in *Caesar and Cleopatra*;[25] two competing onstage bands in *The Devil's Disciple*; a trumpet in *The Simpleton of the Unexpected Isles*; whistling and singing in *John Bull's Other Island*; singing in *Pygmalion* (from Puccini's *La Fanciulla del West*), and songs in *Saint Joan*, *On the Rocks*, and *Passion, Poison and Petrifaction* (a play which specifically calls for an orchestra); a vocal "antiphonal quartet" in *The Simpleton of the Unexpected Isles*; and a carillon, an organ, and flutes in *Back to Methuselah*. And there is Randall Utterword's flute-playing that forms part of the sound-pattern in *Heartbreak House*. Near the beginning of Act 3, Lady Utterword "*is interrupted by the melancholy strains of a flute coming from an open window above*," and, after all the Beethoven-like thundering of the Zeppelin and its bombs, this instrument provides the sound on which the play ends: "*Randall at last succeeds in keeping the home fires burning on his flute*" (*Collected Plays*, vol. v, pp. 161, 181). *Heartbreak House*, with its musical subtitle ("A Fantasia in the Russian Manner on English Themes"), also has the weird chanting at the end of its first act and other kinds of music as well, and there is something to be said for Shaw's comment to Elgar in 1929 that it was "by far the most musical work" he had written (Holroyd, *Bernard Shaw*, vol. iii, p. 14) – although there is, as we have seen, some strong competition.

All of this music in Shaw's plays is not just something added decoratively. Their music – that is, their literal music and their verbal music – is part of their very fabric, and it gives expression to their values and to their form. In an 1894 piece on Wagner's theories about music, Shaw said that "there is a great deal of feeling, highly poetic and highly dramatic, which cannot be expressed by mere words – because words are the counters of thinking, not of feeling – but which can be supremely expressed by music" (*Shaw's Music*, vol. iii, p. 91), and Shaw's music-dramas do express feeling that goes beyond what mere words can convey. If actual music is used in productions, and if dialogue is spoken musically, then the intense feeling in Shaw's work will be given expression. And there is a great deal of intense feeling in Shaw's work, which is not always recognized because much of it is determinedly non-sexual feeling. Shaw's characters tend to be intensely passionate about subjects like improving the world, and often in contexts that lead us to expect something amorous. The sexual feeling has been displaced, as in Barbara's wooing of Bill Walker's *soul* in Act 2 of *Major Barbara*, for example, or as in the non-love scene between Barbara and Cusins late in Act 3, where the tenor and soprano sing lyrically and passionately about what they wish to achieve for society in taking over the munitions business. Another fine example of non-sexual feeling expressed with lyrical intensity in Shaw's work would be any of Juan's arias in the Hell scene of *Man and Superman*. When we hear Shaw's plays as full music-dramas, this element of intellectual ecstasy is much more potent than if they remain mere prose libretti.

And if Shaw's plays are heard as music-dramas, then their sudden contrasts of key, tone, tempo, and volume are more fully evident, as Edmund Wilson has demonstrated in a musical account of the first act of *The Apple Cart*, in which he shows how this act "is an exercise in the scoring for small orchestra at which Shaw is particularly skillful."[26] The importance of contrasting sounds in Shaw's plays is nicely suggested, too, in this passage from his own music criticism – reviewing a performance of Beethoven's Eighth Symphony, which Shaw compares to his Seventh:

> In all subtler respects the Eighth is better, with its immense cheerfulness and exquisite playfulness, its perfect candor and naturalness, its filaments of heavenly melody suddenly streaming up from the mass of sound, and flying away cloudlike, and the cunning harmonic coquetry with which the irresistibly high-spirited themes, after innumerable feints and tantalizing invitations and promises, suddenly come at you round the most unexpected corners, and sweep you away with a delightful burst of joyous energy.
>
> (*Shaw's Music*, vol. III, p. 354)

Here is a passage that tells one more about Shaw's plays than any amount of discussion about social and political issues in them. Attention to their music means attention to their form, and because of the interest that Shaw has always attracted to his social and political opinions there has been too little emphasis on the formal qualities of his plays – on their melody, their harmony, their rhythm, their movements, their changes of key.

It is not enough, then, to read or to see Shaw's plays; you should be able to *whistle* them. And one might continue this paraphrase of the *Richard III* review by saying that it is a positive sin for a director of a Shaw play to give the words without the musical setting, like a Covent Garden libretto. To do so is to deprive Shaw's plays of their real nature as music-drama. As he so often stated, this is the way he himself thought of his work.

> From my earliest recorded sign of an interest in music when as a small child I encored my mother's singing of the page's song from the first act of Les Huguenots . . . music has been an indispensable part of my life. Harley Granville-Barker was not far out when, at a rehearsal of one of my plays, he cried out "Ladies and gentlemen: will you please remember that this is Italian opera."
>
> (*Shaw's Music*, vol. I, p. 57)

NOTES

My quotations from Shaw, unless otherwise noted, are from the following sources:
Shaw's Music, ed. Dan H. Laurence, 3 vols. (London: Max Reinhardt, The Bodley Head, 1981).
The Drama Observed, ed. Bernard F. Dukore, 4 vols. (University Park: The Pennsylvania State University Press, 1993).
The Bodley Head Bernard Shaw: Collected Plays with their Prefaces, ed. Dan H. Laurence, 7 vols. (London: Max Reinhardt, The Bodley Head, 1970–74).
Collected Letters, ed. Dan H. Laurence, 4 vols. (London: Max Reinhardt, 1965–1988).

1 Michael Holroyd, *Bernard Shaw: A Biography*, 5 vols. (London: Chatto and Windus, 1988–92), vol. III, pp. 167–68, 166–67, 164.

2 In "Music and the Man: Bernard Shaw and the Music Collection at Shaw's Corner," *The Annual of Bernard Shaw Studies* 10 (1990), pp. 96–112, David Huckvale reveals the amount of twentieth-century music in Shaw's personal collection of scores at Ayot St. Lawrence. For example, "He had copies of virtually every Strauss opera" (p. 102).

3 Michael Kennedy, *Richard Strauss* (Oxford: Oxford University Press, 1995), pp. 72–73.

4 Bernard Shaw, *Theatrics*, ed. Dan H. Laurence (Toronto: University of Toronto Press, 1995), pp. 85–86.

5 Shaw's diary in the British Library of Political and Economic Science; Kennedy, *Richard Strauss*, pp. 72–73. I thank Dan H. Laurence for information on this subject.

6 Mosco Carner, *Puccini: A Critical Biography* (1958; 3rd edn. London: Duckworth, 1992), p. 212.

7 Quoted in R. F. Rattray, *Bernard Shaw: A Chronicle* (Luton: Leagrave Press, 1951), p. 20n, as something that Shaw said at the 1939 Malvern Festival. This passage is cited in Josephine Lee, "The Skilled Voluptuary: Shaw as Music Critic," *The Annual of Bernard Shaw Studies* 12 (1992), pp. 147–64; and it serves as the epigraph for chapter 2 of Martin Meisel, *Shaw and the Nineteenth-Century Theater* (Princeton: Princeton University Press, 1963). Meisel's chapter, entitled "Opera and Drama," remains the best discussion of musical elements in Shaw's plays.

8 The designation is Shaw's own: "I am myself a composer: that is, a planner of performances, in the special capacity of a playwright" (*Shaw's Music*, vol. III, p. 756).

9 As for Beethoven, see the novel that Shaw wrote in 1881 which includes a major character modeled on the German composer – *Love among the Artists*.

10 In staging the Devil in the Hell scene, and his counterpart Mendoza earlier in Act 3, there is also something to be done with that other popular nineteenth-century musical expression of Faustian conflicts between Heaven and Hell, Boïto's *Mefistofele*.

11 The national issue is implicit in Shaw's reference to French composers in the Epistle Dedicatory to *Man and Superman* when he comments that "one bar of the voluptuous sentimentality of Gounod or Bizet would appear as a licentious stain on the score of Don Giovanni" (*Collected Plays*, vol. II, p. 500). For a

discussion of Shaw's view of Gounod, see Richard Corballis, "Why the Devil Gets All the Good Tunes: Shaw, Wagner, Mozart, Gounod, Bizet, Boïto, and Stanford," *The Annual of Bernard Shaw Studies* 12 (1992), pp. 165–80. This article, one of the few really serious, detailed accounts of musical elements in Shaw's plays, discusses the place of Gounod's *Faust* in the Hell scene of *Man and Superman*, and points illuminatingly to connections between the Hell scene and Bizet's *Carmen*, and also between *John Bull's Other Island* and Boïto's *Mefistofele* (and Sir Charles Villiers Stanford's Irish Symphony as well).

12 In the rather likely event that a tenor cannot be found to play the part of Octavius and to sing "Dalla sua pace" adequately, then something could be done with a recording.

13 [Lorenzo da Ponte], *Three Mozart Libretti*, trans. Robert Pack and Marjorie Lelash (New York: Dover, 1993), pp. 202–03.

14 It is difficult to convey the nature of the music itself, and mere print must of necessity draw too much attention to the "Covent Garden libretto" side of things. I hope that readers will complement my text with musical performances in some form, and in any case it is best to read – or see and hear – *Man and Superman* and *Major Barbara* shortly after listening to *Don Giovanni*, *Faust*, Wagner's *Ring*, and the various other relevant musical works.

15 See Paulina Salz Pollak, "Master to the Masters: Mozart's Influence on Bernard Shaw's 'Don Juan in Hell,'" *The Annual of Bernard Shaw Studies*, 8 (1988), pp. 39–68, for an interesting discussion of structural parallels between *Don Giovanni* and the Hell scene of *Man and Superman*. The *Don Giovanni* here is more da Ponte's libretto than Mozart's score, but Pollak does provide a detailed look at relationships between the Hell scene and the opera.

16 "The Mozart of English Letters he is not – the music of the Marble Statue is beyond him – the Rossini, yes," W. H. Auden wrote of Shaw in 1942. "He has all the brio, the humor, the tunes, the clarity, and the virtuosity of that great master of Opera Bouffe." Auden also described Shaw as "probably the best music critic who ever lived," and said that "For all his theatre about propaganda, his writing has an effect nearer to that of music than the work of any of the so-called pure writers" (rpt. in Louis Kronenberger [ed.], *George Bernard Shaw: A Critical Survey*, [Cleveland and New York: World Publishing, 1953], p. 156).

17 Cf. Shaw's comment to the composer Rutland Boughton in the same year that music that had been proposed for *The Admirable Bashville* would not do because "it spoils *my* music" (*Collected Letters*, vol. II, p. 787). This is one reason why Shaw vehemently rejected musical comedies based on his plays, as he would undoubtedly have done with *My Fair Lady* had he lived long enough to be outraged by it.

18 See the musical analysis of a scene in *Mrs. Warren's Profession*, with careful attention to contrasts in vocal pitch, in Meisel's *Shaw and the Nineteenth-Century Theater*, pp. 52–54.

19 For Barbara, an alternative to playing vigorous hymn music on the tambourine or concertina would have been wasting her life away playing Schumann on the piano. "If I were middle-class I should turn my back on my father's business," she tells Cusins during their final duet in Act 3, "and we should both live in an artistic drawing room, with you reading the reviews in one corner, and I in the other at the piano, playing Schumann: both very superior persons, and neither

of us a bit of use" (*Collected Plays*, vol. III, p. 183). Schumann's music represents the values of the useless leisured middle-class life that Barbara will avoid by taking over the munitions foundry; in *The Quintessence of Ibsenism* Shaw refers to "the sentimental ideals of our amiable, cultured, Schumann playing propertied classes" in Chekhov's *Cherry Orchard* (*The Drama Observed*, vol. IV, p. 1297).

20 Arrigo Boïto, *Mefistofele*, with Nicolai Ghiaurov, Luciano Pavarotti, and Mirella Freni, cond. Oliviero de Fabritiis, London, 410 175–2, 1985 (Libretto, trans. Avril Bardoni, pp. 182–83).

21 And Faust's principal tenor aria in Boïto's Epilogue ("Giunto sul passo"), like Cusins's in Shaw's final big scene, passionately envisions a social transformation to which he wishes to consecrate his life (*Ibid.*, pp. 170–75).

22 For example: J. L. Wisenthal, "The Underside of Undershaft: A Wagnerian Motif in *Major Barbara*," *Shaw Review* 15 (1972), pp. 56–64; Arthur Ganz, "The Playwright as Perfect Wagnerite: Motifs from the Music Dramas in the Theatre of Bernard Shaw," *Comparative Drama* 13 (1979), pp. 187–207; Robert Coskren, "*Siegfried* Elements in the Plays of Bernard Shaw," *The Annual of Bernard Shaw Studies* 2 (1982), pp. 27–46.

23 *The Collected Screenplays of Bernard Shaw*, ed. Bernard F. Dukore (London: George Prior, 1980), p. 93. Shaw's screenplay adds some Salvation Army band and hymn music to what is in the original play.

24 Shaw wanted Toscanini himself to be engaged for this scene; see his letter of September 12, 1939 to Pascal in *Bernard Shaw and Gabriel Pascal*, ed. Bernard F. Dukore (Toronto: University of Toronto Press, 1996), p. 64.

25 Bernard F. Dukore, in his *Bernard Shaw, Director* (London: George Allen and Unwin, 1971), prints a note written by Shaw for directors of *Caesar and Cleopatra*, which carefully specifies the ways the bucina music may be produced – a note that takes for granted the presence of an orchestra in the theatre. Dukore also quotes a 1910 letter in which Shaw offers a number of detailed suggestions for music in *The Dark Lady of the Sonnets* (pp. 166–67).

26 Edmund Wilson, *The Triple Thinkers* (1938, rpt. New York: Oxford University Press, 1963), pp. 182–83.

SELECT DISCOGRAPHY

Beethoven, Ludwig Van, Symphony No. 8 in F, Op. 93, Cond. Bruno Walter, Columbia Symphony Orchestra, CBS Masterworks, CD CB 801, 1985.

Boïto, Arrigo, *Mefistofele*, with Nicolai Ghiaurov, Luciano Pavarotti, and Mirella Freni, Cond. Oliviero de Fabritiis, National Philharmonic Orchestra and London Opera Chorus, London, CD 410 175–2, 1985.

Gounod, Charles, *Faust*, with Nicolai Gedda, Victoria de Los Angeles, and Boris Christoff, Cond. André Cluytens, Orchestre et Choeurs du Théâtre National de l'Opéra, EMI Records, CD CMS 7 69983 2, 1989.

Mozart, Wolfgang Amadeus, *Don Giovanni*, with Thomas Allen, Edita Gruberova, Francisco Araiza, Ann Murray, and Claudio Desderi, Cond. Riccardo Muti, Orchestra and Chorus of Teatro alla Scala, Home Vision, LaserDisc DON 140 LD, 1989.

Rossini, Gioacchino, *Mosè in Egitto*, with Ruggero Raimondi and June Anderson, Cond. Claudio Scimone, Philharmonia Orchestra and Ambrosia Opera Chorus, Philips, CD 420, 109–2, 1992.

Wagner, Richard, *Der Ring des Nibelungen*, with Donald McIntyre, Gwyneth Jones, and Hanna Schwarz, Cond. Pierre Boulez, Orchestra and Chorus of the Bayreuther Festpiele, Unitel, LaserDisc 070–501–1, 070–502–1, 070–503–1, 070–504–1, 1980.

15

ROBERT G. EVERDING

Shaw and the popular context

When Bernard Shaw died in late 1950, he was an international literary figure whose dramatic works were sought by the stage, cinema, radio, and television. A spokesperson for the Society of Authors noted that "a day never passes without a performance of some Shaw play being given somewhere in the world."[1] In 1951 five different Shaw plays appeared on Broadway, while six full-length and eighteen short scripts ran in London. The actors headlining these productions were among the world's most renowned performers, including Laurence Olivier, Vivien Leigh, John Clements, Kay Hammond, Yvonne Mitchell, and Uta Hagen. Shavian drama was so ubiquitous in 1951 that the Shaw estate feared a "debasement of the coinage" and had "for the moment forbidden any further West End productions of Shaw's works."[2]

One reason for this popularity was (and still is) that actors found in Shaw's energetic, articulate characters attractive vehicles by which to showcase their talents, vehicles with the potential for bravura performances. Basil Langton attested that Shavian drama "offered me a multitude of fascinating, meaty and showy roles to act . . . *Man and Superman* is a good play, but above all it has the most glorious role any actor can dream of or wish for."[3] Daniel Massey reflected that "Some of the greatest moments of any theatrical life have been at the service of GBS. It is a thrilling privilege to be able to touch people's emotions through that deep and generous mind."[4] Shaw himself acknowledged his genius for creating extraordinary roles when he remarked that "if you want to flatter me . . . tell me that, like Shakespeare, Molière, Scott, Dumas and Dickens, I have provided a gallery of characters which are realler to you than your own relatives and which successive generations of actors and actresses will keep alive for centuries as their *chevaux de bataille*."[5] This chapter examines Shaw's post-1950 reception with a focus on the multiple ways in which performers and producers used Shaw's characters as actor vehicles. The essay explores not only stage productions but also the film and broadcast media as it charts the evolution of Shaw's growing popularity with the general public.

Broadway and West End revivals depend in large measure on casting that satisfies each generation's desire to see its stage celebrities appear in entertaining roles. Audiences attend these productions primarily to see the star rather than the play, and Shaw's works receive frequent revival in part because his canon offers dominating major parts and satisfies a variety of casting combinations. *Candida* offers an attractive female star turn and thus inspired revivals featuring Katharine Cornell (who appeared in five different stage productions), Olivia de Havilland, Joanne Woodward, and Deborah Kerr. One appeal of *The Apple Cart* is its entertaining Interlude scene, and its two characters attracted pairings such as Noel Coward and Margaret Leighton (1953), Maurice Evans and Signe Hasso (1956), John Neville and Carmen Munroe (1969), Keith Michell and Penelope Keith (1977), Peter O'Toole and Susannah York (1986). *Major Barbara* is a three-character vehicle whose many revivals included such trios as Glynis Johns, Charles Laughton, Burgess Meredith (1956) and Judi Dench, Brewster Mason, Richard Pasco (1970). *Heartbreak House* fulfills the commercial formula for the talent-crusted production that assembles in a single cast an irresistible number of stage, film, and television celebrities. The 1975 National Theatre revival of *Heartbreak House* brought together Colin Blakely (Shotover), Eileen Atkins (Hesione), Anna Massey (Ariadne), Kate Nelligan (Ellie), Alan MacNaughtan (Hector), and Paul Rogers (Magnan). Filling those same roles in the 1983 revival at London's Haymarket Theatre were Rex Harrison, Diana Rigg, Rosemary Harris, Mel Martin, Paxton Whitehead, and Frank Middlemass.

Since most professional revivals exist as star vehicles, these productions are not always well cast, adequately acted, or thoughtfully directed. However, select Shavian characters hold the promise of the exceptional dramatic experience because these roles demand a level of performance that draws only the foremost actors of each era. Saint Joan belongs to this exclusive category, and the litany of stage luminaries undertaking the challenge includes: Uta Hagen, Siobhan McKenna, Ann Casson, Sian Phillips (1950s); Zoe Caldwell, Joan Plowright, Judi Dench, Jane Alexander (1960s); Angela Pleasence, Lynn Redgrave, Eileen Atkins (1970s); Jane Lapotaire, Frances de la Tour, Roberta Maxwell, Nora McClelland (1980s). Each actor sought to place her unique stamp on the role and thereby reserve a place in the theatre's pantheon of renowned actors.

Siobhan McKenna's association with Joan illustrates the professional rewards awaiting the exceptional performance. McKenna describes her initial attraction to the character by noting that "Saint Joan, the most remarkable woman who ever existed, stands for the spirit of freedom. When the Hungarians revolted I thought, 'How great is the human spirit; when it has no chance to survive, it will flame out.' The human spirit is Godlike to me."[6] This association inspired her not only to play the role in 1952 but also to provide the production's Gaelic translation. The following year she performed the play in English at the Gate Theatre in Dublin and appeared two years later in a new West End production. In 1956 she portrayed the French peasant girl at the Phoenix Theatre (New York) and recorded the production for Caemdon records before embarking on the play's European tour. Later McKenna directed the script and continued to perform Joan, most notably in her one-woman show *Here Come the Ladies*.

If actors used Shaw's roles to further their careers, their success repaid the playwright by expanding his popularity. This was particularly true during the 1950s when a plethora of New York and London revivals attracted large audiences primarily because the names appearing atop the marquees were Olivier, Leigh, Coward, Hepburn, Clements, and Laughton. These commercial ventures enlarged the public interest in Shaw which in turn motivated actors to appropriate Shaw's plays and person as sources for their own dramatic creations. These special productions took several forms, including staged readings, epistolary drama, one-person shows, and biographical plays.

The seminal event for these various Shavian offspring was Charles Laughton's 1950 concert-style reading of *Don Juan in Hell* (the third-act dream sequence from *Man and Superman*), a presentation featuring theatrical celebrities dressed in evening attire and seated on stools behind microphones. Called "The First Dramatic Quartette," the cast included Charles Boyer (Don Juan), Charles Laughton (Devil), Agnes Moorehead (Doña Ana), and Cedric Hardwicke (Commander). While the production was eventually hailed as "one of the most exciting experiences of this and any other season,"[7] its prospective success was not immediately apparent, even to its playwright. When Laughton sought permission for the experiment, Shaw cautioned that "the hell scene is such a queer business that I can't advise you to experiment with it, but I should certainly like you to try it."[8]

Laughton proceeded with the project but he looked to the hinterlands rather than Broadway for his audiences. The reading premiered in Stockton, California, followed by a tour of thirty-four university towns in twenty-three states. This grass-roots approach drew an average nightly audience of three thousand patrons and generated an impressive quarter of a million dollars in revenue. The production captured the nation's imagination and created a public response typified in a Los Angeles report that "for a single night the greatest thrill was provided by the First Drama Quartet [*sic*] . . . crowds literally stormed the auditorium to applaud the remarkable Bernard Shaw presentation."[9] The reading was the only American theatre production invited to the Festival of Britain where it appeared in the provinces during the summer months. In September the Quartette resumed its American tour, presenting sixty-two performances before arriving on October 22, 1951 in New York City for one performance each at Carnegie Hall and the Brooklyn Academy of Music. The demand was so frenzied that within eight hours every ticket was sold with the result that the forgotten seats for the critics needed to be repurchased from the public through newspaper appeals. The response compelled Laughton to extend his tour through 1952 and to return twice to Broadway. In total the production played to a half million people in forty-two states with revenues exceeding a million dollars.

Another measure of the popular appetite for this *Don Juan in Hell* was the 1952 issuance of a two-disc album; as Felix Grendon noted, "any Shavian can now have ninety minutes of Hell in his own home at his leisure."[10] This was a significant event because it was the first recorded Shaw play and its popularity initiated a new Shavian marketplace. In 1956 RCA Victor produced the first entire Shaw play, *Saint Joan*, with Siobhan McKenna in the titular role. By 1975 Shaw plays were issued by several different recording labels with the Caedmon catalogue offering seven complete plays including *Pygmalion*, *Misalliance*, and *John Bull's Other Island*.

Given the extraordinary artistic and fiscal success of *Don Juan in Hell*, it is not surprising that others repeated Laughton's formula. In the 1955–56 season Agnes Moorehead directed a Los Angeles production featuring Ricardo Montalban, Kurt Kasmar, Mary Astor, and Reginald Denny. In 1973 Montalban, Edward Mulhare, Moorehead, and Paul Henreid presented their version at Broadway's Palace Theatre for twenty-four performances before undertaking a coast-to-coast tour.

Laughton's experiment also prompted other Shavian creations. Shaw was a prolific and entertaining letter writer, and performances based on his correspondence contain the double appeal of a Shaw impersonation and a glimpse into his personal life. In 1952 Sarah Churchill and Edward Tommen devised and performed *Affair of Letters*, which presented the correspondence between Shaw and the Victorian era's leading female performer, Ellen Terry. In 1959 two other versions were created, one for an unrealized production involving James Mason and another for a Caemdon recording featuring Peggy Ashcroft and Cyril Cusack.

One of the most popular of this genre was Jerome Kilty's *Dear Liar*, which translates into dialogue the charming, forty-year correspondence between Shaw and actor Mrs. Patrick Campbell. The first act centers on their brief love affair and the London premiere of *Pygmalion* that Shaw directed and in which Campbell played Eliza; the second act explores the postwar years and the *The Apple Cart*'s Interlude scene that Shaw based on their relationship. The production includes brief scenes from the two plays and an episodic musical score.

This letter-drama owes its initial commercial success to its star-vehicle potential. The letters were published in 1952, and five years later Kilty created and performed his show for various benefits before seeking playwright Lillian Hellman's advice on professional possibilities. Hellman sent the script to two prominent Shavian performers, Elisabeth Bergner and Katharine Cornell, both of whom eagerly agreed to portray the legendary Campbell. In March 1959 the first professional production of *Dear Liar* opened at the Sombrero Playhouse (Phoenix), starring Katharine Cornell and Brian Ahearn, and then toured small towns and college campuses for two months. In October Elisabeth Bergner premiered *Dear Liar* at the Berlin Festival, while simultaneously Cornell commenced a second tour leading to a Broadway opening. The play was selected as America's only representative to the International Drama Festival, which in turn induced a West End appearance. *Dear Liar* won several distinguished international awards and received frequent productions, including a 1981 Hallmark Hall of Fame television presentation starring Jane Alexander and George Hermann. It also inspired other epistolary dramas including pieces based on Shaw's correspondences with a Catholic nun, the widow of an Arctic explorer, the first English actress of Ibsen, a romantically determined student nurse, and a woman who believed her child was switched at birth.

Another popular form of Shavian entertainment to emerge following his death was the one-person show, a *tour de force* in which an actor impersonating Shaw recalls his life. One of the most enduring and endearing of these vehicles was Michael Vorsey's *An Evening with G.B.S.* (later titled *By George*), which premiered at the 1966 Edinburgh Festival and featured the preeminent classical actor Max Adrian. This biographical portrait uses only three chairs, a table, a hat stand, and two changes of makeup; it draws from Shaw's letters, essays, and criticism to chart his creative life from his 1876 London arrival to a touching television broadcast shortly before his death. Along the journey Shaw discovers Fabian socialism, courts his future spouse, encounters Isadora Duncan, and expounds upon sex, religion, vivisection, doctors, and vegetarianism.

Following the premiere, this living biography played in the West End, toured England and Northern Ireland, and visited the United States. In 1968 Adrian returned to London for three performances at the Queen Elizabeth Hall before embarking upon a world tour. Adrian recorded his performance and continued to present the show until his death in 1973. Three years later Irish actor Donel Donnelly presented a revised version entitled "My Astonishing Self."

The public's fascination with Shaw also spawned scripts based upon the Irishman's life. *The Shaws of Synge Street* (1960) portrays Shaw's adolescence, and *The Bashful Genius* (1958) focuses on Shaw's courtship of his future spouse. *A Fig Leaf in Her Bonnet* (1961) captures the tension of Shaw's 1912–14 flirtation with Mrs. Patrick Campbell, while *The First Night of Pygmalion* (1966) has its two actors portray some forty different individuals involved in the tempestuous rehearsals for the play's London premiere. Shaw's associations with other artists are depicted in stage and television scripts such as *The Magnificent Humbug* (1958), which examines the dramatist's relationship with William Archer and Beatrice Potter Webb; *The Ghost of Adelphi Terrace* (1975), which portrays Shaw's 1911 discussions with fellow playwright and neighbor James Barrie; and *Isadora and GB* (1977), which concerns Shaw and dancer Isadora Duncan. There are even plays concerned with Shaw's afterlife – *Bernard Shaw in Heaven* (1952) and *Bernard Shaw Arrives* (1953).

Actors were not the only artists to mold Shaw's plays and life to their own ends. Film directors and composers also discovered enticing material for their own creations which in turn introduced Shaw to a far larger and different audience.

In 1914 Shaw observed that the cinema will "form the mind of England. The national conscience, the national ideals and tests of conduct will be those of the film."[11] Shaw was a political playwright intent on changing the world, and the cinema offered the opportunity to reach and influence millions rather than thousands of people. While Shaw sought to penetrate this new industry and use it to preach his Fabian ideas, he moved cautiously because of a concern that studios were interested only in his reputation and would reshape his scripts into mere amusements. He refused many film proposals, including a 1920 offer of one million dollars for the film rights to all his plays. He also wrote his own screenplays and crafted contracts to forbid textual alterations. Consequently, the major artistic accomplishments in film versions of Shaw's plays occurred during his lifetime, with the productions of *Pygmalion* (1938), *Major Barbara* (1941), and *Caesar and Cleopatra* (1945). Still, as the fate of *Pygmalion* demonstrates, he was not completely successful in controlling what reached the public.

In 1927 Shaw received a proposal for a silent film version of *Pygmalion* to star Lynn Fontanne, who had appeared as Eliza in a recent Broadway production sanctioned by Shaw. Nevertheless, Shaw rejected the offer because his form of drama rested on witty and thought-provoking dialogue that was not reducible to subtitles. Shaw explained that "asking me to write a dumb show is rather like asking Titian to paint portraits in black and white."[12]

By 1934 sound came to the movies, and it appeared that the first film of *Pygmalion* would be a Franco-Italian production. However, when Shaw read the screenplay, he rejected the proposal. Not only were scenes rearranged and passages transposed but also a new scene was added in which Eliza purchased a necktie for Higgins, an erroneous reading of the play's final moments during which Eliza defiantly refused Higgins's order to buy him new gloves and a tie. This impulse to romanticize Shaw's conclusion began with the play's London premiere when its Higgins tossed a bouquet of flowers from his balcony to the departing Eliza. Mrs. Patrick Campbell compounded the problem on her American tour when she concluded the show by returning to ask Higgins "What size?" Both performers catered to the audience's desire for a Cinderella ending, and future producers continued the practice despite Shaw's protestations, clarifications, and textual revisions. It is little wonder, then, that Shaw rejected the Franco-Italian proposal and set about writing his own screenplay.

Two European film versions of *Pygmalion* appeared during the next three years. Despite a contract forbidding textual changes, the German film added new material including a final scene in which waltz music accompanies Higgins's romantic request that Eliza stay with him. The 1937 Dutch version was equally distasteful to Shaw because it concluded with Higgins following Eliza to church, where the couple exchanged loving glances as they witnessed the marriage of her father. Both films were commercial successes, but the only words Shaw could find to describe them were "blunder," "abomination," and "loathe."

Shaw took a far more active role in the 1938 British film. Its producer was an enigmatic Hungarian who arrived on Shaw's doorstep in 1935, announced that an Indian guru had foretold that he was fated to produce Shaw's films, and demanded *Pygmalion*. Gabriel Pascal won Shaw's confidence and the film rights. Still, despite Pascal's promise that the film would use only Shaw's words, Shaw revised the screenplay and added an unequivocal ending in which Higgins delights at a vision of the future in which the happily married Eliza and Freddy operate a florist shop in South Kensington. Shaw participated in casting, securing his choice for Eliza (Wendy Hiller) but not for Higgins (Charles Laughton), who was portrayed by matinée-idol Leslie Howard. Shaw also attended the first day of filming and sent Pascal notes of advice during the shooting. One missive in particular reflected Shaw's lingering concern: "It is amazing how hopelessly wrong Leslie is. However, the public will like him and probably want him to marry Eliza, which is just what I don't want."[13]

The studio disliked Shaw's ending, and Pascal authorized two alternative versions. The final cut contained a new ending that again subverted Shaw's intention by having Eliza return to Higgins. One might wonder why Shaw did not take legal action to block the film's release. In part he could not because Pascal achieved this effect without altering a line of the text, for he borrowed earlier dialogue (some over the voice recording phonograph in Higgins's laboratory) and directed the actors' facial expressions to leave little doubt about the couple's emotional relationship. The film was extremely popular, earned Shaw £25,000 in a single year, and was re-released in 1944 and again in 1948. It also received several international cinema awards, including the Academy Award for the best screenplay, an Oscar that must have caused Shaw at least a moment of consternation.

The films made following Shaw's death fully justified his caution because for the most part they reduced his scripts to star turns and crowd-pleasing entertainment. *Androcles and the Lion* (1952) with Jean Simmons and Victor Mature, and *The Devil's Disciple* (1959) with Burt Lancaster, Kirk Douglas, and Laurence Olivier devolved into simple love stories. Otto Preminger made a romantic spectacle of *Saint Joan* (1957), while *Great Catherine* (1968) served as a series of farcical opportunities for Zero Mostel and Peter O'Toole. The German versions of *Arms and the Man* (1958) and *Mrs. Warren's Profession* (1960) were without distinction. *The Doctor's Dilemma* (1958) featured Dirk Bogarde and Leslie Caron, while *The Millionairess* (1960) provided a comic vehicle for Sophia Loren and Peter Sellers. The most popular of these Shaw-inspired films was one that Shaw never would have tolerated, *My Fair Lady* (1964).

Shaw had no interest in musical theatre as such. He rejected a lucrative offer to write a libretto for a Cole Porter opera and – in defence of the vocal music inherent in his dialogue – rejected proposals to turn *The Devil's Disciple* and *Captain Brassbound's Conversion* into musicals. He also refused all requests to adapt *Pygmalion*. In response to composer Franz Lehar's plan for a light opera, Shaw wrote "if they attempt to use a word of my dialogue, or to connect my name or my play in any way to their abominable opera I will let loose all the engines of the Copyright law to destroy them utterly." In 1948 Shaw turned down a request to set the play to music, and a proposal involving Noel Coward with the insistence that "My decision as to Pygmalion is final: let me hear no more about it. This is final."[14]

Following Shaw's death, however, Gabriel Pascal secured the rights to musicalize *Pygmalion*. He was the appropriate person to oversee the project because Shaw's will granted him all film rights and therefore the 1938 spectacle scenes that were indispensable to any musical version. With the assistance of the Theatre Guild, Pascal obtained the full rights in April 1952; however, there were still sizable obstacles in writing and casting.

The major difficulty was the incompatibility between Shaw's play and the prevailing formula for a Broadway musical. The main story contained no love interest; the subplot lacked onstage development; and the cast provided no ensemble for dancing and choral numbers. Richard Rodgers and Oscar Hammerstein worked on the project for a year before concluding that they could not shape Shaw's script into the kind of musical expected by Broadway audiences. Other composers approached without success included Frank Loesser, Howard Dietz, Cole Porter, and Gian-Carlo Menotti. In 1952 Alan Jay Lerner and Frederick Loewe worked for six months before also abandoning the project. In 1953 a discouraged Pascal sought unsuccessfully first to interest Leonard Bernstein and then to sell his option to Otto Preminger. It was only following Pascal's death and after Lerner secured the rights from both the Shaw and Pascal estates that the musical proceeded.

My Fair Lady also faced serious casting problems because many leading performers believed that a Shavian musical would fail and hesitated to jeopardize their professional reputations. Lerner and Loewe wrote the music and lyrics with Mary Martin in mind, but she refused the role; Deanna Durbin and Dolores Gray were also considered before eighteen-year-old Julie Andrews was selected. Similar problems plagued the casting of Higgins. Michael Redgrave declined the role and Rex Harrison was not initially enthusiastic because he was not a singer. Other actors considered included George Sanders, John Gielgud, and Noel Coward.

My Fair Lady (cockney slang for the Mayfair Lady that Eliza aspires to become) opened on March 15, 1956 and ran for six and a half years on Broadway (2,717 performances) and six years in London (2,281 performances). The ticket demand was so large for the 1957 national tour that one observer quipped that the musical "will probably go down in theatrical history as the show that had to turn back more money than it took in."[15] The response in Detroit, for instance, was that "*My Fair Lady* actually became a household word in our city. Never before has such interest been shown for any attraction in the city's 169-year history."[16] The show remained popular with Broadway audiences after it closed in 1962, for its first revival came only twenty months later and again in 1968, 1976, and 1981.

The Warner Brothers' film version opened in 1964 amid controversy because the studio passed over Julie Andrews, who it believed lacked the star status required for the international marketplace. Instead, Audrey Hepburn played Eliza and Marni Nixon dubbed her songs. The studio first sought Cary Grant to play Higgins, but he responded that not only would he not accept the role but he would not see the film unless Rex Harrison appeared. The studio also considered Rock Hudson for Higgins and James Cagney for Doolittle. The film won numerous awards including both the American and British academy awards for best picture of the year; but ironically the Oscar for best actress that year went to the rejected Julie Andrews for her performance in *Mary Poppins*.

The musical's extraordinary popularity stirred interest in other Shavian scripts. As Lerner whimsically observed, "I was told the day after *My Fair Lady* opened that there was not a theatrical agent available in New York. All of them were at the library" reading Shaw's other plays.[17] Those seeking to replicate the success of *My Fair Lady* soon discovered, though, that Shaw's plays do not easily adapt.

Androcles and the Lion was the next Shaw script to receive a musical treatment. With a book by Peter Store and music by Richard Rodgers, this work premiered to a nationwide audience on November 15, 1967 in a ninety-minute NBC television special featuring Norman Wisdom, Inga Swenson, and Noel Coward. The production radically abridged Shaw's text to accommodate the time limitations, commercials, and musical numbers. A larger problem was Rodgers's music, which lacked the satire and wit needed by a Shavian composer. Despite solid acting performances, critical reaction was very unfavorable.

The following year a musical based on *Caesar and Cleopatra* fared little better. *Her First Roman* opened on Broadway starring Leslie Uggams and Richard Kiley and including eyebrow-raising musical titles such as "What Are We Doing in Egypt," "Hail to the Sphinx," and "Caesar is Wrong." Clive Barnes encapsulated best perhaps the general critical reaction when he wrote that "Speaking frankly, I think you would be better advised to hang around until 'Her Second Roman' turns up."[18] The production closed after seventeen performances and lost $575,000.

It was a decade before another Shavian musical appeared and then only on the regional theatre level. In 1979 Peter Ekstrom set two Shaw one-act plays to music in *Matrimomium: Overruled Passion, Poison, and Petrifaction* that premiered at the Actors' Studio of Louisville. The first act set *Overruled* to music with appropriately bombastic song titles such as "Oh, Guilt! How Great Thou Art," while the second act presented *Passion, Poison, and Petrifaction* with playful tunes such as "What Do You Think of My Bust?" and "Sleep, Dear Adolphine, Sleep!" The production ran for nine performances.

The most persevering effort to create musical adaptations of Shaw's plays involves Benny Green. His first effort, a musical biography entitled *Boots with Strawberry Jam*, premiered at the Nottingham Playhouse to a less than enthusiastic response. In 1983, however, Green and Dennis King premiered *Bashville*, a musical version of Shaw's stage adaptation of his novel *The Admirable Bashville* at Regent's Park Open Air theatre; the show was so popular that it was revived at the same venue the following summer. Green turned his attention next to *You Never Can Tell* with the result that in 1992 *Valentine's Day* premiered at the prestigious Chichester Festival before transferring to London's West End.

While the cinema and the musical introduced Shaw to new audiences, it was the mass media that brought him into millions of homes. In its long Broadway run *My Fair Lady* played to some three million people; on one night in 1959 a television version of *Misalliance* reached approximately twenty million viewers. It was this potential audience that attracted Shaw to the broadcast media, and it was these media that were most responsible for the expansion of the Shaw audience in the years immediately following his death.

Shaw participated in the early development of both radio and television. British radio broadcasting commenced in 1922 and immediately sought Shaw's assistance to lend his international reputation to its struggle for credibility. In 1924 Shaw appeared in person to read *O'Flaherty VC*, assuming the different characters' voices and even singing "Tipperary." Two years later the first Shaw play was acted on radio. Shaw also appeared on BBC television's inaugural program on November 2, 1936, and eight months later *How He Lied to Her Husband* became the first televised Shavian play. While Shaw encouraged and approved subsequent radio and television presentations, he did so only if producers presented his plays in their entirety and without alterations. He also insisted on approving the costs and monitored broadcasts. He reacted to a 1929 production of *Captain Brassbound's Conversion* by writing to the BBC director that the broadcast's "infamy was such that I hereby solemnly renounce, curse, and excommunicate everybody who had a hand in it. . . If the producer has not already been shot, I will pay for the cartridges."[19]

Shaw's restrictions caused fewer difficulties in England because both radio and television were government controlled and therefore able to schedule without concern for rigid time blocks or advertising interruptions. This freedom allowed BBC radio to present Shavian productions such as the complete *Saint Joan* starring Constance Cummings (1941 and 1947). In the United States, however, Shaw's conditions severely constrained the airing of his plays. A 1946 radio broadcast of *Pygmalion* was only possible by dividing the presentation into two parts; the first televised Shaw play did not occur until 1946 when the sketch *Great Catherine* filled a sixty minute program slot.

Following Shaw's death, however, radio immediately embraced the Irish playwright because his plays were now free from production limitations. On May 6, 1951 Katharine Cornell starred in a one-hour radio version (with commercials) of *Candida*. BBC radio broadcast Shaw's plays both in complete and abridged form including a Shaw festival that presented twelve Shaw masterpieces in a six month period (1952) and the complete *Back to Methuselah* (1958). Shaw was a staple of British radio drama, for between 1950 and 1975 BBC radio presented forty-one Shaw plays and ten programs about Shaw for a total of nearly two hundred performances.[20]

The lifting of Shaw's restrictions came at a propitious time for the American television industry because it was just entering its boom years. In 1951 network television linked the country, but the industry lacked programming. Live drama came to the rescue as the industry wed shrunken versions of established masterpieces with popular radio and film celebrities. In the next seven years "over five thousand dramas in a new form with a new emphasis were broadcast to the largest audiences in history."[21]

The Shavian drama found a prominent place on television because it provided the kind of entertaining theatre and star vehicles that attracted audiences. In January 1952 NBC's Robert Montgomery Presents televised *Cashel Byron's Profession*, featuring Charleton Heston and June Lockhart. CBS responded with Omnibus, which over four seasons presented truncated versions of *Arms and the Man* (Nanette Fabray), *Man of Destiny* (Alan Badel), the trial scene from *Saint Joan* (Kim Hunter), and *Androcles and the Lion* (Bert Lahr). NBC replied with a Cameo Theatre presentation of *Inca of Perusalem* (Cedric Hardwicke), and a Playhouse 90 broadcast of *Misalliance* (Claire Bloom, Robert Morley, Siobhan McKenna).

The networks' competitiveness is reflected in its varied approaches to *Caesar and Cleopatra*, a script particularly well known to audiences because of the 1952 Broadway revival starring Laurence Olivier and Vivien Leigh. In 1956 NBC's Producer's Showcase presented the play with a star-studded cast including Claire Bloom, Cedric Hardwicke, Cyril Richard, Farley Grainger, Anthony Quayle, and Judith Anderson. ABC sought to capitalize on the public's anticipation by showing the 1945 film version of the play the day prior to the NBC event. In 1959 CBS presented its own production starring Maurice Evans and Piper Laurie.

The majority of these early television dramas did little justice to Shaw's plays. Producers generally emasculated his scripts into amusing episodes that fitted between advertisements and that spotlighted performers who too often lacked the training to handle Shaw's language. Reviews for the ninety-minute Omnibus *Arms and the Man*, for example, complained that the textual cuts were diabolical, the production poorly cast, and the comedy totally lost. Moreover, with commercials and a long introduction by Alistair Cooke, barely an hour was devoted to the play itself. Still, an estimated thirteen million viewers saw the production.

In the 1956–57 season magnetic taping replaced live productions, but the drama remained a popular programming element. Its most prestigious representative was the Hallmark Hall of Fame because its careful casting, high production values, and uninterrupted presentations produced quality television drama. Its first Shavian offering was a ninety-minute version of *The Devil's Disciple* (1955) with Maurice Evans, Ralph Bellamy, Theresa Wright, and Margaret Hamilton. Over the next dozen seasons, the series presented *Man and Superman* (1956) with Maurice Evans and Joan Green-wood; *Captain Brassbound's Conversion* (1960) starring Greer Garson, Christopher Plummer, George Rose, and Robert Redford; *Pygmalion* (1963) featuring Julie Harris; and *Saint Joan* (1967) with Genevieve Bujold, Maurice Evans, Raymond Massey, Roddy McDowall, and David Birney. Also notable was the WNDT–TV (New York) *Sunday Showcase* production of *Heartbreak House*, presented in its entirety with only one-minute uncommercial breaks and sponsored by the Bristol-Myers company; the distinguished cast included Maurice Evans (Shotover), Lois Nettleton (Ellie), Eileen Herlie (Hesione), Margaret Leighton (Ariadne), Edward Mulhare (Hector), and George Rose (burglar).

British television also made extensive use of Shaw's plays during the decade following his death. Constance Cummings's 1951 appearance in *Saint Joan* was arguably the television event of the year. By 1956 the BBC reported that it had virtually achieved its goal of providing television broad-casting to the entire United Kingdom. That year viewers enjoyed productions of *Pygmalion*, *You Never Can Tell*, and *The Dark Lady of the Sonnets*; in 1957, *The Devil's Disciple* and *Getting Married*; and in 1958, *The Apple Cart* and *Heartbreak House*. Also in 1956 commercial television com-menced, and its initial theatrical presentation was *The Man of Destiny*. In subsequent years British television offered the public Shavian productions cast with prominent stage figures. In 1968 Maggie Smith and Eric Porter appeared in *Man and Superman*; subsequently John Gielgud portrayed King Charles and Captain Shotover. Other notable performances include Lynn Redgrave as Eliza Dootlittle, Geraldine McEwan as Candida, Judi Dench and Zoe Caldwell as Major Barbara, and Peter O'Toole as John Tanner.

One result of these Shavian broadcasts was a considerable increase in the popular appreciation of Shaw's dramatic works, an increase that led literary critic Edmund Wilson to pronounce that "There is now an automatic Shaw audience."[22] This development stimulated the emergence of another cultural avenue by which Shaw reached the public, the dramatic festival.

A festival is a larger-than-usual number of plays offered in a condensed time period for the purpose of honoring the dramatist. Perhaps the best known drama festival opened in 1879 at Stratford-upon-Avon, England, to recognize William Shakespeare. Stratford became the world center of Shakespearean production, and patrons made the pilgrimage to this cultural retreat to visit its museum and library as well as to attend productions staged by its resident professional company. In 1929 Sir Barry Jackson began the Malvern Festival and dedicated it to Shaw's genius. Unlike Stratford, though, Malvern possessed a patron who supplied the festival with new plays and mingled with its audiences. The first season lasted two weeks and presented in repertory the English premiere of *The Apple Cart, Heartbreak House, Caesar and Cleopatra*, and the five plays of *Back to Methuselah*. Birmingham Repertory Theatre (also founded and directed by Barry Jackson) supplied the core acting company that included Cedric Hardwicke and Edith Evans. The festival was presented in a newly renovated nine-hundred seat theatre where a different play was staged each evening so that the one-week visitor could attend the entire season's offerings. In 1934 the festival expanded to four weeks. In its initial eleven seasons Malvern presented a total of nineteen Shaw scripts (including two world premieres) as well as the works of forty other playwrights.

A visit to Malvern offered more than theatrical incentives. Located in an idyllic spa town in the Malvern hills and with particularly pleasant summer weather, the festival presented a tantalizing array of recreational, social, and educational activities. Professors presented morning lectures about that evening's play, while guest artists offered entertaining afternoon tea talks. There were hikes and donkey rides into the hills; folk dancing, putting, swimming, boating, bowling; garden parties, traveling exhibitions, films, and a marionette theatre. Following the evening performance, there was a pool for night swimming or an orchestra for dancing.

The Malvern Festival ended with the outbreak of war, but it inspired the creation of other Shaw festivals. In 1934, for example, Jasper Deeter and his Hedgerow Theatre outside Philadelphia presented a professional Shaw festival comprised of six Shavian works produced in repertory. Deeter repeated the festival each summer and created innovative programming such as the 1937 season that ran for four weeks and presented twelve Shaw plays chronologically to focus attention on Shaw's intellectual and drama-turgical development. The theatre's 1939 season included a production of the complete *Man and Superman* that began at seven-thirty and ended in time for patrons to catch the one-thirty trolley. The festival existed for ten summers, ceasing only after the draft depleted the acting company. In England during the war the Lyric Theatre (Hammersmith) produced a mobile version of a Shaw festival when its Touring Bernard Shaw Repertory Company traveled for fifteen weeks throughout the island presenting five Shavian works. In 1951 Basil Langton attempted to create a permanent Shaw festival on the island of Martha's Vineyard (Massachusetts), but the venture lapsed after two summers. By the early 1960s, however, there were calls for the establishment of a permanent professional Shaw festival, and the coming years saw the creation of Shaw festivals in rural, suburban, and urban settings.

In 1962 Brian Doherty, a Toronto lawyer with twenty-five years of experience as a theatre producer and playwright, founded an annual Shaw festival in the small town of Niagara-on-the Lake, Ontario, Canada, where he resided. The initial season assembled a company of local actors and presented four performances each of *Candida* and *Don Juan in Hell* in a small theatre located in the town's Victorian courthouse. By 1966 a professional company headed by Barry Morse and including Zoe Caldwell, Pat Galloway, Leslie Yeo, and Paxton Whitehead presented a nine-week season of *Man and Superman*, *Misalliance*, and *The Apple Cart*. Today The Shaw (as the festival is informally called) offers an April–October season of some ten plays and over seven hundred performances in three theatres by a resident professional company of seventy actors under the artistic direction of Christopher Newton. The festival presents not only Shaw's plays but also those written by dramatists during Shaw's long lifetime. In 1995, the theatre sold more than 290,000 tickets for a season presenting three Shaw plays, two musicals, a murder mystery and four classics from the modern repertory.

The Shaw is far more than a commercial enterprise; it serves as a center of Shaw study and appreciation. The festival offers a lunchtime reading series, Friday chats, Saturday conversations, and post-performance talk-back sessions. Its Academy sponsors public educational activities such as annual Shaw seminars, teachers' days, and young audience programs. Moreover, its productions reach for more than entertainment and homage; they seek to enlarge the understanding of Shaw's dramaturgy by mining unexamined textual areas and by exploring how his scripts address contemporary concerns. One value of a cultural institution like The Shaw is its ongoing engagement with a script with the result that each new

28 Thematic interpretations – a laboratory of language: Michael Ball as Colonel Pickering, Andrew Gillies as Henry Higgins, and Joan Orenstein as Mrs. Pearce in the Shaw Festival's 1992 production of *Pygmalion*

production develops upon and contributes to a richer understanding of a text and its production possibilities. *Pygmalion* has been staged four times, once in each of the past four decades, all with different directors and all markedly different in tone and thematic focus. This continuous textual reexamination saves Shaw's plays from being relegated to amusing period pieces and permits provocative new staging approaches that allow Shaw's ideas to continue to address and influence the modern world.

The festival's 1993 production of *Saint Joan* provides a salient example of the power of theatrical revisionism. Director Neil Munro shifted the play's location from fifteenth century France to a modern, eastern European combat zone not unlike Bosnia. The stage world of this production was composed of a raked floor, two large rotating columns, and a giant crucifix, to which individual scenes added the accouterments of modern warfare such as machine guns, a jeep, field telephones, computers, paper shredders, and amphibious fighter craft. The dress was modern with Joan appearing at various times in khaki, camouflage, a bomber jacket, and a dress uniform. Munro explained that "I'm not interested in history; I'm interested in living today . . . I'm always looking for new ways to approach old subject matter and make it relevant – give people a really thoughtful evening of what we are, where we've come from, how we're handling it (and) 'Are we indeed any different now than where we were then?'"[23] By transforming the script's Hundred Years' War into a Bosnian-like holocaust, Munro sought to have the audience not only identify more fully with the social chaos and political agendas that explained the emergence of a Joan and the conservative reaction that destroyed her but also understand the immediate relevance of Shaw's epilogue argument that, despite the current reverence for the image of Joan, society would execute her again if she returned because her ideas are still too threatening.

Munro did not begin his rehearsals in the traditional manner of a cast reading of the script; he showed film footage of atrocities committed during the Bosnian war and then provided the actors a period of personal contemplation in a nearby church. He also did not begin his production with Shaw's initial scene, but added a prologue composed of a violent dumb show in which modern refugees wearing hospital gowns were gunned down by militia carrying automatic weapons. The curtain then lowered and the prologue's staccato, pulsating music continued until the curtain rose again, this time on Shaw's opening scene.

Having prepared the audience to view the action with contemporary sensibilities, Munro provided a *mise-en-scène* that placed the plot's events in a modern time frame. Joan's initial meeting with the Dauphin occurred before a military map that she ripped from its easel in her eagerness to raise the siege of Orleans. While she and Dunois awaited favorable conditions for crossing the Loire, they sat upon the hood of a jeep examining maps and planning strategy. Cauchon and Warwick met below the massive wingtip of a military bomber in the English camp (see illus. 19) where the two sipped tea and plotted Joan's downfall; their discussion was punctuated by nearby gunfire and heavy artillery that at moments drowned the dialogue. Joan's confrontation with the French court occurred around a long conference table under fluorescent lighting. The inquisition scene was transformed into a public hearing in which Joan sat with her back to the theatre audience facing a panel that presented its questions over microphones in a conversational tone and included references to ethnic cleansing in the former Yugoslavia; two banks of four large monitors provided a close-up picture of Joan's face and compelled spectators to follow her emotional journey as though seated at home before their own television sets. Only in the epilogue did the production return to Shaw's time scheme with its medieval dress and its single 1920 emissary, an effect enhanced by an audience conditioned to see the present-day relevance of Joan's final prayer "O God that madest this beautiful earth, when will it be ready to receive Thy saints? How long, O Lord, how long?"

29   Updating Shaw with modern media: Troy Skog as an English Soldier and Mary Haney
as Joan in the Shaw Festival's 1993 production of *Saint Joan*

This production's effort to guide the spectator to discover the source of today's tragic world situation in his or her own lack of faith and imagination succeeded with at least one patron. During the inquisition scene at one performance, an audience member rose to his feet and shouted angrily at the investigating panel, "What are you people trying to do? What are you trying to say?" The actor playing the chief investigator banged his gavel and called for order, and the play continued without further interruption. For that viewer, Shaw's word touched a contemporary nerve.

There have been other efforts to create an annual Shaw festival, one of which I began in 1979 at the University of Houston-Clear Lake. The Houston Shaw Festival was located in a suburban area midway between Houston and Galveston. The festival's mission was to highlight Shaw's contemporary relevance, and its commitment was to produce the complete canon before repeating any script. This mission guided both the festival's play selection and directorial approach, for each season sought to bring Shaw's insights to bear upon issues relevant to the lives of the community. Fortunately Shaw's plays are richly textured and allow multiple perspectives. While I preferred to keep the plays in period, my casting and staging

30   Updating Shaw with modern media: Michael Ball as Cauchon and Barry MacGregor
as The Inquisitor in the Shaw Festival's 1993 production of *Saint Joan*

decisions moved to the foreground those textual elements that underscored that season's theme while allowing the remainder of Shaw's ideological composition to resonate in the background. In 1983, for example, the festival staged *Misalliance* and *Fanny's First Play* in order to address the local community's heightened concern over adolescent behavior. Both festival productions focused on the parent–child relationships in Shaw's texts and emphasized the children's shared predicament and the contrasting manners in which the parents (especially, the fathers) respond to their rebellious offspring. The directorial intent was to focus audience perception on this aspect of the plays and thereby allow Shaw to contribute to the discussion of a current social problem.

The festival's initial summer season consisted of twelve repertory performances of *Getting Married* and *Arms and the Man*. A discussion with the audience followed each performance, and special activities occurred on July 26 to commemorate Shaw's birthday. Subsequent seasons were built around Shaw's views on various subjects – religion (*Major Barbara* and *Androcles and the Lion*), happiness (*Heartbreak House* and *Too True to Be Good*), marriage (*Candida* and *The Philanderer*), childrearing (*Misal-*

liance and *Fanny's First Play*), the human will (*You Never Can Tell, Village Wooing, The Man of Destiny*).

The season that focused on religion engendered considerable controversy in large part because Shaw's ideas clashed so directly with one of the most pervasive and entrenched value systems of the American south, Christianity. At the time there was considerable media attention given to the exodus from mainstream religions and the search for spiritual fulfillment in various eastern theologies and sects. I felt Shaw had insights to offer about this sociological trend, and I selected a season that highlighted his religious views. My program essay sought to aid the audience to view the play's action in terms of their world rather than the Edwardian one in which Shaw set the piece. I cited Shaw's preface comment to *Major Barbara* that "Creeds must become intellectually honest. At present there is not a single credible established religion in the world. That is perhaps the most stupendous fact in the whole world situation," and then appended my own observation that "we are still searching for a relevant creed – one that actively confronts the world's miseries, one that welcomes changes as realities change, one that makes of religion a lifelong obligation rather than a once-a-week diversion." Not all of our audience were ready to consider the faults of Christianity let alone a humanistic substitute called "the Life Force." At two different performances audience members exited during the Salvation Army scene, a particularly visible form of protest given the production's intimate thrust staging. The post-performance discussions were the most vociferous of my time at the festival. One evening the talkback session lasted almost an hour in an often heated debate over the flaws and viability of contemporary religion. Were Shaw in attendance, he would have delighted at the unruly spectacle although undoubtedly he would have also plunged into and dominated the discussion.

Like Doherty, I formed my first company from community actors as an initial step in the creation of a resident professional company. The artistic director and design staff were faculty members. In 1985 actors were paid and in 1988 the first Equity actors appeared. Two years later the festival became an Equity II small professional theatre. During this period the audiences grew, necessitating a move from the University's smaller arena theatre into its 500-seat auditorium. Unfortunately, the University announced the termination of its theatre program after the festival's 1992 season and thereby brought an end to the Houston Shaw Festival after thirteen seasons.

Actor Montgomery Davis created a moveable, urban, non-summer Shaw festival in 1983 when he presented productions of *Don Juan in Hell* and *Dear Liar* as part of his Milwaukee Chamber Theatre's season. This professional company's name derives from its initial existence as a touring group that performed in various intimate, informal spaces. In 1993 it established residence in the 360-seat Broadway Theatre Center where it offers each winter a four-week Shaw festival of some twenty-four performances as part of its subscription season. Each festival examines a contemporary theme through the staging of one or more Shaw plays as well as non-Shavian works that provide a perspective on that theme. In 1989, for instance, the season explored the Irish question through its productions of *John Bull's Other Island, O'Flaherty VC, The Admirable Bashville*, and Ray Hutchison's powerful 1984 drama *Rat in the Skull*. Recently festival alumni formed a fringe troupe that enhanced the festival by presenting a bill of short plays by Shaw and his contemporaries. The festival also has an active educational component including public lectures, panel discussions, audience talkback sessions, and a school outreach program. Including the 1997 season, the company has staged a total of twenty-six of Shaw's plays, and Davis announced that he plans to produce the complete *Back to Methuselah* for the millennium year.

The 1989 season with its focus on the Irish question provides an example of how this festival emphasizes the contemporaneousness of Shaw's plays. The festival joined three Shaw plays about Ireland with a 1984 drama in an examination of the historical attitudes that are embedded in the individual Irish and British consciousness and fuel today's antagonism and violence. *John Bull's Other Island* provided insight into what Shaw viewed from his historical context as the incompatible national character of and mutually exploitative relationship between the two nations. *The Admirable Bashville* offered a satiric look at the disturbing disjunction between the British attitude toward boxing as a sport and as an aggressive habit, while *O'Flaherty VC* captured Ireland's deeply seated suspicion and hatred of England. From these perspectives, the spectator would hopefully see the deeply embedded attitudes that underlie and motivate the act of police brutality at the center of Ron Hutchinson's penetrating drama and thereby understand more fully the complexity of the modern Irish troubles. This process was enhanced by a public lecture and radio call-in program presented by Tom Hadden, a criminologist from Northern Ireland and the founder of a political periodical in Belfast, who brought together the various threads of English colonialism, religious prejudice, and terrorism that appeared in the four plays. These issues then served as the flashpoints for the post-production talkback sessions with the audience.

It is now almost a half century since Shaw's death, and today he remains popular through many of the same avenues by which he reached audiences in the 1950s. In the present decade star-vehicle revivals have included Mary

Steenburgen appearing as Candida and both Imogen Stubbs and Maryann Plunkett as Saint Joan. *Heartbreak House* returned again to London's Haymarket Theatre with a cast of Paul Scofield, Vanessa Redgrave, Felicity Kendal, Imogen Stubbs, Daniel Massey, and David Calder. *Don Juan in Hell* was presented in a 1991 Los Angeles reading (Ricardo Montalban, David Carradine, Lynn Redgrave, and Stewart Granger) and the 1992 "Second Drama Quartet" (Harry Yulin, Rene Auberjonois, Judith Ivey, and Ed Asner), which undertook an extensive nationwide tour before opening in New York where Dianne Wiest replaced Judith Ivey; Laughton's experiment also returned in 1993 to Carnegie Hall (Weill Recital Hall) where literary luminaries Gay Talese, Gore Vidal, Susan Sontag, and Norman Mailer (Kurt Vonnegut was originally cast but became ill) provided a reading as a benefit for the Actors Studio with tickets priced between five hundred and one thousand dollars. *Dear Liar* appeared off-Broadway with Julie Harris and Alvin Epstein, while Donel Donnelly performed *My Astonishing Self* frequently, including visits to the Canadian Shaw Festival and the Library of Congress's celebration of Shaw's 125th birthday. New off-Broadway biographical plays included Marty Martin's *Shaviana* (1993), which explored Shaw's adolescent years in Ireland, and Jesse Torn's *George Bernard and Stella* (1994), which presented still another version of the Shaw–Campbell relationship.

My Fair Lady experienced continual revival during the 1990s including two major professional productions, one in England starring Edward Fox and the other in the United States featuring Richard Chamberlain. In 1993 America issued a postage stamp honoring *My Fair Lady*, while during the following year Warner Brothers celebrated the musical's thirtieth anniversary by releasing a restored version of the film. There were also new attempts to musicalize Shaw's plays: Goodspeed Opera House and the Great Lake Shakespeare Festival both staged *Blanco!*, music and lyrics written by Skip Kennon; *The Admirable Bashville* (adapted by Charles Marowitz) premiered at the Texas Stage Company; drama critic Benedict Nightingale and director Tony Branch completed a new musical version of *You Never Can Tell*; and the College of Marin (California) premiered *Wings of Fire*, a musical adaptation of *Saint Joan* created by Patsy Garlan and Nicholas Scarim.

Shaw has also remained popular with cinema, radio, and television audiences. While the major studios long ago lost interest in Shaw, *Pygmalion*, *Caesar and Cleopatra*, and *Androcles and the Lion* remain particular favorites at film festivals and on television. British broadcast media have aired new productions of Shaw's plays as well as biographical specials such as the 1993 BBC production of "Mister Shaw's Missing Billions" starring Ian McKellen.

In 1905 Shaw wrote to an actor that "a part that is any good can be played fifty different ways by fifty different people."[24] This observation accounts in large measure for Shaw's post-1950 popularity because, as the previous listings of theatrical luminaries illustrates, actors have readily embraced both Shaw's roles and the persona of Shaw himself as star vehicles. Whether on stage or television or recordings, performers have turned to his extraordinary gallery of characters as resources for displaying their talent and enlarging their professional reputations. One byproduct has been a considerable expansion of a Shavian audience that has discovered and enjoyed the witty old Irishman and raised him to the status of a theatrical icon. This general popularity has rested, however, on a reductive view of the playwright. It was as though two Shaws existed: the comic genius who entertained and made us laugh, and the social gadfly who shocked and made us think. Popular culture wanted only the compelling stories and the benign humor; hence it reshaped his plays, simplified his ideas and romanticized his life. However, to the same degree that commercial enterprises sought to capitalize on Shaw for their own ends, Shaw sought to capitalize on the mass audience for his sociopolitical aims. He battled to maintain the complete Shaw by blocking unworthy projects and insisting that productions link laughter to insight. As the fate of *Pygmalion* suggests, though, the power of the popular will can be overwhelming. Today the tension between the complete Shaw and the popular version continues, for each new production begins with a decision about its *raison d'être*. Some ventures simply celebrate the icon of the witty and entertaining old man; other productions discover that the icon has penetrating eyes and a knowing smile. It is at these moments that Shaw again uses the popular context for his purposes and thereby continues to enrich our culture and influence our lives.

NOTES

1 John O'Hare, "How the Play Reached Publication," *Theatre Arts Monthly* 40 (August 1956), p. 22.
2 Harold Hobson, "Dramatist of the Year: Shaw," *Christian Science Monitor*, February 24, 1951 p. 15.
3 Basil Langton, "A Shaw Repertory Theatre," *The Shaw Bulletin* 3 (May 1952), p. 6.
4 Daniel Massey, "Some Thoughts on the Acting of Shaw," *The Annual of Bernard Shaw Studies* 8, ed. Stanley Weintraub (University Park: The Pennsylvania State University Press, 1988), p. 133.
5 Langton, "A Shaw Repertory Theatre," p. 6.
6 Siobhan McKenna, "Siobhan McKenna on Saint Joan," *Theatre Arts Monthly* 41 (March 1957), p. 89.

7 Quoted from Simon Callow, *Charles Laughton: A Different Actor* (New York: Grove Press, 1987), p. 212.

8 *Ibid.*, p. 211.

9 Edwin Schallert, "The Season in Southern California," in John Chapman (ed.), *The Best Plays of 1950–1951* (New York: Dodd, Mead and Company, 1951), p. 51.

10 Felix Grendon, "The Quartette in John Tanner's Dream," *The Shaw Bulletin* 4 (Summer 1953), p. 15.

11 G. Bernard Shaw, "The Cinema as a Moral Leveller," *The New Statesman* 3 (June 27, 1914), p. 1.

12 Daniel Costello, *The Serpent's Eye: Shaw and the Cinema* (Notre Dame, IN: University of Notre Dame Press, 1965), p. 11.

13 "Shaw on Leslie Howard," *The Independent Shavian* 19, no. 3 (1982), p. 71.

14 *Bernard Shaw: Collected Letters: 1911–1925*, ed. Dan H. Laurence, vol. III (New York: Viking, 1985), p. 730.

15 *Bernard Shaw: Collected Letters: 1926–1950*, ed. Dan H. Laurence, vol. IV (New York: Viking, 1988), p. 817.

16 Leota Diesel, "The Traveling 'Fair Lady'," *Theatre Arts Monthly*, 41 (October 1957), p. 63.

17 *Ibid.*, p. 64.

18 Alan Jay Lerner, "*Pygmalion* and *My Fair Lady*," *The Shaw Bulletin* 10 (November 1956), p.7.

19 Clive Barnes, "*Her First Roman*, A Musical, Opens Here," *New York Times*, October 21, 1968, p. 53.

20 Shaw, *Collected Letters*, pp. 164–65.

21 Warren P. Smith, "Some Vital Statistics on GBS – 25 Years After – 1950–1975," *The Shaw Review* 18 (September 1975), p. 90.

22 Francis W. Sturcken, "An Historical Analysis of Live Network Television from 1938 to 1958," unpublished PhD dissertation, University of Minnesota (1960), p. iii.

23 Edmund Wilson, *The Sixties: Last Journal, 1960–72*, ed. Lewis M. Dabney (New York: Farrar Straus Giroux, 1993), p. 205.

24 Sean Condon, "*Saint Joan* meets CNN in this Season's Shaw Opener," *Saint Catherine's Standard*, Ontario, May 21, 1993, p. D2. This article furnished by Special Collections, University of Guelph Library, Ontario, from its Shaw Festival collection.

25 *Bernard Shaw: Collected Letters: 1898–1910*, ed. Dan H. Laurence, vol. II (New York: Dodd, Mead, 1972), p. 583.

FURTHER READING

Day, Arthur R., "The Shaw Festival at Niagara-on-the-Lake in Ontario, Canada, 1962–1981: A History," unpublished PhD, dissertation, Bowling Green University, Bowling Green, Ohio (1982). Detailed account of the festival's evolution with informative discussions of programming, economics and community relations.

Doherty, Brian, *Not Bloody Likely: The Shaw Festival – 1962–1973*, Toronto: J.

M. Dent & Sons (Canada) Limited, 1974. Reflections on the early years of the Canadian Shaw festival by its founder.

Dukore, Bernard F. (ed.), *The Collected Screenplays of Bernard Shaw*, Athens: University of Georgia Press, 1980. A detailed, well-documented introduction presents a history of Shaw's involvement with the cinema.

Elliot, Vivian, "The Malvern Festival Tradition," *Shaw's Plays in Performance: Annual of Bernard Shaw Studies 3*, ed. Stanley Weintraub, University Park: Pennsylvania State University Press, 1983. Discussion of the Malvern Festival from its inception through its brief revival in 1949.

Garebian, Keith, *George Bernard Shaw and Christopher Newton: Explorations of Shavian Theatre*, Oakville, Ontario: Mosaic Press, 1993. Examination of the Canadian Shaw Festival's first twelve seasons under artistic director Christopher Newton with a focus on how this artistic director approached Shaw's texts in order to address modern audiences.

Haverkorn, Monique A, "A Theatrical History of the Houston Shaw Festival 1979–1992," unpublished MA thesis, University of Houston–Clear Lake, TX (1993). Detailed record of the beginning, growth, and demise of the festival.

Rae, Lisbie, "Making Sense of Shaw: Newton at the Shaw festival, 1980–1993," *The Annual of Bernard Shaw Studies 15*, ed. Fred D. Crawford, University Park: Pennsylvania State University, 1995. Examination of the Canadian Shaw Festival's artistic direction under Christopher Newton.

INDEX

334

Index

Bland, Edith, Hubert, Rosamund, 12, 26, 184, 185

Blake, William, 16, 127, 137, 194, 290

Blakely, Colin, 310

Blanco!, 330

Bloom, Claire, 320

Bloom, Harold, 128–29, 140

Bogarde, Dirk, 316

Boïto, Arrigo, 299–300, 306n11; *Mefistofele*, 299–300

Bond, Edward, 177

Bonner, Arthur, 30

Boots With Strawberry Jam, 319

Boughton, Rutland, 306n17

Boyer, Charles, 311

Branch, Tony, 330

Brand, 57

Brecht, Bertolt, 177, 202, 203, 213; "Three Cheers for Shaw," 213

Brieux, Eugène, 32, 51n1, 112, 122n13, 264

Bright, Golding, 115

British Society for the Study of Sex Psychology, 20

Broadway Theatre Center, 329

Brooke, Henry, 198

Brooke, Rupert, and Ranee, 184, 185–88

Brooklyn Academy of Music, 312

Brough, Fanny, 116

Buchanan, Robert, 85

Buckle, Henry Thomas, 202, 210

Bujold, Genevieve, 321

Bunyan, John, 127, 230

Butterfield, Herbert, 203

By George, 313

Cagney, James, 318

Calder, David, 330

Caldwell, Zoe, 310, 321, 323

Calhoun, Eleanor, 79, 97n16

Calvert, Louis, 268, 273, 275

Cambridge Theatre, 193

Camille, 117

Campbell, Mrs. Patrick, 4, 21, 70, 90, 141n9, 180, 188, 193, 313, 314, 315

Carnegie Hall, 312, 330

Carlyle, Thomas, 128

Carpenter, Edward, 12, 17

Carroll, Lewis, and *Alice Through the Looking Glass*, 133, 190

Carte, D'Oyly, 124

Carton, R.C., 72

Caron, Leslie, 316

Carradine, David, 330

Casson, Ann, 269, 273, 310

Casson, Sir Lewis, 266, 268, 269, 270, 272, 273, 276, 277, 280

Caste, 65

Cenci, The, 199

Chamberlain, Richard, 330

Chekhov, Anton, 32, 181, 182, 183, 189, 279

Cherry Orchard, The, 182, 183, 184

Chesterton, G.K., 3, 255

Chiswick Press, 45

Chichester Festival Theatre, 246, 319

Cholmondeley, Mary, 240

Chu Chin Chow, 193

Churchill, Sarah, 312

Churchill, Sir Winston, 187

Clements, John, 309, 311

Clouds, The, 183

Cobden-Sanderson, Thomas, 41

Collins, Wilkie, 65

Comedy Theatre, 93

Congreve, William, 133

Constable & Co., 47

Cooke, Alistair, 321

Cornell, Katherine, 310, 313, 320

Cotterill, Erica, 187, 188

Country Wife, The, 112

Court Theatre, 20, 111, 182, 183, 186, 261–80

Coward, Sir Noel, 310, 311, 316, 317, 318

Cox, Katherine, 186

Cromwell, 199

Cummings, Constance, 319, 321

Cusack, Cyril, 312

Cusins, Sir William, 295

Cymbeline, 61, 63, 70

Dalton, Hugh, 184

Daly, Arnold, 116

Darwin, Charles, 59

Davis, Montgomery, 328–29

Dear Liar, 313, 328, 330

Death of Tintagiles, 263

Deeter, Jasper, 322

Degeneration, 79, 86,

Dench, Judi, 310, 321

De Havilland, Olivia, 310

De la Tour, Frances, 310

De Maupassant, Guy, 85

Dent, Joseph, 45

Denny, Reginald, 312

Dervin, Daniel, 4

Dickens, Charles, 66, 309

Index